Poisoners
of the Seas

K.A. Gourlay

Foreword by
Stanley Clinton Davis

Zed Books Ltd.
London and New Jersey

Poisoners of the Seas was first published by Zed Books Ltd,
57 Caledonian Road, London N1 9BU, UK, and
171 First Avenue, Atlantic Highlands, New Jersey 07716, USA,
in 1988.

Copyright © K.A. Gourlay, 1988.

Cover designed by Andrew Corbett.
Cover photograph copyright © Greenpeace/Gleizes.
Typeset by EMS Photosetters, Rochford, Essex.
Printed and bound in the United Kingdom
by Biddles Ltd, Guildford and King's Lynn.

British Library Cataloguing in Publication Data

Gourlay, K.A.
  Poisoners of the seas.
  1. Oceans. Pollution
  I. Title
  363.7'394

  ISBN 0-86232-685-0
  ISBN 0-86232-686-9 Pbk

Contents

Figures

Foreword

It is an obvious truth that the seas are among our planet's most important resources. They are at the heart of the earth's ecology. They are the home of abundant and diverse life. They are one of the chief driving forces behind our weather and temperature patterns – patterns upon whose stability our entire culture and economy depend.

But it is a truth that we are in danger of forgetting. As this book shows, mankind has got into the habit of treating the seas as a bottomless dustbin. They are not. And in some areas – the Mediterranean, the North Sea – the waste is now rising perilously high.

With the seas, as with other global resources, mankind must learn a new approach, and learn it quickly. If he does not, future generations will pay a heavy price. The pollution of the seas is not principally a scientific or an economic problem. It is a political problem. The behaviour of Governments, corporations and people has to be changed. In admirably clear language, this book shows why.

Stanley Clinton Davis
Member of the Commission of the European Communities with special responsibility for the Environment, Consumer Protection and Nuclear Safety

Acknowledgements

In a work such as this, where one is entirely dependent on others for information, it may appear invidious to single out any individual or group for special acknowledgement. I would, however, like to express my indebtedness to three bodies of experts on whom, as the numerous chapter references show, I have relied considerably for factual data, even when I have not always accepted their conclusions: the UN Joint Group of Experts on the Scientific Aspects of Marine Pollution (GESAMP), the compilers of the *Times Atlas of the Oceans*, and the writers of the reports produced by UNEP's Regional Seas Programme. I have also drawn freely on the excellent accounts given by environmental and scientific correspondents of the press. Without the help of these and all others listed in the Bibliography this book could never have been written. My experience in working for the Advisory Committee on Pollution of the Sea (ACOPS) in London proved invaluable in directing my attention to the main sources of information, and the Committee's Annual Reports and Yearbooks were particularly helpful in writing the account of oil pollution. The final version of the text owes much to the editing of Ralph Smith, whose meticulous attention to detail I much appreciated.

Note from the Publisher

The manuscript of this book was completed, apart from minor amendments, by May 1987. We would like to make it clear that the delay in publication until Summer 1988 was due to circumstances entirely beyond the author's control.

Note to the Reader

Measurements
I have tried to be consistently *metric* but the sea's traditions inevitably break in. Distances at sea thus appear at times in *nautical miles* (nm) rather than kilometres. No one ever calls a *200-mile Exclusive Economic Zone* a '320-km EEZ'. The following list of equivalents may interest anyone who is capable of visualizing them:

1 statute mile = 1.61 km = 0.87 nautical miles
1 km = 0.62 statute miles = 0.54 nautical miles
1 nautical mile = 1.15 statute miles = 1.85 km

Tonnage
Except for the tonnage of ships, the term *ton* is used throughout to refer to the avoirdupois weight of 20 hundredweight or 2,240 lb, while *tonne* is used for the metric ton of 1,000 kg, i.e. 0.984 ton; conversely, one ton equals 1.016 tonnes.

Confusion arises over the tonnage of ships because the *deadweight tonnage* (dwt), i.e. the weight of the cargo, fuel, freshwater and stores it can carry, is usually given in *weight* tons as defined above, while the *Gross Registered Tonnage* (GRT), i.e. its internal capacity under the tonnage deck together with certain 'over deck' spaces for the bridges, accommodation, etc. is calculated in *measurement* tons at 100 cu ft per ton.

There are further complications in that, if an item of cargo weighs more than 40 cu ft per ton, freight charges are based on volume rather than weight, and that, under a recent convention which took effect from July 1982, GRT is no longer expressed in tons of cu ft but in cubic metres. I have, however, avoided both of these in an attempt to achieve clarity, even at the risk of obsolescence.

References
In order to reduce the number of references I have, where possible, grouped together the sources used in acquiring data for a particular section or topic and given only the reference for actual quotations used.

Newspapers referred to are English newspapers (*The Times*, the *Guardian*, etc.) unless specified (e.g. *Le Figaro*, Paris) or obvious from the title (e.g. *New York Times*).

Technical Terms
These are explained when first used. The less familiar of those in italics are included in the Glossary.

Less Familiar Metric Terminology

Prefix	*Symbol*	*Factor/Power Notation*	*Normal Notation*
Above unity		Multiplied by	Multiplied by
mega	M	10^6	1,000,000
giga	G	10^9	1,000,000,000
tera	T	10^{12}	1,000,000,000,000
Below unity			Divided by
micro	μ	10^{-6}	1,000,000
nano	n	10^{-9}	1,000,000,000
pico	p	10^{-12}	1,000,000,000,000

Acronyms and Abbreviations

ACOPS	Advisory Committee on Pollution of the Sea (UK)
AEA	Atomic Energy Authority (UK)
AEC	Atomic Energy Commission (USA/India)
AFERNOD	Association Française pour l'Etude et la Recherche des Nodules
AIFC	Amoco International Finance Company
AIOC	Amoco International Oil Company
ALARA	as low as reasonably achievable
BCL	Bougainville Copper Ltd.
b/d	barrels per day
BHS	γ–hexachloro cyclohexane
BNFL	British Nuclear Fuels plc
BOD	Biological Oxygen Demand
BP	British Petroleum
BPG	byproduct phospho–gypsum
Bq	Becquerel(s)
CAPL	Coastal Anti Pollution League (UK)
CEA	Commissariat à l'Energie Atomique (France)
CEGB	Central Electricity Generating Board (UK)
CFCs	chlorofluorocarbons
Ci	Curies
Ci/a	Curies per annum
CLC	Civil Liability Convention 1969
CNEXCO	Centre National pour l'Exploitation des Océans
COD	1) Concise Oxford Dictionary; 2) Chemical Oxygen Demand
CRASH	Computerized Risk Analysis of Shipping Hazards
Cu	Curie
cu ft/d	cubic feet per day (of gas)
DDT	dichloro–diphenyl–trichloro–ethane
DoE	Department of the Environment (UK)
DOMA	Deep Ocean Minerals Association
DOMCO	Deep Ocean Mining Company Ltd.
DORDCO	Deep Ocean Resources Development Company Ltd.
DOT	Department of Trade (UK)
DTI	Department of Trade and Industry (UK) (formerly DOT)
dwt	deadweight tonnage
EC	European Communities
EEC	European Economic Community
EEZ	Exclusive Economic Zone

ENI	Ente Nazionale Idrocarbi
EOD	Explosives Ordnance Disposal
EPA	Environmental Protection Agency (USA)
EURATOM	European Atomic Energy Community Treaty 1957
FAO	Food and Agriculture Organization (UN)
FC	Fund Convention 1971
FOC	Flag(s) of Convenience
FRG	Federal Republic of Germany
GBq	GigaBecquerel
GESAMP	Joint Group of Experts on the Scientific Aspects of Marine Pollution (UN)
GRT	Gross Registered Tonnage
HCH	hexachlorocyclohexane
HELCOM	Helsinki Commission
HLW	High Level Radioactive Waste
HNS	Hazardous and Noxious Substances
HSE	Health and Safety Executive (UK)
IAEA	International Atomic Energy Authority (UN)
ICES	International Council for Exploration of the Sea
ICI	Imperial Chemical Industries
ICRP	International Commission for Radiological Protection
ICSU	International Council of Scientific Unions
ILO	International Labour Organization/Office
ILW	Intermediate Level Radioactive Waste
IMCO	Intergovernmental Maritime Consultative Organization (see also IMO)
IMDG	International Maritime Dangerous Goods [Code]
IMO	International Maritime Organization
ISA	International Sea-bed Authority (LOSC)
IUCN	International Union for the Conservation of Nature and Natural Resources
JCL	Jayshree Chemicals Ltd.
LDC	London Dumping Convention 1972
LLW	Low Level Radioactive Waste
LNG	Liquid Natural Gas
LOF	Lloyd's Open Form
LOSC	Law of the Sea Convention 1982
LPG	Liquid Petroleum Gas
m	metre(s)

MAFF	Ministry of Agriculture, Fisheries and Food (UK)
MARPOL	International Convention for the Prevention of Pollution from Ships 1973
MEK	methyl ethyl ketone
mg/kg	milligrams per kilogram
mg/l	milligrams per litre
ml	millilitre
MOU	Memorandum of Understanding
mSv	milliSievert
MWe	megawatts of electricity
µg/g	micrograms per gram
µg/l	micrograms per litre
NASA	National Aeronautics and Space Administration (USA)
NEA	Nuclear Energy Authority (OECD)
ng/l	nanograms per litre
NII	Nuclear Installations Inspectorate (UK)
nm	nautical mile(s)
NNOC	Nigerian National Oil Corporation
NOAA	National Oceanic and Atmospheric Administration (USA)
NDP	Norwegian Petroleum Directorate
NRC	Nuclear Regulatory Commission (USA)
NRPB	National Radiological Protection Board (UK)
NUS	National Union of Seamen (UK)
OBO	ore–bulk–ore [carrier]
OECD	Organization for Economic Co-operation and Development
OILPOL	International Convention for the Prevention of Pollution of the Sea by Oil 1954
OMA	Ocean Mining Associates
OMCO	Ocean Minerals Company
OMI	Ocean Management, Incorporated
OO	ore–oil [carrier]
OSIR	Oil Spill Intelligence Report
OTEC	Ocean Thermal Energy Conversion
PAH	polycyclic aromatic hydrocarbon
PCBs	polychlorinated biphenyls
PIP	Preparatory Investment Protection [scheme] (LOSC)
PNAH	polynuclear aromatic hydrocarbon
PNG	Papua New Guinea
ppm	parts per million
PPP	polluter pays principle
PSC	Port State Control
PVC	polyvinyl chloride
PWR	Pressurized Water Reactor

RAPS	Rajasthan Atomic Power Station
RCEP	Royal Commission on Environmental Protection (UK)
Ro–Ro	roll on–roll off [carrier/ferry]
RSPB	Royal Society for the Protection of Birds (UK)
RSPCA	Royal Society for the Prevention of Cruelty to Animals (UK)
RSRS	Regional Seas Research Studies (UNEP)
RTZ	Rio Tinto–Zinc
SAR	International Convention on Maritime Search and Rescue 1979
SI	Système Internationale [of radiological units]
SMN	Société Metallurgique de Nickel
SNS	Société Nationale de Siderurgie
SOLAS	International Convention for the Safety of Life at Sea 1974
SPREP	South Pacific Regional Environment Programme
STCW	International Convention on Standards of Training, Certification and Watchkeeping for Seafarers 1978
Sv	Sievert
TAO	Times Atlas of the Oceans
TAPS	Tarapur Atomic Power Station
tb/d	thousand barrels per day
TBq	TeraBecquerel(s)
TBT	tribultyn tin
TGWU	Transport and General Workers Union (UK)
THORP	Thermal Oxide Reprocessing Plant
UNCHE	United Nations Conference on the Human Environment (Stockholm)
UNCTAD	United Nations Conference on Trade and Development
UNEP	United Nations Environment Programme
UV	ultra-violet
VLCC	Very Large Crude Oil Carrier
WCED	World Commission on Environment and Development (UN)
WHO	World Health Organization
WWF	World Wildlife Fund

Glossary

absorbed dose (of radiation): see *dose*.

abyssal zone = bathyal zone: the region of the sea between 1,000 and 3,000 m in depth.

abyssopelagic zone: the region of the sea between 2,000 m in depth and about 100 m above the *deep sea floor* (q.v.) as distinguished by its *fauna* (q.v.).

adsorption: the process by which a substance attaches itself to the surface of another, e.g. oil to particles of solid matter (as opposed to *absorption* by which a substance enters into and becomes part of another).

aerosol: in scientific explanations the terms refers to a gas containing microscopic particles of a liquid or solid; in the discussion of CFCs in Part 3 it refers to the familiar aerosol spray.

aliphatic chlorinated hydrocarbons: a combination of the atoms of a *hydrocarbon* (q.v.) with those of chlorine in the form of a straight line chain.

alkane = paraffin: a form of *hydrocarbon* (q.v.) in which seven atoms of carbon are linked together in a straight chain; each of the five internal atoms is linked to two hydrogen atoms, while the ones at each end are linked with three.

aromatic hydrocarbon: an *unsaturated* (q.v.) form of *hydrocarbon* (q.v.) in which some carbon atoms have a double link with each other, e.g. benzine.

ataxia: medical term for a condition in which human beings lose control of their limbs and other bodily functions, e.g. speech, sight, touch and hearing as the result of poisoning by heavy metals, e.g. mercury.

bathyal zone: see *abyssal zone*.

bathypelagic zone: the region of the sea between 1,000 and 2,000 m in depth as distinguished by its *fauna* (q.v.).

benthic zone: the region of the sea immediately above the sea-bed extending from the *inter-tidal zone* (q.v.) to the ocean depths.

benthos: living creatures inhabiting the *benthic zone* (q.v.).

biodegradation: the process of being broken down by living matter, especially bacteria. Hence *(bio)degradable*, capable of being broken down in this way and *(bio)degrade*, the action of doing so.

biological oxygen demand: (BOD): The amount of oxygen required to decompose organic matter; used as a measure of the oxygen requirement of bacteria in a water sample and thus as an index of pollution.

biomass: all the creatures living in the sea.

bioturbation: disturbance of sediments by creatures living in or on the ocean bed.

bottom water = deep water: water at the bottom of the ocean.

chemical oxygen demand: the amount of oxygen required to degrade non-living substances in the sea through oxidation.

collective dose: (of radiation): see *dose*.

continental margin: the bottom of the sea adjoining the land, comprising the *continental shelf* (q.v.), *continental slope* (q.v.) and *continental rise* (q.v.).

continental rise: the rise in level of the sea floor beyond the *continental slope* (q.v.)

caused by the piling up of masses of sediment.

continental shelf = sub-littoral: the shallow platform forming the bottom of the sea between the *inter-tidal zone* (q.v.) and the *continental slope* (q.v.).

continental slope: the sudden descent of the sea-bed at the end of the *continental shelf* (q.v.).

convergence: the coming together of different types of water.

Coriolis effect: the deflection of the path of a moving object, e.g. a current of the sea, as the result of the earth's rotation.

critical group: people most at risk from contamination by radioactivity.

critical pathway: the means by which radioactivity is transferred from a contaminated source to human beings, e.g. through the food chain.

current: movement of water in a particular direction and with sufficient continuity to be distinguished from other water, e.g. surface currents, such as the Gulf Stream, caused by a dominant wind.

cyclo–alkane = naphtheme: an *alkane* (q.v.) in which the carbon atoms at the ends of a linked chain join up to form a circle.

deep sea floor = ocean floor: the land at the bottom of the sea in the ocean depths, i.e. where the water is between 1,000 and 3,000 m deep.

density: the weight of a given volume of water; heavier water tends to sink towards the bottom of the sea and be replaced by lighter water.

diagenesis: the term used for the collective chemical, physical and biological processes undergone by matter reaching the *deep sea floor* (q.v.).

divergence: the separating of two types of water (opposite of *convergence* – q.v.).

dose: the amount of radiation received by a person or object.

— *absorbed dose:* measures the energy deposited in a specific unit of matter, e.g. one joule of energy absorbed per kilogram is designated a 'gray'.

— *dose equivalent:* the *absorbed dose* multiplied by a quality factor that will indicate the biological effect, usually at a point in a tissue.

— *collective dose equivalent:* the estimated quantity for the total exposure of a group of individuals to a radiation source.

— *effective dose equivalent:* indicates the risk of death from any form of radiation and includes both direct bodily harm and the hereditary effects from two generations.

Eckman layer: the surface layer of the sea affected by the wind.

effective dose: (of radiation): see *dose*.

epipelagic zone = euphotic zone: the region of the sea immediately below the surface to a depth at which photosynthesis becomes impossible.

estuary: an arm of the sea at the mouth of a tidal river where the tidal effect is influenced by the river current.

euphotic zone: see *epipelagic zone*.

eutrophication: enrichment of the sea by nutrients, causing rapid growth of organic matter. If carried too far, this causes undesirable effects. The correct term for this is *hypertrophication*, but 'eutrophication' is often loosely used to cover both processes.

Exclusive Economic Zone (EEZ): the area beyond the *territorial sea* (q.v.) over which a state has sovereign rights for the purpose of exploration, exploitation and management of the resources of the waters, sea-bed and subsoil.

fauna: a collective term for the living creatures (as opposed to plants) of a particular area.

flocculation: the physical process by which two particles join together.

foreshore: see inter-tidal zone.

hadal zone: the area of the sea in deep ocean trenches below 6,000 m in depth.

half-life: the time taken for the activity of a *radionuclide* (q.v.) to be reduced by half through radioactive decay.

homologue: a compound in a series characterized by graded changes in structure and properties.

hydrocarbon: a compound of hydrogen and carbon only, e.g. petroleum, coal, asphalt.

hypertrophication: see eutrophication.

inter-tidal zone =foreshore or *littoral:* the area of the sea and land between high and low water marks.

isomer: a chemical substance with the same composition and molecular weight as another but with a different structure and thus different properties.

isotope: atoms of an element which have the same atomic number but a different atomic mass. Isotopes of a particular element have identical chemical properties.

littoral: see inter-tidal zone.

mesopelagic zone: the area of the sea between 100 and 1,000 m in depth, the upper limit of which is determined by the *epipelagic zone* (q.v.) and the lower by the extent to which light can penetrate.

methane: a *hydrocarbon* (q.v.) consisting of one atom of carbon and four atoms of hydrogen.

naphtheme: see cyclo–alkane.

nuclear fission: the chain reaction set off when a neutron strikes a uranium atom, splitting it and releasing other neutrons to strike more atoms, thus producing large amounts of energy in the form of heat.

ocean floor: see deep sea floor.

paraffin: see alkane.

petroleum products: substances produced in refining crude oil by heating it to different temperatures, e.g. liquid petroleum gases, petrol, kerosene, etc.

plankton: the most prolific form of small life found in the sea. *Phytoplankton* are microscopic forms of plant life, *zooplankton* of animal life. *Plankton blooms* or *red tides* are sudden vast population explosions caused by the injection of abnormal amounts of nutrients into the sea, e.g. through sewage. See also *eutrophication, hypertrophication.*

polycyclic aromatic hydrocarbon = polynuclear aromatic hydrocarbon: the most chemically active *hydrocarbon* (q.v.) consisting of a number of linked circles (see *cyclo–alkane*) while remaining *unsaturated* (q.v.).

pore waters: water filling small openings and channels in rocks or sediments, particularly those of the *deep sea floor* (q.v.).

radionuclide: any *isotope* (q.v.) of an element that is unstable and undergoes natural radioactive decay.

red tides: see *plankton blooms*.

reprocessing: the process of recovering and recycling plutonium and uranium from spent fuel.

sub-littoral: see *continental shelf*.

synergism: combined effect, e.g. of two heavy metals in conjunction, that exceeds the sum of their individual effects.

territorial sea: that part of the sea nearest to land which is treated for legal purposes as if it were part of the state concerned, normally up to three nautical miles from low water mark. The 1982 LOSC permits a 12 nm territorial sea measured from specified baselines.

thermocline: the layer of the sea below the surface which is marked by an abrupt change in temperature and found only outside higher latitudes.

turbidity current: underwater avalanche caused by earthquakes or the effect of gravity on loose masses of sediment.

unsaturated: used of a *hydrocarbon* (q.v.) in which carbon atoms are not linked to hydrogen atoms but to each other.

upwelling: the process by which colder water from the depths rises towards the surface as the result of *divergence* (q.v.) or by winds driving surface water away from the coast.

Introduction

This book is about poisoning the seas. It is also about words and their users; about *euphemisms*, soft words designed to conceal hard meanings; *technical terms* that confuse the reader with science; and *jargon*, the outworn language of specialists who have lost the ability to use plain words. Sometimes the three combine or interchange; a technical term becomes jargon – or even a euphemism. Their effects are constant – to make non-specialists think the subject beyond their understanding, and to make them feel that things are better than they are.

The users are either scientists or lawyers, experts in understatement and the euphemistic phrase, who sprinkle their pages with technical terms, construct sentences from scientific or legal jargon and, through language, establish a monopoly over the subject which others attribute to knowledge. This book aims to break that monopoly.

Scientists and lawyers prefer the term 'marine pollution', high-sounding words derived from Latin, a common euphemistic trick to soften unpleasantness or confer respectability. The rat-catcher becomes a 'rodent operative', the dustbin-man a 'refuse collector'. 'Poisoning the seas' is nasty, blunt and sensationalist, a loud-mouthed cry of alarm; 'marine pollution' is objective and scholarly, an authoritative pronouncement of the quiet-voiced specialist.

Are poisoning and pollution two different things? Or is the difference only a choice of words?

The United Nations Joint Group of Experts on the Scientific Aspects of Marine Pollution, usually known as GESAMP (acronyms are another symptom; we no longer call things by their names, only by their initials), defines pollution of the sea as

> introduction by man, directly or indirectly, of substances or energy into the marine environment (including estuaries) resulting in deleterious effects such as harm to living resources, hazards to human health, hindrance of marine activities, including fishing, impairing quality for use of sea-water and reduction of amenities.[1]

The Concise Oxford Dictionary defines 'poison' as a 'substance that when introduced into or absorbed by a living organism destroys life or injures health, especially one that destroys life by rapid action even when taken in small quantity'; a 'slow poison' is one 'of which repeated doses are eventually injurious'.

Neither GESAMP nor the compilers of the COD appear able to define long words without using equally long ones. 'Poisoning', we conclude, causes either death or sickness – as does 'pollution'. The GESAMP definition is of further interest – it shows what happens when scientists use words. Ignoring the 'introduction by man', we ask how the pollutant can be introduced other than 'directly or indirectly' and thus whether these words are necessary, note the scientific inclusion of 'energy' as well as 'substance', translate 'marine environment' into 'sea', wonder how the straightforward term 'estuaries' crept in (surely 'tidal reaches of the marine environment intruding into the land-surface' would be better!) and reach the core of the definition in 'resulting in deleterious effects', a piece of redundant jargon, 'results' and 'effects' being synonymous, with a high-sounding Latinism 'deleterious' instead of 'harmful'. As the remainder of the definition consists only of examples ('such as'), all the scientists are saying is that pollution is putting something harmful into the sea.

The question is: if a poison 'destroys life or injures health', how 'harmful' must a substance be to qualify for this category? GESAMP is careful not to go too far; 'harm', 'hazards', 'impairing' and 'reduction' are words which, while not excluding ultimate destruction – '*harm* to living resources' could, though it need not, mean killing fish; '*hazards* to human health' range from a cold to a cancer; 'reduction of amenities', i.e. fouling beaches with oil or sewage, could include a reduction to zero – leave a cumulative impression that things are not as bad as they might be.

This is no accident, but a reflection of the way establishment scientists think. The report in which this definition occurs is called *The Review of the Health of the Oceans*. 'Health', it can be claimed, is a neutral word; one can have good health, bad health or suffer permanent ill-health (though 'healthy' does not allow such permutations). Yet the tenth session of GESAMP defined the Working Group's objective as (among others) providing 'a periodically updated review of the *state of pollution* of the world's oceans' (my stress); only in the Group's terms of reference does the 'health of the oceans' appear, and then in the context of advising 'on the extent to which potentially harmful substances, processes or activities' may affect it.[2] The title, however, refers simply to health. Did the Group, one wonders, ever consider calling their report 'The Review of the Diseases of the Oceans'? Or even 'The State of Pollution of the World's Oceans'? Our attention is directed to health, not disease. Whatever the Group's intentions, scientific 'objectivity' is, in effect, suggestibility. Euphemism rules – and all's OK!

A GESAMP favourite is the word 'local'. It occurs on nearly every page of the Executive Summary with which their report begins. Large volumes of waste, including 'food and beverage processing wastes, pulp and paper mill effluents, woollen and cotton processing wastes', etc. 'have a local impact' on the sea. Sewage 'problem areas are *local* rather than global'. The effects of oil and metals on fishing 'tend as yet to be *local* or *regional*'. In semi-enclosed seas 'living resources have been *locally* contaminated to such a degree that fisheries have been stopped in *limited* areas'. Oil spills and blow-outs from offshore platforms or the mining of minerals on the sea-bed have caused pollution, but 'at present the effects are *localized*'; in the 'coastal zone' 'detrimental effects can already be detected in the *local* disruption of habitats'. Even the 'hot spots' of the world, where 'further work' is needed to discover how much poison reaches the open sea, 'may be regarded', at least 'initially', as a *restricted or local* problem'.[3] (My stress throughout.)

Concerned with 'global' problems and long-term effects, the scientists' lofty perspective enables them to give the oceans a generally clean bill of health. The Ekofisk blow-out in the North Sea on 22 April 1977 may have discharged 30,000 tons of oil into the sea before it was stopped, but 'no long-term damage to open-sea ecosystems has been detected'.[4] Any unpleasantness, we are assured, is purely local or restricted.

Behind this assessment is the same attitude of mind as that which celebrates VE-Day 1985 as marking 40 years of peace. The wars in Korea, Vietnam and Afghanistan are only local affairs; military intervention in Nicaragua is even more restricted. And the atomic bombs on Hiroshima and Nagasaki, like the Ethiopian famine, produced only local consequences.

Except, of course, for the men, women and children concerned.

Poisoning the seas may at present be only 'local'. Must the human beings affected, the fishes poisoned and birds killed, the contaminated beaches, ruined mangrove swamps and coastal reefs, and estuaries made uninhabitable through industrial effluent be ignored because the entire world has not yet suffered their fate? As the ultimate cause, uncontrolled industrialization, spreads to the Third World and restrictions now imposed in the West are by-passed in the rush for 'development', the disease will spread. Even the muted tones of GESAMP's scientists carry a warning. 'If a high proportion of a given habitat becomes affected, then the pollution could become global in the context of that habitat'.[5]

If euphemisms induce assurance, technical terms provoke bamboozlement. Faced with 'eutrophication', the 'thermocline', 'benthic' or 'euphotic' zones or communities, 'biogeochemical', 'diagenesis' and 'oleophilic contaminants', the non-specialist gives up, especially when this unfamiliar terminology is embedded in an impersonal, 'scientific' prose, constant reading of which induces a form of hypnosis that begins by causing a decrease in one's attention and ends by sending one to sleep.

The rules of the game of 'writing scientifically' are simple: whatever happens, avoid the personal; insert a technical term at every opportunity; never use the active voice when you can use the passive; take advantage of the impersonal 'it' construction; unless absolutely certain (which is rare) do not commit yourself but use a vague expression or 'may', 'seems' or 'appears'; and, if these are not enough, fall back on jargon.

Take a comparatively simple sentence and examine it: 'Marine plants and animals may be involved in air–sea interchange in a number of significant ways'. 'Marine' is inevitably used for 'sea'; 'may be involved' combines the passive with the non-committal – they may possibly not be involved after all; the 'air–sea interchange' takes place at that other technical term, now familiar to all computer-users, the 'air–sea interface', i.e. what happens where air and sea meet; while 'a number' is unspecified and 'significant' undefined (the two together are common scientific jargon) – to whom, or what, are they significant, and what *is* their significance? (The rest of the paragraph gives possible answers.) Two paragraphs later we find the impersonal 'it' introducing another passive: 'It has been demonstrated that . . .' Why not 'Scientists have shown/proved . . .' with a reference naming the scientists?

As soon as we discover how scientists use language, we can begin the counter-game of translation into plain words. The accounts in this book of the sea and how it works are basically 'translations' from 'scientese', the expression in simpler English of the otherwise incomprehensible.

Unlike jargon, however, technical terms have their merits; properly used they save time and energy. It is simpler to say 'benthic' than to write 'having to do with the bottom of the sea', 'diagenesis' than 'physical and chemical changes that take place in sediments while they are being, and after they have been, deposited on the ocean floor but before they have reached a settled state', or 'eutrophication' for the process by which the addition of certain substances to the sea provides the food necessary for increasing the growth of some sea creatures but which, if carried too far (hypertrophication), causes undesirable effects – in short, it resembles eating and over-eating. The price for this is that one has to know what the terms mean and make the necessary adjustment when half a dozen occur in the same sentence.

The perpetual use of Latin- or Greek-derived words can go too far. 'Anthropogenic' is clumsy and lengthy compared with its Anglo-Saxon equivalent, 'man-made'. And the use of an everyday word in a specialized sense can be baffling. 'Aerosol', for example, is not only the familiar spray but the 'gaseous suspension of ultramicroscopic particles of a liquid or a solid'.[6] In describing the sea and how poisons act in it we have, therefore, used technical terms (and provided a glossary) when we consider them useful, and avoided them when they are likely to be confusing.

Jargon is to lawyers what technical terms are to scientists, though the lawyers would doubtless claim that legal jargon is merely the correct use of technical terms and that the scientist's technical terms are a form of jargon. What happens is that, when an event occurs that resembles a previous event, a term used to describe the first is taken over and used not only for the second but on all similar occasions. This process saves lawyers from having to think and enables them to understand each other. International conventions, national laws or departmental regulations never 'take effect' or 'come into operation' from a certain date: they always 'enter into force'. A pollutant that reaches the sea from the land is said to come from 'land-based sources', just as pollution from ships is always 'vessel-source pollution'. Pedantically – and legally – the statement is, of course, correct; the pollution *is* from a source on the land. One is disappointed that the process of dropping poisons into the sea from aircraft has become 'dumping from aircraft'; presumably some legal expert was sufficiently alert to the humorist who expected 'flying sources'!

This type of phraseology starts with the best intentions – to avoid any possible misconstruction – and ends in the inflated or ridiculous. The lawyer's world does not allow metonymy. Everyone knows that 'the kettle boils' is not true; it is the water inside it. Yet in everyday life the expression is accepted as meaningful. If the pedant insists on 'It is I' instead of 'It's me', the lawyer would inform us that 'the water inside the kettle has reached the temperature which scientists have established as its boiling point.'

A recent book on United Kingdom marine pollution law explains the working of section 27(1) of the 1936 Public Health Act as follows:

> . . . no person may discharge into a sewer or drain communicating with a public sewer any matter likely to injure it or to interfere with its function, or any chemical refuse or waste steam, or any liquid with a temperature of more than 110°F, which will either by itself or when mixed with other contents of the drain or sewer be dangerous, the cause of a nuisance or prejudicial to health, unless such matter is trade effluent that is discharged into the sewer in accordance with the consent of a water authority.[7]

This far from extreme example is perfectly clear – provided one can tune in on the right wavelength to understand it. The difficulty arises from the attempt to be *too* clear and inclusive. It is as if the writer, having made one statement, realizes its incompleteness and adds another, the inadequacy of which necessitates further additions. Prohibiting discharges into a public sewer is not enough; a drain may lead to the sewer, so that too, must be included. The types of offending matter are spelt out in detail, together with their possible effects. The matter must not 'injure' the sewer or 'interfere with its function', i.e. prevent it from working properly. Having banned 'any liquid with a temperature of more than 110°F' if it is dangerous, the writer realizes that, while the liquid may not itself be a danger, it may become one when mixed with other contents of the 'drain or sewer'; so *that* also is included. The effect may not merely be 'dangerous' (whatever that means) but include those two other standbys which will provide opportunity for argument in court – 'the cause of a nuisance' and 'prejudicial to health'. Finally, we reach the positive aspect, expressed in the form of an exception. What the whole paragraph boils down to, in fact, is that *only* trade effluent for which the authorities have given permission can be discharged down a sewer or drain connected with it.

'Legalese' reaches its greatest heights (or depths) in international conventions or declarations, particularly in the opening preambles. The accepted form for these is to string together a series of dependent clauses which the prospective reader must then wade through before reaching the nitty gritty. The Declaration on the Protection of the North Sea issued after a ministerial meeting in Bremen on 31 October and 1 November 1984, for example, begins by describing the participants as

> *Aware* that the North Sea, and in particular its natural resources, constitute an important, irreplaceable environment;

> *Recognizing* that the North Sea is bordered by densely populated and highly industrialized states and crossed by much frequented shipping routes;
> *Conscious* that man can alter nature and endanger natural resources as a result of his activities, in particular through pollution and its consequences;
> *Convinced* that special attention should therefore be given . . .[8]

and so on, for 35 phrases, which take up almost five pages of the typed declaration. Nine of these phrases tell us that the ministers are 'conscious', seven describe them as 'recognizing', five maintain that they are 'convinced' or 'aware' (the distinction between this and 'conscious' is not clear), two stress that they are 'emphasizing', while the remaining seven (with one example each) refer to them as 'concerned', 'expecting', 'noting', 'confirming', 'affirming' (a subtle distinction here?), 'recalling' and 'recalling the importance', the only difference between the last two being that 'the importance' is stressed on one occasion and not on the other. If our stamina has been sufficient to get us this far, we discover at last what these conscious, concerned, convinced, etc. ministers actually do: they *declare their firm determination* (underlined in the original) to do various things, which are then enumerated in a series of paragraphs beginning 'to make every effort', 'to implement', 'to ensure', 'to prevent', 'to develop', etc., thus providing a formal counterpoint to the opening participial phrases and hiding in a mass of words the simple fact that none of them are really committing themselves to doing very much.

Bamboozled by the legal phraseology of parliamentary or diplomatic draughtsmen and by the technical terms of scientific documents, the non-specialist is cowed into accepting the image of these experts as superior beings who alone have access to a truth that can be expressed only in the esoteric languages of science or the law. The idea that, in their own field at least, scientists and lawyers 'know best' is fostered not only by respect for their lengthy training but also by publicly promoted and TV-sponsored images, one of a white-coated figure in a laboratory, surrounded by test tubes, flasks, retorts, flowing rainbow-coloured liquids, flickering lights and the inevitable computer, the other of a wigged and gowned advocate, expert in minor points of legal procedure, whose penetrating cross-examination à la Rumpole or Perry Mason causes witnesses to contradict themselves, while his masterly oratory sways the jury into acquitting or convicting the accused according to his wishes.

The reality is different. International lawyers are not barristers, nor do the scientists with whom we are concerned have much time for laboratory work, except, if they are lucky, in their own restricted specialities.

What then qualifies them as specialists in 'marine pollution'?

The answer is that they *read*.

That lawyers read legal documents, reports of cases, commentaries and the criticisms or proposals of fellow lawyers is only to be expected, but to say that scientists are also primarily 'readers' goes against the whole concept of empirical research. In practice, they have little option. Research within their own particular fields is the most that they have time or the qualifications to carry out. Since knowledge of the sea requires the coming together of many specialists – physicists, chemists, biologists, geographers, geologists, hydro-logists and climatologists (and even specialists within these spheres – marine biologists, for example, rather than those interested in the biology of human beings) – the most that anyone can do is to read what others have written. The GESAMP Report includes the statement, 'Written contributions forming part of the scientific background material have been given by both nominated Working Party Members and especially invited scientists . . .'[9] The Independent Review Body set up by the UK Government to report on the disposal of radioactive waste in the north-east Atlantic began their investigations by compiling a 'list of questions relating to the issues', which they submitted to 'known sources or . . . the responsible authority'. Inevitably, 'the major part of our task involved the reading of a vast quantity of literature'.[10]

The implications for the non-specialist and members of the thinking public are obvious. The qualifications for acquiring similar knowledge are at bottom basic literacy and a modicum of intelligence and perceptiveness. The future of the seas, and of the human beings who depend on them, need not lie with politicians, scientists or lawyers but with men and women who care enough to find out about them.

This book is only a beginning. Its success will be measured less in terms of sales than in the number of those who go on to conduct their own research and use it to bring pressure on the poisoners of the seas. The task involves a threefold approach: first, one must obtain the essential literature to enable one to keep up to date. The bibliography to this book comprises a selection of background reading matter from which one can start. Secondly, one must be capable of translating into the language of everyday communication the scientific and legal jargon in which essential data are often – but not always – cloaked. This book is itself an example and one can only hope that by the time the reader reaches the end, s/he will be aware of the methods involved and capable of producing his/her own translation. Thirdly, one must acquire the ability to assess the value of a contribution both in terms of facts and through perception of the attitude of the writer.

Facts, it may be thought, are facts, irrespective of who writes them. This is the modern fallacy of 'scientific objectivity'. There are two issues: one has to decide whether or not to accept the 'fact' as 'true'; and one has to examine how the facts are presented. There is a difference between the GESAMP figure of '71,287,000 tonnes' as the world total nominal catch of fish in 1979[11] and their statement on dumping that 'even where an effect can be clearly demonstrated on an isolated dumping ground, this effect will usually be restricted by the nature of the dumping operation to a relatively small area, so that only a small part of the commercial fish stock will be exposed to contamination'.[12] The figure for total fish stocks is precise (perhaps *too* precise) but open to verification; the comment on dumping is an expression of values masquerading as 'science'. At one level killing off 'a small part of the commercial fish stock' may suggest little cause for concern, and we may be thankful that the 'small part' is not larger. At another level, the same 'fact' may mean loss of livelihood, even starvation, to the men, women and children of a fishing community.

Scientists, like ourselves, are human beings, even if, like politicians, some have lost their humanity. They may persuade themselves that they are more objective than their fellow men and women and that, in consequence, their 'truth' is the 'real' truth. In practice, like the rest of us they see what they want to see because their training and experience allow no alternative. A scientist who has spent his working life in the oil or nuclear power industries or even in a government ministry and so acquired expertise in a particular field of marine pollution also acquires a particular perspective on these issues which, more often than not, he fails to recognize because to him it has become the 'objective', 'scientific' and therefore 'correct' view.

Perceptiveness on the reader's part is necessary to recognize that this view is no more valid than his or her own. One must learn to see through not only the technical jargon and scientific terminology but also the *mode* of the presenter. Ultimately it is a question of values. If one is establishment-minded, a supporter of the *status quo*, a believer in respectability and Victorian values, the attitude of mind which these produce will be reflected in one's work. If one is radical, progressive and forward-looking, the 'facts' will be presented differently. The perceptive reader quickly comes to recognize whether the source is 'for us' or 'against us'. That is why the ability to understand words and their uses is fundamental to acquiring knowledge of the poisoning of the seas.

References

1. GESAMP 15 p. 9
2. Ibid. pp. i–ii
3. Ibid. All examples are from pp. 3–5
4. Ibid. p. 4
5. Ibid. p. 5
6. Ibid. All examples from p. 99
7. Bates 1985 p. 127
8. Official text of the Declaration on the Protection of the North Sea issued on conclusion of the International Conference in Bremen, FRG, 31 October–1 November 1984
9. GESAMP 15 p. 103
10. Holliday 1984 p. 2
11. GESAMP 15 p. 58
12. Ibid. p. 61

Prologue: The Death-Bringers

The *Torrey Canyon*

Ships approaching the Scilly Isles, twenty miles off the coast of Cornwall, on their way to the Bristol Channel or South Wales, have three choices. They can go to the west of the islands between the lighthouse at Peninnis Head on their southern tip and that at Bishop's Rock to the west; pass to the east through a five-mile gap between the Scillies and the Seven Stones reef; or go further east through a ten-mile passage between the Seven Stones light-vessel and the Longships lighthouse.

On Saturday 18 March 1967 the Liberian oil tanker, *Torrey Canyon*, 297 metres long and fully loaded with 119,000 tonnes of crude oil which it was bringing from Mina al Ahmadi in Kuwait to Milford Haven in Wales, did none of these. Instead, it grounded on the Seven Stones reef, ruptured a number of its tanks, and initiated the most massive oil spill that British and French beaches had ever experienced.

We now know in detail what led to the disaster; what happened afterwards is less certain.

Four days before the crash the *Torrey Canyon* passed between Tenerife and Grand Canary Island off the West African coast and set a course by which it would pass five nautical miles (nm) *west* of the Scillies. At 2.30 a.m. on the 18th, with the islands not yet in sight or detected by radar, the master went off duty, leaving an order to be called when this happened and, in any case, not later than six o'clock. The wind was moderate north-westerly with visibility 10 nautical miles.

The master was duly called at six, only to be told by the chief officer that there was still no sign of the Scillies. At 6.30 the islands were detected by radar, approximately 24 nm to port (i.e. on their left). The ship was several miles east of where it should have been but there was time to put this right.

Accordingly, at 6.55 the chief officer altered course to head for what he thought was the radar echo from Bishop's Rock to the west of the Scilly Isles but which was actually the eastern Scillies. At seven the master came on to the bridge and, on being told that their original course would take them east of the islands, ordered them to resume it. The tanker was now heading directly for the Seven Stones reef, but the master intended altering course to pass either through the five-mile gap between the reef and the islands or to the east through the ten-mile passage between the reef and Longships lighthouse.

Thirty-five minutes later they sighted Bishop's Rock lighthouse to the west. At eight o'clock the ship's position was allegedly fixed by taking two bearings and a radar range, and the third officer relieved the chief officer. Twelve minutes afterwards they passed Peninnis Head lighthouse on the southern Scillies $4\frac{1}{2}$ nm to their left.

At 8.18 the *Torrey Canyon*'s position was fixed at 4.7 nm east of Peninnis Head and the master ordered the course to be changed to bring them nearer the coast. They sighted a number of fishing boats, two of them between the tanker and the land. Seven minutes later the position was again fixed and the course altered to bring the ship nearer land, but the action was less effective than expected as the tide was running strongly to the east.

At 8.30 the tanker again altered course, this time to the east, to avoid a fishing vessel. At 8.38 the third officer plotted their position – incorrectly – but the master realized it and called for fresh observations. Two minutes later their position was fixed from the Seven Stones light-vessel – the tanker was now only 2.8 nm from the rocks ahead.

At 8.42 the master switched from automatic steering to manual, altered course to port to pass to the left of the reef, and returned the steering to automatic. At 8.45 the third officer, who was now under stress, took a bearing, forgot it, and took it again. The position showed that the tanker was less than a mile from the rocks.

The master ordered hard to port. The helmsman ran to the wheel and turned it but nothing happened. He shouted to the master, who checked the fuse and found it in order. The master tried to telephone the engineers to check the steering gear – and got a wrong number. As he dialled again, he noticed that the steering was on automatic. Switched quickly to manual, it began to turn the ship, but had completed only about ten degrees when, still travelling at its full speed of $15\frac{3}{4}$ knots, at 8.50 the *Torrey Canyon* grounded on Pollard's Rock. Immediately crude oil spread round it from the ruptured tanks, and, since the grounding occurred near the time of high water, as the sea level fell, the massive tanker settled further on to the rocks.[1]

Salvage operations began almost at once, but heavy seas caused the *Torrey Canyon* to become a complete wreck. An explosion on board killed one member of the salvage team, the only human life lost in the disaster. Within 24 hours it was estimated that 30,000 tonnes of crude oil had spilled into the sea; within a week a further 20,000 tonnes were released, and another 50,000 when the tanker broke up on 26 March. Finally, despite the fact that the vessel was a Liberian ship and that the accident took place outside British waters, the UK Government ordered the Royal Air Force to bomb the vessel in an attempt to burn up the remaining oil. The bombs started several fires but only a small proportion was burnt away before the *Torrey Canyon* finally sank on 30 March.[2]

Meanwhile the oil spread slowly towards the British and French coasts. By 3

April it was 40 km north-west of Guernsey; on the 10th slicks had reached Brittany and by the 12th oil was reported from the north coast of Finistère where, on some beaches, it was lying a foot deep. On the other side of the Channel, over 100 km of Cornish coastline were affected.

Both British and French Governments acted immediately – if not always wisely. The British attempted to use detergents to disperse the oil, producing huge quantities of froth of which the wind then took hold. Because the problem was larger than any previously experienced, the authorities were forced to use large numbers of unskilled operators, whose excessive and inefficient use of emulsifiers, solvents and cleaning agents had a disastrous effect on sea creatures and exacerbated rather than relieved the extent of the poisoning. The French preferred manpower to chemicals, and, though they stocked 250 tons of detergents at Brest, under pressure from the owners of oyster and mussel beds, they promised not to use them. The Government massed over 30 ships between Brest and Cherbourg to dump sand and sawdust on floating patches of oil, sent 3,000 troops to clean up polluted beaches, asked primary school children to spend their day's holiday catching birds and taking them to hospital, and earmarked 15,000 francs to fight the oil menace. To the chagrin of deputies and senators from Brittany they refrained from declaring the event a national catastrophe – which would have meant that the Government footed the bill.[3]

Meanwhile, others took advantage of the ubiquitous oil slicks to follow the tanker tradition of adding their own. An RAF plane on reconnaissance patrol photographed two Norwegian tankers discharging oil; the first, the *Harwi*, bound for Africa, was just outside British territorial waters; the second, the *Stolt Vesfonn*, left a trail of oil 10 km long and a kilometre wide opposite Beachy Head. Others were doubtless more fortunate. The French *Journal de Dimanche* summed up the situation in a typically Gallic cartoon: from the deck of a large tanker labelled *Torrey Canyon* a sailor adds his own water to that of the sea, while an officer cries in consternation, 'Everyone's doing it now!'[4]

Everyone was certainly doing something, if only to help the victims. In Britain, as soon as the accident was reported, the Royal Society for the Prevention of Cruelty to Animals (RSPCA) placed its staff on the west and south coasts on the alert and drafted in additional helpers. So great, however, was the number of oiled birds washed ashore that the RSPCA centres and those of local naturalists were unable to cope. Their difficulties brought a great army of enthusiastic, if inexperienced, well-wishers to the West Country and a gigantic operation of 'washing' birds began. With many it would have been preferable to end the wretched bird's sufferings by putting it out of its misery. But 'washing' had become an *idée fixe* with the enthusiasts, who set up 'cleansing stations', to which the terrified and exhausted birds were carried in sacks, only to be tipped out into pens, frightened further by the presence of curious spectators, then seized and scrubbed, all with the best of intentions. The survival rate – one per cent of 7,849 birds treated by the end of the year – showed the futility of their actions.

How many deaths did the *Torrey Canyon* cause? The answer will never be known. In England it was estimated as a minimum of 10,000 known deaths, chiefly guillemots and razorbills, but, if one adds those lost at sea, the total could have been anything between two and ten times as large. Other species killed include puffins, great northern divers, black-throated divers, cormorants and kittiwakes. In France, the month after the disaster the French League for the Protection of Birds gave a first estimate of 4,400 puffins as having perished on the island of Reuzic alone, where the population was reduced from 5,000 to 600, razorbills reduced from 800 to 100, and guillemots to 100.[5]

The *Torrey Canyon* disaster was an accident; but it was not the first, nor was it to be the last. And it had no effect on the practice by which tankers persistently and deliberately dumped oil at sea when washing out their tanks. 1967 was a bad year, but the public could not claim that they had not been warned. On 20 January the London *Daily Mirror* published the repulsive picture of an oil-covered seagull under large headlines 'THE CRUCIFIED SEAGULL, a picture that tells better than words the tragic truth about oil on our beaches'. Beneath the picture it wrote:

> A seagull lies dead on the sands. Its wings, drained of all their strength, are spread out cross-like.
> The symbolism is not inappropriate. For this little bird has been stripped of all its dignity, all its grace.
> Its life has ebbed slowly away, its flesh burning. A victim of the 15-mile long patch of oil swept by the sea up on ten miles of beaches in West Sussex and Hampshire.[6]

Ten days later – two months before the *Torrey Canyon* – the *Mirror* resumed its attack:

> Oil is the scandal of Britain's beaches. It is swept ashore year after year, with horrifying results.
> Millions of seabirds have died, trapped in oil patches. Their deaths are slow and agonizing.
> In the worst slaughter 100,000 seabirds are believed to have died in the Atlantic as oil was swept slowly along by the Gulf Stream.
> The oil has ruined holidays for countless Britons who have found their clothes and their bodies marked with oil. It has cost holiday resorts enormous sums of money – in cleaning costs and lost bookings from visitors. This is the scandal. And the real tragedy is that most of the damage need never be caused.[7]

Sensationalism and sentimentality? The *Mirror* is at times given to overstatement but anger at the sight of oiled birds was real enough, as was the tourist's displeasure at finding favourite beaches covered with tarballs, the hotelier's concern at cancelled bookings and the local authority's worry over clean-up costs.

The *Torrey Canyon* was the symbol of a deeper, worldwide disease. As the *New York Times* wrote a month after the disaster:

> The break-up of the *Torrey Canyon* was an accident; but it has long been the practice of tanker crews to wash out their tanks at sea and pump the contaminated waste overboard before calling at the next loading port with

clean tanks. Almost three tenths of one per cent of a tanker's cargo is routinely wasted through such cleaning operations on each voyage.[8]

The *Torrey Canyon* had other consequences. At the request of the United Kingdom Government, the Intergovernmental Maritime Consultative Organization (IMCO), the United Nations body responsible for the seas of the world, met in extraordinary session on 4–5 May to adopt a comprehensive plan for international agreement in the routeing of ships, navigational aids, ship construction, the training and certification of seafarers, watchkeeping standards, liability and compensation, and, arising from concern over the bombing by Britain of a Liberian ship outside British waters, intervention on the high seas when there was a threat of pollution. Within the next five years half a dozen conferences had been held and, through IMCO's Marine Safety and Legal Committees, new conventions drawn up or adopted. Yet, as the London-based Advisory Committee on Pollution of the Sea (ACOPS) commented in its 1967 Annual Report: 'It is somewhat ironical that exactly three months before the 1962 amendments to the [1954] International Convention for the Prevention of Pollution of the Sea by Oil came into force, the stranding of the *Torrey Canyon* caused the greatest pollution yet experienced and the provisions of the Convention deal solely with "deliberate" or controlled discharges, . . . not with oil which escaped into the sea as the result of an accident'.[9]

Undeterred by the *Torrey Canyon*, on 11 August 1967 Esso International announced an expansion programme for five super-tankers of the 140,000-dwt class. These 1,000-ft tankers, the largest ever to be built in Europe, would be placed under foreign flags, though no decisions had been taken on which company would operate them.[10] The following month it was reported that Italy planned to build two 227,000-ton tankers for the Societa Mediterranea Raffineria Siciliana Petroli of Palermo, while American interests had placed an order with a Japanese shipyard for a 276,000-ton tanker and Standard Oil (New Jersey) ordered several 240,000-ton tankers from a West German yard.[11]

The crucified seagull would not be alone . . . .

The Minamata Fishermen

Most peoples are not big eaters of seafood. Taking a global view, GESAMP scientists calculate that, in an estimated world population of 4,150 million in 1977, the average man or woman eats 3.5 grams of protein daily, out of a total of 68.8 grams, in the form of fish or shellfish. To acquire this one has to eat 20 grams of actual fish a day or 140 grams, about one fish meal, a week.

The 'average man or woman' is, of course, a statistical illusion, but the figure provides a useful standard. It enables the United Nations Food and Agriculture Organization (FAO) to point out that, by comparison, small island populations eat large quantities of seafood. The 40,000 inhabitants of the Faeroe Islands, for example, obtain 38.6 grams of protein daily from 193 grams of seafood, which suggests that they eat more than one seafood meal a day. Among countries with large populations the Japanese eat most fish (on average); within all populations fishermen eat more than other people, and the fishermen and their families of Minamata used to eat 800–1,500 grams or between 20 and almost 40 times the average amount eaten daily in Europe (38 grams).[12]

In the 1950s and 1960s their dependence on a fish diet brought disaster to the Minamata fishermen and their families.

Twenty years later one may be excused for not having heard of Minamata. Fodor's current *Guide to Japan* does not mention it; writers of travel books express amazement at the country's industrial progress, but one will not find it either in the index or on the map in Bartholomew's *World Atlas*. It would almost seem as if Minamata is a dirty word, not to be used in polite company. Yet Minamata was no small fishing village, but a town of some 50,000 inhabitants on the east coast of the southern island of Kyushu. Many of these were fishermen, though the town's economic prosperity depended on the Shin-Nihon Chisso Hiryo chemical factory which produced, amongst other things, large amounts of vinyl chloride and acetaldehyde.

GESAMP summarizes the events that took place as follows: 'In Minamata Bay, Japan, methylmercury from a chemical plant was discharged to the bay for at least 30 years up to 1968. Severe mercury intoxication affected human consumers of fish and there were a number of deaths'.[13] Precision seems to have deserted our scientists – the 'chemical plant', which appears to operate without human responsibility, is unnamed, the 'number of deaths' unspecified, and the incident drowned in euphemisms. In plain words, the 'human consumers of fish' were the wretched fishermen and their families who ate poisoned fish; the 'severe mercury intoxication' with which they were 'affected' may sound as if they got drunk – but it killed at least 43 of them.

What actually happened at Minamata?[14]

The Chisso chemical factory had been discharging methylmercury into the sea for 15 years before what became known as 'Minamata disease' appeared in 1953. Three years later it had become epidemic. Doctors suspected that it was a contagious form of meningitis and isolated the victims. Isolation, however, failed to stem the spread of the disease.

Under Dr Hosokawa, director of the factory's hospital, a study commission investigated the patients and discovered that all had similar symptoms. The illness began with numbness in the lips and limbs. After two weeks the victim's senses of touch, speech and hearing were impaired; his gait became irregular, he walked as if drunk (intoxicated) and was unable to stop suddenly or to turn round (in medical terminology, he suffered from *ataxia*). The most disturbing symptom was a narrowing of the field of vision.

The suffering can be imagined. What made it worse was that the expected end was not a return to health, but madness, death or permanent disability.

From the symptoms Professor Shimanosuke Katsuki of Kuomoto University inferred that the cause of the illness was heavy metal poisoning. The questions remained: how had the victims acquired the poison, and what was its source?

All those who became ill, it was noted, ate a lot of fish. This was not surprising; they were fishermen and, like their ancestors, lived largely on a fish diet. What was difficult for them to understand was that, if eating fish had not affected previous generations, why were they suffering now?

The answer came from the local cats. The moggies of the quays were also fish-eaters, scroungers of scraps that the fishermen threw away. Many of them showed the same symptoms, even before these appeared in human beings. In desperation they jumped into the sea and drowned. With more concern for human than feline life investigators fed fish to healthy cats and produced the same results, thus demonstrating that the cause of the disease was food-poisoning from eating fish or shellfish.

At the beginning of 1957 the authorities placed a ban on fishing in the bay. That year no one contracted the disease. In 1958 there were only three cases. Up to that time, of 116 officially recorded cases – and there must be many unrecorded – 43 had died. Few of the survivors recovered completely; many had permanent disabilities. By 1972 almost 300 were officially listed as victims.

The search for the poison and its source took three years. The chemical company refused to give information about its production processes and to submit its waste water for analysis. Even when, in 1960, investigation showed that the discharge contained methylmercury, they denied all responsibility. The Japanese chemical lobby supported the local firm and succeeded in preventing official recognition of the findings. A government largely representative of business interests took no action.

Only in 1969, sixteen years after the disease first appeared, was it possible to prove beyond doubt that mercury in organic compounds had caused the poisoning. Meanwhile, the fishermen had achieved publicity – and public sympathy – through direct action. In desperation at the absence of relief or compensation and convinced that the Chisso factory was responsible, they stormed into the Annual General Meeting of the company to demand an end to the poisonous discharges. Twenty-eight families went further and began legal proceedings against the company, which eventually closed down the equipment causing the poisoning, but continued its refusal to admit responsibility.

In 1965 a similar, if less prolonged or disastrous, incident occurred at the mouth of the River Agano in the district of Niigato. Thirty people became ill, five of them died. The source of the poisoning was traced to mercury-containing waste from the Kanose factory of Showa Denko, which had again reached its victims through the fish they ate. The families took the company to court, not only claiming compensation but also charging it with polluting the environment. After four years and three months of legal argument, they received £312,000 in damages from the company.

In 1970, when the smog of Tokyo and other industrial cities made environmental issues unavoidable, the government introduced a series of protective measures. In the Third World, however, as industrialization increases, the lesson of Minamata is still unlearnt.

In the early 1980s the Institute of Science in Bombay revealed that industries on the banks of the Kalu River on the outskirts of Bombay were creating the conditions for another disaster. 'The spectre of Minamata stares in the face of the village population that consumes fish and food from or near the Kalu river', declared the leader of the investigating team, Dr B. C. Haldar.

The Kalu is a small river which flows from the Western Ghats through the industrial suburbs of north-east Bombay to reach the sea 50 km north of the city. During its course it receives effluent from over 150 small industries; the ten-kilometre stretch between Ambivali and Titwala, which was examined in detail, received toxic waste containing mercury, lead, copper, cadmium, chloride, dyes and organic acids from a rayon factory, paper mills, a dye factory and a chemical plant. Dr Haldar was in no doubt of the potential consequences. 'The water at the point of discharge into the Kalu river has a mercury content equal to that at the centre of Minamata Bay'.

A study of fish from seven sources in Bombay revealed that the bones and muscles of certain species contained concentration of mercury greater than the accepted safety limit of 500 nanograms (one nanogram = one thousand millionth of a gram). But, as in Japan, it is the industrial lobby, not the environmentalists, who decide events. Senior officials of the Maharashtra Board for Prevention and Control of Water Pollution have reputedly resigned after being frustrated by politicians in their attempts to ensure that industries along the banks of the Kalu conform to existing regulations.[15]

Indian and Japanese power groups opposed to pollution control are at least open in their hostility. There are other, more subtle, ways of deflecting anger. The last word on Minamata must surely go to GESAMP, whose discussion of the 'geochemical cycle of mercury' enables it to reach 'certain general conclusions', the third of which reads:

> Direct toxic effects may result from these increased concentrations, especially when they are accompanied by changes in local conditions [sic]. In extreme cases, these may give rise to local problems [sic] that may reach epidemic proportions, as for example, at Minamata, where the sequence of increased mercury flux, increased local concentration, and increased production of methylmercury, combined with a special human diet, has . . .

Has what? Led to an epidemic or major disaster? Brought about 43 deaths of fishermen? Killed off many of the local cats?

The important result, as seen by GESAMP, is none of these. The sentence ends – 'has . . . been unequivocably quantified'.[16] The 'unequivocably' has a touch of genius.

The *Stella Maris*

The year after the *Torrey Canyon* disaster, scientists in Western Europe, investigating the extent to which the North Sea was used as a dustbin for industrial waste, produced some alarming results. They showed that the Dutch poured in 3,600 tons of sulphuric acid and 750,000 tons of sulphur dioxide each year; the West Germans dumped 375 tons of sulphuric acid and 750 tons of iron sulphate daily, 40 tons of chlorinated hydrocarbons and 40–50 tons of polyethylene every month, and 200,000 tons of gypsum every year.[17] These were the official figures; one can only assume that, through clandestine dumping, the actual amounts were much greater.

In 1970, Scandinavian scientists showed that *aliphatic chlorinated hydrocarbons* were present in both the open Atlantic and in Norwegian coastal waters. These toxic wastes from the manufacture of the plastic PVC (polyvinyl chloride) were particularly dangerous to sea creatures, and eventually to human beings, through their persistency.[18]

Fishermen were again involved – in both directions. While some fished up barrels containing a variety of toxic substances, particularly off the coasts of Holland and West Germany, their less scrupulous colleagues found it profitable to take on board illicit canisters and dump them there.[19] The scope of dumping needed to dispose of the waste required more than the co-operation of a few crooked fishermen. Reports quickly circulated of ships setting out from harbours in the Netherlands loaded with drums of industrial waste. Allegedly bound for such destinations as the Sargasso Sea or even the United Kingdom, they returned within a few hours – after dumping tens of thousands of drums near the Dutch coast.

As the International Council for the Exploration of the Sea (ICES) reported that huge amounts of waste were being discharged into the North Sea, in April 1971 an article in the London *Observer*, headlined 'Big Business Moves into Sea Dumping', maintained that a company intended to collect chemical effluents from West European ports and dump them at sea.

Alarmed at this increasing dumping of harmful substances, for which no international regulations existed, the Norwegian Government expressed its concern to the British Government, discussed the issue with other Scandinavian countries, and on 11 June put into effect a ban on the dumping of persistent and harmful substances which they had agreed between them. Supported by other Nordic countries, Norway convened a conference for October, to which Western industrialized states, together with Portugal, Spain and the USSR, were invited.[20]

Before the conference took place, on UK initiative, representatives from Belgium, the Federal Republic of Germany, France, the Netherlands and the UK met informally in London in June, and in Paris on 23 July. It was necessary for the countries most responsible for waste dumping to determine their attitude to the Norwegian proposal. The complete ban proposed by the Nordic group was going too far; the question was where to draw the line.

At the second meeting the leader of the Netherlands delegation, Rob van Schaik, proposed in his opening statement that they discuss the *Stella Maris* affair. The others, however, rejected his proposal.

What, then, was the significance of the *Stella Maris*? Why were the Dutch so concerned?

A week before the Paris meeting the freighter *Stella Maris* had left

Rotterdam loaded with 650 tonnes of chlorinated hydrocarbons which, in accordance with his contract with the Dutch AKZO vinyl chloride factory, the captain had informed the harbour authorities would be dumped near Halton Bank, 60 nautical miles (110 km) west of Norway in the north part of the North Sea. Half the waste consisted of trichlorethane, five per cent of dichlorethane, and the rest of tar products from the production of vinyl chloride. Nor would the process end there, for the company intended making regular trips to dump waste.

Recalling that previous cargoes assigned to more distant destinations had been dumped within a few miles of the coast, the Dutch authorities took no chances. A ship from the Royal Dutch Navy followed the *Stella Maris* until it was north of the Dutch part of the continental shelf. Meanwhile, the Netherlands sent word to the Norwegian Shipping Directorate that the *Stella Maris* was to dump its waste off the Norwegian coast. According to one report, an error in the telex gave the figure as 30 miles instead of 60! Whether true or not, the news caused consternation in Norway as the proposed dumping site was near important fishing grounds. The Norwegian Government promptly demanded that the Netherlands stop the dumping. As the *Stella Maris* was not breaking any international law – there were no international laws to break – the most the Dutch Government could do was to ask the company voluntarily to reconsider its action.

The company obliged – and rescheduled the dumping to take place at a point in the Atlantic Ocean 1,600 km from the Icelandic and Irish coasts. Although distant, this new site was near an area in which the United States industry was in the habit of dumping waste, and, when the *Stella Maris* called at the port of Torshavn in the Faeroe Islands to take on coal for the Atlantic trip, the local fishermen prevented it from bunkering and forced it to leave.

The Governments of both Iceland and Ireland then protested against dumping at the new site. The British Government expressed concern and opposed a suggestion that the freighter should take on coal at Stornoway in the Hebrides. The Irish acted more dramatically; in case the ship intended entering Irish waters, they threatened it with a warship.

It was while the *Stella Maris* was on its way to the second site that the Paris meeting took place. By lunchtime delegates had failed to reach agreement on a common policy and it looked as if they would wait for further Scandinavian proposals before deciding. At that point the Netherlands delegation again raised the issue of the *Stella Maris*. Adopting a different tactic, they suggested that, as none of the governments represented was prepared to negotiate an international agreement, they would presumably have no objection to the *Stella Maris* continuing to dump industrial waste at authorized sites. Put this way, this disconcerting, if logical, alternative to inaction, together with the fact that, through press stories of the 'Flying Dutchman', their respective publics were alerted to the danger, produced an immediate response. As no one could be seen to approve of continued dumping, the other representatives were not only forced to express their disagreement but accepted a Dutch invitation to send experts to a meeting at The Hague on 16–17 September to prepare specific proposals for regulating dumping.

For the *Stella Maris* there was no alternative. On 25 July the freighter returned to Rotterdam, where the lethal cargo was unloaded to avoid further publicity. Later it was handed over to a Belgian firm. The day before its return, under the heading of 'Marine Dustbin', the leader of the London *Daily Telegraph* was not optimistic.

> As the public outcry against pollution goes up in most western countries, Governments are being nudged into a show of action and industrial firms appear to exercise greater discretion in the disposal of their waste chemicals and other obnoxious refuse. Not that any noticeable impression is being made on a menace that increases inexorably with the growth of industrialization. The effect of such restrictions within national territory, however, is to encourage resort to the open seas as a free garbage pit for the disposal of industrial detritus. Only in the most glaring cases, such as the highly publicized Stella Maris with its 600 tons of chemical waste, is any positive action taken, and then only as the result of diplomatic intervention by the countries most concerned. Judging by the difficulty of securing compliance even with navigation rules in the world's busiest shipping lanes in the English Channel, the chances of achieving international agreement to limit the pollution of the wider seas are remote. The best hope lies in regional co-operation, in the appeal to national self-interest of the coastal countries most immediately threatened.[21]

Despite the *non sequitur* of the penultimate sentence – 'securing compliance', i.e. ensuring that international agreements are enforced, is a different issue from 'achieving agreement' in the first place – the *Telegraph* was right on two counts: poisoning of the seas is no accidental or transient issue but an inevitable concomitant of increased industrialization; and only when a disaster occurs or there is an immediate threat do governments and the public rouse themselves – a poor outlook if humanity needs a *Torrey Canyon* or a *Stella Maris* every year to spur it to action.

Sellafield 1983[22]

On the morning of 14 November 1983 four divers from the Greenpeace ship, the *Cedarlea*, were taking samples of silt near the end of the 2.4-km pipeline in the Irish Sea near Sellafield, Cumbria, through which British Nuclear Fuels plc (BNFL) discharge radioactive waste. As they approached the pipeline the readings on their geiger counters leapt from the normal four to ten counts per second to more than 500, then went over the maximum on the dial. The source of the radioactivity appeared to be an oily substance discharged down the pipeline.

Greenpeace immediately recalled the divers, but 24 hours later the men's clothes and the inflatable dinghy from which they worked still showed high readings. The National Radiological Protection Board (NRPB), which is responsible for protection against radioactive contamination in the UK, asked the men to have a check-up and tested their equipment to try to identify the substance that had caused the accident. The divers' clothing had to be destroyed, but the dinghy, affected mainly by ruthenium, was later decontaminated and returned to its owners.

Five days later heavily contaminated items were found on a stretch of beach near the pipeline. Between these two events a visiting inspector from the Department of thé Environment (DoE) had been told of the existence of an 'oil slick' but not that it was radioactive and on the 20th the authorities declared the beaches free of pollution.

On the 24th a review of BNFL's monitoring techniques led the DoE to ask for further checks. These resulted in the discovery of high-level radioactivity near the surface of the water and of highly radioactive debris; the public were again warned of the danger of using the beaches.

Meanwhile Greenpeace attempted to carry out their aim of stopping discharges by blocking the pipeline with specially prepared bungs. On 18 November the *Cedarlea* sailed from London with a crew of 15, including the four divers previously contaminated, only to find a Liverpool tug, the *Buckmaster*, anchored near the pipeline. Two other boats later joined it. After playing cat and mouse for most of the day, ropes from the Greenpeace ship eventually fouled the tug's propeller. Greenpeace divers freed it and, diving into 26 m of water, discovered that it had been anchored over the pipe. A few minutes later they located the end of the pipeline, only to find that two metal rods had been welded to the diffuser so that their bungs were useless. Radioactivity in the area with a geiger counter reading of 150 counts per second hastened their withdrawal.

BNFL, who had obtained a legal injunction against Greenpeace not to interfere with the pipeline, now sought a sequestration order. During proceedings in the High Court on 1 December, Mr Justice Comyn invited the environmentalists three times to give an undertaking that they would not interfere with what he called the 'Windscale radioactive pipeline'. On each occasion they refused, maintaining that, while they had no wish to show contempt of court, they had been through all the normal channels to try to stop the discharge of nuclear waste into the Irish Sea and had no alternative. The judge fined Greenpeace £50,000 plus costs and gave them until 1 February to pay.

Eight days after the High Court action the DoE extended its previous warning. Originally a 200-metre stretch of beach had been sealed off when an oil slick was washed ashore. Now they warned the public against 'unnecessary use of the beaches' over a 40-km stretch. Further debris, including seaweed, pieces of plastic, string and herbage had been found with 'higher than normal' levels of radioactivity between St Bees and Eskmeals. The contamination was actually higher than during the previous month – 100 to 1,000 times the normal level. The Ministry of Agriculture, Fisheries and Food (MAFF), who are responsible for monitoring radiation, acknowledged that some samples of mussels contained significantly higher levels of radioactivity than usual, though the 'significance' was not clear as it went on to maintain that, even on the most pessimistic assumption, the resulting doses to the most exposed members of the public would not approach the limits recommended by the International Commission on Radiological Protection (ICRP). Public confidence was not increased by reports that the Ministry had withheld details about radioactive contamination of fish and solid waste that it had received.

Shortly before Parliament adjourned for the Christmas break, the Secretary of State for the Environment, Patrick Jenkin, announced that, as the Sellafield leak involved a possible breach of the law on discharges, he had referred the matter to the Director of Public Prosecutions, Sir Thomas Hetherington. Meanwhile, on the advice of the NRPB, the beaches would remain closed. The Board's memorandum revealed that items capable of giving a year's permissible dose of radiation to the skin in less than an hour were still being found. The most highly contaminated were not, as at first thought, seaweed, but porous items such as corks, pieces of rope and string, a rubber mat and other flotsam, such as feathers. Scientists were puzzled by the discovery that, while they had expected a decline in the amount of contaminated material coming ashore, the rate had continued at the same level. They had also been forced to revise their prediction that tidal movements would trap such material and return it to beaches near the pipeline. The first items had come ashore south of the plant; now they were arriving both north and south, and there was the possibility that general movement of the water, together with customary winds, would carry some material north to the Solway Firth. MAFF reported increased radioactivity in mussels near the pipeline but no other changes, and the Minister responsible, John MacGregor, expected that levels would be back to normal 'within a matter of weeks'. Others were less sanguine. The MP for Workington, the constituency in which the incident occurred, Dale Campbell-Savours, spoke of the great damage done to the tourist and fishing industries, called for compensation, and demanded that the discharge be reduced to zero. Kenneth Warren warned of the 'magnification effect' being investigated by Harwell scientists by which the level of radioactivity in sea-spray becomes ten to twenty times greater than that of the sea.

What, then, actually happened at Sellafield? The Reports of the Radiochemicals Inspectorate of the DoE and the Health and Safety Executive (HSE), published on 14 February 1984, give details which show the extent of BNFL's negligence and guilt. There were three separate discharges, on 11, 13 and 16 November, during washing-out operations. Tanks that have contained highly radioactive waste products are cleaned out with solvent but, 'because of what appears to be a failure of communication between shifts' (HSE Report), instead of the water, solvent and crud (the mixture containing the radioactive material) being returned to the original waste tank for separation so that the less radioactive watery liquid could be discharged to the sea, the whole of the water, solvent and crud was passed to sea tanks and the valves opened for discharging. At that point the alarms sounded.

BNFL decided to isolate the highly radioactive crud, which they assumed was floating on the surface, by discharging some of the contents into the sea.

The next step was to pump the material back through the system. Some of it stuck to the sides of the pipes, causing radiation to rise, and BNFL finally resorted to flushing out the pipes. This was done on the three occasions mentioned; each time the radiation level rose again. When the HSE inspectors reported, there was still no satisfactory explanation of how this happened. Their report refused to accept BNFL's figures for the amount of radioactive waste discharged and argued that the figure could be up to five times as much as BNFL's estimates.

The Radiochemicals Inspectorate were uninhibited in their condemnation of the Sellafield management. They maintained that existing controls were inadequate and accused BNFL of not considering the consequences of discharging highly active particles of waste into the sea before deciding to do so, and of failing to notify the appropriate government departments as soon as possible, even when there was potential danger to the public. The procedure for communicating information between managers was 'inadequate, prone to error and not sufficiently formalized'. Some tanks had no instruments for detecting radioactive crud, sampling was inadequate, specified procedures were not followed and, in considering the options for dealing with the emergency, BNFL had not borne in mind their duty to keep radiation exposures as low as reasonably achievable. BNFL had considered only the total amount of radioactivity, not the substances which contained it, and how they would behave when flushed out to sea.

At the beginning of March the NRPB reported that the initial drop in the amount of contaminated material had not been maintained and that a new tar-like substance containing spots of radioactivity had been found on the beaches. There were three possible causes: a further leak; the tides had uncovered material already on the beach; or material in the sea had now been brought ashore. BNFL denied a leak but identified the possible source as one of their pipelines which had been used just before discovery of the bitumen; at the DoE's request they were testing it.

On 21 March BNFL announced a week-long beach cleaning exercise and was confident that the ban on using the beaches would be lifted by Easter. The following day they pronounced the popular Cumbrian beach, St Bees near Whitehaven, free from contamination. The DoE and MAFF preferred to carry out their own monitoring before making a decision.

As April opened an independent inquiry showed that the beaches near Sellafield were still between three and thirty times more radioactive than before the November leak. On 15 May the Environment Secretary announced a considerable improvement and that the risk was now negligible. Government scientists, however, expressed misgivings over the continued uncertainty and in June employees at the Ministry of Defence experimental station at Eskmeals, seven miles south of Sellafield, detected radioactivity above normal background levels. Not until the end of July, almost nine months after the incident, did the DoE give the all-clear for the public to use the beaches, though monitoring would continue and any further contaminated material be removed.

Meanwhile the Director of Public Prosecutions had still not decided whether to prosecute BNFL, whose Radioactive Waste Management Advisory Committee published its Fifth Annual Report that month. The report is of interest as it covers 1983; admittedly the November incident is mentioned – it would be difficult not to include it – but the extent of the discharge is lost in the averages and overall context. BNFL had already maintained that only 1,500 curies of radioactivity reached the Irish Sea during the November discharge and pointed out that, as their annual authorization was 300,000 curies, they were still within their approved limits. The concept of a 'local incident' could hardly be taken further. Others might have suggested that nine months' closure of adjoining beaches could be considered a 'local' time period – if viewed in relation to a century! On 22 August, to demonstrate his trust in government pronouncements, Giles Shaw, a junior minister at the Department of Energy, went so far as to take a well-publicized swim in the sea. 'Local' hoteliers, publicans and shopkeepers were reportedly not impressed and announced plans to claim compensation for loss of trade. Nor were 'local' birds: for some reason, at nature reserves on the Ravenglass estuary there had been a decline in breeding among six species of seabirds. Black-headed gulls had declined from 12,500 breeding pairs in the 1960s to only 1,500 and had failed to breed in 1982 and 1984. Breeding terns had moved away, and there were now only 30–40 pairs of ringed plovers and 10 breeding pairs of oystercatchers – none producing chicks. No red-breasted mergansers had bred successfully and only two pairs of shelduck had raised young. The only bird not to have declined as a breeder was the lapwing. Perhaps there was significance in the fact that it fed inland.

After nine months' investigations, in August 1984 the DPP announced that BNFL were to be prosecuted under the Radioactive Substances Act 1960 and the Nuclear Installations Act 1965 on six counts: three of them concerned failure to keep adequate records – of operations at the plant, of radioactive material kept stored or accumulated, and of disposal by discharge to sea. The other failures were: to control radioactive material so that it could not escape control; to keep radiation exposure as low as was reasonably achievable; and to take all reasonable steps to minimize the exposure of persons to radiation. The offences carried penalties of five years' imprisonment or unlimited fines.

When the case came before the Carlisle Crown Court in June 1985, BNFL pleaded guilty to the charge of failing to keep adequate operational records but not guilty to the remainder. During the three-day trial, at which 40 witnesses gave evidence, it was revealed that a log sheet showing the amounts of low-level liquid waste being prepared for discharge had 24 alterations or corrections. After more than five hours' deliberation the jury found BNFL guilty on a number of counts.

Mr Justice Rose fined the company £5,000 for failing to keep discharges as low as possible, £1,500 for failure to keep records of discharges, £2,500 for failing to take all reasonable steps to minimize exposure of persons to radiation and £1,000 for not keeping adequate operational records – a total of £10,000 (with £60,000 towards costs). In making his assessment he said: 'I bear in mind that the discharge to the sea, which is at the heart of this indictment, was within the company's authorized limits. I bear in mind the fact, of particular importance in this case, that should not be lost sight of, was that there was no harm or risk of harm to any member of the public. That is not what this case has been about'.

Sceptics quickly asked why, if the case had not been about the harm or risk of harm to any member of the public, BNFL had been fined for failing to take all reasonable steps to minimize exposure of persons to radiation. They asked further why, if there was never any risk of harm to the public, the Secretary of State for the Environment had considered it necessary to warn people against using the beaches for a period of eight months. Recalling the £50,000 fine imposed on Greenpeace, the more mathematically minded calculated that, in contemporary monetarist values, it was five times as cheap to let poison get into the sea as to try to prevent it.

The Problem Stated

The incidents described in this section illustrate four of the major poisons deposited in the seas of the world – oil, heavy metals such as mercury, hazardous chemicals from industrial waste, and radionuclides. They also illustrate ways in which these reach the sea – from ships, either by accident or deliberately, by discharges of effluent through pipelines and outflows from land, and by dumping at selected sites in the sea. Finally, they illustrate some of the effects – destruction of bird life, illness or death of human beings, poisoning of fish with loss of food and livelihood for the men and women of fishing communities, and ruining of beaches that provide pleasure and relaxation for thousands of people and employment for those in the tourist industry. There is a fifth, more common pollutant for which we are all ultimately responsible, if not for the way in which it reaches the sea – human waste in the form of sewage. The poison may not be conspicuous in Western Europe, where there is more concern over dogs fouling pavements, but some coastal areas of Third World countries – and even some European ones – are literally in the shit!

The plan for this book thus largely determines itself. We must begin with the seas themselves, examine the poisons and their effects and finally determine who is responsible and what can be done about it. Chapter 1 gives an outline description of the seas and oceans of the world both spatially and 'in depth'. It describes the characteristics of different geographical water masses and the different levels of which they are composed, explains briefly the type of life found in each and its value in the ecological scheme, and shows how the waters at different levels interact with each other, with the air above, with the sea-bed beneath and with adjoining land masses.

Chapter 2 relates the sea to humanity by discussing present and potential uses – exploitation through fishing or sea-bed mining and mineral extraction, the transport of goods and people, in both civil and military operations, the potential value of the sea as a source of energy, and the use of coastal areas and islands for recreation and relaxation. This leads to the major theme – use of the seas as a dustbin for human waste.

Each of the four chapters in Part 2 deals with a particular poison – Chapter 3 with oil, Chapter 4 sewage, Chapter 5 industrial and agricultural poisons – hazardous chemicals, heavy metals and pesticides – and Chapter 6 with radioactivity. The structure of each chapter is broadly the same: a description of the nature and characteristics of the poison is followed by accounts of major accidents or operations by which it reaches the sea, the effects of the poison on living creatures, including human beings, and on the environment, and surveys of the current situation in both the industrialized and the Third World.

In Part 3, The Deeper Malady, we extend our analysis to investigate the future of the sea itself, examine attempts at amelioration through legal agreements at international and regional levels, and, drawing on the data from our survey in Part 2, attempt to diagnose the underlying causes of the dangers that now threaten not only the seas but our planet itself.

References

1. Source: *TAO* pp. 108–9

2. Ibid. and p. 169; ACOPS 1967 p. 4

3. *Le Figaro*, Paris, 4 April 1967; ACOPS 1967 pp. 4–5; *The Times* 13 April 1967; *Le Journal de Dimanche*, Paris, 2 April 1967; *Evening Standard* 13 April 1967

4. *Le Journal de Dimanche*, Paris, 2 April 1967

5. ACOPS 1967 pp. 9–11; *L'Homme et L'Oiseau* April 1967

6. *Daily Mirror* 20 January 1967

7. Ibid. 30 January 1967

8. *New York Times* 21 April 1967

9. ACOPS 1967 p. 5

10. *New York Times* 12 August 1967

11. Ibid. 17 September 1967

12. GESAMP 22 pp. 6–8

13. GESAMP 15 p. 51

14. Sources: Gerlach 1976 pp. 605–6; Moorcraft 1972 pp. 89–90

15. Agarwal et al. 1982 p. 22

16. GESAMP 15 p. 37

17. Moorcraft 1972 pp. 95–6

18. Gerlach 1976 p. 613

19. Ibid.; Moorcraft 1972 p. 96

20. This account combines those of Van der Burgt 1984 pp. 1–4 and Gerlach 1976 p. 613.

21. *Daily Telegraph* 24 July 1971

22. Sources: *Guardian* 17, 22, 24 November 1983, 2, 9, 22 December 1983, 14 January 1984, 15 February 1984, 2, 21, 23 March 1984, 3 April 1984, 16 May 1984, 7, 8 June 1984, 27 July 1984, 1, 2, 23 August 1984, 6, 8 June 1985, 24 July 1985; ACOPS 1983 pp. 7, 11–12; DoE Radiochemicals Inspectorate 1984; Health and Safety Executive 1984

Part 1: The Seas and Humanity

1.   The Oceans and How They Work

Land, Air and Water

The first thing to strike one about the sea is its size – 361,740,000 sq km or 70.92% of the total earth's surface.[1] The Pacific Ocean alone covers almost 32% of the globe, more than all the land masses put together; three-fifths of the northern hemisphere is covered by water. Of the human inhabitants of the land seven out of ten live within 320 km of the seashore.[2]

The sea has not only extent but depth – 11,524 m (or over seven miles) in the Mindanao Trench of the Pacific. Scientists have estimated its total volume as 1,205,600,000 cu km (308,400,000 cu miles) of sea-water. Not only is its surface area greater than that of the land, its desirable 'living space' is also greater. For inhabitants of the land only 20.9% of the earth's surface is lower than one kilometre above sea-level; for those of the sea the least inhabitable region – between four and five kilometres below the surface – occupies only 23.2% of its total volume.[3]

The very size of the sea gives potential poisoners their strongest argument. The command 'Get Lost' to a canister of deadly chemicals or radioactive waste has a better chance of being obeyed in the vast ocean depths than on land, or even at the bottom of the deepest mine. Any challenge to this argument must begin by studying the sea in relation to humanity.

Of the sea itself, four facts are axiomatic: 1) despite the divisons by which geographers have labelled the waters of the earth – oceans, seas, gulfs – and so compartmentalized our conceptualization of them, there are no separate seas, only one interlinked world ocean; 2) even this concept is inadequate, for the world ocean does not exist in isolation; throughout its length and breadth it has an intimate and complex relationship with the air around it. 'Oceanic circulations depend upon atmospheric motions and also help maintain those motions. In a sense, the atmosphere and the oceans constitute a single system of two fluids interacting with each other'[4]; 3) if the 'spatial' facts are obvious, where poisons are concerned the 'time' factor is equally important; for example, plutonium-239, which is produced by the nuclear industry, has a 'half-life' of 24,400 years[5] (see Chapter 6). Even if the chemical composition of the seas has remained relatively stable for millions of years, the addition of a long-living poison may affect it for millions to come; 4) finally, despite the recent exciting discoveries of the *Glomar Challenger* and scientific research into the ocean depths, our knowledge of the sea, of how it 'works', and of its relation to land-dwelling human beings is far from complete. Of even such a familiar feature as the tides the compilers of the *Times Atlas* write: 'The complex behaviour of the tides is still not fully understood',[6] and comment, in almost the same words, on the constancy of the relative proportions of the elements in sea-water: 'the chemical balance of the oceans is not yet fully understood by scientists'.[7] On the question of how substances are carried through the sea GESAMP experts conclude: 'Knowledge of fundamental processes is not extensive enough for the identification or quantification of the oceanic pathways for many substances';[8] in non-scientific language, if we drop something into the sea, we cannot be certain where it will arrive or how much of it will get there! The simple and ultimate verdict upon those who regard the sea as a permanent and bottomless dustbin is that they know not what they do.

Descriptions of the sea tell us as much about those who write them as about the sea itself. Fishermen view it in terms of fish; navigators in relation to channels, rocks, lighthouses, typhoons, tsunamis, wrecks and the speed of wind and water currents; industrialists are concerned only with extracting oil, gas or minerals from beneath the sea-bed or with dumping dangerous waste on or into it; holiday-makers notice whether the tide is in or out, how far they must walk for a swim and whether jellyfish or human excrement is the more likely hazard; impressed by its majesty, the poet apostrophizes it – 'Roll on, thou dark and deep blue ocean, roll' – meticulously choosing open-vowelled sounds whose effectiveness is obvious if one substitutes 'Splash' for 'Roll'. Even those 'objective' analysts, the scientific community, offer different 'seas' for our inspection: the surface geographer writes of oceans, seas, bays, embayments, estuaries, straits, sounds, channels, etc; the chemist analyses the composition and salinity of sea-water; the investigator of ocean basins divides his sea into the continental shelf, slope and rise, and the deep ocean with its abyssal hills, seamounts and guyots; to the marine biologist it consists of euphotic, mesopelagic, bathypelagic and abyssopelagic zones according to the types of plants and animals found in each, while students of ocean movements introduce yet a further system with divisions such as the Eckman layer, the thermocline and deep (or 'bottom') water. The only 'sea' we know is that created by humanity's perception of it; the only way to understand what is meant by 'poisoning the seas' is to discover the relevance of each of these partial views.

The View from Above – with a Glance Below[9]

In the 1980s we have a better chance of appreciating the extent of the world ocean than had previous generations. Our television screens show us the earth viewed from space – a watery planet on which the land appears as a geological afterthought. The spaceman's view is of interest to potential poisoners since it distinguishes large areas of water from small. These the earth-bound geographer labelled respectively 'oceans' – from the Greek *okeanos*, the stream which his forebears believed encircled the earth, i.e. the land – and 'seas', if it was not always clear which was which. The 'seven seas' of history – the Arctic, Antarctic, North Pacific, South Pacific, North Atlantic, South Atlantic and Indian – are now 'Oceans' in their own right, even though, with the realization that there is only one world ocean, it becomes increasingly difficult to decide where one ends and another begins, and present practice has reduced the seven to five, or even three.

The largest surface area of water, 165.4 million sq km or almost 40% of that of the total world ocean, is the ironically named Pacific, bounded on the east by the coastline mountain ranges of North and South America, which effectively block the flow into it of any major rivers, thus limiting the amount of sediment reaching it from land, and on the west by a series of smaller seas off the land masses of eastern Asia and Australia. Its greatest length, from north to south, is estimated at 11,000 km, its greatest width, from east to west, at 16,000 km. It is also the deepest ocean, both on average (4,200 m) and absolutely (11,524 m). In general it is deeper in the west, particularly near the island groups where major trenches occur, than in the east.

If the Pacific owes its name to the sailors who dared its perils, the Atlantic belongs to Greek myth as extended by later history. The word *Atlantikos*, derived from the giant Atlas-antos who held up the pillars of the universe and whose name was later applied to the mountains of north Africa, came to denote, as 'atlas', a book of maps, then the sea near those mountains, and finally the expanse of water between Europe and Africa in the east and the Americas in the west. With a surface area of 82.2 million sq km the Atlantic is only half the size of the Pacific; in the north its greatest width, between Morocco and Florida, is 7,200 km; it is shallower than the Pacific, with an average depth of 3,600 m and a maximum of 9,560 m in the Puerto Rico Trench. In contrast again to the Pacific, a number of major rivers, the Amazon, Congo, Niger, Mississippi and St Lawrence, flow, either directly or indirectly, into the Atlantic, bringing with them large quantities of sediment from land as well as both fresh and poisoned water.

The third major ocean, the Indian, at least lives up to its name, for its character is largely determined by that land mass to the north. Unlike the other oceans, the greater part of its 73.6 million sq km is in the southern hemisphere. At its greatest width, between Tasmania and Cape Agulhas in the south, it is as extensive as the southern Atlantic (9,600 km). On average it is slightly deeper (4,000 m) though its greatest depth, in the Amirante Trench (9,000 m), falls slightly short of that of the Atlantic.

As for the Arctic and Antarctic, or, as the latter is more generally called today, the Southern Ocean, their major characteristics are well-known. The Arctic is more clearly definable as it is surrounded almost entirely by land. Of its 12.2 million sq km the largest part is covered by ice 3–3.5 m thick, which is more complex in form and lasts longer than that of the Antarctic.

In contrast the Southern Ocean is almost three times as large, approximately

35 million sq km, of which almost two-thirds freezes over each winter. The land-mass of Antarctica, a continent in itself, is surrounded by sea and buried beneath an ice sheet that covers about 13.5 million sq km with an average thickness of about two kilometres. In this most inhospitable part of the globe is found 90 per cent of the earth's permanent ice. From our present viewpoint, the importance of these oceans is their effect on the movement of the world ocean as a whole.

The seas of the world are those smaller areas of the world ocean which, because they are partly surrounded by land, have acquired distinguishing labels. Of the 14 largest, three are designated by colour, if for different reasons – the Black, Red and Yellow; others, like the East China, South China and Sea of Japan, take their names from the adjoining land; two are not even 'seas' – Mexico is a 'Gulf' and Hudson a 'Bay'. The Baltic aside, Europe's seas reflect ethnocentricity and politics; the Mediterranean was once 'the centre of the world'; early twentieth century atlases show not the 'North Sea' but the 'German Ocean'.

Compared with oceans, seas are minuscule. Only three – the Mediterranean, South China and Bering – exceed two million sq km in surface area, while the Black, Red and Baltic Seas are less than 500,000 sq km. Similarly with depth: the Caribbean has the deepest point (7,100 m) but only two others, South China and Bering, exceed 5,000 m, while the greatest depth of the North Sea is 661 m, of the Baltic 460 m, and of the Yellow Sea a mere 91 m. It is this comparative shallowness and smallness, coupled with their proximity to highly populated and industrialized countries, that makes seas particularly susceptible to poisoning. The Mediterranean and the Baltic are among the most highly poisoned waters of the world.

The View from Below – the Shape of Ocean Basins[10]

In relation to the land that adjoins or lies beneath them all oceans and seas have similar features. Starting from the land, the first definable area is that portion of the earth's surface which land and water share between them – the *inter-tidal zone*, *foreshore* or *littoral* between high and low water marks. This varies from gently sloping beaches with extensive littorals, over which the incoming tide must travel several kilometres, to precipitous cliffs, where the difference in water level is more vertical than horizontal, from estuaries or deltas with mud flats or sand dunes to busy ports and harbours; from ice shelves in the Southern Ocean to coral lagoons in the tropics. It is at this point that humanity, either through direct disposal of waste into the sea or indirectly through rivers, has its greatest impact.

Beaches are the result of accumulated sediment, mainly sand, sometimes gravel or shingle, that waves bring up and deposit on the underlying rock. Where waves are small, beaches tend to be stable, but continual large waves have a dramatic effect on their shape and structure. In the perpetual interplay between sea and land, humanity is generally the loser. Where the sea advances, human habitations, built safely a mile or more from the shore, now perch perilously on a cliff edge; where it retreats, the sea drags with it the livelihood of a one-time busy port, its harbour silted up, its wharves useless.

Technically the shoreface extends to a depth at which waves no longer affect the movement of sediment, usually where the sea is 12–20 m deep. Beyond this is the *continental shelf* or *sub-littoral*, a shallow platform that is really an extension of the land. Like the land also it may be irregularly shaped, with small 'hills', valleys and basins, but for the most part it is relatively smooth and gently sloping. Much of the sea-bed consists of sands or gravels deposited thousands of years ago either from rivers or by coastal erosion and thereafter subject to the activity of waves or tidal currents. Such sediments are either silicate minerals – gravel, sand, silt and clay, thus inciting human beings to exploit them by dredging – or carbonates with a high potential for encouraging the growth of life in the sea. In depositing sediments the sea at times traps oil or gas in pockets beneath the earth – hence the undersea oilfields of the Gulf and the North Sea. Among the fascinating features of the continental shelf are coral reefs, found only in the tropics where the water temperature is never less than 18°C. The actual reef consists of an upper layer where thousands of polyps live on top of the whitened skeletons of previous generations which form the deeper layers.

At depths varying from 35 m to over 350 m there is an abrupt change. The sea-bed descends to the depths down the *continental slope*, which varies in gradient from one in forty (off deltas) to a steep one in three. The slope is often marked by deep V-shaped valleys, probably formed by erosion during the last ice-age and since widened by *turbidity currents*, underwater avalanches caused by earthquakes or simply by the effect of gravity on huge, loose masses of sediment. On their journey to the ocean depths these plough furrows down the slope at speeds of 80–100 km an hour, assisted in their impetus by the relative steepness of the upper slope, and carrying with them material that eventually finds its way thousands of kilometres out to sea.

Over the centuries these vast masses of sediment have piled up at the foot of the slope to form a third distinctive feature, the *continental rise*, with gradients varying from one in fifty to one in 1,800. These long wedges have now accumulated so that in places they are several kilometres thick.

Collectively referred to as the *continental margin*, these three features are found in all oceans, while, because of their relative shallowness, the basins of many seas are no more than continental shelves. The oceans, however, have different characteristics; the Atlantic has wide continental shelves of up to 1,500 km, the Pacific narrow ones of 20–40 km; in the Atlantic the slope may be marked by deep, underwater canyons, in the Pacific there is more likelihood of a steep descent to a trough or trench (over 6,000 m). In both the Atlantic and Indian Oceans continental rises tend to be wide, in the Pacific narrow or absent.

Beyond the continental margin lie the ocean depths. Scientists designate the area between 1,000 and 3,000 m as the *bathyal* or *abyssal zone* and deep trenches below 6,000 m as the *hadal* zone. More commonly, if less technically, they talk of the *ocean* or *deep sea floor*, or simply of the *ocean basin*. The floor itself may consist of mile upon mile of flat, rolling plains, broken by hills, some of which are several kilometres high and up to ten kilometres in diameter. They are caused either by geological folding or through volcanic activity. The plains themselves are unique in flatness with gradients of less than one in a thousand. In the ocean depths turbidity currents that have produced the continental rise become weaker and the sediments finer as particles settle to form a blanket of ooze over the earth's crust that varies in thickness from 500 m in the Atlantic to 300 m in the Pacific. This sediment comes from two sources – sea-life itself, as the skeletal remains of millions of microscopic sea creatures from the surface waters sink slowly downward to pile up on the remains of earlier generations, and, on the borders of the oceans, by deposits from land, some of which may have been carried by ice as it drifted away.

The most remarkable features of the deep ocean are the huge mountain *ridges* which form a continuous chain through the three main ocean basins and occupy about a third of the total area. The summits of these ranges are from one to four kilometres above the ocean bed and two to three kilometres below the surface of the water. Even more remarkable, these ridges are accompanied by deep trenches, throughout the length of which there is volcanic activity. Basaltic rocks, thrust up from deep inside the earth, form new oceanic crust at the crest of ridges which then spreads sideways. Oceanic *rises* differ from ridges in that they are not formed by volcanic activity but by a gentle upwarping of the earth's crust. Again the Atlantic and Pacific are in contrast, the former is now passive and aseismic, the latter active and seismic.

The explanation for this phenomenon lies in the theory of continental drift, put forward in 1912 by the German scientist Alfred Wegener, and now developed into the science of tectonics. According to this the present continents were originally more or less one great island surrounded by sea; the island fractured into a number of plates which have 'drifted', and are still drifting, apart. The driving force behind this process is the volcanic activity taking place along the ocean ridges. The 'passivity' of the Atlantic is explained by the fact that it is all on the same tectonic plate. In contrast the Pacific floor is on different plates and the Pacific/Nazca boundary has the fastest spreading rate of over 16 cm yearly. When one plate moves under another, the result is a long, narrow but exceptionally deep trench, which in practice occurs near the margins of continents as on the western coast of South America, or near some island arc system. Hence the great depths of the Mindanao (11,524 m) and Marianas (11,022 m) Trenches. The 'obvious' solution to poisonous waste disposal – dropping it into the deepest parts of the sea – is thus a non-starter. As the plates are still in motion, it would imply defying the movement of the earth itself.

The Waters Between – a Chemist's View[11]

Between the sea-bed and the air is the sea itself, which the non-scientist thinks of as 'water', or, if just back from a swim, as 'salt-water'. But what exactly is this 'salt sea' apart from the poisons that humanity has placed in it and the living creatures to which it is a natural home?

Chemical analysis shows that sea 'water' is a complex solution, the most remarkable feature of which is its relative stability, i.e. the proportions of all major and several minor elements found in it are constant except in special areas such as estuaries or the bottom of enclosed waters, such as the Black Sea. Scientists have estimated the total quantity of solids dissolved in the world ocean as approximately 5,000 million million tonnes, of which sodium and chlorine account for more than 85% by weight, while there are large amounts of sulphate, magnesium, calcium and potassium. They have discovered about 80 of the naturally occurring elements in seawater, although in theory all of them should be present, either brought from land by rivers or discharged into the sea by volcanic activity. In addition to the substances mentioned, which are dissolved in the water in the form of electronically charged ions, there are small amounts of those nutrients which enable plants and animals to exist, together with gases from the air. Many substances of importance to humanity, e.g. lead, zinc, copper, nickel, manganese, cobalt and phosphorus, can be obtained from minerals formed in the sea or from living organisms, such as seaweed, which concentrate these elements more effectively than we can. This ability is, however, both a benefit and a danger; if the seas remain our only source of that essential substance, iodine, 'it is the very ability to concentrate elements that poses special dangers from certain types of pollution, such as organochlorines and heavy metals'.[12]

From our present viewpoint the 'saltiness' of the sea is more than an interesting phenomenon; it is associated with both life and death. But for the nutrient salts dissolved in water, there would be no life, yet poisons can also exist 'in solution' and so reach their victims. Addition of fresh water, e.g. from rivers, decreases the salinity of the sea, while evaporation, especially in hot climates, increases it, thus producing, in conjunction with differences in temperature and pressure, changes in *density*, i.e. the weight of a given volume of water. As 'more dense' water is heavier than 'less dense', the heavy water sinks towards the ocean bed, to be replaced by lighter water – and the sea, which so far we have examined as a static object, is set in motion, carrying with it whatever poisonous or non-poisonous substances it contains.

The Moving Waters – Ocean Circulation[13]

Movement of the sea – and its contents – is a highly complex process brought about by the interplay of internal changes, e.g. in density, and external forces, e.g. the atmosphere. Surface waters are affected mainly by the wind; mid- and bottom-waters by internal factors.

Wind blowing over the surface has a number of effects. Near the coast it produces waves, i.e. *wind-waves*, as opposed to the *internal waves* which are caused by differences in density. Further out to sea wave movement takes the form of *swell*, that 'up-and-down' motion whose unfortunate effects are familiar to sea travellers.

The wind also causes surface water to drift in the same direction as it blows and so to form *currents*. At this point another phenomenon intervenes – the rotation of the earth. Because of what is known as the *Coriolis effect* this rotation deflects the movement of water so that eventually it flows at an angle of 45° to the direction of the wind. In the northern hemisphere water flows to the right of the wind direction, in the southern to the left. The surface water then communicates its movement to the water beneath it by friction, but the effect lessens with depth, while that of the earth's rotation remains constant. Eventually the two forces 'cancel' each other and the water does not move at all. What may happen to any object in the water thus becomes increasingly unpredictable.

As movement of the wind-driven layer of the sea – the *Eckman layer* as it is known, after the Swedish hydrologist who first analysed it – and that of the lower waters affected by it depends on the wind, its direction will be that of the prevailing winds. In the tropics these are trade winds, which blow from the north-east in the northern hemisphere, from the south-east in the southern, and converge on the equator; in middle latitudes the dominant winds are westerlies; and in the north Indian Ocean, the China Seas and the western North Pacific, there are reversals of direction brought about by the monsoon. In summer the land is hotter than the sea so that the wind blows from sea to land; in winter the opposite occurs.

The effect of these dominant wind patterns is to produce a number of well-marked surface currents, the best known of which are the boundary currents on the western sides of the oceans, e.g. the Gulf Stream in the Atlantic, the Kuroshio in the Pacific and the Agulhas Current in the Indian Ocean off southern Africa. All these are permanent water movements; off East Africa, however, the Somali Current flows in a similar direction only between May and October when the winds are south-westerly.

An important effect of such major surface currents is to produce zones of *convergence* or *divergence*, i.e. a coming-together or separating of different types of water. Of these perhaps the best known is the Antarctic Convergence between latitudes 50° and 60° south, which marks the meeting of cold, ascending and extremely productive water with warmer waters. When divergence occurs, there is a vertical upward movement of colder waters rich in nutrients such as nitrates and phosphates that promote the existence of plankton (see next section). This vertical movement, known as *upwelling*, occurs also when the wind blows parallel to the coast, causing the surface water to be driven away from it and allowing colder, richer water to rise. The phenomenon is particularly important off the western coast of South America and is directly responsible for the Peruvian fishing industry (see Chapter 2).

Outside higher latitudes there is a further ocean layer, the *thermocline*, distinguished by an abrupt change in temperature, which occurs at depths of a few hundred metres according to latitude, weather and time of year. The main effect of the thermocline is to act as a 'stopper' and impede the mixing of surface water with the *deep* or *bottom water* below. Like that of the surface, the lower water flows in currents, which are strongest at the western edges of the oceans (20 cm per second) but elsewhere very slow indeed.

As part of the world ocean, seas have some of the same features. The Mediterranean, for example, with its clear skies and sparse rainfall for most of the year, has a large amount of evaporation uncompensated by the entry of river water. This leads to increased salinity and density of the surface water, which then sinks, to be replaced by less dense water. As the extent of evaporation increases between Gibraltar in the west and Turkey in the east, the surface water moves generally eastward, while a bottom current of dense salty water is formed which flows over the sill at the Strait of Gibraltar into the North Atlantic. So strong is this flow that, during World War II, German submarines were able to be carried into the Atlantic with engines stopped, thereby avoiding detection by Allied radar. The salty water then flows southward with the North Atlantic deep water and is replaced by a comparatively shallow surface layer from the Atlantic.

In considering the movement of the oceans – and of anything deposited in them – we may know the general features, but we cannot predict the details. Maps showing average or mean conditions thus

> provide no information about the ever-changing meanders, eddies and filaments which are now known to be characteristic elements of oceanic circulations in both surface and deep water. Many of the eddies and fragments of current are very extensive, not uncommonly covering several thousands or even tens of thousands of square kilometres. They can also be remarkably persistent as identifiable features.[14]

In investigating the pathways of poison we cannot take the average or mean as our standard. It is the exceptional that causes major disasters; the average is important for its cumulative effect.

Life in the Sea – the Marine Biologist's View[15]

Of the many amazing characteristics of the sea, perhaps the most surprising is the fact that, considering its depth and extent, the whole of it is inhabited by living organisms (the *biomass*). Despite its size, however, the number of different species of plants and animals is distinctly limited. Scientists have differentiated more than a million animal species on our planet, but only about 16% of them are found in the sea, and only two per cent live in mid-water. The size of their environment, however, enables them to exist in millions. Copepods, for example, those small, shrimp-like creatures which vary in length from 0.15 to 17 mm, are found throughout, the larger types mainly at depths between 1,000 and 5,000 m, the smaller in shallower waters.

The occurrence of different species at different depths enables marine biologists to produce their own division of the ocean by layers. From the surface to a depth of about 100 m they distinguish the *euphotic* or *epipelagic zone* by the fact that within it photosynthesis can take place. Most of the world's fisheries (see Chapter 2) are in this zone; among copepods found are krill, the largest species of which grows to about 60 mm and swarms in huge shoals in the Southern Ocean. Between 100 m and 1,000 m, the *mesopelagic zone* is bounded by the extent to which light can penetrate. Many creatures living here migrate daily to higher waters in search of food, which is either carried back by them or sinks in the form of dead bodies or faecal matter from those living above. Scarlet or deep red deep-sea prawns, for example, travel upwards from depths of 500 m or more during the day to within 100 m of the surface at night. As their main concern is to find food without becoming food for others, many inhabitants of this zone have developed protective camouflage such as reflective surfaces or flashing lights, e.g. squid, which have cells that change colour and give out light.

In the *bathypelagic zone*, between 1,000 and 2,000 m, there is a general decrease in both the number of different species and in the total population. Fewer creatures have light organs, though angler fish use them to attract prey. The most typical creatures are black fishes, red shrimps and gelatinous squid; at these depths few creatures show much movement, but pass their time conserving energy. Below 2,000 m, in the deep waters of the *abyssopelagic zone*, there is an even further decrease in living matter until about 100 m from the sea floor where an unexpected change takes place – a sudden increase in living creatures, as we encounter a new community associated with the sea-bed, the *benthos*.

To the non-scientist this appears an anomaly, for the *benthic zone* extends the whole length of the sea-bed from the foreshore to the ocean depths. There are, however, different benthic communities according to depth and variation in sediments, from the sands and gravels of the coastal region and continental shelf to the finely grained calcareous or siliceous oozes of the deep ocean. In coastal areas and along the mid-ocean ridges there are also rocky outcrops which provide a home for those creatures that spend their lives clinging to rocks.

In the inter-tidal zone of the benthos, plants and animals are exposed to both air and sea, and adapt themselves accordingly, thus producing the different bands of texture or colour found on rocky coasts. On the upper continental slope down to about 1,500 m live the sponges, corals and starfish; slow-moving eaters of detritus, including typical deep-sea creatures such as rat-tailed fishes, also appear. Inhabitants of the lower continental slope (1,500–3,500 m) and the deep-sea abyssal plains (4,000–6,000 m) such as sea-cucumbers depend mainly on detritus for food. On the deep-sea floor itself most creatures are no more than a millimetre in length and live buried in the sediment. Previously biologists had thought that food in the form of dead bodies and faecal matter from mid-ocean reached the sea-bed as decomposed small particles, but research during the last twenty years has led to the discovery of a highly mobile group of deep-sea scavengers, varying from amphipod crustaceans and shrimps to different types of fishes and larger sharks, which move rapidly towards any newly arrived food, irrespective of size.

Even more remarkable was the discovery in the late 1970s that special forms of life exist in volcanic deep trenches 11,000 m below the surface. Water entering fissures in the sea-bed becomes heated and acquires hydrogen sulphide and other chemicals which are then used by bacteria to produce organic matter from carbon dioxide, thus by-passing the normal process of photosynthesis. This activity enables the existence of creatures unknown elsewhere, e.g. a clam which grows up to 20 cm in length, and giant tube-worms several metres long and 2–3 cm in diameter. That these discoveries are so recent and contradict previous 'knowledge' of life in the ocean depths is yet a further reminder of the need for caution in passing judgements on the sea.

Basic to life in the ocean are *plankton*. *Phytoplankton*, the most important form of plant life in the sea, are microscopic algae which float freely in the mid-ocean depths or live in the surface layers of the open ocean. Their abundance is determined by the supply of nutrient salts, which, as we have seen, is controlled by the mixing of cold deep waters with warm shallow waters, thus bringing salts to the surface layers. Over continental shelves and in shallow waters the supply of phytoplankton is affected by currents and the stirring of waters during storms. In the polar region, where there is no thermocline layer, storms and currents also bring up nutrient-bearing depth water with comparative ease. In the sub-tropics and tropics, however, where surface temperatures would encourage production, the strong thermocline keeps the water layers separate so that only when upwelling occurs do supplies increase.

Zooplankton are animals that feed not only on phytoplankton but also on themselves and are in turn fed on by such fish as herring and mid-water shrimps. The category includes all main animal types, from protozoa to larval fishes, and all sizes from the microscopic to large jellyfish. As their main diet is phytoplankton, their distribution in the world ocean is similar. They are found at all ocean depths but live mainly in the upper thousand metres where many migrate daily upwards. To humanity they are important as a link in the chain between plants and commercially exploitable fish – the chain along which poisons dumped in the sea return to plague us.

Pathways of Poison

The Coastal Zone and the Continental Shelf[16]

What happens to any substance entering the sea in the coastal zone is determined by a complex interaction between the substance itself, the sea at that point, and the coastal area, each of which offers a number of variables. Geologically, the coastline may vary from a large bay surrounded by high cliffs to a low-lying delta. Economically, it may be a scene of industrial activity or fishing, of ports, harbours and transport, or of tourist beaches, each with its distinctive type of waste. The sea is affected not only by internal factors – the complex interplay of currents, wind and wave movements, the tides, and even the inflow of waters from the deep ocean – but by direct discharges of poisonous and non-poisonous substances from land outfalls and pipelines, from the atmosphere and through rivers, the 'fresh' water alone of which would lead to further complications as it mingles with the sea. As for the substance itself, it may either be dissolved in the water or take the form of minute particles of suspended matter.

Faced with this complexity, even GESAMP's scientists admit that 'the pathways of many materials . . . are only beginning to be understood as analytical techniques have recently reached the state that allows measurements made at various times and places to be compared'.[17] They are at least reasonably certain about what happens to matter entering the sea as particles – nine-tenths of it sinks to accumulate on the sediments of the continental shelf, the remaining tenth finds its way to the open ocean. In plain terms, we may think we have got rid of some nasty waste by discharging it into the sea, only to find out that most of it remains at the bottom just off our doorstep.

What happens to material dissolved in the water is even more complex. If its chemical properties permit, it may be changed through such processes as oxidation or reduction. Physically, it may attach itself to particles, which then join together – a process known as *flocculation* – and follow the path of other particles to the bottom. The process may even be reversed. The arrival of river water leads to a dilution in the sea's salinity, which in turn causes changes in solubility and so affects flocculation. To the non-scientist the whole process appears as a perfect example of what is meant by things being 'in flux', a conclusion reinforced by GESAMP's assessment that

> the primary sedimentation zone probably never reaches equilibrium and its chemical and physical transport properties involve different time scales that are still to be determined. Consequently, it is difficult to make predictions about the total amount of a contaminant that will reach, or has been reaching, the open ocean.[18]

This area of the sea, which is of the greatest importance to humanity and of which our knowledge is also perhaps greatest, remains unpredictable. We know that considerable mixing of waters and of the substances carried by or dissolved in them occurs, together with various chemical changes, but the end result may not be what the experts forecast. We know that movements of light fresh water entering the upper layers of the sea from rivers bring up heavier, more saline water from below. We have seen already how winds set up surface currents and how these are deflected by the Coriolis effect. We have noted also the influence of the tides, which can cause the circulation of residual matter in large bays and the mixing of different layers of water in shallow areas. Yet the very complexity of these processes, even without interference from humanity, makes it rash indeed to predict with assurance what will happen to any substance entering the sea.

The Surface of the Sea[19]
We stated at the outset that the ocean and the atmosphere form a single system of two interacting fluids. In considering the pathways of poison from the air into the sea (and vice versa) we encounter yet another 'zone' – the ocean surface itself. This is actually a very thin layer, generally less than a millimetre thick, which not only contains a unique community of organisms but is extremely

important in determining the rates of movement of solids, liquids and gases, both from air to water and from the sea into the atmosphere.

From our landlubber's viewpoint, it comes as a surprise to discover that, for some substances, the same or even greater quantities reach the sea through the air as are discharged into it by rivers. More than half the total amount of zinc, cadmium, lead, mercury and selenium reaching the sea travels by air in the form of *aerosols*, in which ultra-microscopic particles are suspended as a gas. The process extends to man-made substances such as chlorinated hydrocarbons and the radionuclides of plutonium and americium. A remarkable feature is that this is a two-way activity. Heavy metals, sulphates, radionuclides and micro-organisms reaching the sea as precipitation and beginning their journey to lower levels are brought back to the surface by air bubbles which collect material as they rise and eject it into the atmosphere, along with their gaseous contents, as they burst at the surface. Even more remarkable is the process occurring in that other form of sea–air transport, sea-spray; the poisons carried back to air – and land – by this method have *increased* in toxicity!

Microscopic plants and animals found in the surface layer also play a part in this sea–air traffic. They produce organic matter which forms a surface film that in turn attracts oils and heavy metal compounds, a process of particular importance in oil spills. Compared with the water beneath it, this surface layer is highly poisoned, but again there are limits to our knowledge. 'Relatively little information exists on levels of pollutants in the organisms inhabiting this zone – the pleuston that live on the surface and the neuston that live immediately beneath it'.[20] What is important is the capacity of these organisms as a 'pathway of poison' to lower levels of the sea, either through predation or excretion; if the organisms themselves are not eaten, their faeces sink as minute particles to form food for other organisms.

In this way, or dissolved in the water itself, all substances entering the ocean across the air–sea boundary may be carried downwards. How rapidly this removal of poisons from the surface layer takes place depends both on the extent of mixing that occurs in the upper ocean and on what happens in deeper waters.

The Open Ocean[21]

Because of their extent and depth, our knowledge of what happens to a substance in the wide ocean expanses between the surface layer and the sea-bed is limited. Scientists admit frankly that most of it is deduced from what we know of the physical movements of the ocean. Sharp differences in temperature at the polar regions cause colder, heavy water to sink and spread in slow-moving currents throughout the ocean basins. At the same time winds cause the major surface currents along the western sides of the Atlantic and Pacific. Upwelling also mixes the waters.

From the physical viewpoint most mixing occurs horizontally along layers of the same density rather than vertically. This was demonstrated after the atmospheric testing of atom bombs in the 1960s, when tritium discharged was sampled during the Geochemical Ocean Section Study of 1972–73. Water masses from the same source have also been traced along the same density layer throughout the oceans.

Substances may also move vertically, both downward and upward, with the additional complication already noted that they may be dissolved in water, attached to particles, or even carried by living creatures. Particles vary in size from 1–100 micrometres (μm); the smaller, mainly skeletal remains or inorganic detritus, travel at the rate of only several hundred metres a year; the larger, mainly faecal pellets and dead matter, reach the sea-bed in a few days. On their way to the ocean floor they may add to or remove elements dissolved in the water. The extent of this activity varies with the amount of inorganic matter entering the water and the number of creatures living in the upper and middle waters.

So far scientists have been more successful in identifying these different and highly complex processes than in quantifying them. We know, for example, that chemically active elements metamorphose between the form of particles and the state of being dissolved in water at different stages of their journey. While each horizontal layer may show a certain consistency, the physical processes already noted may upset the vertical pathway. Some elements, such as phosphorus and cadmium, are released when the organic matter carrying them is destroyed on its journey; conversely, copper, which becomes more concentrated the deeper it sinks, becomes attached to fine particles. Some trace elements reaching the open ocean from either land or air are recycled several times, proceeding both up and down again, before finally settling on the sediments of the sea-bed. As for transport by living creatures, that process is mainly upward and responsible for the return of poisonous substances to humanity, a subject to which we shall return.

The Sea-bed[22]

Even at the bottom of the sea the process continues. Obviously what happens depends on the point at which a substance reaches the sea-bed. What happens on the sands and gravels of the continental shelf, where the water is comparatively shallow and currents and tides cause considerable movement and mixing, differs from what takes place on the ocean ridges with their rocky masses and volcanic outpourings. Here we will consider only the vast abyssal plains of fine sediment which form the greater part of the sea-bed in the ocean depths.

Materials reaching the ocean floor undergo a variety of physical, chemical and biological processes, known collectively as *diagenesis*, which may continue for millions of years. The chemical processes include decomposing, dissolving in water, undergoing a reduction in oxygen content, and being added to or separated from other matter. A further possibility is the formation of completely new substances. Materials that escape being deposited on the sediments by dissolving in the water form a suspended boundary layer some tens of metres thick, which lies above the sea-bed and, at the ocean edges in particular, is mixed by movement of the water.

Two processes account for the fact that the sediments themselves accumulate only slowly. Where there are relatively strong bottom currents, material already deposited may be stirred up again and resuspended to mix with the thick layer of newly arriving matter. The second is the work of the benthic community – those creatures living on or in the sediment itself, which depend for their food on the one to three per cent of organic matter that travels from the surface to the depths. In their struggle for existence they not only stir up the sediment (*bioturbation*) but pump water into it, thus increasing the exchange of the *pore waters* that fill the narrow channels between particles.

The process by which a substance reaches its final resting place in the deep sediments is slow indeed and depends on how quickly it escapes resuspension, the molecular processes which it must undergo to diffuse into deeper sediment, and the rate at which it is buried by newly arriving deposits. Man-made substances tend to enter the sediments relatively rapidly, but unless they then undergo chemical or radioactive change, they will remain available for future interaction with the waters above – and their contents.

How the sediment is affected depends on the amount and composition of the material it receives. In the deep ocean, oxygen enters the sediments at the same rate as it is used up in the decomposition of organic matter. In shallower waters, where there are many living creatures, decomposing matter enters the sediments and affects the pore waters as microbes use up all the oxygen available before turning to other matter. The result is the foul-smelling hydrogen suphide and toxic methane associated with stagnant waters.

The fate of the living benthic community depends on adequate supplies of uncontaminated matter. While scientists speculate on their possible use as indicators of the extent to which the oceans are poisoned, to the majority of humanity their importance is as the first stage of a chain by which the sea enacts its retribution, and poisons considered safely disposed of begin their return to guilty and innocent alike.

References

1. *TAO* p. 226
2. Anon. 1984a
3. *TAO* pp. 27, 226
4. Ibid. p. 44
5. RCEP 6 p. 24
6. *TAO* p. 60
7. Ibid. p. 66
8. GESAMP 15 p. 3
9. Source: *TAO* pp. 26–7, 62, 226
10. Source: *TAO* pp. 26–9, 42–3
11. Source: *TAO* pp. 66, 116
12. Ibid. p. 118
13. Source: *TAO* pp. 44–6, 49, 51–5, 58–61
14. Ibid. p. 51

15. Source: *TAO* pp. 68–73
16. Source: GESAMP 15 pp. 12–15
17. Ibid. pp. 14–15
18. Ibid.
19. Source: GESAMP 15 pp. 15–18
20. Ibid. p. 16
21. Source: GESAMP 15 pp. 18–21
22. Source: GESAMP 15 pp. 21–3

2. Humanity and the Seas

To the seas humanity is the great exploiter. As long as there have been human inhabitants of the earth, they have helped themselves to its living resources – finfish, shellfish and plant life. Before the invention of the aeroplane, the sea was the only means of carrying goods and people from the old world to the new or between islands in both worlds, and is still used for heavy cargoes such as oil, grain or coal. More recently we have extended our activities below the waters, extracting oil and gas from the sea-bed; today industrialists are assessing the possibilities of using sea power as an alternative source of energy and of seizing the vast mineral wealth of the ocean depths. To others the sea and its coasts offer opportunities for recreation – swimming, sunbathing, snorkelling, yachting, surfing, making friends with dolphins and whales or taking an archaeological cruise. And, as industrial and human wastes increase with the growth of new factories and population, the sea is increasingly used as humanity's dustbin. Before turning to this aspect we examine those other possibilities that the sea offers humanity – exploitation of its living and non-living resources, transport of goods and people, as a source of energy, and tourism – to discover *their* effects on the ocean ecosystem.

Harvesting the Seas

Fishing, like farming, is an occupation of extremes: on one side, the traditional, or, as they are more frequently called, artisanal fishermen, using small dugouts, canoes or sailing vessels, hunting with line, net or spear, and salting or drying their catch for their own use or that of their neighbours; on the other, the modern industrial enterprise, using sonar equipment to locate its prey, computerized assessment of the size of shoals, and factory ships in which the catch is treated, refrigerated and stored for the journey to a distant port. Traditional fishermen watched the birds or scanned the surface of the sea to discover where fish were 'biting'; they were craftsmen, skilled in a knowledge of the natural world, of the sea and its moods, against which, at times, they needed to pit their courage and cunning. Fishing communities tended to be closely knit, people with common experiences, background, culture. They knew – and lived *with* – the sea in a love–hate relationship, which modern technology makes as impersonal as itself. Today, the majority of the world's fishermen, eight out of ten, some 40 million people, especially in Asia and the Pacific, still follow traditional ways, but the majority of the world's catch is taken by the developed nations. The pattern is repeated in Third World countries undergoing industrialization. In Thailand new trawlers form only 15% of the fleet but take 70% of the catch, making their impact on 64,000 village fishermen. At Muncar, in Indonesia, fishermen destroyed nets, boats and engines in protest against the use of mechanized vessels and attacked the crews of trawlers who ventured too close to traditional fishing grounds.[1] To the fishermen they were not only a threat to their livelihood but to their way of life, to which the only response was a negative, Luddite protest.

It is inevitable that technologically advanced countries should lead the world in fish production. In 1982 Japan produced nearly 11 million tonnes, the USSR almost $9\frac{1}{2}$ million and the USA nearly four million.[2] Not all of this was caught at sea – Japan derived almost a million tonnes from aquaculture in 1980, and this was only a quarter of the output of the world's leading country in fish-farming, China[3] – but, despite the difficulties of obtaining statistics on home-bred fish, which, in some Third World countries, where peasants have fishponds for home use, is like trying to calculate how much firewood is collected, it is estimated that at least seven-eighths of it came from the sea.

How much fish do the world's seas supply, and what are current trends? According to the United Nations Food and Agriculture Organization (FAO),[4] the average annual catch between 1950 and 1954 was 21.6 million tonnes. By 1970–74 this had almost trebled to 60 million tonnes per annum. In 1983 the annual catch was 67.7 million tonnes, an increase of only 12.8%; in the North Atlantic and the South Pacific it had actually declined – by 11% and 20% respectively.

The rapid rise in the world catch between 1950 and 1970 was due to three causes: an increase in world population from 2.5 to 3.7 billion, accompanied by an increase in average income; new developments in fishing technology; and cheap oil. The last two made possible the use of distant water fishing fleets. The overall optimism of the time made people think of the seas as containing an inexhaustible supply of fish. Estimates of its potential rose as high as 200 million tonnes per year – or even 400 million.[5] The whole human race would satisfy its animal protein needs from fish breakfasts, fish lunches and fish dinners!

The collapse of the Peruvian anchovy industry in the south-east Pacific from an average annual catch of 9.8 million tonnes in the five years before 1970 to 0.8 million in 1980, and a further decline to 0.1 million in 1983, suddenly woke people to the facts of sea life. We noted in the last chapter how, when the wind blows parallel to the coast, it causes upwelling; colder water, rich in nutrients and plankton, rises to the surface. Where there is food, there will be fish; where there are fish, people will catch them. The Peruvian anchovy industry owed its existence to upwelling; its collapse was due partly to the ocean–atmosphere system taking its revenge through the phenomenon of *El Niño* ('The Child'), as the anomalous behaviour of the Peru Current is called. For no apparent reason upwelling stops, as in 1957–58, 1965, 1972–73 and again in 1976.[6] The collapse was also due to human greed – overfishing, not to provide adequate protein for the inhabitants of South America, but to amass bigger profits for the fishmeal industry.

This introduces a further factor: the use of inferior, non-table species for feeding pigs or chickens, as fertilizer, in the preparation of fish oil, or, as in Japan and Thailand, as food for higher-value fish in aquaculture. Almost 30 per cent of the world catch, some 20 million tonnes annually, is used in this way.[7] Establishment of processing plants, however, requires not only initial capital investment but, if profits are to be maintained, a guaranteed supply of fish, irrespective of the sea's capacity to produce it. In the 1930s Peruvian fishing was small scale, but capital investment in processing factories resulted in a fourteenfold increase in the catch in the five years between 1957 and 1962. In the next five it increased only by half, the 1965 *El Niño* causing an actual decline. In 1968 the catch rose to 10.6 million tonnes and in 1970 to 12.6 million, although a team of FAO experts estimated the maximum sustainable yield as 9.5 million tonnes. At this point, the Peruvian Government, alarmed at the prospects of overfishing and the dependence of the industry on one species, stepped in, banned fishing for three months, and imposed a limit of 10 million tonnes on the catch, which was then reduced to two million tonnes of fishmeal and exported for cash. As all sizes of fish can be used in this process, it is inevitable that fish which are too small to eat and would traditionally have been rejected are taken irrespective of the effect on replenishment of the population. In 1971 the government actually restricted fishmeal production; its aim, however, was not conservation, but keeping up prices on the world market. Even this did not save the industry from collapse, and by 1980 the anchovy catch was down to 0.8 million tonnes. As the numbers of fish declined, an associated export industry – guano from seabirds that depended on anchovy for food – also collapsed, leaving barren rocks where once birds nested and deposited their droppings.[8]

The same factor, without the assistance of *El Niño*, affected fisheries elsewhere. The problem is that, while, according to the FAO, over 100 species of finfish, shellfish and crustaceans are caught commercially, six of these alone – herring, cod, jack, redfish, mackerel and tuna, together with their associates – account for more than 45 million tonnes or over 60% of the total catch. A decline in any of these thus affects total availability. The largest group – North Atlantic herring, sardines, anchovy and pilchards – yields over 16 million tonnes, most of which goes for fishmeal. The second group, of almost 11 million tonnes, includes Atlantic cod, now heavily overfished, hake, haddock and Alaska pollack, which has recently risen in importance.

In their *Review of the State of World Fishery Resources*, published in mid-1983, the FAO report eleven major oceanic fisheries that have become depleted – six in the Atlantic and five in the Pacific. The highest estimated loss from mismanagement, after Peruvian anchovy, is of 1.27 million tonnes for Atlantic herring in the north-east Atlantic, to which should be added a further 76,000 tonnes of herring in the north-west Atlantic. Then come 762,000 tonnes for

Atlantic cod, 601,000 tonnes for pilchard and 461,000 tonnes for capelin, the first and third in the north-west Atlantic, the second in the south-east. In the Pacific there was a loss of 184,000 tonnes of Pacific Ocean perch and 149,000 tonnes of salmon. The countries mainly responsible were the developed nations or those traditionally relying on fishing as a means of livelihood – Canada is listed for six areas, the United States and the Soviet Union for five, Japan for two, with Denmark, Finland, France, GDR, Greenland, Peru, Poland, Spain and Sweden sharing the guilt. Nor can the Third World escape blame. The *Review* points out that expanded fishing activities by India and Pakistan in the western Indian Ocean are threatening several species, and catches of shrimps in the Gulf–Arabian Sea area have decreased considerably.[9]

Changes in the Indian fishing industry illustrate the impact of attempts to maximize production irrespective of cost in human terms or availability of supplies. India has six and a half million artisanal fishermen and an annual sea catch of 1.9 million tons. Government policy allowed mechanized trawlers owned by big business and multinational companies to operate in inshore waters. Between 1961 and 1980 the number of mechanized fishing boats increased from 2,161 to 16,100. In Goa alone, while the number of trawlers rose from four to 200 between 1964 and 1974, the actual fish catch decreased from 40,000 tons in 1971 to 26,597 tons in 1979 as the result of concentrating on catching shrimps for export. In ten years the shrimp catch actually increased from five tons to 663 tons, of which 500 tons was exported – at the cost of depleting stocks of other species, for the large trawl nets scooped up both eggs and immature fish indiscriminately. For the fish-eating population of Goa no more fish were available than before; the only difference was that they had become exceedingly expensive.[10]

The Indian example illustrates clearly one of the problems of what is euphemistically termed 'fish management'. Any disturbance of the ocean ecosystem may have other, unforeseen but more damaging, effects. Overfishing of one species can cause the depletion of other, associated species, especially where there are decreasing returns. The decline of a fishing industry, with subsequent loss of profits, makes governments reluctant to impose quotas in the interests of conservation, especially where exports are involved; increased fishing efforts to overcome the decline lead only to a further decrease in stocks, culminating in the inevitable collapse.

The phenomenon is not entirely due to human greed. Lack of data on fish stocks and reproduction rates, misinterpretation of existing data, unforeseen changes in water temperature resulting in an accelerated decline, the reluctance of governments to impose necessary restrictions, increased waste discharges from agriculture, industry and municipalities – all affect availability. In addition, there is the operation of the ecosystem itself, particularly the food chain by which larger fish feed on smaller fish, while smaller fish, as the FAO point out, eat small individuals, including eggs and larvae, of larger fish.[11] While Indian shrimp catching caused a decline in the number of other fish available, the reverse is also possible; a decline in one species may cause an increase in another. The most efficient way to ensure a supply of krill in the

Southern Ocean, now being caught in increasing numbers, is to eliminate the whales that feed on them! In economic terms the choice for humanity in some areas may be whether to allow larger fish for human consumption to survive at the expense of smaller fish, used mainly for fishmeal, or to adopt the opposite policy. One cannot have one's fish and eat it; one cannot also have one's fish to eat and expect to have others for pigs and chickens.

Recent developments, particularly the establishment of 200-mile fishing zones or, under the 1982 Law of the Sea Convention, of *Exclusive Economic Zones* (EEZs), have provided an opportunity both to take stock, in the literal and figurative senses, and to exercise more control. With almost 99% of the world catch coming from waters either already or potentially within EEZs,[12] opportunities for international regulation of fishing, including the protection of declining species, are obviously greater than when countries controlled only a narrow 3–12 miles stretch of territorial sea, and major fishing grounds in the open ocean offered a free-for-all until declining economic returns forced them to accept voluntary arrangements. The key question remains the extent to which developed countries will continue to dominate the economies of the Third World. Among these uncertainties one fact is inescapable – the sea can be ruined as much by what one takes out of it as by what one puts into it.

Beneath the Waters – Oil and Gas

Not content with depleting the living resources of the sea, humanity has turned to the non-living. In Chapter 1 we saw that sea-water contains almost every known element. The sea's 'saltiness' has led to the extraction of sea salt for over 4,000 years by the simple process of evaporation in large pans on the shore. Today six million tonnes are produced annually, mainly around the coasts of Africa, South America and South-East Asia. More recently the reverse process of removing 'sea salts' to produce fresh water for drinking or irrigation has led to the setting up of desalination plants, particularly in desert areas such as the southern Mediterranean, the Red Sea and the Gulf. More ingenious is the idea of towing large icebergs from the Antarctic to the desert coasts of southern Africa, Asia, South America and Western Australia; small icebergs were actually towed northward from southern Chile in the 1890s. Commercially, the only elements extracted on a large scale from the sea itself are magnesium, which, as the lightest available structural metal, is widely used in the chemical industry, and bromine, used in antiknock compounds in petrol. If the idea of extracting gold from the sea as a means of paying Germany's World War I reparations was abandoned as uneconomic, the possibility remains of obtaining uranium for nuclear power plants – Japan has shown interest[13] – after which the cycle will presumably be completed by dumping the resulting waste back in the ocean.

To date the most important extractive industries are not from the sea itself but from the land beneath it – sand and gravel, coal, and, above all, oil and natural gas. Without the sea, however, these resources would not exist, and, in extracting them, humanity has increased the dangers to the world ocean.

Trapped by shifting sediments, pockets of oil and gas exist beneath both land and sea (Chapter 1). Near the coast they originated at the time when the sea covered the land, dragging back organic matter with it as it retreated. Alternatively, they may have been formed by upwelling, which caused a growth of plankton and its subsequent burial.[14] Early attempts at extracting oil from beneath the sea, like those to obtain coal, were extensions of land activities. In 1896 drillers in the Summerland field of southern California worked from wooden piers extended over the sea to bring up the first oil. In the 1920s offshore wells began production in Lake Maracaibo, Venezuela, and in 1938 in the Gulf of Mexico, off the Louisiana coast. But it was not until the development of new technology, increased demand and the sudden upsurge in world oil prices in the 1960s and 1970s, as Third World producers attempted to show their strength, that production extended to deeper waters. Offshore sites, previously considered uneconomic, gained immediate commercial and political importance.[15] Oil companies – and governments – prepared themselves for a big bonanza. By 1985 there were more than 6,000 platforms in place around the world, 130 of them in the North Sea alone.[16] Starting production, however, was easier than stopping it. Capping an oil well on land is no easy task; how much more difficult in a floating platform, assaulted by gales and surging waters! The oil continued to flow – and the world found itself faced with a glut.

Obviously offshore production is more costly than on land. Not only must there be exploratory drilling – from jack-up rigs in shallow waters, semi-submersible platforms with retractable legs at deeper levels, or drill ships able to operate at any depth – but special structures are needed for recovery – platforms of steel that are towed into place and anchored to the sea-bed with piles, or of reinforced concrete ('gravity platforms') held in place by ballast in huge tanks fixed to their feet.[17]

Once extracted, oil must be taken from site to shore. Hence the construction and laying of continuous pipelines capable of withstanding the hazards of more than 200 m of water and, in nearshore areas, conforming to regulations designed to prevent fouling of ships and fishing nets. Supplementing all this is a huge servicing operation – supply vessels and helicopters for transport of goods and men, pipe-laying barges, barges for scouring trenches, crane barges, accommodation ships, fire-fighting and stand-by vessels. Finally, there are the onshore installations – storage tanks, repair sheds, warehouses, transport facilities, refinery and port operations. Given the initial cost of setting up these essentials, it is not surprising that much offshore working developed as an extension of onshore activity. Where it has not, as in the North Sea, it has transformed coastal towns into new areas of activity.

By 1980 offshore production was running at almost 14 million barrels a day (b/d), more than 20% of total world production.[18] Known offshore reserves represent a quarter of the world total, about 90% of it being under continental shelves.[19] Unlike deep ocean fisheries and the yet unexploited mineral resources of the ocean depths, oil supplies are thus almost all within the jurisdiction of coastal states, especially where they have applied EEZs under the Law of the Sea Convention. This introduces a further contradiction: developing countries have the resources but not the means to exploit them; industrialized countries have the means but are already using them to exploit their own resources. The result is the inevitable 'co-operation' which, as with fisheries, means in practice dominance by multinational corporations, export of technical equipment from developed countries, enrichment of local business communities and corporations, and continued reliance on cheap local unskilled labour.

The complex industrial structure needed for exploration and production is dominated by the major US and West European oil companies. Subsidiaries specializing in high technology now operate worldwide in exploratory drilling, well-logging and the design and installation of offshore facilities. Supplementing this is the offshore engineering industry, dominated by the major civil engineering and shipbuilding companies of Western Europe, which specialize in building exploration rigs, production platforms and unmanned modules. By extending their activities throughout the world they aim to lessen their dependence on any one area.[20]

Despite incompleteness of data (no figures are available for Iranian oil production in 1983), Figure 2.1A shows clearly two recent trends[21] – an overall rapid increase in offshore production, followed by a levelling off, and a change in regional levels favouring the industrialized world. This picture of offshore production should be set against total world production; estimated at 57,210 thousand barrels per day (tb/d) in 1976, this rose to 59,812 tb/d in 1980 and fell to 53,259 tb/d in 1983 as demand slackened. The result was a net increase in the proportion of offshore production from 16.9% to 25.7% of the world supply.

The increase, however, as Figure 2.1A shows, took place mainly in developed countries at the expense of the Third World, as major industrialized users attempted to exploit local resources and overcome their previous dependence on others. While Third World offshore production rose by 22%, that of developed countries more than doubled. Between 1976 and 1983 production in Denmark and the UK quadrupled and in Norway rose by 150%. Elsewhere in Europe Italy showed a 130% increase through its activities in the Adriatic and off Sicily, and Spain a 76% rise through Mediterranean production. Other countries varied in their response: in the USA, already advanced in this field, production rose by only 18%; in Australia and New Zealand it stayed at the same level, while in the USSR it fell by 20% and in Japan dropped by two-thirds.

Similar variations affected Third World countries, whose share in offshore production fell from three-quarters in 1976 to under two-thirds in 1983. Middle East countries cut back offshore production by amounts that varied from 25 to 80%; West African production remained constant as reductions by the two largest producers, Nigeria and Gabon, were offset by newer, if smaller, operations in Angola/Cabinda, while those in Congo rose by 150%. In Central and South America, Venezuela and Trinidad & Tobago obtained up to a third less oil from offshore sources in 1983 than in 1980, but this was again countered by a rise in Brazilian output from 35,000 to 197,000 b/d and by Mexico, where

Figure 2.1.   Offshore Production

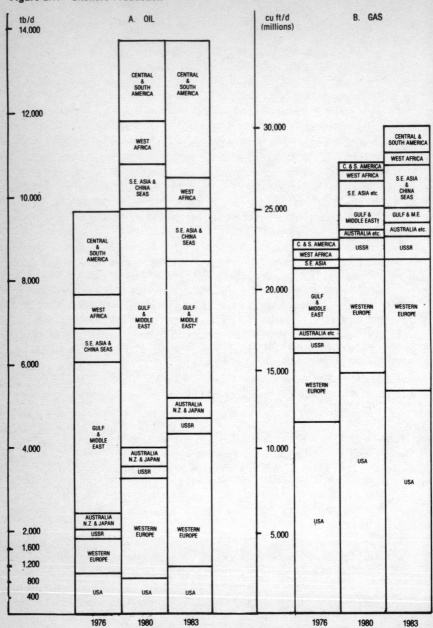

* Excluding Iran

† All Saudi Arabian gas flared

production rose from 45,000 b/d in 1976 to 1,674,000 b/d in 1983.

So with natural gas (Figure 2.1B). Between 1976 and 1983 total world production from offshore sources increased by 29%, but this figure conceals disparities. While Western Europe almost doubled production (from 4,458 million cu ft/d to 8,714) and Australia and New Zealand more than doubled their smaller output (from 293 million cu ft/d to 787), Third World countries showed an actual decrease. This was due largely to Saudi Arabia's decision to flare off all its gas so that a daily rate of 3,825 million cu ft in 1975 dropped to zero. In South-East Asia and Central and South America, however, there were major programmes of expansion, particularly in Indonesia, Thailand, Brunei, Malaysia, India, Mexico, Trinidad & Tobago, and Brazil.

From the sea's viewpoint fluctuations in the production of oil and gas are less important than the existence of man-made platforms that punctuate its surface. Potential blow-outs and operational oil spills apart (see Chapter 3), these structures themselves present two problems that humanity has not yet solved. First, there is the risk of a collision between a ship and an offshore platform. As some North Sea oil platforms have storage space for up to a million barrels of crude oil,[22] while the *Amoco Cadiz* spilt 1,300,000 barrels in 1978 when it grounded in heavy seas off the coast of Brittany, the results of a collision would need stronger terms than 'disaster' or 'catastrophe' to describe them, especially as most oil rigs are not far from coasts.

Improbable as the prospect of a collision may appear, a group of computer experts from the UK's Department of Energy, working on 'risk assessment' under the ominous title of CRASH (Computerized Risk Analysis of Shipping Hazards), concluded that 'if a platform is near a heavily used route the risk of collision from passing ships is sufficiently high to be a matter of concern'.[23]

The second problem is: what will happen to platforms when the oil runs out? It has been estimated that, by the year 2010, in the British sector of the North Sea alone, as many as 40 oilfields, each with many platforms, will be exhausted.[24] Already the lawyers are at work, 'dismantling' the 1958 Geneva Convention on the Continental Shelf, which states clearly that 'any installations which are abandoned must be *entirely removed*'[25] (my stress), a prospect which the oil companies argue is technically impossible and financially crippling.

At the 1981 session of the Law of the Sea Conference, 31 states supported a British amendment so that Article 60(3) of the Convention now reads that abandoned or disused installations or structures 'shall be removed to ensure safety of navigation . . .' Removal must be carried out in such a way as to protect fishing interests, the environment and the rights and duties of other states, and publicity be given to 'the depth, position and dimension of any installation or structure not entirely removed'. In short, 'removal' has passed from the domain of common usage into that of the law and now means that you must take it away but that you can also leave some of it behind!

Fishermen are not impressed and want the sea-bed cleared. They are concerned not only with static obstructions but with ropes that foul propellers.

floating or semi-submersible debris and the thousands of miles of pipelines on the ocean bed. The suggestion that toppled platforms could act as artificial reefs and attract fish is greeted sceptically, a reaction supported by scientists who maintain that below 40 metres there is too little light for photosynthesis to take place. The Japanese have turned disused jacket platforms into angling centres, but no one knows what fish elsewhere think of their proposed new habitat.[26] In the UK MAFF scientists, not convinced that the 'Rigs to Reef' concept will help increase fish stocks, have found allies in the Ministry of Defence who argue that not only would sunken rigs be a hazard to their submarines but advantageous to hostile ones who could use the reef for sonar confusion. Owners of merchant shipping are likely to want platforms removed, especially from busy shipping lanes, but ships' captains are ambivalent – a static object at sea is a potential hazard to be avoided, if platforms are allowed to remain in position; but it also quickly becomes a useful landmark for navigation.

The North Sea presents especially difficult problems and so far only one small gas platform from West Sole E is known to have been removed. In the USA, where there is considerably more experience and conditions are better, redundant platforms are removed and dumped in areas designated by the US Government. Officially they are first dismantled.[27] One can only hope that, as the lawyers would put it, the action is subject to adequate surveillance.

Beneath the Waters – from Aggregates to Nodules[28]

It is unfair to blame the sea for those monstrous concrete structures that now dominate the cities of the world. Only human beings could perpetrate such ugliness. Yet without the sea many of them would not exist. As land sources of sand and gravel are depleted or become too expensive to work, more and more countries are turning to the sea for these essential ingredients of the ubiquitous concrete.

Today, 'aggregates' – sand, gravel, or shell deposits – are quantitatively the most important hard minerals obtained from the sea. Deposited on recently formed beaches through cliff erosion or on continental shelves by glacial action, wave movement and tidal currents to mingle with the fragmented remains of shells, aggregates are extracted by modern suction dredgers, working to a depth of 35 metres, and brought to land. Among the potentially rich areas for mining are the North Sea, already divided into areas licensed by the governments of the UK, Belgium, the Netherlands and France, and both coasts of the United States, where, as the result of glacial action in the Pleistocene age, there are nearly 500 billion tonnes on the Atlantic side and another 900 billion on the Pacific.

The costs are more than the 'economic' expenses entered in the balance sheets of the dredging companies. One cannot remove part of the sea-bed and expect the sea to ignore it. Uncontrolled dredging can lead to coastal erosion as waves and currents adopt new courses, destroy the habitats of fish that depend on gravel for their existence and, in the true spirit of competitive technological capitalism, compete for territory with oil or gas pipelines and submarine cables.

Nor is mining of aggregates humanity's only activity on the continental shelf. There are also 'placers', deposits of heavy minerals that have weathered from the ore that once contained them and resisted chemical action by the sea. Off the harsh coast at Nome, Alaska, gold deposits, known to exist since the late nineteenth century, have been sampled by drilling through the ice that covers the sea. Off Sumatra, Indonesia, extend deposits of tin, already worked inland and now expanding to depths of 50 metres out at sea. Forty per cent of the 1.6 million tonnes of tin estimated as available may eventually be extracted from beneath the waters. Placer deposits of tin occur also in Malaysia, magnetite in Japan and titanium in Australia, Brazil, Florida, India and Sri Lanka.

The oldest industry of all in undersea mining is, of course, coal, but as this has been mainly an extension of activities from land as seams are followed under the sea and uses methods that are less technologically exciting than oil rigs and unmanned modules, it is often overlooked. Perhaps when scientists have evolved the means of extracting the good quality coal now known to exist below the gas-bearing rocks under the North Sea, more than 7,000 m beneath the sea-bed, we shall enter another 'age of coal'. The extraction of many minerals from beneath the waters belongs as much to the future as their formation did to the past. Only recently, however, with continued research into plate tectonics (see Chapter 1) has that past – and its results – been deciphered. We now know where to look, even if we do not always have the means to grab, and, as humanity continues to demonstrate its infinite capacity for ingenuity and stupidity, the means will undoubtedly be found – when there is money to be made out of it.

Knowledge in itself is harmless, and what we now know is that, as the land masses drifted apart and the ocean flowed between, sections of the earth's crust were thrust upward to form the sea-bed, as in the Red Sea. As the distance between land masses increased and the oceans appeared, a second upsurge of volcanic activity produced the mid-ocean ridges, as in the Atlantic. Finally, at the point where plates meet, oceanic crust collides with continental crust and is 'subducted' beneath it. In all three areas a combination of volcanic and hydrothermal activity causes the depositing of hard minerals which humanity now assumes were placed there for its benefit.

In 1963 what scientists refer to as 'metalliferous muds' were discovered in the northern and central parts of the Red Sea. Although the contents vary, there are concentrations of up to six per cent zinc, one per cent copper and 100 parts per million (ppm) silver to be found in sulphide, oxide and silicate. The only area of present commercial interest is the Atlantis II Deep, about 60 sq km in extent, where the muds, varying in thickness from two to 25 m, are some 2,000 m below sea level. The Deep lies within the EEZs of Sudan and Saudi Arabia, who set up a joint Red Sea Commission and in 1979, with support from the West German Ministry of Science and Technology, examined the possibilities.

To overcome problems of transport, storage and disposal of waste on land, they carried out the first stage of processing on board ship and discovered that, if they were to reach commercial levels of production, as much as 367,000 tonnes of tailings would need to be discharged daily. Dumped directly into the sea, waste of this volume would seriously damage coral reefs and their inhabitants; discharged down a pipeline at a depth of 400 m, it could start circulations that would affect the chemical structure of the water. Humanity is learning the hard way that the sea will not give up its riches without a struggle.

In 1978, as part of the programme of oceanic exploration, a manned submersible discovered massive deposits of sulphide on the East Pacific rise in the hills near to hydrothermal vents that were still in action. The deposits, roughly cylindrical in shape and varying in size from three to ten metres in height and five metres in diameter, contained large concentrations of iron, zinc and copper sulphides. More recently similar deposits have been found on the Galapagos Ridge between the islands and Ecuador and on the Juan de Fuca Ridge off Oregon. As yet we do not know whether these discoveries have any commercial importance but, on past precedent, it will doubtless be found.

Of more immediate importance is the search for phosphorite – rocks and marine sediments containing significant quantities of the phosphate mineral (apatite) and thus the only suitable source of phosphorus for manufacturing phosphate fertilizers and chemicals. Phosphate is graded according to the proportion of phosphorus pentoxide (P_2O_5) it contains, marketable material usually having a content of more than 30% P_2O_5. To date, because of their vast land reserves, the USA and Morocco have dominated world production and sea mining is at present a theoretical possibility rather than a practical reality. On the sea-bed phosphorites usually occur as nodules, varying in size from pebbles to gigantic boulders, but may also appear as muds, sands, slabs or even continuous pavements. They occur mostly on continental margins and the upper parts of continental slopes at less than 500 m depth, mainly between 40°N and 40°S of the equator. Off the coast of California they were first dredged in 1937 and it is now estimated that there are about 50 million tonnes of nodules and 12.5 million tonnes of phosphatic sands with P_2O_5 contents varying from one per cent to 31.4% awaiting extraction. South Africa need have little fear of a phosphate shortage as the Agulhas Bank was one of the earliest sites to be discovered – by the *Challenger* Expedition of 1872–76 – and the nodules have a content of between 10 and 25% P_2O_5. That the nodule-carrying area extends northward on the Atlantic side along the coast of Namibia, with estimated resources of four billion tonnes, may not be without effect on the political future of that country, a feature reflected on the other side of the Ocean, where the world map shows a potentially large area of deposits between Argentina and the Falklands/Malvinas. Commercially, the main immediate possibility is in the Chatham Rise to the east of New Zealand, where nodules with 15–25% P_2O_5 could eventually provide an alternative supply.

Ironically, the aspect of sea-bed exploitation that has most captured the public imagination, aroused commercial interest, caused political dissension and almost wrecked the United Nations Law of the Sea Conference, is now the least likely to happen. The *Challenger* discovered not only phosphates in the Agulhas but large quantities of manganese nodules scattered over the sea floors of the great ocean basins. Apart from scientific interest there was neither the technology nor further incentive to retrieve them from the depths. Only in the 1950s did industrialized countries realize that the nodules contained not merely manganese but nickel, copper and cobalt in sufficient quantities to make them worth a second look. The realization was further prompted by the fact that, while the USA and the USSR jointly led the world in copper production, neither the USA nor the countries of Western Europe were among the top ten producers of cobalt and nickel. The greater part of the world's cobalt came from Zaire with an annual output of 14,700 tonnes, followed by Zambia with 3,300. Alarmed by the prospect that the central African states might do for cobalt what OPEC did for oil, industrialists in countries using the largest amounts of cobalt – France, the USA, the UK, the FRG and Japan together use more than Zaire and Zambia could supply – decided that it was time to seek out the riches of the deep.

Unfortunately, there were three snags – one geological, the second political, or perhaps more correctly, since it is rarely possible to use the word, idealistic, and the third technological. Geologically, the contents of the nodules varied considerably. Only if the combined nickel and copper content exceeded 1.75% were they of commercial interest. As the majority of nodules in the world's oceans fell below this standard, industrialists turned their attention to the only area of promise, the Clarion–Clipperton fracture zone in the north-east Pacific, from which it was estimated that they could extract some 8–25 million tonnes of nickel, 6–23 million tonnes of copper, 0.9–3.5 million tonnes of cobalt and 144–530 million tonnes of manganese.

The industrialists were not the only ones with their eyes on this prospective bounty. At the third United Nations Law of the Sea Conference 1974–82, the Maltese Ambassador, Arvid Pardo, introduced a new concept by suggesting that the wealth of the sea beyond national boundaries was 'the common heritage of mankind' and should be used for the benefit of humanity as a whole. Extraction of mineral riches from the ocean might be possible only by those with the technology to achieve it, but the riches themselves should go towards alleviating the increasing gap between the already rich and the developing nations. Third World countries, who formed the most numerous group at the Conference, quickly realized the possibilities. The final Convention includes provisions for an International Sea-bed Authority (ISA) to be responsible for the 'Area', i.e. the whole of the world ocean outside national jurisdiction, with an operating arm, the 'Enterprise', to undertake deep sea mining and an International Tribunal of the Law of the Sea, whose Sea-bed Disputes Chamber would have responsibility for handling the inevitable problems that might arise. The complexities of a system designed to satisfy both those who would provide the technology and those who would share in the gain do not concern us here, except in so far as they demonstrate what can be achieved by statesmen of vision, determined to achieve consensus through compromise.

The consensus was achieved – and accepted – until the Reagan Administration re-interpreted 'the common heritage of mankind' as meaning the traditional heritage of US exploitative capital, refused to sign the Convention, and the Thatcher Government in Britain, which had previously given its acceptance, followed its example.

Meanwhile, one of the final acts of the Conference was to pass Resolution 2: this set up the Preparatory Investment Protection (PIP) scheme guaranteeing exclusive rights in certain defined areas to those 'pioneers' who had already invested in research, once the Preparatory Commission, set up to continue the work of the Conference, had granted them that status on the sponsorship of a member government.

The 'pioneers' included four international consortia of private companies and a number of state-owned enterprises. First in the field, in January 1974, were Ocean Mining Associates (OMA), in which the four participants – Essex Minerals Company, a subsidiary of the US Steel Corporation, which was concerned about the supply of manganese for use in iron and steel processing, Union Seas Incorporated of the Belgian Union Minière, Sun Ocean Ventures of the US Sun Company, Incorporated and·Samin Ocean, Inc. of the Italian Ente Nazionale Idrocarbi (ENI) – each held 25% of the shares. In contrast, the Kennecott Consortium, formed in May the same year, is dominated by the US Kennecott Minerals Company, with a major interest in copper, which has a 40% shareholding in the company, while British Petroleum Development Ltd. holds a further 12%. RTZ Deepsea Enterprises Ltd. and Consolidated Gold Fields plc, both subsidiaries of the British Rio Tinto–Zinc Corporation Ltd., each hold 12% as do Noranda Exploration, Inc. of the Canadian Noranda Mines, Ltd. and the Japanese Mitsubishi Group.

Ocean Management, Inc. (OMI), formed in February 1975, comprises four partners with equal shareholdings – the Canadian Inco, Ltd., who are the world's leading producers of nickel, the West German AMR, the US SEDCO Inc. and the Japanese Deep Ocean Mining Company, Ltd. (DOMCO), a consortium of 23 companies. The Ocean Minerals Company (OMCO), formed in November 1977, is US-dominated in that each of the three participants – Amoco Ocean Minerals Co., Lockheed Systems Co. Inc. and Ocean Minerals, Inc. – is either wholly or partly US-owned, the remaining members of the consortium being the Dutch Billiton BV (Royal Dutch/Shell group) and the Dutch BKW Ocean Minerals, a subsidiary of the Royal BOS Kalis Westminster Group, NV. Additionally there are the state-owned enterprises: the French Association Françoise pour l'Etude et la Recherche des Nodules (AFERNOD), formed in 1974, comprising the Centre National pour l'Exploitation des Océans (CNEXO), the Commissariat à l'Energie Atomique (CEA), the Société Metallurgique de Nickel (SMN) and the Chantiers de France-Dunkerque; and the Japanese Deep Ocean Resources Development Co., Ltd. (DORDCO), which in 1982 absorbed the earlier Deep Ocean Minerals Association (DOMA), a loose association of companies, financed primarily by the Government, with contributions from about 50 companies.

Between them the consortia and their government backers have already spent billions of dollars on research – the OMA more than US$130 million, the Kennecott Consortium US$50 million before 1976, of which US$1.5 million was a loan from the UK Government to the two British companies; OMI some US$50–100 million, mostly before 1980, the Government of the FRG assisting the Germany company with US$27 million between 1970 and 1982, while the Japanese Government made loans to DOMCO; and OMCO US$120 million, although Billiton has announced its intention of withdrawing from the group and BOS Kalis has not contributed to activities since 1981. AFERNOD has spent an estimated US$50 million, the French Government contributing US$17 million in 1982, when the programme was redirected towards new exploration techniques. Finally, India, the People's Republic of China, the USSR, and the Republic of Korea have all shown interest and France, Japan, India and the USSR have applied to the Preparatory Commission for registration as pioneer investors.

The third problem, developing adequate technology, has not yet been solved. If a project is to be commercially viable, it is necessary to lift 10,000 tonnes of nodules a day continuously. Any breakdown in the system or pause for repairs would make it useless. In practice, as the nodules are on the ocean floor rather than under it, the operation is not so much mining as dredging. From single buckets scraped along the bed of the sea and hauled laboriously to the surface, the technicians have progressed to Continuous Line Buckets and self-propelled collectors – modules to retrieve nodules – so far without an adequate answer.

Changes in the economic situation were equally influential in dampening initial enthusiasm. Urged on at first by the increased demand for nickel, the price of which rose in the mid-1970s together with those of copper and cobalt, as energy costs increased at the end of the decade, industrialists were less enthusiastic as land production doubled, prices stabilized and, for copper, fell. Dredging the ocean depths no longer appeared the priority need it had seemed and in 1980 the consortia announced a slowdown in research and development which they have shown no inclination to reverse.

So far the sea has been spared – but of what is uncertain. Scientific opinions on the effects of sea-dredging differ. Because the scoops will disturb the sediments only slightly and be spaced at wide intervals, one group maintains that the operation will have little or no effect. Another stresses the disasters that could come to previously unknown benthic creatures, particularly to those minute objects that live on the nodules themselves. Nor is it only the act of collection that is dangerous; discharging unwanted solid material 20 metres above the sea-bed would produce a plume of particles that could stifle sponges or bivalves, while discharges of waste just below the surface would blot out sunlight, prevent photosynthesis and so affect both phytoplankton and the creatures that feed on them. The final stage of what happens when waste is deposited in shallower waters from plants operating on shore has still to be investigated.

Who and What goes to Sea – and Where?

There are four main types of vessels travelling either on or under the sea today: fishing boats, of which there are millions, varying from the small craft of artisanal fishermen and sportsmen to giant factory ships; merchant ships of 50 different types, carrying liquid or solid cargoes, almost 60% of which are tankers or ore and bulk carriers; military surface vessels, ranging from small patrol boats to huge aircraft carriers; military submarines, which may be either diesel–electric or nuclear-powered and armed with weapons that range from torpedoes to ballistic missiles.

No one knows how many vessels are on or under the sea at any moment, or what they dump into it. *Lloyd's List* provides daily reports of arrivals and departures at major ports and 'casualties' for merchant shipping – the depressing record of groundings, collisions, ships adrift or laid up in port awaiting repair – and the world's major surface navies cannot escape satellite surveillance. But the fishing fleets of the world are too numerous to count, and only military commands know where their submarines are – and they are unlikely to tell.

Despite this, we can form a general picture. Fishing vessels, for example, can be divided into the vast majority of artisanal or sporting boats and the much smaller, but more economically important, commercial fishing fleet proper, which can be further sub-divided according to the gear carried, the kind of fish caught, or the geographical range. Using the last method of classification, there are four main types: firstly, nearshore fishing boats, which operate around the coasts and concentrate on such species as shellfish or salmon; secondly, inshore/offshore vessels, operating on the continental shelf within a 200- to 300-mile limit from the coast, which provide the basis for the fishing industry in many developing countries, especially where they have set up Exclusive Economic Zones (EEZs); thirdly, distant water fishing fleets, based on distant continental shelves, e.g. North Atlantic trawlers in search of cod, which are usually more specialized but whose operations have in places been cut back by the establishment of EEZs; and, fourthly, long-distance fleets operating from remote shore or floating bases, as used by the USSR, Japan, Poland and East Germany, which include the huge factory ships and the Antarctic whaling industry, and which have also been affected by the new EEZs.[29]

Merchant ships over 100 GRT (gross registered tonnage) now number more than 40,000 and have a total tonnage of over 400 million. Of these (in terms of percentage tonnage) in 1985 32.4% were tankers and 26.5% ore and bulk combination carriers, with bulk/oil carriers, chemical tankers, container ships and liquid gas carriers forming a further 13.3%. In short, 72.2% of the world merchant fleet, over 300 million GRT, is involved in carrying potentially dangerous materials around the world.[30]

What exactly are these ships? Are their numbers increasing or decreasing? And who owns them?[31]

The most notable type of tanker in use today is the *Very Large Crude Oil Carrier* (VLCC) such as the Turkish *M Vatan*, which is 370 m long and was loaded with 300,000 tons of Iranian crude oil when it was hit by an Iraqi missile on 9 July 1985 during an incident in the Gulf War. VLCCs are in fact no more than floating oil tanks; the major part of their structure consists of compartments for holding oil, which are separated by bulkheads running the length or breadth of the ship. The oil is often discharged through under-deck pipelines and, despite their size, VLCCs can discharge their cargo in less than 24 hours.

Combination carriers or *oil/bulk carriers* can carry either crude oil or solid bulk cargoes such as coal, grain, sugar, bauxite or phosphate. The *Ore-Bulk-Ore* (OBO) carrier uses the same holds for different types of cargo and needs to be cleaned out between trips; the *Ore-Oil* (OO) carrier avoids this by keeping separate compartments for dry cargo and others for oil.

Ore and bulk carriers carry solid cargoes. Bulk cargoes have large hatchways and holds to make handling easier, while ore carriers are usually strengthened and have ballast tanks along their whole length on each side of the cargo.

Chemical tankers are designed specially for carrying liquid chemicals in bulk and have a number of tanks which are separated from the main structure of the ship.

Liquefied gas carriers have specially constructed insulated tanks for carrying either liquefied natural gas (LNG) at its boiling point of $-161°C$, or liquefied petroleum gas (LPG) which can be pressurized, so that LPG carriers are usually smaller than those for LNG.

Container ships are designed to carry packaged solid goods. Their holds take standard-sized containers, usually 20 ft long by eight feet wide and eight feet tall, so that they can be loaded in 24 hours. Other vessels are *Roll-on/roll-off* (RoRo) container ships, used for general cargo on ocean routes; part of these may be for RoRo cargo, the remainder for containers. They should be distinguished from the smaller *RoRo ferries*, used for short sea transport of commercial vehicles and private cars.

In 1913 the world tanker fleet totalled 1.4 million tonnes; in 1938 it was 11.6 million. The vast increase in tanker traffic in the 1960s and 1970s and its recent diminution in comparison with other types of shipping are shown in Figure 2.2, where the 1980 peak, when tankers were 41.7% of the world merchant fleet, represents 175 million in terms of tonnage. By 1983, as demand for oil decreased, this had fallen to 157.3 million and in 1985 to 134.9 million, but at 32.4% of world tonnage was still the largest single category of vessel at sea. The fall in tonnage for tankers from 1980 onward is countered by rises, over the fifteen-year period (1970–85) in ore and bulk carriers from 16.8 to 26.5% (38.3 million tonnes to 110.3), in container ships from 0.8 to 4.4% (1.9 million tonnes to 18.3), in liquid gas carriers from 0.6 to 2.4% (1.4 million tonnes to 18.3) and in chemical tankers from 0.2 to 0.8% (500,000 to 3.4 million tonnes), while bulk/oil carriers, after rising from 8.3 million tonnes in 1970 to 26.2 million in 1980 remained steady at 26.0 million in 1983 and fell slightly to 23.7 in 1985. The net effect is that merchant shipping outside these categories, which formed 40% of the world fleet in 1970, was constant at 27.1% in both 1980 and 1983 and rose only slightly to 27.8% in 1985.[32] In short, even with fewer tankers in

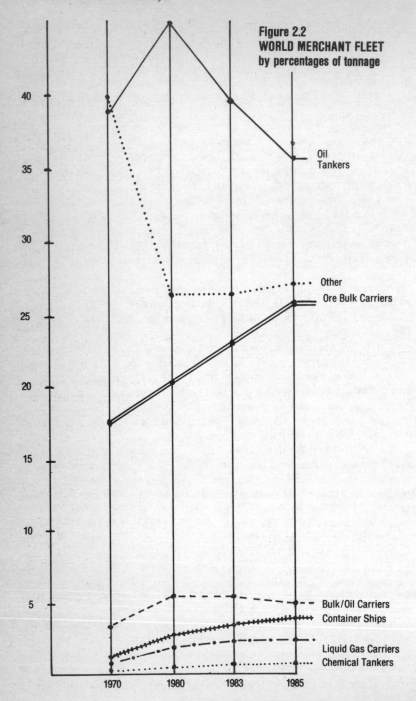

Figure 2.2
WORLD MERCHANT FLEET
by percentages of tonnage

service, the prospect of danger to the sea shows little change if considered solely in terms of cargo carried. Indeed, it can be argued that the increase in chemical and liquid gas carrying capacity, while much smaller in actual tonnage than the decline in oil, has increased the opportunities for more deadly poisons to reach the sea.

Oil, chemicals, or liquid gas are no more likely of themselves to fall into the sea than any other type of cargo. Danger arises only when there is an 'incident' – a grounding, collision, fire, explosion or Act of God, as when in 1981 two tankers were struck by lightning, fortunately after unloading.[33] Some accidents in bad weather are beyond human control, but the majority are due to causes that could be avoided – ships that fail to reach adequate standards of safety, or deficiencies in the training and skills of those who operate them. Here recent trends are not reassuring.

The trouble began at the end of World War Two when the USA, which had become the world's largest provider of merchant shipping, turning out vessels by the hundred, found itself with nearly 30 million GRT of shipping for which there was no immediate use. The result was the growth of the Flags of Convenience (FOC) system, whose main operators, Liberia, Panama and Cyprus, offer open registries. Between 1945 and 1953 eleven million tonnes of US shipping were transferred to foreign registration, mostly to Liberia or Panama, while, in order to secure American loans to replace ships lost during the war, many Greeks were forced to register them under flags of convenience. Owing to what they labelled 'political uncertainty' the Americans would not make the necessary loans available for Greek-registered ships. By using flags of convenience the actual owners made considerable financial gains; they could employ crews at lower rates of pay, avoid corporation tax and even circumvent international regulations.[34] For the British there are other advantages. As recently as January 1986 British Petroleum announced that it would be using 'manning agencies', i.e. hiring labour where it pleased, and 'flagging out' its 30-vessel bulk fleet to Bermuda. In the British House of Commons the Minister of State at the Department of Trade, David Mitchell, commented:

> The differences in operating costs arise because for its own crews BP has to pay national insurance contributions, train cadets, make contributions towards pension schemes and because of substantial leave entitlements, employ considerably more seafarers than are actually at sea at any one time. Manning agencies outside the UK are likely to have to make much smaller welfare payments to the state, they incur no training or pension costs, and directly at least they do not pay for leave.[35]

The system is obviously convenient – at least to the oil companies, and, it can be argued, to the public in that petrol prices can be kept down. It is less convenient to British merchant seamen, whose insurance contributions will now presumably go towards paying their unemployment benefit. The question at issue here, however, is whether assigning shipments of oil to an FOC country makes its transportation more dangerous.

Flags of convenience have been criticized at the United Nations Conference

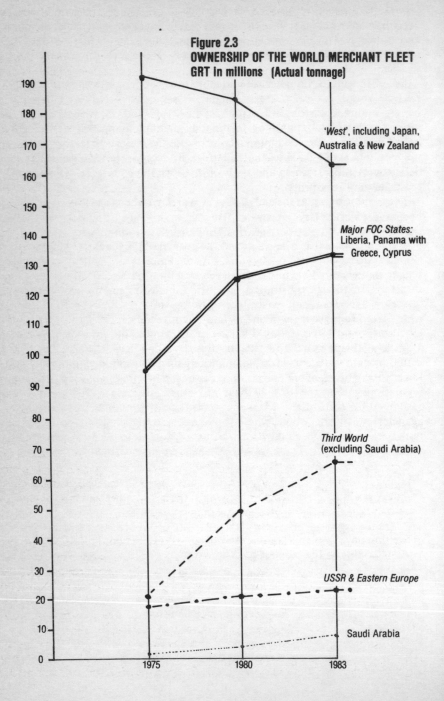

Figure 2.3
OWNERSHIP OF THE WORLD MERCHANT FLEET
GRT in millions   (Actual tonnage)

'*West*', including Japan,
Australia & New Zealand

Major FOC States:
Liberia, Panama with
Greece, Cyprus

Third World
(excluding Saudi Arabia)

USSR & Eastern Europe

Saudi Arabia

on Trade and Development (UNCTAD) on economic grounds with delegates arguing that countries whose flags are used do not receive sufficient economic benefit, while Third World countries are frustrated in their efforts to build their own fleets.[36] So far as danger is concerned, a lower paid crew is not necessarily an inferior crew (higher skills do not automatically command higher wages) any more than a vessel registered under an FOC is automatically a sub-standard ship – but statistics support common sense in suggesting a connection. Of ships over 100 GRT lost between 1976 and 1980 the ranking order of flags was Panama (291), Greece and Japan (between 200 and 250), Cyprus, USA and South Korea (100–120) with the largest FOC state, Liberia, in ninth position. In terms of tonnage, however, the largest losses for the period were for Greece (over two million tonnes), followed by Liberia (over 1,800,000) and Panama (over 1,600,000) with Japan and Cyprus in joint fourth place with just over 300,000 tonnes.[37] Of the 15 major incidents of ships involved in oil spillages in 1985 four concerned US ships, three Liberian and three Panamanian, while other countries were limited to one each.[38]

A potentially disturbing feature is revealed in Figure 2.3, which shows trends in ownership of the world merchant fleet (in actual tonnage) between 1975 and 1983 for the major areas of the world.[39] While the proportion owned by 'Western' industrialized countries has declined from 190.1 million tonnes in 1975 to 160 million in 1983 (almost entirely as the result of a 31.3% fall in Western Europe) and that of the Eastern bloc has risen slightly from 27.3 million tonnes to 36.2 million (7.7% of the world total to 8.6%), the Third World has made substantial progress in increasing its tonnage from 32.7 to 76.8 million, or, if Saudi Arabia is included, from 32.9 to 82.1 million. The most spectacular increase, however, is for the major FOC states. Panama has increased its tonnage from 13.7 million in 1975 to 34.7 in 1983, while Liberia, which rose from 65.8 million in 1975 to 80.3 in 1980 still remains the leading FOC state with 67.6 million tonnes of shipping. If Greece and Cyprus are added, then the proportion of world shipping potentially in this category has risen from 29.6% to 34.0%. In practice not all Greek ships operate under flags of convenience, but these figures make no allowance for those ships owned by nationals of other nations which work under the system. Even without firm figures it would appear that, far from being phased out, flags of convenience are increasing – and the dangers to the sea with them.

Our third and fourth categories, military vessels, whether on or under the ocean, are usually described in terms of superpower rivalry or 'strategic capability' – in plain words, their ability to eliminate humanity from the earth's surface. The seas, however, are non-discriminatory: if a nuclear-powered submarine ends up on the ocean floor, what matters is not whether it carries the stars and stripes or the hammer and sickle but that it is 'nuclear', both in its means of propulsion and in the warheads it may be carrying.

Naval commentators also stress the trend by which most armed vessels have now moved under the water rather than travelling on its surface. In the sense that there were 2,889 surface vessels and 669 submarines in 1950 compared with

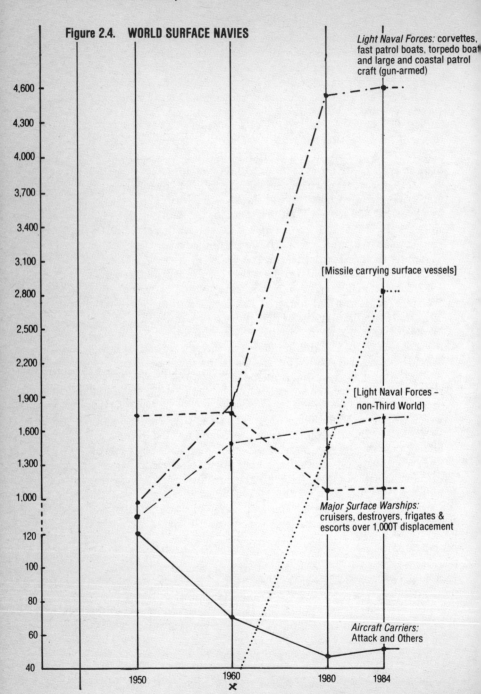

Figure 2.4.   WORLD SURFACE NAVIES

Light Naval Forces: corvettes, fast patrol boats, torpedo boats and large and coastal patrol craft (gun-armed)

[Missile carrying surface vessels]

[Light Naval Forces – non-Third World]

Major Surface Warships: cruisers, destroyers, frigates & escorts over 1,000T displacement

Aircraft Carriers: Attack and Others

5,705 and 1,233 submarines in 1984, i.e. surface vessels formed 81.2% of world naval forces in 1950 and 82.2% in 1984, this is not strictly true. Focusing attention on submarines does, however, deflect it from the dominant fact, namely that the number of armed vessels for use at sea has almost doubled during the last thirty years. The number of armed surface vessels has risen by 97.5%, of submarines by 95.0%.[40]

This overall figure conceals the great disparities between different types. As Figures 2.4 and 2.5 reveal, the tendencies have been for larger surface ships to decrease in numbers, and for there to be a rapid rise in the numbers of both missile-carrying surface vessels and nuclear submarines.

Of the world's surface naval ships, aircraft carriers have suffered most. In 1950 there were 119, by 1984 only 47, though this was four more than in 1980. Major surface warships – cruisers, destroyers, frigates and escorts of over 1,000 tons displacement – show a less spectacular decline of 39.6% from 1,783 to 1,077 but this is offset by the increased proportion of those able to carry missiles. None are listed for 1950, only 18 for 1960, but 686, i.e. 63.7% of ships of this type, by 1984. The outstanding increase, however, has been in the numbers of 'light naval forces' – corvettes, fast patrol boats, torpedo boats and large and coastal patrol craft armed with guns – from 987 in 1950 to 4,581 in 1984, of which almost a quarter are missile carrying. Almost two-thirds of the total (65.3%) are assigned to 'developing countries', where numbers have risen from 124 in 1950 to 2,985 in 1984, but the industrialized world, who between them deployed 86.8% of ships of this type in 1950, have almost doubled the actual numbers at their disposal, from 822 to 1,586.

So far as submarines are concerned, the most 'striking' increase has been in the numbers of large 'strategic submarines' armed with medium- or long-range ballistic missiles. In 1960 only 17 of these existed, of which seven were 'nuclear'; by 1984 there were 133, of which only 17 were 'conventional'. The greatest numerical increase is in nuclear-powered 'Attack Submarines', a singularly honest title, even if their activities are controlled by the less appropriately named Ministries or Departments of Defence. These include Cruise missile carrying submarines and now number 235. Twenty-five years ago in 1960, the world total was 15; in 1955 there was only one. Not surprisingly the USA and the USSR own over 90% between them in almost equal proportions. 'Patrol submarines'. i.e. post-World War II vessels of 700 tons or more displacement, have more than doubled in numbers – from 355 in 1950 to 790 in 1984, while the proportion of them that are nuclear-powered has risen from just under three per cent in 1960 to just under 30% in 1984.

Not all stories in the submarine world, however, are of increases. The good old 'coastal subs.', conventionally powered with less than 700 tons displacement, of the type that achieved heroic or villainous status in World War II films, are 'down', if not completely 'sunk'. The decline of 76% from 313 in 1950 to 75 in 1984 is almost the same as that for conventional warships (78.1%). Indeed, the most significant transformation, as Figure 2.5 reveals, is the change from 'conventional' to 'nuclear', irrespective of type. In 1950 there was *one* nuclear submarine, in 1960 37; in 1984 there were 585 or almost half

Figure 2.5. WORLD SUBMARINES

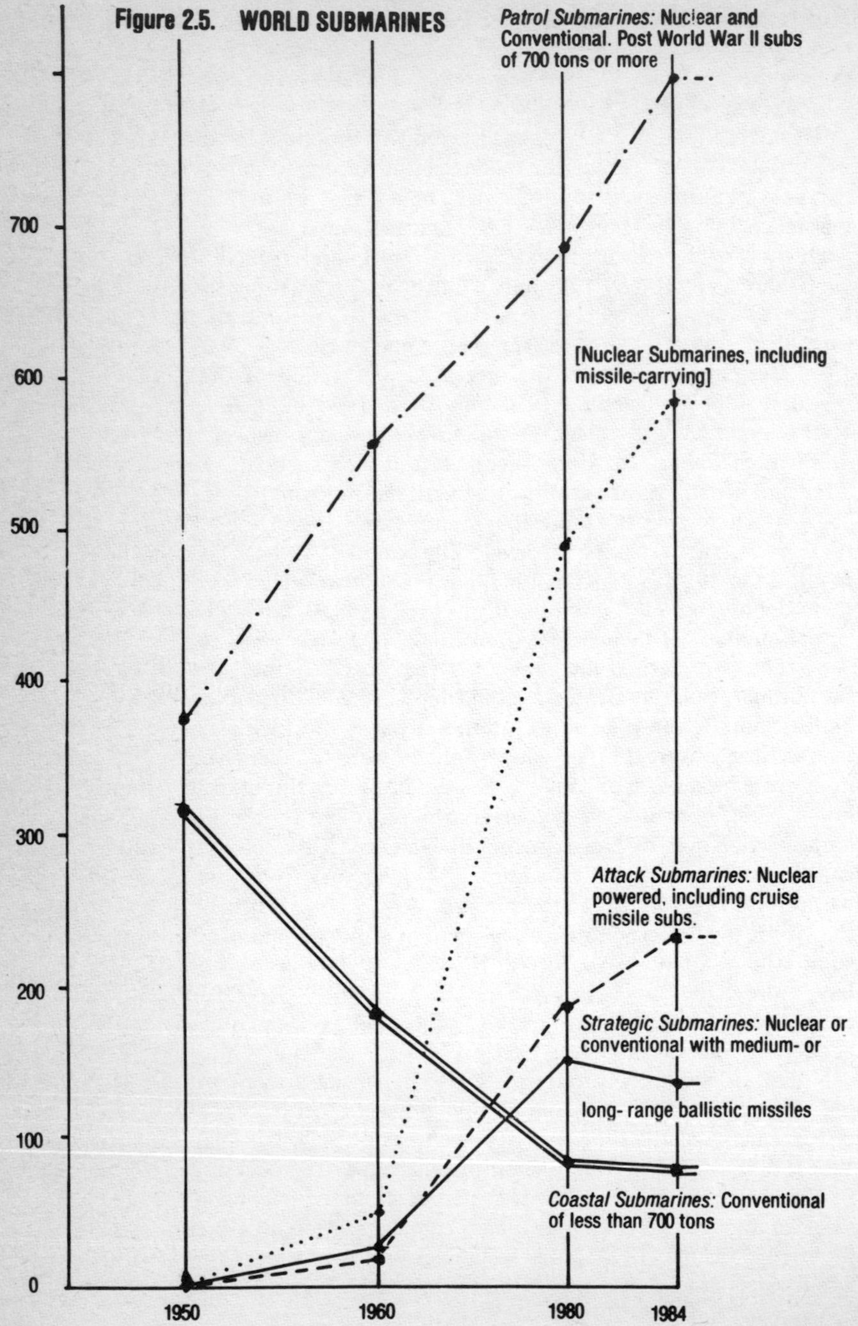
Patrol Submarines: Nuclear and Conventional. Post World War II subs of 700 tons or more
[Nuclear Submarines, including missile-carrying]
Attack Submarines: Nuclear powered, including cruise missile subs.
Strategic Submarines: Nuclear or conventional with medium- or
long- range ballistic missiles
Coastal Submarines: Conventional of less than 700 tons
700
600
500
400
300
200
100
0
1950
1960
1980
1984

(47.4%) of the total. Compared with the immensity of the oceans, the space they occupy is minimal, but one is less sanguine about their contents (see Chapter 6).

The final word on ships and the sea must, however, go to GESAMP. After pointing out that the revenue from sea transport is considerably larger than the revenue from the fishing industry, it adds that 'much of the sometimes large volumes of beach litter is derived from this source' and concludes by drawing our attention to a previously unnoticed poison: 'a large vessel may contribute one ton of copper to the sea each year from its anti-fouling paint'.[41] As there are approximately 40,500 merchant ships over 100 GRT and another 1,100 large surface naval vessels, even if we ignore submarines, fishing boats, pleasure vessels and light naval forces, this means that 41,600 tons of copper may be deposited in the sea annually simply by ships sailing on its surface.

Energy from the Oceans

The seas, we saw in Chapter 1, are almost everywhere in motion. Viewed objectively, the fact that waves, tides, currents, surges and swell rarely cease is one of the most remarkable phenomena on this earth. How is it possible that this movement should continue without end? We have explained the action of wind in causing ocean currents but the ultimate cause is solar energy, which, in reaching the earth, sets the winds in motion. Almost three-quarters of this energy itself is absorbed by the sea.[42] Surely it should be possible to retrieve some of this invisible force and to take advantage of the movement of the waters.

The tides have long aroused the curiosity and ingenuity of human beings. Throughout the world, particularly in upper latitudes, there are long narrow inlets into the land up which the sea rushes twice a day, causing the water level to rise and fall, and, just as streams on land were dammed and then released to turn water wheels that provided power for grinding corn, so in early times in Europe people made similar uses of the sea.[43]

Today the prospect of using the sea to turn generators for producing electricity has superseded the turning of mill wheels and the technological resources at our disposal now make it possible. The principle, however, remains simple. A dam or barrier is built across a narrow arm of the sea where the incoming tide raises the water level by more than five metres. The dam allows the incoming tide to flow through it into an artificial reservoir. As the tide ebbs and the water level falls, the water behind the dam is released under control and by passing through pipes is made to turn a turbine or generator and thus produce electricity. With the next incoming tide the reservoir is again filled and the process repeated. As long as the dam survives and the generators are maintained, there would appear no reason why the cycle, like the tides, should not continue indefinitely. The only snag – once money for building is obtained and the technical problems of construction solved – is the sea itself. As water cannot be flowing both in and out at the same time and the times of tides vary by 50 minutes in a 24-hour cycle, there must be breaks in production, which will not always coincide with the demand for electricity. To rely solely on immediate generation is futile; people would want to switch on lights or use electric cookers only to find the tide coming in and the power off. In short, some means of storing the electricity generated is essential.

Despite these advantages only one site in the world at present uses tidal power to produce electricity commercially – at the mouth of the River Rance, Brittany, France, where its 24 turbines and generators have operated since 1967 with low costs and little corrosion of equipment. The barrier across the river has sluice gates that open to allow the basin to be completely emptied and filled, and the newly formed lake behind it has become a tourist attraction for yachtsmen and sightseers.[44]

As the demand for electricity has increased and production at fossil-fuel burning power stations has become more costly or been condemned as a danger to the environment, interest in tidal power continues to grow. Already three sites in the Bay of Fundy, Canada, have been chosen and in the UK the Severn Estuary Barrage Tidal Power Committee has recommended the construction of a barrier across the Severn from Weston-super-Mare to the Welsh coast; tidal power would enable the production of about six per cent of British electricity.[45] Experimental stations now operate in the USSR at Kislaya Guba on the Barents Sea, and at Xiamen (Amoy) in China. Over 40 possible sites have been identified throughout the world where the tidal range is from five to twelve metres and the physical features of the land make possible the building of a barrier across the inlet. Six of these are in North America, nine on the east coast of South America and two on the west, three border the Indian Ocean, three are in the Far East and a further three on the north coast of Australia with one on the north island of New Zealand. In the UK, in addition to the Severn, the Solway Firth is considered a possibility and in France there are additional prospects in Brittany. The only site in Africa is at Abidjan, Ivory Coast.[46]

Wave movement is more complex than the in–out–up–down action of the tides, but the energy available is huge, especially in latitudes north and south of 30° from the equator where the 'best' waves for this purpose are found. To date there are three proposed types of energy converters: those using the vertical rise and fall of waves to force air or water into operating turbines; those using the rolling, pitching or heaving action of waves to activate cams which work similarly; and wave focusing, which concentrates available energy at one point. One type of this, 'surge funnelling', channels shoaling waves into a storage basin and the hydraulic head produced is used to run a turbine.[47]

The idea of using waves to provide power for remote navigation buoys, first developed in Japan, is now being extended to a larger project run by Japan and the International Energy Agency. This uses a ship-like rectangular structure with 24 openings in its base through which waves move water up and down, forcing air through valves into a turbine which in turn drives an electric generator. Wave focusing is being studied in Norway and the United States, where the Lockheed 'Dam-Atoll' is a saucer-shaped structure which focuses water to drive a turbine at its centre.[48] A further development is 'passive' wave energy which it is proposed to apply in Mauritius. A coral reef would be built up so that waves top the wall created and produce a hydraulic head within the reef that would be used to drive a turbine at the outlet.[49]

Wave power has the advantage over tides of greater persistence and no unavoidable breaks in supply. Even bad weather can be turned to good use as waves are conveniently more plentiful in winter when demand for electricity increases. Scientists have estimated that a quarter of the electricity used in the UK could be obtained in this way without extra energy storage and that, if the wave power around the coasts of Britain and Ireland was fully used, it could supply more than five times the present UK demand.[50]

More ingenious – and more limited in availability – than either tidal or wave energy is sea thermal power or Ocean Thermal Energy Conversion (OTEC). This uses the difference in temperature between hot surface waters and cold waters in the depths as a means of producing energy. Such differences occur only in tropical climates between 20°N and 20°S of the equator, and the existence of broad continental shelves in some areas means that the necessary cold water is found only many miles out to sea. Technically, the problems are, first, to produce a structure that can be moored in deep water and has powerful pumps for obtaining supplies of both types of water, and, secondly, to transmit the energy produced to land by means of a cable.

Theoretically, the actual process is simple – given a fluid with a sufficiently low vaporization point, e.g. ammonia or Freon. Liquid ammonia is vaporized by heat from the warm surface water and under pressure made to turn a turbine for generating electricity. The vapour then passes through a condenser where cold water from the depths reconverts it to a liquid and the cycle is repeated. Practically, there is less agreement. GESAMP maintains that, for a 40 MWe commercial station, the cold-water pipe must be approximately 10 metres in diameter and reach to a depth of 1,000 m; the *TAO* gives a pipe of 20 m diameter but only 500 m long.[51] Attempts to construct plants in Hawaii, Tahiti, Japan and the Caribbean are still experimental, but already the experts have identified a number of potential sites. GESAMP lists 74 'developing countries' – 22 in Africa, 28 in Latin America and 24 in the Indian and Pacific Oceans – where the temperature range between surface waters and those at 1,000 m depth is sufficient. Unfortunately the distance the 'resource' would have to be from the shore is not always encouraging. Cuba, the Dominican Republic, Haiti, the Lesser Antilles, the US Virgin Islands, Guam, the Pacific Islands Trust Territory, the Philippines and the Seychelles are listed as 'one kilometre', but for Sierra Leone and Australia (sic) the figure is 100 km, and for French Guiana and Surinam 130 km.[52] The prospect of mooring a platform at this distance from the coast and connecting it by cable to land is unlikely to attract many investors.

OTEC's supporters have stressed not only the generation of electricity but the possibility of other uses. The cold waters of the deep ocean, we have seen, are rich in nutrients; pumping them to the surface creates an artificial form of upwelling that could be used for setting up fish farms at sea. On the industrial level, by extracting hydrogen from sea-water by electrolysis and combining it with nitrogen from the air, the plant could produce ammonia both for its own operation and as a saleable commodity for use in producing fertilizer. Countries with deposits of bauxite ore could use the OTEC plant for producing aluminium, while yet further developments would be the production of alternative fuels such as methanol and of fresh water by desalination.[53]

The final possibility is to use, not the sea, but its contents – the 'marine biomass'. Commercial methods have still to be developed but the 'macro-algae', i.e. kelp, at present harvested for animal feed, fertilizers or emulsifiers, could be used to produce methane gas,[54] a highly useful, and renewable, source of power.

How benign are these activities? Assuming that these new sources of energy are ever developed on a large scale, will there be no undesirable results?

Harnessing tidal power by damming an inlet of the sea obviously interferes with the natural movement of the waters, especially when it creates a large artificial lake. If, as the French example shows, this provides additional recreational facilities, while the smaller tidal range makes for easier working in harbours and the region is now able to avoid extremely high tides, these benefits are offset by disadvantages. The mean water level behind the barrage is now higher than previously and the waters of the basin are exchanged less frequently with the sea. In consequence, sewage and industrial waste formerly washed quickly out to sea tends to linger and, unless given additional treatment, can rapidly cause pollution. Heavy metals in particular are caught up by suspended sediment and collect on the bottom, where movement is also reduced, thus affecting bottom-living creatures. Add to this changes in the salinity of the water and it is obvious that, whatever precautions are taken, some effect on fisheries in inevitable.[55]

Using waves to produce energy may appear harmless but, on a large scale, could have more far-reaching effects. As the energy extractors act as a breakwater – whatever energy they take from the waves does not pass beyond the point of extraction – they could produce a calm sea between them and the shore. This would make navigation easier and decrease land-erosion in the immediate area. On the other hand, coastal sediment previously carried away by the sea would accumulate and the resulting changes in currents, assisted further by the wave-breaking machinery, could cause erosion elsewhere. Creation of a calm-water area would attract new types of fish and other sea creatures, whose increased activities could result in fouling of the structure, followed by the application of anti-fouling coatings which in turn could harm marine life. The greatest possible danger is from a passive wave energy plant making use of a coral reef where changes in natural workings could affect the whole ecosystem with subsequent damage to fisheries and to the corals themselves.

As for OTEC, the main concern is the 'large' quantity of water required. 'A 5 MWe plant would need to pump and discharge the same amount of water as a nuclear power plant of about 1,000 MWe capacity.'[56] Whatever this implies in total terms, an extremely large volume of water will be in perpetual motion. In practice there are three types of water in movement – the cold water drawn up from the depths, the warm water from near the surface, and the 'warmed' effluent returned to the sea after it has carried out its cooling work. What happens to this effluent depends on its density and the speed at which it is discharged. If it comes out of the discharge pipe with sufficient force, it will continue in the same direction, dragging some of the surrounding water with it until its impetus is exhausted, then move either up or down until it finds waters of the same density. The disturbing feature is that, according to GESAMP's estimates, this large quantity of water will carry with it *nine times* its own volume of sea-water. What may happen if the plant is near the coast or in shallow water so that the discharge reaches the sea-bed before mixing with the ocean is of sufficient concern to cause even GESAMP to comment that 'this general situation will require caution to avoid deleterious effects on exposed substrates and biota'. In non-euphemistic language, there will be an ecological disaster. Elsewhere, sea creatures dragged along by the discharge may continue with it until the level of 'neutral buoyancy' is reached, by which time they may be literally out of their depth, i.e. in regions where it is impossible for them to live.

Meanwhile both cold water from the depths and warm surface water, together with their contents, are being pumped into the plant. Organisms will be sucked in by both intakes, and either pumped through the plant or caught on screens 'to prevent the clogging of heat exchangers'. Attempts at nuclear and other power plants to divert 'juvenile and adult fish' from the screens 'have had only limited success'; the outcome is either immediate death or destruction when the screens are cleaned. Not only fish but both phytoplankton and zooplankton are endangered species, the extent of their peril varying according to the time of day, the level of illumination and the 'attractive effects of the OTEC structures'.

Finally, if the plant is to work efficiently, the heat exchangers must be kept clean and free from biological growth. This will necessitate not only 'mechanical cleaning' but 'intermittent use of biocides', the present choice for which, both because it is effective and can be manufactured on site, is chlorine. Mixed with sea-water, chlorine reacts rapidly with bromine in the water and later produces halogenated organic compounds. Toxicity is expected to be low in the large volume of water discharged but 'cumulated or regional effects of long-term use with possible accumulation of persistent residual compounds remains speculative'. One would have assumed that, if you put poison into the sea, little speculation is required to predict what may happen.

GESAMP is concerned only with 'normal working conditions'; 'accidental catastrophic incidents' are omitted as beyond their scope. For a new and unknown source of energy this is rather like making an assessment of nuclear power without mentioning Chernobyl. They admit, however, that 'catastrophic events cannot be fully excluded'. As a 10 MWe OTEC system uses between 230,000 and 300,000 litres of ammonia or three to four times that volume of

Freon, an accident leading to a sudden release of either chemical would not be the most welcome event in human history. With an ammonia leakage

> the effects would be acute and short-term. The most unfavourable circumstance would be a sudden release from a large installation near a population centre on a calm day, creating a toxic cloud that could pose a serious threat to nearby population centres. In the case of a Freon leakage, a concern would be the long-term effects on the ozone layer and thereby on global increases in transmitted ultra-violet (UV) radiation'.[57]

No one can accuse GESAMP of being 'sensationalist' – at least in expression. Perhaps we should have mentioned Bhopal as well as Chernobyl.

Beside the Seaside – On, In and Under the Sea

In the eighteenth and nineteenth centuries, only privileged young men with titled or monied parents set out from London, Paris or Berlin on the Grand Tour of Europe as part of their education. Their marine activities went little further than sun-bathing by the Aegean or swimming in the Hellespont. In the UK the discovery of medicinal springs and the alleged health-giving benefits of sea-bathing combined with the rise of an affluent middle class to produce the first seaside resorts, Scarborough and Brighton. The development of rail travel ensured their success. In 1833 only 50,000 visitors, travelling by coach, went to Brighton; in 1840, when the railway opened, there were 360,000.[58]

Before World War II, railways remained the major means by which the masses of northern Europe went to the nearest seaside resort for sun, sand and sea. Increased use of cars, cheap airflights and packaged holidays in the last 40 years have turned almost the whole world into a Travel Agent's commodity and produced a new phenomenon, the Tourist Industry. According to the World Tourism Organization international arrivals alone rose from 25 million in 1945 to some 280 million in 1980 out of a total of 3,000 million arrivals annually, 90% of whom were internal. Receipts from tourism rose from US$6.9 billion in 1960 to US$100 billion in 1982. Despite economic depression, hunger and starvation, tourism continues to expand at five per cent a year and the demand will have doubled before the year 2000. Some 600 million people throughout the world now receive 'paid leave', and the International Labour Organization (ILO) works constantly to increase the number. Even if domestic travel remains between two and ten times more significant than international travel, as popular beaches become more and more overcrowded, those who can afford it take off for the Galapagos Islands or the lower slopes of the Himalayas.[59]

Not all tourists visit the sea, but it remains the great magnet for the majority, and to offset those who go elsewhere there are others to whom the sea is primarily a means of recreation as distinct from tourism proper. Between 1851, when the America's Cup was run over a 27-nautical-mile series, and 1978, no fewer than 14 major ocean races have been established, ranging from local events such as the annual Cowes Week in the UK or the Sydney to Hobart race in Australia to the 2,500-nm single-handed Transatlantic and the 20,000-nm Whitbread Round the World. The sport is perhaps the most expensive and specialized in the world, its impact on the seas minimal.[60]

Equally widespread geographically in its use of the sea's surface, but restricted also to those who can afford it, is the ocean cruise. Today's journeys vary from port-to-port voyages to round the world cruises, from 'Cruise and Fly' holidays, in which the tourist flies out to the port of departure or returns home by air, to 'educational cruises' that include trips ashore to visit archaeological sites or study wildlife.[61] These minority activities also have little effect on the sea.

Discovery that the sea's surface would carry not only ships but suitably equipped human beings led to the development of surfing, now carried out by over three million people. The major sites are on open coasts exposed to great expanses of ocean, where the waters have time to collect before thrusting themselves towards the shore – southern Australia, both coasts of North and South America, and the north-western and southern tips of Africa. More widespread than ocean yachting because less financially demanding, surfing, except in the Caribbean, remains largely a perquisite of the developed world and takes place within its boundaries.[62]

The surfer, however, does not stay permanently at sea. Like other marine and coastal recreations swimming, sand-yachting, canoeing, dinghy sailing, wind surfing, water skiing or snorkelling – his/her activities take place within the surf zone or just beyond it. Add to these the millions of people who visit the sea because it is there or, if they have pinko-grey skins, expose as much of their bodies as permissible to acquire a tan, and problems arise of how they are to get to the coast, and where they are to eat, sleep and defecate. The response is the tourist industry.[63]

All these activities take place within that most vulnerable area of the sea – the coastal zone or on the continental shelf, where ports, industry and sea-fishing have already posed their own particular threats. Few studies have been carried out and, when the tourist industry realized the dangers of unplanned expansion and instituted a series of reviews of the 'carrying capacity' of national parks, forests and inland waters in the 1970s, there were few references to the coast.[64] In a more recent assessment, Pearce and Kirk point out that: 'Most tourist development along coasts has been undertaken by a multitude of developers with little overall co-ordination and planning, especially in the period of rapid growth of the 1960s and early 1970s.' At the same time, 'coasts, particularly beaches, are amongst the least stable and most physically changeable of the Earth's landform systems . . . Any factor, natural or man originated, which alters the supply, throughput and loss of sediments and/or the distributions of wave energy and currents in time and space, will have its repercussions on the form and position of the shoreline.' They conclude: 'It has been common that development of coasts has proceeded with little awareness of either the nature of beach systems generally, or detailed knowledge of local states of stability.'[65]

As long as the tourist operator could make a quick profit and the holiday-maker return home satisfied, the environment could be disregarded – until both sea and shore reached the stage where continued maltreatment threatened the industry itself. The most readily visible sign was sewage. We shall consider this in more detail in Chapter 4, but the problem of 'disposal of effluent' is particularly exacerbated by tourism when the population of an area, for which disposal facilities are normally adequate, is considerably increased for a short period of the year. 'The capacity of public sewage treatment systems along France's 930 coastal communes was reported in 1979 to be able to cope with the needs of about seven million people. This was sufficient for a winter population of about six million but clearly inadequate for the summer peak which sees the population double.'[66] Seas – and tourist areas – such as the Mediterranean are particularly susceptible because of the small tidal range and long water renewal period (see Chapter 1).

Pearce and Kirk mention a less familiar factor, the destabilization of sand dunes and their subjection to 'great stress from intense use, tracking, fire, vegetation depletion by pedestrian traffic and off-road vehicles, and "landscaping" for building sites, car parks and the like'. Foredunes, they point out, are active parts of beach systems which 'accumulate reservoirs of sand in fair weather and . . . yield it to the sea through scour in time of storm thus offsetting and limiting the extent of erosion'.[67] They act as a buffer, or shock-absorber, whose capacity is reduced if they are landscaped or the retaining cover vegetation is removed. The results are shore erosion or exposure of the hinterland to blowing sand and even inundation by the sea. Ironically, dune control and protection is not particularly expensive, at least in contrast to failing to protect them. The first essential is for tourists – and tour operators – to recognize their purpose – and respect it.

But it is the sea, and its resources, on which tourism has the greatest impact. Salt-water fishing is now a worldwide recreational sport with an effect on the economy of some areas greater than that of commercial fishing. During 1975 in the USA, 22 million anglers spent 4.5 billion dollars on the sport and so increased demand that some recreational stocks are now as overfished as commercial stocks. In 1935 catches of Californian barracuda were 14 lb (6.35 kg) per angler; in 1970 they had dropped to 2 lb and the fish is now designated a 'depleted sports resource'.[68]

Nor are the problems limited to developed countries. In Kenya 'sports fishing by visitors off the coasts and on the inland lakes has had some adverse effects on conservation, in particular of endangered species . . . ships trawling shallow creeks on the coast often accidentally kill dugong and marine turtles. The dugong population along the entire Kenya coast is now barely fifty individuals, yet even those do not enjoy adequate protection because their habitat is outside the existing marine parks and reserves.'[69] In the Caribbean there are signs that the spiny lobster is being overfished, not as a tourist sport, but to fill tourists' stomachs. The island of Anguilla, where the local people are not traditional lobster eaters, has become an exporter of seafood to the tourist economies of the US Virgin Islands and the French territories. And the demand for seafood shows no signs of diminishing.[70]

Sewage problems affect Barbados and Antigua. Barbados has an area of 431 square kilometres and a population in 1982 of 251,000. Three-quarters of the land is used for agriculture, mainly sugar-cane, leaving a highly urbanized 35-km stretch on the south and west coasts, approximately a sixth of the country, to accommodate its 7,000 hotel rooms and 303,800 tourists (1982). The results are inevitable: frequent traffic jams, difficult access to beaches or movement along them because of buildings and the construction of groins to protect property, impaired views of the sea that have led to a 'windows on the sea' project, and degraded habitats attributed to inadequate septic tank sewage disposal, to remedy which a major public sewage disposal and treatment system is being installed. At Dickinson Bay, Antigua, a sewage treatment plant for two hotels broke down through inadequate maintenance and was out of action for over a year. Two oxidation ponds were used temporarily but the 'treated' effluent was allowed to trickle into McKinnon's pond, into which there had previously been leaks from a nearby oil refinery. During a dry spell the stench downwind from the pond was so great that it forced guests to leave hotels at nearby Runaway Bay.[71]

Beaches have also suffered erosion, threatening beach hotel tourism. Grand Anne and Levera, Grenada, and Dickinson Bay, Antigua, all have unusual erosion rates; at Levera this was 3.6 metres a year between 1970 and 1984. The causes may be natural, but extraction of sand from beaches for use in concrete building structures is not without effect, and is thought to have caused the loss of a beach at Dickinson Bay.[72] In Kenya the reverse has happened – hotels have hampered tourists! 'The annihilation of beaches through the massive construction of beach hotels coupled with a monopoly of beach sites has progressively diminished public access to beaches'.[73]

The most damaging effect of tourism is probably on coral reefs, particularly as the result of a spectacular increase in skin diving. Between 1972 and 1981 the number of resorts in the Maldives in the Indian Ocean increased from two to 37, while the number of tourists exceeded 60,000. Kenya's marine parks attract about 25,000 people a year to snorkel and dive, while about a million visit the Virgin Islands National Park in the Caribbean. As a result tourists and sportsmen have damaged reefs in the Comoros, Kenya, Madagascar, Mauritius, Réunion, Seychelles and Tanzania in the western Indian Ocean and in Malaysia, Sri Lanka and Thailand to the north-east. Not only do ship's anchors and chains smash corals in landing or dredging – in one visit alone an anchor destroyed almost 20 square metres of large fragile corals – but tourists trample on the reefs, crushing the delicate branching forms, or attack them with crowbars or spears to collect corals and shells. Tourists who do not themselves go diving are in part responsible for additional damage by walking along reefs at low tide or supporting the lucrative industry which sells them corals and local shells, or even exports them to Europe. Actual diving is in fact probably less damaging than 'sedimentation, commercial collection of reef organisms for the ornamental trade, explosive fishing, coral mining, and entanglement of fishing nets'.[74] The common factors are human greed, ignorance and selfishness, the assumption that the seas and their contents exist solely for human exploitation.

Realization that such policies are ultimately self-defeating, and greater environmental consciousness, have brought about recent changes in practice and attitudes. Setting up marine parks and protected areas and providing glass-bottomed boats for visitors, as in the St Anne Marine National Park in the Seychelles,[75] make both commercial and environmental sense. Entrance fees bring in over US$22,000 a year, the tourists are satisfied – and so are the corals.

At the Manila World Tourism Conference of October 1982, 107 states agreed unanimously that:

> The satisfaction of tourism requirements must not be prejudical to the social and economic interests of the population in tourist areas, to the environment, or above all the natural resources, which are the fundamental attraction of tourism . . . The protection, enhancement, and improvement of the various components of man's environment are among the fundamental conditions for the harmonious development of tourism.[76]

The satisfaction of tourism requirements must not be prejudicial to the social precedence over local people, and the effects of a tourist invasion on that most susceptible of local phenomena, their 'cultural interests', are not mentioned. Perhaps it is too much to expect a recognition that human beings should live in total harmony with the environment of which they are part, at least when, as with tourism, it is the environment that brings in the dollars.

The world ocean is vast. Faced with these different types of human activity in isolation, it could doubtless survive the onslaught on its resources. But what of their cumulative – and potential – impact?

The sea's most plentiful creatures, fish, are endangered not only by commercial fishing but by the new generation of salt-water anglers; they have to face not only traditional dangers but new hazards from offshore structures, suction dredging for aggregates, the use of anti-fouling paint on ships and yachts and, potentially, the barely known effects of damming inlets for tidal energy or the creation of artificial lagoons by harnessing the waves. Lesser sea creatures are even more at risk, particularly from proposed developments: dredging for nodules, discharging effluent from an OTEC plant or the unwanted tailings of a mining operation, obliteration of air and sunlight and even changes in the movement of ocean currents may have consequences of which humanity is but little aware. The whole coastal ecosystem and the continental shelf, particularly beaches, sand dunes and, in the tropics, coral reefs are endangered by dredging, mining, the thoughtless actions of tourists in search of sea or spoil and the additional human effluent discharged into near shore waters. The oceans themselves are at greater risk than at any time in human history from those who sail on or under the waters – from increased numbers of oil tankers, chemical or liquid gas carriers, nuclear-powered or nuclear-armed ships and submarines, and the many sub-standard ships with underpaid and undertrained crews. The erection of structures to extract oil or natural gas and the potential erection of others to produce thermal energy are not only hazards to shipping and additional sources of danger when they are dismantled, but potential sites for accidental catastrophes – blow-outs of oil rigs or discharges of toxic gases into the atmosphere, the ultimate effect of which could be the deaths of many human beings or even climatic change.

Yet, these are only the beginning – humanity's 'normal' relations with the sea. Whatever their effects – and the only certainty is that nothing is certain – they are merely a permanent, if increasingly cumulative, hazard to enhance the greater danger, to which we now turn – the accidental or deliberate discharge of poisons into the sea.

References

1. *TAO* pp. 80–81, 99
2. FAO *INOFISH 5* 1983 p. 1
3. Brown 1985 p. 84
4. FAO *Yearbook*. Various years
5. Brown 1985 p 74
6. *TAO* p. 53
7. FAO *Yearbook*. Various years. Quoted Brown 1985 p. 74
8. Moorcraft 1972 pp. 32–3
9. FAO *Review* 1983
10. Agarwal et al. 1982 pp 115–18
11. FAO *Review* 1983
12. Gulland 1984 p. 359
13. *TAO* pp. 118–19
14. Bruce 1985 pp. 62–3
15. *TAO* pp. 104–5
16. Bell 1986 pp. 36, 40
17. *TAO* pp. 104–5; Bell 1986 p. 38
18. *TAO* p. 102
19. Bruce 1985 p. 62
20. *TAO* p. 104
21. Constructed from *TAO* p. 104 and Borgese and Ginsburg 1985 Tables 20, 40, from which figures quoted in the text are taken
22. *TAO* p. 106
23. Anon. 1986a p. 6
24. Bell 1986 p. 36
25. Quoted Brown 1982 p. 25
26. Bell 1986 p. 40
27. Kasoulides 1986 p. 7
28. Sources: Borgese and Ginsburg 1985 pp. 472–5; Kimball 1985 p. 74; Sanger 1986 pp. 162, 164–7, 189, 191; *TAO* pp. 110–15, 117
29. *TAO* pp. 86–7
30. All statistics from *Lloyd's Register of Shipping Statistical Tables* with acknowledgement
31. Source for types of merchant ships: *TAO* pp. 138–9
32. *Lloyd's Register of Shipping*; Borgese and Ginsburg 1985 p. 500

33. *TAO* p. 164
34. *TAO* pp. 140–41
35. *Hansard.* House of Commons. 22 January 1986
36. *TAO* pp. 140–41
37. Ibid. p. 162
38. ACOPS 1985–6 pp. 6–7
39. Constructed from Borgese and Ginsburg 1985 pp. 502–7, Table 3E, based on *Lloyd's Register of Shipping*
40. All statistics from Borgese and Ginsburg 1985 Tables 1G–7G, based on Moore 1983, 1984 and Albrecht 1983
41. GESAMP 15 p. 65
42. *TAO* p. 120
43. Ibid.
44. Ibid.
45. Ibid. and later TV news report on the Committee's proposals
46. *TAO* p. 120; GESAMP 20 p. 8
47. GESAMP 20 p. 8
48. *TAO* p. 121
49. GESAMP 20 p. 8
50. *TAO* p. 121
51. GESAMP 20 p. 2; *TAO* p. 121
52. GESAMP 20 Table 1 pp. 5–7, p. 11
53. Ibid. pp. 22–3
54. Ibid. p. 24
55. Ibid. p. 27; *TAO* p. 120
56. GESAMP 20 pp. 12–19 from which all quotations following are taken
57. Ibid. pp. 8–10
58. Romeril 1984 p. 4
59. Anon. 1986b
60. *TAO* p. 217
61. Ibid. p. 216
62. Ibid. p. 217
63. Ibid.
64. Pearce and Kirk 1986 p. 3
65. Ibid. pp. 3–4
66. Ibid. p. 5
67. Ibid.
68. *TAO* p. 217
69. Sindiyo and Pertet 1984 p. 19
70. Jackson 1986 p. 9
71. Ibid. pp. 8–9
72. Ibid. p. 9
73. Sindiyo and Pertet 1984 p. 19
74. Salm 1986 p. 11
75. Ibid.
76. Anon. 1984b

Part 2:
Poisoning the Seas

3. The Black Death – Oil

In the summer of 1985 appeared two reports on the effects of oil at sea. The first, the result of ten years' work on a worldwide basis by the US National Research Council, updates and expands a 1975 report to conclude that there has been 'no evident irrevocable damage to marine resources on a broad oceanic scale' from either major spills or chronic sources, i.e. regular discharges from industry or ships. As scientists, however, the experts are unwilling to commit themselves; more research is needed before they can make an 'unequivocal assessment' on the effect of oil on the environment, especially for 'specific environments and conditions'.

The second report deals with a 'specific environment'. Following a two-year study, the West German Deutsches Hydrographisches Institut concluded that at least half the 8,750 dead seabirds found along West German beaches between August 1983 and April 1984 died from oil pollution – and most of the oil came, not from tanker accidents or offshore oil rigs, but from normal shipping operations. 'All oil-induced losses of sea birds reported so far are caused by small oil quantities.'[1]

Neither report made headlines in the world press. Oil is no longer front-page news; interest is in fluctuating prices, not effects. The *Torrey Canyon* with its loss of 95,000 tonnes in 1967 and the even more disastrous *Amoco Cadiz* which spilt its entire contents of 220,000 tonnes of crude oil and several thousands of bunker oil in 1978 have become historical incidents, superseded by Sellafield and the *Mont Louis* which sank, with its nuclear cargo, off the Belgian coast in 1984 (see Chapter 6). Is oil then a back number? Does it cause 'no irrevocable damage' in the long run? Or have we merely become dulled by disasters, immunized into inaction by other and greater threats from nuclear or chemical catastrophe?

Oil, Hydrocarbons and Others

Motorists talk simply of 'oil', the working fluid that needs to be regularly checked and topped up; scientists write of 'hydrocarbons'; industrialists use esoteric terms such as 'Bunker-C', 'Ninian crude', or 'naphtha oil', while pollution control experts have a vocabulary of technical terms – 'sheen', 'chocolate mousse', 'adsorption' or 'biodegradation' – with which to baffle the non-specialist. Wrapped up, and frequently lost sight of, in the jargon are the simple facts that oil in the sea leads not only to such obvious, and pitiful, disasters as the deaths of thousands of seabirds, but has longer-term, more potentially far-reaching, effects on mammals, fish, plankton, plant life, and, through the food chain, may even affect human beings. Plankton such as copepods, writes GESAMP, 'are an important component of marine food chains . . . (their) population levels can be reduced by oil at concentrations found in the immediate vicinity of offshore platforms. *The possible long-term effects of this in the sea have yet to be assessed*' (my stress).[2] In short, there are aspects of oil pollution about which we are still ignorant.

What then is oil? How much do we really know about it and its effects?[3]

We have seen how oil and coal were produced when organic matter deposited at the bottoms of primeval lakes and seas was trapped by overlaying strata. Heat, pressure and time did the rest. Sediments deposited in fresh water became coal, those in salt water oil, with natural gas forming a huge bubble above it and the salt water remaining below.

The oil found in natural deposits is *crude oil* or *petroleum*, a complex mixture of chemical compounds, mainly *hydrocarbons*, i.e. combinations of hydrogen and carbon in different proportions, together with nitrogen, copper and traces of metals such as nickel and vanadium. The composition of different crude oils varies according to where they are found – with consequent variations in their poisonous effects – while the size of the molecules determines whether the oil is dense or light – again with variations in its effects.

Refining of crude oil to obtain *petroleum products* is made possible by the fact that the components of the mixture do not all boil at the same temperature and can be drawn off separately as more heat is applied. The proportions of each product vary according to the type of oil but the order in which the 'cuts' occur is constant. First come the petroleum gases, mainly propane and butane, which are sold in liquefied form as liquefied petroleum gases (LPGs) and used for heating. The 'light gasoline' that follows is more familiar as motor fuel or petrol. The 'naphtha cut' is used for making petrochemicals or, with further treatment, in blending with motor fuel; the 'kerosene cut' for domestic heating and as the basis for aviation fuel; diesel fuel for heavy transport, and the residue can be further distilled and used in lubricating oils or blended with kerosene to produce lighter fuel oils. When all products, including petroleum waxes, have been extracted, the residue is bitumen.

Further complexities arise from the properties of hydrocarbons themselves. Carbon atoms have the ability to link up ('bond') not only with hydrogen atoms but *with each other*. The simplest combination, *methane*, consists of one atom of carbon and four of hydrogen (CH_4). A straight line chain of seven atoms of carbon linked together and each bonded with two atoms of hydrogen except for the two at the ends, which are bonded with three, produces an *alkane* or *paraffin*, in this case, heptane (C_7H_{16}). If the carbon ends of the chain link up to form a circle, the result is a *cyclo-alkane* or *naphtheme*, in which each carbon atom is bonded with four atoms, i.e. the adjoining carbon atoms and its associated hydrogen atoms. When this happens, the compounds formed are said to be saturated.

Complications, however, do not end here. Some carbon atoms may lose their hydrogen partners and form a double bonding between themselves. The resulting compounds, referred to as *unsaturated*, are more chemically active than saturated ones. The most common types in crude oil are cyclic compounds known as *aromatic* hydrocarbons, of which the simplest is benzene. Finally, where the compound has a number of linked circles and is unsaturated, we have a *polycyclic aromatic hydrocarbon* (PAH), or *polynuclear aromatic hydrocarbon* (PNAH) as GESAMP calls it, such as Benzo(a)pyrene. According to the UK Royal Commission on Environmental Pollution, 'Benzo(a)pyrene and some other PAHs found in crude oil are known carcinogens',[4] or, as GESAMP states with polysyllabic precision, 'of known mammalian carcinogenicity'.[5] In short, they are cancer-producing poisons.

The deadliness of oil is not, however, limited solely to its toxicity. Oils can be dense or light and the smothering, or clogging, effects of dense oil are often the cause of more deaths, particularly among seabirds, than its actual toxicity. Before examining these consequences, we must first discover how oil gets into the sea.

Purveyors of Pollution

Attempts to discover how much oil is in the sea lead to three discoveries – that all sets of figures are estimates, that no two sets of figures agree, and that, despite these disparities, there is general agreement as to the sources and the relative contributions of each. As the US National Research Council points out in its report, the fact that it has revised its 1973 estimate of oil entering the sea from 6.1 to 3.2 million tonnes per annum does not mean that the quantity has almost halved in two years, merely that its estimating methods have improved![6]

In practice, humanity is responsible for considerably less than half the oil in the sea. Since hydrocarbons are natural products, this is not surprising. The UK Royal Commission on Environmental Pollution (RCEP) estimates that, given the average hydrocarbon content of phytoplankton as 0.03% of dry weight and their global production as 86 billion tonnes a year, they produce 26 million tonnes of hydrocarbons annually.[7] To this we can add production on land from emissions by growing plants or from their decay, much of which reaches the sea by run-off through rivers, or hydrocarbons resulting from fires, particularly large forest fires, which reach the sea through the air. Finally, there are leaks from the land itself, 'natural seeps' from which oil eventually reaches the sea. All sources agree that the latter account for between seven and ten per cent of oil entering the sea, while a similar proportion reaches it through the atmosphere, i.e. almost a fifth of the input is outside our control.

Of the remaining four-fifths more than half – approximately 45% of the total – enters the sea from land, the greater part through river run-off, including urban and inland municipal waste, the remainder being similar coastal discharges or those from coastal refineries. With just over one per cent from offshore oil operations, this leaves transportation with slightly less than 40% of the total. Non-tanker ships account for 7–10% and tankers for between 20% and 25% of the total. Of tanker discharges fewer than four per cent of the total are the results of accidents; the remainder – 22.2% in the 1985 figures – are from operational discharges.

Why then the outbreaks of public indignation after a *Torrey Canyon* or an *Amoco Cadiz*? Are these the result of popular ignorance fanned by media sensationalism? And why, if so much oil enters the sea naturally or is actually produced there, label it 'pollution' or 'poison'?

The simple answer is that, while hydrocarbons produced in the sea are evenly distributed throughout the ocean expanses and those received through the air are diffuse, oil spills lead to unnatural concentration in a restricted area. Moreover, many hydrocarbons found in crude oil are not only different from those formed by the metabolic processes of living organisms, but toxic to such organisms.[8] As for natural seeps, research at Kimmeridge Bay, Dorset, England, and at Coal Point, Santa Barbara, California, where oil enters the sea at a rate of up to 27 tonnes a day, reveals that, so far as its effect on fauna and flora is concerned, there is 'no difference between areas of seepage and normal regions of shore of similar type'. The Kimmeridge Bay research went further: laboratory experiments showed that barnacle cyprids, 'the most sensitive of settling larvae to environmental influence', actually preferred to settle on slate panels with thinly oiled surfaces rather than on unoiled ones, while the hydrocarbon content of limpets grazing in the oil seep area was 'not significantly higher than in limpets from a clean site'. With the larger quantities of oil at Santa Barbara the only harmful effects of weathered oil came not from toxicity but through smothering.

It is the combination of the two and their concentration that makes even small accidental spills of oil so deadly in their effects.

Tanker Accidents

The *Times Atlas of the Oceans* lists 176 tanker incidents between 1970 and 1981, each of which caused a spill of 10,000 barrels (1,360 tonnes) or more. To these may be added a further ten to the end of 1985, giving a total of 186. With few exceptions, all occurred in busy shipping lanes near coasts or even in ports, i.e. at the places where they were most likely to cause damage. Twenty-four were off the North American east coast, a further 24 in the Gulf of Mexico and the Caribbean, 29 in the high traffic areas of the North Sea, English Channel, Irish Sea and Bay of Biscay, 22 in the Mediterranean and Black Sea, 9 off the coast of southern Africa, 15 in the Gulf and Indian Ocean to the west of the Indo-Pakistan land mass, 15 in Indonesia and 9 in the area of Japan, the Philippines Sea and the South China Sea.[9]

Not all caused massive pollution. The *Castillo de Bellver*, for example, which caught fire some 65 km off the South African coast in August 1983, drifted shorewards, broke in two and threatened the breeding sites of jackass penguins on Dassen Island, did not lead to the disaster predicted. The stern half of the ship sank, but the bow, with up to 50,000 tonnes of oil in it, was towed out to a point 190 km from the coast and sunk by explosives.[10] Conversely, the *ARCO Anchorage*, which ran aground in Port Angeles harbour, Washington, in December 1985 and lost 612 tonnes, i.e. half the amount that would have qualified it for inclusion in the *TAO* list, affected over 1,500 birds, together with sea lions and harbour seals, and heavily oiled the salmon-rearing pens in Port Angeles harbour.[11]

The largest spill, however, from the *Amoco Cadiz*, in March 1978, was one of the most disastrous. Now that the Hon. Frank J. McGarr, the presiding judge into the lengthy legal inquiry that followed, has given his assessment of liability (April 1984) we can correct some of the myths and rumours of the time and name the real poisoners of the seas.

In outline the facts are as follows: the *Amoco Cadiz*, a VLCC of 232,182 dwt, loaded with 120,000 tonnes of light Iranian crude oil and 100,000 tonnes of light Arabian crude, and carrying several thousand tons of her own fuel, was en route from Kharg Island in the Gulf to Rotterdam and intended unloading part of her cargo at Lyme Bay, Dorset, England. On 16 March 1978, as it was proceeding along the coast of Brittany, the steering gear failed and the vessel drifted in heavy seas. Attempts by the salvage tug *Pacific* to tow it out to sea failed and the *Amoco Cadiz* grounded on the Portsall Rocks, later breaking in two; the entire cargo was lost and the French coast, which was just recovering from the *Torrey Canyon* disaster, was polluted to an even greater extent.

At the time French anger was directed at the masters of both vessels, Captain Bardari of the tanker and Captain Weinert of the salvage tug, who were arrested and ordered not to leave the quayside. An interim report presented in May and signed by the French premier, Raymond Barre, maintained that 12 hours were wasted while Captain Bardari was in contact with the owners and one or more salvage firms but made no attempt to warn the French authorities of the danger. According to this report the *Amoco Cadiz* asked for help at 10.15 a.m., the company agreed a salvage contract with the tug operators at 4 p.m., but not until 11.18 p.m., when the ship was firmly aground, was French assistance sought. The story of time wasted while the ship's owners and the salvage company haggled over terms was quickly taken up. Even the London *Times*, perhaps recalling the incompetence that had led to the *Torrey Canyon* disaster, commented: 'Most tanker accidents, it is now generally accepted, occur not because of mechanical or structural failure of the vessel, nor through unduly lax navigational rules, but as a result of human error'. So far as the *Amoco Cadiz* was concerned, 'it is already apparent that the human element played a considerable part, not least the considerable time-wasting which seems to have occurred at various stages'.[12]

In general terms *The Times* is correct. The massive poisoning of the French coast was ultimately due to human error. But it was not the negligence of the two individuals immediately concerned, as Judge McGarr's report now makes clear.

The main parties to the legal dispute are:

- the Standard Oil Company (Indiana) ('Standard') – now the Amoco Corporation – a corporation with its main office in Chicago, Illinois;
- the legal owners of the tanker, the Amoco Transport Company ('Transport'), a Liberian corporation operating from Bermuda, all of whose stock was indirectly owned by Standard through a chain of wholly owned subsidiaries;
- the Amoco International Oil Company ('AIOC'), a Delaware corporation, also wholly owned by Standard, and operating from Chicago;
- Amoco Tankers Company ('Tankers'), a Liberian corporation, all of whose stock was indirectly owned by Standard through subsidiaries;
- the builders of the vessel, Astilleros Españoles, S.A. ('Astilleros'), a Spanish corporation based in Madrid;
- the operators of the tug *Pacific*, Bugsier Reederei und Bergungs, A.G. of Hamburg, FRG;

Of the major characters Captain Pasquale Bardari was an experienced seaman. He had become an officer in 1963, served on Amoco vessels since 1970 and become a master in 1975. On this occasion he was accompanied by a retired Royal Naval officer, Leslie-John Maynard of the British Marine Safety Service, who acted as Safety Officer; the engineering officers of the *Amoco Cadiz* appear to have been thoroughly competent, while Captain Hartmut Weinert had salvaged over 65 ships, was supported by an efficient crew, and in the *Pacific* commanded a vessel that, when built in 1963, was the largest and most powerful tug in the world. Whatever happened, there was no prima-facie reason to attribute it to incompetence or inexperience.

The initiating factor was the ultra-severe weather of 15 March with rough seas and winds so strong that they caused the ship to roll considerably. Despite this there were no steering problems or other signs of trouble.

At 9.45 a.m. on 16 March, when the *Amoco Cadiz* was about 15 km north-west of the island of Ushant, the steering gear failed. Captain Bardari ordered the engines to be stopped, broadcast a VHF message, repeated at intervals, to all ships to keep clear and sounded an alarm. Although the French authorities later claimed that they had not been informed until after the ship grounded, in practice they were aware almost as soon as the incident occurred. Five navy watchtowers followed the ship's course as it drifted, two radio stations picked up the message, and the Molene watchtower between Ushant and the mainland followed the progress of the tanker and tug but did not inform Navy headquarters. The watchtower at Stiff also plotted their positions, noted a change in direction, and also failed to inform Navy headquarters. At dusk the staff at both watchtowers 'closed down their stations and went off duty in violation of their instructions not to shut down when observing an incident at sea.'[13]

Attempts to repair the steering gear and prevent the rudder from swinging across continued under the chief engineer's supervision until about 11.20 when it was decided that repairs were impossible. Captain Bardari then sent a radio call for tugs, while Maynard contacted Radio Le Conquet, who replied that the *Pacific* would be coming to assist. Action thus far is standard procedure: the master of a vessel does not call for help until advised by his chief engineer that he cannot repair a malfunction.

At 11.25 a.m., as the *Pacific* was travelling from Brest to the Strait of Dover, its radio operator picked up a broadcast from the *Amoco Cadiz*. Captain Weinert, from both humanitarian and financial incentives, immediately turned round and proceeded at full speed towards the tanker. At 11.28 the *Pacific* informed the *Amoco Cadiz* of its action and offered salvage assistance under Lloyd's Open Form (LOF), which provides for London arbitration of any disputes and was the only type of salvage contract which Bugsier allowed Captain Weinert to accept. Weinert informed Captain Karl Gunther Meyer at Bugsier's of his changed course. The latter alerted a second tug, the *Simpson*, then in the English Channel, before calling his London agent to request assistance in obtaining an LOF from Amoco. There was no reply to a phone call at what was 6 a.m. in the USA, so a telex was sent at 12.04. The reply came at 14.20 – a preference for a towage contract rather than a salvage agreement; this was unacceptable to Bugsier and at 15.15 Amoco agreed to the LOF. At 16.00 the *Amoco Cadiz* informed the *Pacific* of the arrangement, which was later confirmed by telex. Despite the delay, 'no time was lost by the *Pacific* in rendering assistance to the tanker',[14] as the timetable of events shows.

The *Pacific* had reached the *Amoco Cadiz* at 12.26 and attempted to shoot a towing line on to her foredeck so that she could be towed out to sea by the bows into the wind. In practice, this meant towing at a right angle and had never been previously attempted with a ship of that size. The effort went on for over two hours, from 14.10 to 16.19, during which time the tanker's southerly drift changed to east-north-easterly; although Captain Weinert used 80–90% of the tug's available power and, on two occasions, the bow of the *Amoco Cadiz* turned slightly to starboard, he did not succeed in turning the tanker into the wind and seas. At 16.19 the towing chain snapped.

By 17.20 the remains had been retrieved and a spare towing chain was in place. At 18.40 the *Pacific* was ready for a second attempt. Meanwhile, the *Amoco Cadiz*, at Captain Weinert's suggestion, had restarted her engines astern to try to keep the tanker away from the shore, despite the danger that the swinging rudder might come off and damage the propeller. It was now clear, however, that unless the tug could tow it out to sea, the tanker would go aground when the tide changed about 22.00.

The *Pacific* began her second attempt at 18.50, the tanker's engines being stopped for the reconnection, this time at the stern. It took four shots between 19.00 and 19.36 before the connection was made – and only 25 metres of heaving line and 110 metres of heavier messenger line had been hauled aboard before it dropped back into the water. The *Amoco Cadiz* then dropped an anchor, the effect of which was to swing the stern away from the *Pacific* but not to stop the tanker from drifting towards the east.

The fifth attempt, at 19.57, was successful and by 20.55 they were ready for towing but unable to heave in the anchor. At 21.00 the tug began towing on about 700 metres of wire, but at 21.04 the *Amoco Cadiz* grounded. The *Pacific* tried to pull her away from the coast and she appeared to start drifting again. At

21.10 the tanker's lights went out and radio contact was lost. At 21.50 oil was both smelt and seen, the tug called Brest for helicopters, increased its speed to full power and at 22.12 the towing connection broke for the second time.

Although he had lost contact with the tug, Captain Bardari on the *Amoco Cadiz* was able to inform Radio Le Conquet of the grounding and to request helicopters to lift off the crew. At midnight French naval helicopters began the hazardous evacuation. Despite the effects of gas, Captain Bardari and Maynard remained on board. Only at 4 a.m., when they realized that the ship was breaking up and there was danger of an explosion did they seek help. At 05.00 a French naval helicopter lifted them from the wreck and attention turned to the havoc on shore.[15]

Who then was to blame? With the benefit of hindsight, it was suggested that, had Captain Weinert towed the *Amoco Cadiz* from the stern in the first place and the tanker used its engines in reverse, it could have been held off the coast until the *Simpson* arrived. In his assessment Judge McGarr accepts this as a probability. He points out, however, that, with a swinging rudder, towing from the bow was a 'reasonable' strategy and that, as no one had attempted to tow or turn a VLCC in storm conditions, Captain Weinert may have made a misjudgement, but his action was not 'culpable negligence'. Neither did Captain Bardari object to the bow towing as he also was in no position to know whether the tug was capable of turning the tanker out to sea.

Was this then just an 'accident' for which no one was blameworthy? Judge McGarr answered this question by asking another: why, in the first place, did the hydraulic steering gear fail? Its successful operation, as specified in the manual provided by the builders, Astilleros, depended on complete changes of oil after every 1,000 hours of operation for the first three changes, then after every 3,000 hours, together with periodic cleaning of filters.

Judge McGarr found that AIOC had never acted

- to ensure that the filters were cleaned as required;
- to ensure that the steering-gear oil was changed as required;
- to make arrangements for having samples of oil analysed;
- to ensure that the system was periodically purged of air or shut down to allow air to separate out;
- to take steps to ensure that the gravity tank and sump pumps were cleaned;
- to rectify the damp and dirty conditions of the steering-gear room, although these had been reported on several occasions by their inspectors.

AIOC's negligence in respect of maintenance and repair thus 'impaired the reliability of the system', 'contributed to the presence of voids in the system' and 'thus to the failure of the De Flange studs'. AIOC's Marine Operations Department also failed to provide the necessary training and instruction to crew members in the following: emergency action after a breakdown, cleaning of filters, changing oil periodically, taking samples of hydraulic fluid for analysis, cleaning pumps, removing sediment from the gravity tank, not using an open bucket for filling the gravity tank, knowing the acceptable amount of fluid consumption, and being familiar with emergency drills for blocking the rudder. The crew had actually painted the ram cylinder valves so that they would not close completely!

Who then was AIOC? It was a subsidiary of Standard, who owned 100% of the voting stock, and had responsibility for carrying out Standard's day-to-day business outside North America. AIOC provided no services for anyone outside the Standard organization. 'Transport', the legal owners of the *Amoco Cadiz*, also had no publicly owned stock but was owned by subsidiaries of Amoco International Finance Company (AIFC), 80% of whose shares were directly owned by Standard, the remaining 20% by AIOC and Amoco Chemicals Corporation, another wholly owned subsidiary of Standard. 'Standard, AIOC, Transport and other Standard subsidiaries were managed by a network of interlocking directors and officers . . . Standard treated its subsidiaries' operations as its own; its officers and directors had little or no perception of separateness with respect to the various Standard companies'.[16]

Judge McGarr's conclusion leaves no doubt as to guilt.

The failure of *Amoco Cadiz*'s steering gear is directly attributable to an improperly designed, constructed and maintained steering-gear system, and AIOC knew or should have known of the unseaworthy condition . . .

The negligence of AIOC in failing reasonably to perform its obligations of maintenance and repair of the steering-gear system was a proximate cause of the breakdown of the system on March 16, 1978, the grounding of the vessel and the resulting damage.

AIOC is thus liable for the damages suffered by the plaintiffs, as is Transport, the 'nominal owner'.

In practice it is the 'integrated multinational corporation', Standard, which is liable since it 'exercised such control over its subsidiaries AIOC and Transport, that those entities would be considered to be mere instrumentalities of Standard'.[17]

Never has a multinational corporation been damned in the dock as a purveyor of poison with a comprehensiveness equal to its own ramifications. The story was not yet over. In April 1986 action began to determine the damages. On 11 January 1988, almost ten years after the disaster, Judge McGarr issued a 400-page report and ruling in which he awarded the French victims of pollution US$85.2 million in damages against Standard, now the Amoco Corporation, as partial compensation towards the US$2 billion clean-up costs.

Ironically, other and less disastrous incidents had more immediate effects. On 15 December 1976 the Liberian-registered *Argo Merchant*, on its way from Venezuela to Salem, Massachusetts with 28,000 tonnes of dense fuel oil, ran aground on the Nantucket Shoals off the east coast of the USA.[18] Bad weather hampered attempts to salvage the ship, which was abandoned two days after grounding without loss of life. The tanker broke up and an offshore wind carried most of the oil out to sea. The effects were greater on land, where expensive precautions were taken. Already there had been a number of incidents near the United States, public pressure for action was increasing, and the *Argo Merchant* grounding finally spurred President Carter into calling for international action. In 1978 two protocols were added to existing legislation (see Part 3, Figure 7.1). Cynics were not slow to suggest a connection between presidential action and the proximity of the incident to the USA.

On this occasion also there were faults in the tanker. The *Argo Merchant* itself was 23 years old and the Liberian Marine Investigation Board found that the gyro-compass was faulty, as was the course recorder, and a radio direction finder may not have been working properly. The main cause of the incident, however, was 'navigational incompetence'. The master received three clear warnings of impending danger: positions taken on the two days before the accident showed that the tanker was heading for the point where it grounded; the Nantucket light-vessel, by which it was intended to pass, was neither sighted nor picked up by radar when expected; and three hours before grounding depth soundings showed that the tanker was running into shallow water and was thus off course. Despite warnings from the chief officer, the master changed neither direction nor speed – and the *Argo Merchant* grounded.

There were different problems with the 12,680-ton Greek tanker *Eleni V*, split in two after colliding in thick fog with the French ore–bulk–ore carrier *Roseline* off the coast of Norfolk, England, on 6 May 1978, less than two months after the *Amoco Cadiz*. At least, there were problems with the bow section. The stern portion, which contained the engines, accommodation and three-quarters of the cargo, and was almost intact, was towed to Rotterdam after the 39-member crew had been rescued by lifeboat, and the oil was later sold. The sunken bow section continued its underwater odyssey at about a mile an hour, shedding oil as it went, passing over two pipelines from Bacton to the Shell, Phillips and Amoco (*sic*) platforms in the Hewett and Deborah North Sea gas fields, and grounding on Happisburgh Sands for 7–8 May. From 9–13 May, still spilling oil, it beached on Southcross Sands, while the Department of Trade (DoT) discovered that it had no large-scale contingency plans and the salvage companies argued amongst themselves and with the UK Government over whether it was worth while attempting to retrieve the oil. On 13 May the half-*Eleni V* floated off the sandbank, was secured by tugs on the 14th and taken to a deeper channel nine miles off shore. Meanwhile the oil slicks which the DoT had predicted would not come ashore did so, dispersants used in large quantities proved to be only 15% to 25% effective, and the Norfolk holiday resorts attempted to drum up business by advertising polluted beaches as a novel attraction and opening stations along the front for issuing cleaning liquid and rags to those with oil on their skin or clothes.

A week later, on 21 May, the *Eleni V* was taken and beached on Holm Sands less than 3 km off shore with the intention of pumping out the oil. Next day it was removed after it was discovered that its position was too unstable for the work, and on 23rd again dragged into a deeper channel 14 km off shore. Over 25th and 26th Dunwich Sand was surveyed as a possible offloading point, only to be deemed unsafe. On 27th South Whiting Sands were suggested as a possibility, but later abandoned. On 28th the hulk was towed to a point 42 km off Lowestoft and, after being held up by fog on 29th, at 4.30 a.m. on 30 May,

25 days after the collision, Royal Navy divers fixed $2\frac{1}{2}$ tons of explosives to it and the *Eleni V* disappeared in a ball of fire, a huge column of smoke and spray, and a bang that was heard 70 km away and rattled the windows of the pollution crisis headquarters on Gorleston pier. Not having learned the lessons of ineffective bombing of the *Torrey Canyon*, the Navy optimistically hoped that much of the oil would be vaporized in the fireball, and a dozen less optimistic spray-ships moved in to try to break up oil rising to the surface. Aerial surveillance showed a 300-yard slick, and oil continued to come ashore.

The Parliamentary Select Committee on Science and Technology, which reported on the affair in October 1978, was far from complimentary about the handling of events. 'The main cause, we feel, of these delays was the failure of the DOT to anticipate future events . . . Whilst these delays did not cause extra pollution, they suggest DOT did not display the urgency which this situation needed in order to resolve it as quickly and effectively as possible.' The Secretary for Trade, Edmund Dell, was criticized for giving inadequate consideration to the possibility of blowing up the wreck, and his defence – that bombing the *Torrey Canyon* had been a *last* resort – dismissed on his apparent inability to distinguish between a final bombing and a controlled explosion. Alternatives discussed at a meeting on 16 May and described by the Committee as 'wholly unworkable options' might be more appropriately labelled macabre. One plan, which should 'never have been considered', was to beach the wreck on Dunwich Bank near the Sizewell nuclear power station. The Committee's objections to this, however, were to cost rather than risk. 'If the wreck had spilled any of its load in the area, and this had penetrated Sizewell's underwater cooling inlet, then the cost of closing down the nuclear power station would have been £130,000 a day, plus the cleaning cost.' One can only speculate whether this would have been the only result. At least there is no doubt on the Committee's second objection, that 'the selected part of Dunwich Bank was even closer to Minsmere Bird Reserve . . .' If oil from a wrecked tanker fails to destroy birds at sea, the policy is presumably to give it a chance to have a go at those on land!

Administratively the DoT is criticized for dictating to local officials and for giving insufficient powers of decision to the men on the spot. Local authorities complained that meetings with the DoT were not for genuine consultation, merely to inform them of what the DoT proposed to do – at least after they had referred all policy decisions to London. The division of responsibility was in any case nonsensical. Local authorities were responsible for clearing oil from beaches and up to one mile at sea, at which point the DoT took over. As the oil had not been informed of this arrangement, it continued to drift over the demarcation line regardless of either party.

On the technical level the Committee pointed out that there were virtually no preparations for dealing with the problems caused by spills of heavy fuel oils. It was common knowledge that dispersants were 90% ineffective on such oils; the French had decided against using them when the German tanker *Böhlen* ran aground off the coast of Brittany in October 1976 and had tried to recover oil using a modified drill ship. Despite this, the DoT ordered a spraying operation, using up to 19 ships at one time, and making no attempt at manual recovery. Spraying of beaches was also largely unsuccessful and in the end local authorities had to fall back on manual labour. Not only had scientists failed to find an effective dispersant, the Department of Energy's Warren Springs Laboratory was criticized for a three-day delay in taking samples of the spillage.[19]

At least the technical lesson was learnt. When heavy oil poisoned the seas off South Wales in 1985 after the *Bridgeness* grounding, the Marine Pollution Control Unit of the Department of Transport, who were then responsible, did not use dispersants. On this occasion they were criticized by the Royal Society for the Protection of Birds for *not* spraying!

The *Christos Bitos* incident of 12 October 1978, which coincided with the Select Committee's report, displayed the now familiar features – large-scale pollution and the deaths of many seabirds and seals, defective or inadequate equipment on the ship, and 'human error' – and added a further problem: what to do with a stricken tanker (as opposed to only part of a tanker as with the *Eleni V*). The Greek Government's inquiry into the grounding and loss of the vessel showed that:

- the ship's main radar set, a 19-year-old model, was not working;
- the second radar broke down five hours before the ship grounded;
- the radio direction finder had not been adjusted for four years, and its margin of error had grown so wide that it was not used;
- the gyro-compass was working, but not the repeaters on the bridge, so that the helmsman had to rely on the magnetic compass;
- the distance run indicator on the bridge was not working; and
- the ship did not carry a Decca Navigator system, but relied on Loran which is not as accurate in European waters.

Despite these defects and inadequacies, the *Christos Bitos* might have cleared the rocks but for the master's behaviour. Although the radar was out of action and fog restricted visibility, the captain did not order a reduction in speed from the ship's 14 knots, did not sound appropriate signals to warn other vessels, and failed to post adequate lookouts. He did not use the echo sounder, which was working, to warn him of approaching shallow water, but continued on his course without taking bearings on lighthouses, buoys or other landmarks. The inquiry decided the captain had been grossly negligent, but the Greek merchant navy disciplinary council took no action and he remained free to command ships anywhere in the world.

The disaster could have been worse as, thanks to the weather clearing and remaining calmer, over 30,000 tons of oil were transferred to other vessels, leaving 1,000 tons in the tanks. The question remained: which port was prepared to accept a damaged tanker with this quantity of potential poison aboard? Which port, in fact, had the facilities for doing so? Obviously the owners would be asked to provide a huge indemnity against pollution before any port authorities would accept, even if, as the United Towing company maintained, the ship was salvageable. The answer was no one, and, as a last resort, dictated by expediency, the *Christos Bitos* was towed out into the Atlantic and sunk 330 miles (520 km) west of the Fastnet Rock, off the southern coast of Ireland. Even this was not according to plan; the actual sinking took place at a point 200 miles (320 km) short of the position agreed by the British and Irish Governments.[20]

The *Esso Bernicia* and *Betelgeuse* incidents, which took place within ten days of each other at the end of 1978 and the beginning of 1979, both occurred at oil terminals but differed in scope and the problems raised. The 190,000-ton *Esso Bernicia* was being manoeuvred into position at the Sullom Voe oil terminal in the Shetland Islands off the north coast of Scotland, when fire broke out in the engine room of one of the tugs engaged in the operation. The tanker collided with a jetty and spilt about 1,100 tons of heavy bunker oil. Next morning a boom was placed across the entrance but collapsed four days later, 600 tons of oil escaped into Yell Sound and 30 miles (48 km) of coast were polluted with the inevitable loss of bird life. The incident raised the question of dealing with spills in a remote, low temperature, biologically sensitive area in mid-winter. Pumps and dispersants proved useless in coping with the heavy oil and in the end it was necessary to fall back on mechanical and manual methods.

Nor were sub-Arctic conditions the only problem. The escape of oil into open waters provided the same opportunity as did the *Torrey Canyon*. Despite anti-pollution regulations, tanker captains quickly seized their chance to get rid of oil-contaminated ballast water, 'justifying' their actions by the knowledge that reception facilities at the terminal would not be working for a further six months. Who would take on the task of policing these remote northern waters? The question is still not satisfactorily answered.

The *Betelgeuse* incident on 9 January 1979 at the Gulf offshore terminal near Whiddy Island in Bantry Bay on the south-west coast of Ireland was considerably more serious in its loss of human life. An explosion on the tanker, followed by fire, caused the deaths of 51 people – all 43 of the crew, a technician on board and seven employees of Gulf Oil Terminals (Ireland) Ltd. Nor was this Bantry's first experience of catastrophe. Between 1968, when Gulf opened its million-tonne storage terminal, and 1975 there were 24 oil spills, including the *African Zodiac* which was punctured by a tug while docking and lost 115,000 gallons (430 tons) of oil on 10 January 1975. A spill the previous October had ruined the fishing fleet's whole season and the herring fleet had only been back at work five days when the January spill brought a further stoppage and caused the Irish Minister of Transport and Power, Peter Barry, to declare that he would be looking at Gulf to see if they were worth keeping at Bantry.[21] After the spill Gulf allegedly installed more sophisticated pollution control equipment.

The *Betelgeuse* had unloaded 80,000 tons of Arabian oil before the explosion and much of the remaining 40,000 was burned off in the fire. The ship split into three sections: the bow, containing some 4,000 tons of oil, remained afloat and the oil was salvaged within a few weeks; the mid-section with an unknown quantity of oil in it, which was not salvaged until August 1979; and the stern section containing accommodation and engines, which sank in 110 feet of water and was successfully raised in the summer of the following year. Over 60 miles of coastline suffered chronic pollution from seeping oil from January to the end of September, despite extensive large-scale aerial spraying, which was halted periodically when it was feared that the chemicals would cause more harm than the oil itself. Clean-up operations went on around the shores until September 1980, 21 months after the accident. Despite the pollution, the effect on seabirds was minimal. Fishing, of course, was suspended. The long-term effects of chemical spraying have still to be assessed.

The findings of the Tribunal of Inquiry, published by the Irish Government in July 1980, place the blame squarely on Total, the owners of the ship, and on Gulf Oil as operators of the terminal. The hull of the *Betelgeuse*, seriously weakened from inadequate maintenance and under excessive stress by incorrect ballasting, had buckled, causing explosions in the permanent ballast tanks. The ship's back broke, followed by fire, a massive explosion and extension of the fire to the aft of the ship, the oil jetty and even across the water towards the storage tanks on Whiddy Island.

The report condemned the management of Total for deciding not to renew corroded longitudinals or replace spent protective cathodes in the ballast tanks, thus seriously weakening the vessel's condition. These repairs would have taken a week and cost about £155,000. Civil claims for damages as a result of the incident were estimated at £100 million. In addition, there was no 'loadicator' or similar instrument for calculating stresses during loading and ballasting. Total knew that this caused problems for the ship's chief officer. Neither did the *Betelgeuse* have an inert gas system, such as prevented the *Energy Concentration* from catching fire at Rotterdam when a similar incident occurred within days of the report's publication.

Gulf were criticized for poor safety standards and for attempting to cover up the absence of one of their employees from the control room. They went so far as to take active steps to suppress the truth, falsified logs, gave false accounts to the inquiry and to other investigators, and attempted to avoid making statements to the police. The report condemned the previous management decision to moor stand-by tugs, which, when the terminal was built, were placed close to the jetty, 4.5 km from it and out of sight. In consequence, it took the tug 20 minutes to reach the tanker after a radio warning. Had it been moored nearby, it could have stopped the initial fire from spreading and perhaps even prevented it. Gulf also failed to provide suitable escape craft on the offshore jetty, which could have averted loss of life, and had removed steps and ladders to water level from the western mooring pile which was not damaged by fire or explosion and could have offered an escape route. Finally, Gulf were criticized for their decision to discontinue keeping fire mains under pressure because of maintenance problems. Instead, pumps to provide water had to be turned on by the control room's despatcher who, when the fire broke out, was missing – and the jetty crew were unable to use the mains.[22]

As with the *Amoco Cadiz*, ultimate responsibility for the disaster lay with the oil corporations who were prepared to risk men's lives, the loss of cargo, and subsequent poisoning of the seas rather than spend a meagre sum on maintenance, only to be faced with claims for damages far exceeding any loss. Even in monetarist terms it doesn't make sense, and one can only conclude that arrogant over-confidence had ousted business acumen.

Before the oil from the *Betelgeuse* had been mopped up the collision between two VLCCs, the 292,666-dwt Greek-registered *Atlantic Empress* and the 210,000-dwt Liberian *Aegean Captain*, 32 km north-east of Tobago on 19 July 1979 produced only slight variations – those of a hot climate spillage – on a now familiar theme. Twenty-six seamen died in the incident and both ships caught fire. The fire on the *Aegean Captain* was extinguished after two days and the ship towed to safety; the *Atlantic Empress* burned for ten days before sinking, the larger part of the cargo still in her tanks qualifying her for the greatest oil loss to date, over 281,520 tons. In reality only some 90,000 tons escaped to produce an oil slick which it was feared would be swept on to the shores of Tobago. Fortunately, strong winds blew it north of the island so that it drifted into the southern Caribbean. The remainder sits at the bottom of the Atlantic Ocean, awaiting the day when the confining walls of its tanks will corrode and allow it to seep into the waters.

During the last few months of 1980 the Liberian Bureau of Maritime Affairs in London held a public inquiry into the cause of the collision. Their findings are likewise familiar. The chief officer on watch on the *Aegean Captain* at the time had no proper radar training and did not take the usual seamanlike precautions during a heavy squall and reduced visibility. The officer on watch on the *Atlantic Empress* was a radio officer without qualifications as a deck officer. He also failed to keep an efficient radar watch and observe international regulations in poor visibility.[23]

We could continue our account of tanker incidents for the remaining pages of this book but the main causes of pollution, whether on the open sea or in harbour, are now obvious – sub-standard ships and human error. For neither of these is there any excuse. Our selection of examples illustrates different contexts but leads always to the same causes. We will conclude this survey with an incident not recorded among 'Great Spills of the World'. The actual spillage was small, the pollution non-existent, the potential implications hazardous.

On 11 January 1980 the 33,287-GRT Greek-owned and registered tanker *Scenic* was loading North Sea crude oil at Sullom Voe terminal. Two hundred gallons of oil, i.e. just over three-quarters of a ton – compared with the 220,000 tonnes of the *Amoco Cadiz* or even the 90,000 tons of the *Atlantic Empress* – were spilt, yet the ship's master was fined £3,830, of which £2,830 went to cover clean-up costs. Behind this lay a series of further incidents. The day before the spill, crew members were reported to be smoking on deck and loading was suspended. Inspection by the terminal's marine adviser showed that fire extinguishers were not available, the scuppers were leaking, and the anchors had been secured so that they could not be used in an emergency. Matches and lighters were confiscated and the ship inspected. The oil pollution control officer reprimanded the master for her dirty condition and loading was resumed, only to be stopped when the spill occurred.

After completing loading on 12 January, it was found that the vessel was over-loaded by more than 3,000 tons as a segregated ballast tank, i.e. one allegedly used for ballast water only, had not been emptied. Permission to discharge this into the harbour was refused when it was found that the 'ballast' contained 18 ppm of oil. In the end the surplus 3,000 tons of oil was pumped back into the terminal's tanks.

A further inspection by the Department of Trade found a number of defects:

- the port lifeboat engine would not start and caused a small but severe electrical fire during attempts to do so;
- the gas-tight covers of emergency lights were open, exposing naked electric light bulbs;
- crude oil was leaking from a deck hatch.

On 14 January the *Scenic* was allowed to leave – but banned from ever returning to Sullom Voe in such a condition. The next day, while 48 km east of Shetland, an explosion in the engine room injured five members of the crew and disabled the ship; it drifted for three days while repairs were made, then set off across the Atlantic. Further research showed that the *Scenic*, built in Japan in 1965, had already been involved in 14 incidents, including another fire and explosion in the boiler room, boiler trouble, and repeated strandings. Five other tankers from the same company are also reported to have caused problems at Sullom Voe.[24]

One may be excused from wondering at times how oil actually succeeds in reaching its destination.

Blow-Outs and Pipelines

Rig blow-outs are more potentially disastrous than tanker accidents because they are more difficult to control. The world became aware of the danger in January 1969 with a blow-out of the underwater oil drilling in the Santa Barbara Channel off the Californian coast of the USA. For twelve days oil gushed out at the rate of 21,000 gallons a day and a black slick spread over 1,200 sq km of the Pacific Ocean. Over thirty beaches were affected, and hundreds of birds died, as did seals and dolphins. Wildlife experts called it the worst disaster to hit California's bird life.

A further incident occurred between 14 and 21 December, causing more pollution and raising the question of the cumulative effect of repeated spills. Wildlife and sea creatures might recover partially from one disaster; could they survive a second? Rincon Point held a colony of 4,000 grebes before the first blow-out. When the birds returned from their migrations in the autumn, there were only 200; after the December incident, only a scattered few.[25] The poisoners applied the principle 'If at first you don't succeed . . .'

Two months later seven wells leading to the offshore drilling rig of Chevron Oil Company near Louisiana caught fire, causing a leak of an estimated 1,000 barrels a day between 10 February and 31 March. Slicks covered about 80 sq km of the Gulf of Mexico.[26]

In 1977 the European public became aware that offshore drilling brought perils as well as profits. On 22 April a blow-out occurred at Well B–14 of the *Bravo* platform in the Ekofisk oilfield of the Norwegian sector of the North Sea. An estimated 20,000–30,000 tons of crude oil escaped before it was stopped after eight days; at one time the oil slick covered 240 sq km. An inquiry commission headed by Judge Johan Fr. Mayer of Bergen attributed the disaster to 'human error' and blamed both the operating company, Phillip's Petroleum, and the Norwegian Petroleum Directorate (NPD), which was responsible for offshore operations. Ironically, the blow-out occurred while blow-out preventers were being installed following the removal of valves on the production deck in order to withdraw some 10,000 feet of production tubing from the well. An additional safety device, a down-hole safety valve, had been fitted about 500 feet below the production deck. It was eventually found on one of the decks of the platform, having been blown out of the tubing. During the installation of this safety valve there were operational problems so that it was left unlocked for several hours. Instead of pulling it out again, the operator assumed that it had been locked and finished his work. By that time he had not slept for 30 hours. Failure to lock this valve into its seating and so prevent the flow of fluids when the well became unstable caused the blow-out.

The Commission concluded that:

- the accident was to a large degree due to human error;
- there were certain technical weaknesses but these were only peripheral;
- the underlying cause was that the organizational and administrative systems were on this occasion inadequate to ensure safe operation.

In broader terms the Commission enumerated the faults as

- improper practice in documentation of the installations, the identification of equipment and the preparation of instructions on their use;
- weaknesses in the approved programmes of work operations in the producing well;
- improper planning of work at the platform;
- improvisation of procedures instead of revision of the programme;
- misjudging of the critical situation;
- weak leadership and control; and
- unreasonably long working hours for some people.

There had been two days of warning signs from the well but these were ignored. The Norwegian Petroleum Directorate was criticized for failure to ask for an organizational plan of the workout during which the incident occurred, including information about the qualifications of the personnel.[27]

The largest spill of all time, almost twice the amount lost by the *Amoco Cadiz*, came from the *Ixtoc I* exploration well owned by Petroleos Mexicanos (Pemex). The well was in the Gulf of Campeche, 80 km off the Mexican town of Ciudad del Carmen. In the early hours of 3 June 1979, as the final segments of the drill string, including the heavy collars above the drill, were being pulled up through the rig floor, a sudden rise in pressure caused gas and oil to flow. The safety devices in the blow-out preventer failed to contain the pressure and within minutes the gas and oil ignited. Fifteen hours later the substructure supporting the derrick and holding equipment collapsed. On 4 June the rig was pulled away from the site and its burnt-out remains subsequently scuttled.

In late June there were a number of unsuccessful attempts to control the well. On the 24th the flow of gas and oil was cut off and the fire on the sea surface extinguished, but as cement was being pumped into the well-head, oil and gas gushed out from a rupture below the blow-out preventer. This time they were deliberately set on fire to keep down pollution. In July and August attempts to seal the well by injecting steel balls into the top also failed. Relief wells were begun on 11 June and 1 July and by mid-October were almost ready to intercept the flow. In November one actually made contact but succeeded only in effecting a temporary stoppage. Not until 24 March 1980, almost ten months after the blow-out, was the well finally capped.

Meanwhile oil was lost at between 20,000 barrels and 40,000 barrels (2,740–5,480 tons) a day. Within a week a slick 180 km long and up to 80 km wide had formed. By August it had broken into several segments, each up to 110 km long, and had reached the Texas coast where it caused damage to seabirds and marine life. Some parts of the slick were sinking and later rising again so that it became difficult to assess both the size of the slick and its movements. Pemex reputedly spent US$133 million in capping the well and containing the environmental damage. The US Coast Guard spent US$8.5 million in clean-up. Assessment of the environmental effects was delayed by differences between the US National Oceanic and Atmospheric Administration (NOAA) which spent US$2 million on a research cruise, and the US Bureau of Land Management, which was not helped when the US Congress refused to provide the NOAA with a further US$7.9 million. The Mexican National Confederation of Fisheries Co-operatives claimed that large quantities of fish and other commercial stocks had been damaged, but Pemex maintained that Mexican fish catches had been good.[28] Amid these controversies one factor was indisputable – the tropical climate ensured that the effects were less far-reaching than in the North Sea as the oil evaporated or dispersed more quickly in the higher temperature.

Two other major blow-outs in hot regions had different results – *Funiwa 5*, 8 km off the Nigerian coast, and the *Hasbah 6* incident in the Gulf. The *Funiwa 5* blow-out occurred on 17 January 1980 soon after a new well had penetrated the oil reservoir. The well, owned by the Nigerian National Petroleum Corporation and operated by Texaco Overseas Petroleum Co., spilled about 200,000 barrels (27,000 tons) before it 'bridged' a fortnight later, i.e. the borehole wall collapsed and plugged the well. Reports at the time underestimated the effects. According to early investigators the oil reached the shore near the Fishtown and Sangana Rivers in the Niger Delta. Some mangrove seedlings were affected and the oil had tainted crabs and periwinkles living among the mangroves, even killing some of them. Later it became clear that the oil had poisoned the islands and channels of the Delta, ruining the drinking water and food supply of up to

250,000 fishing people, many of whom were forced to seek refuge elsewhere. The effect on the mangrove swamps was even more ecologically disastrous (see p. 107–8).[29]

Hasbah 6, owned by the Arabian American Oil Company (Aramco), about 100 km off the Saudi Arabian coast, blew out on 2 October 1980. Nineteen workers on the jack-up drilling rig *Ron Tappmayer* died when hydrogen sulphide fumes were released along with the oil and gas, but the remainder were safely evacuated. By the time it was capped on 10 October the well had spilt between 5,000 and 13,000 tons of heavy crude oil; at one point the slick covered 25,000 sq km, making it the largest in surface area after the *Ixtoc I*. Immediate danger was to the north-western coast of Bahrain, which had been seriously polluted by a 15 sq km slick of unknown origin the previous August. This slick had already killed about 1,000 birds, contaminated beaches and restricted fishing. By late October wind and currents carried the oil towards Bahrain itself; 12 km of the coast were affected and tar balls were washed ashore along 100 km of the northern coast of Qatar. At the end of November 320 km of the Qatar coast were affected, 30 km severely. The tropical climate both hindered and helped. At first calm weather and low wave energy prevented dispersants from working properly, but by the end of October fresh winds and choppy seas helped to break up the slick. Costs of cleaning up the Qatar coast alone were estimated at US$7 million.[30]

Leaks from pipelines are likely to be more disruptive than dangerous. On 6 April 1980, following a drop in pressure in the 11-km pipeline linking the British National Oil Corporation Thistle and the Royal Dutch Shell Dunlin A platforms in the North Sea and the appearance of an oil slick, a leak was discovered. Next day the Thistle oilfield was completely shut down and, as a further precaution, the platforms on the Brent, Dunlin and Cormorant fields were later closed. The leak, which led to a loss of 460,000 gallons (1,700 tons) of crude oil, was caused by the dragging of an anchor, almost certainly from a supply ship, well within the 500-metre safety zone around the Dunlin platform. Subsequently eleven companies – ten as owners and Shell UK Exploration and Production Ltd. as operators of the pipeline – were charged in Lerwick Sheriff Court under the 1971 Prevention of Oil Pollution Act. The case against Shell was dismissed, but the problem remains. In their 1981 Report, the RCEP points out that burying pipelines in the sea-bed would offer no protection from the type of anchor used by such vessels and that fishing gear could also be dangerous, at least to smaller lines.[31]

More insidious is the sea itself – movements of the sea-bed or the corrosive action of salt-water, especially in hot climates. The danger is obviously greater, the nearer to the shore. On 3 December 1985 a pipeline fractured from 'metal fatigue' about 2.5 km from the coast in the Gulf of Suez, leaving a gap of 100 metres between the ends. Normally the line carries 40,000 barrels (5,400 tons) of oil a day from offshore wells to onshore storage tanks. About 11,000 gallons (1,500 tons) of medium crude oil spilled into the Gulf of Suez. On this occasion there was no 'significant' damage to the environment,[32] but as pipelines get older and potentially more dangerous, we can no longer claim that we have not been warned.

'Normal' Operations

Tanker accidents and oil well blow-outs cannot be hidden; the quantity of oil discharged ensures detection. Discharges at sea from both tankers and merchant ships, whether accidental or deliberate, are not only greater in total quantity, if less immediately damaging, but also less easily detectable. Beach pollution from sources of 'unknown origin' symbolizes the more underhand, sneaky methods of poisoning the seas adopted by unscrupulous or careless masters of ships. Inevitably, as the RCEP comments, 'there is a surprising dearth of hard evidence on this subject . . . At first sight, tankers are the obvious culprits . . . But all vessels generate, and need to dispose of, oily wastes, and many ordinary merchant vessels spend a much larger part of their working lives closer to shore than tankers'.[33] If even a Royal Commission had difficulty in finding 'hard evidence' for a comparatively well policed area such as the waters around the UK, how much more difficult is it to discover what happens in the vast ocean expanses or off the coasts of developing countries!

The causes at least are known. With a tanker there is, first, the problem of oily residues that have settled in its tanks during a lengthy voyage and which need to be cleaned out before it takes on its next cargo. With a large tanker these may amount to a thousand tons or more, while pumps and pipelines contain several hundred tonnes. The traditional method was to flush tanks and other parts with sea-water and discharge the contents, including oil, into the sea.

Secondly, there is ballast. After discharging its oil a tanker needs to replace it with water to ensure proper operation; otherwise it rides too high and becomes unmanoeuvrable. How much ballast is needed depends on the length of the voyage and the weather – more is obviously needed if there are likely to be rough seas – but ballast can amount to 20–50% of a tanker's carrying capacity. Again, traditional practice results in pollution. Placed in tanks that previously contained oil, the water becomes contaminated by the residues, is discharged at sea, and replaced by fresh water that can then be emptied into the harbour on arrival. Not entirely unsurprisingly oil slicks are more common along the world's major tanker routes than elsewhere. Of the total quantity of oil carried at sea in 1979, 58% was shipped from Middle East countries, much of it across the Arabian Sea and either through the Mozambique Channel round South Africa to the west or across the southern Bay of Bengal through the Malacca Strait to the Far East and Japan. 'The effect of oil spills (*sic*) is seen on the beaches of every country in the form of deposits of tar-like residues . . . . The amount of floating tar in the Arabian Sea has been estimated at 3,700 tonnes, and about 1,100 tonnes along tanker routes across the southern Bay of Bengal. This is roughly proportional to the difference in tanker traffic.'[34]

Thirdly, there are deliberate discharges from ships other than tankers to clean out oily waste from bilges in engine rooms and other places where there are leaks of fuel or lubricating oil. While shipping companies argue that the amount discharged at any time is relatively small, at least compared with that from tankers, the RCEP points out that 'frequent small discharges of oil on busy shipping routes relatively close to shore could lead to a chronic pollution problem'.[35]

Again, fuel tanks in non-tanker ships may be used for ballast, and though vessels over 80 GRT are now required to have oily water separators to prevent excessive discharges of oil into the sea, not all oil can be separated and re-used. In theory, any waste is taken to reception facilities at the port; in practice, as the RCEP comments, 'there is little doubt that . . . much of this waste goes overboard instead'.[36]

The problem is exacerbated by the type of oil concerned. Fuel oil is more persistent than the crude oil carried by tankers, which, if released far out at sea, disperses fairly quickly. The operation thus poses a triple danger – from the type of oil itself, from the fact that such discharges often take place on shipping routes near the coast, and from the cumulative effect produced by the quantity of this traffic. Most dangerous of all is our ignorance. For the greater part of the world we do not know how much oil goes into the sea in this way. Only in advanced industrial countries, where the problem has become inescapable and opposition vociferous, is there any attempt to find out. Even for the UK, where surveys have been made since the early 1960s, the Royal Commission commented in 1981: 'The difficulty we have had in assessing this problem suggests strongly that more work needs to be done . . . to obtain information about the sources of oil in the sea. We do not see how it is possible to reach a satisfactory view of the adequacy of existing controls over different sources of discharge without such knowledge.'[37]

Nor are these the only causes of 'operational' discharges; there is always 'human error' or 'equipment malfunction'. With a tanker at sea, the transfer of oil from one tank to another to assist balance or improve stability can lead to what is euphemistically called 'overfilling' but could more aptly be described as 'overflowing' as the surplus finds its way into the sea. Similarly with 'lightening', the transfer of oil at sea from one ship to another to reduce its draught in order to conform to port regulations or for the redistribution of cargo. (The *Amoco Cadiz*, we recall, was on its way to Lyme Bay for 'lightening'.) Here the main risk is failure of a connecting hose so that oil pours into the sea instead of reaching the receiving vessel. Forecasts that 'it is unlikely that more than about ten tonnes of oil would escape before the pumps were stopped'[38] reflect the optimism of assumed efficiency rather than experience.

Operational problems at sea are replicated in ports and harbours, where the greater number of ships also increases the danger of collisions and groundings. On 30 April 1985, while the Liberian tanker *Golar Petrograde* was moored at No. 2 jetty in the port of Rotterdam, over 130 tons of crude oil were discharged into the harbour. The pumpman had opened a tank to correct a starboard list and allowed some of its contents to drain out. He was under the impression that it contained ballast water![39]

So much for 'human error'; as for 'operational malfunction', when the French tanker *Folgoet* was loading cargo at Donges, France, on the last day of 1985, it spilled 326 tons of fuel oil. For 'undetermined reasons', a 70mm-diameter plug in the bottom plates on No. 3 port tank had 'dropped out'.[40]

These are not episodes from ancient history, when, from our superior 20th-century viewpoint we would affect not to be surprised at ignorant seamen or faulty plumbing; they occurred in 1985. Neither did they happen in some far away backwater port where one might expect anything to occur, but in well-equipped ports of France and the Netherlands.

As for 'operational spills' from those isolated structures, oil platforms, available figures are not encouraging. According to information supplied by the UK Department of Energy to the London-based Advisory Committee on Pollution of the Sea (ACOPS), in 1983 there were 72 incidents involving oil spills in the UK sector of the North Sea oilfields, in 1984 66 and in 1985 91. These represent respectively 18% of the total number of incidents reported to ACOPS for the UK in both 1983 and 1984, but 25% in 1985. Despite the decrease in the number of incidents in 1984, the actual quantities of oil spilt show a continuous rise: the 1983 figure was 23% higher than that for 1982, the 1984 25% higher than for 1983 and the 1985 20% up on the previous year.[41]

These, of course, are official figures. How far do they represent the truth? A report presented by the Dutch Government to the contracting parties to the Bonn Agreement (see Part 3) Working Group on 21 April 1986 gives the results of four aerial surveillance flights carried out over the Danish, Norwegian and UK offshore exploration areas, using remote sensing equipment, between 1984 and 1986. The report concludes that 'most oil discharges were generally not reported by the offshore operators or by others'. It maintains further that the quantity detected during 31 flight hours on 3–4 February 1986 – 466 cu m – greatly exceeded that officially reported as uncontrolled or accidentally spilled for the entire year 1983 (316.5 cu m).[42] Either there had been a sudden upsurge in the discharging of oil, or the previous official figures were an underestimate. The latter explanation is more probable.

Once again we are confronted by lack of firm knowledge – or at least by gradually diminishing ignorance. And if this is the best that can be achieved in one of the most technically advanced areas of the world, what of the situation where there are no government departments providing official statistics, no voluntary bodies collating them, and no aerial surveillance to check their accuracy? One would have to hold an idealistic view of humanity indeed to believe that operators, motivated by concern for the safety of the seas, refrained from tipping their oily wastes and drilling muds back into the water, if they were confident the act would pass undetected.

Oil in the Waters[43]

The proverbial injunction to pour oil on troubled waters was obviously formulated before the *Amoco Cadiz* and *Ixtoc I*. Our accounts of the complex nature of hydrocarbons and the equally varied character of the sea suggest that what happens when oil is poured on water depends on the type of oil and the type of water. A spill of light petroleum in a hot climate is a different phenomenon from the loss of heavy crude in the Arctic. The massive pollution expected after a blow-out in the Nowruz oilfield in the Gulf in 1983 and rocket attacks on other oil wells in the area ended in the embarrassed newspaper whimper 'The Oil Slick that Disappeared'.

Enough is now known to predict what can happen to oil in the sea. In the first place, given calm water and no wind, it spreads. The extent of spreading depends on the type of oil, how dense it is and how much there is of it. In ten minutes a cubic metre of Middle Eastern crude oil will form a circle 48 m in diameter and 0.5 mm in thickness; in 100 minutes the circle will be more than twice as wide but only a fifth of the thickness. How far the oil spreads depends on how quickly the volatile components (fractions) in the hydrocarbons evaporate and the thicker, more viscous, remainder breaks up to form floating 'islands'. High temperatures and rough seas assist this process, which affects primarily the light alkanes and aromatic components of the oil. The natural forces that contributed to the *Amoco Cadiz* disaster also caused 90,000 of the 233,000 tons of oil lost to be dispersed by evaporation.

Oil slicks, however, do not stay put but drift under the influence of tides, currents and wind. In the open sea the wind dominates, and sudden changes of direction, as with the *Castillo de Bellver*, have turned potential disaster into fortunate escape. In estuaries and along enclosed coasts, tides and currents have more effect. Not all the oil remains on the surface. The lighter, saturated aromatic hydrocarbons dissolve in the water under a slick, thus both reducing its extent and, because of their high toxicity, increasing the danger to life in the waters.

The remainder, especially in rough seas, mixes with the water to form an emulsion. If the water predominates, the result is an oil-in-water emulsion that is easily dispersed by currents and water turbulence. If the oil is heavy or has lost its lighter fractions, the outcome is a highly persistent water-in-oil emulsion of semi-solid lumps known as 'chocolate mousse', which eventually forms the tar-balls washed up on beaches. A third fate is for the oil to attach itself to particles of matter (*adsorption*) which then sink to the bottom to join existing sediment, where further change is exceptionally slow.

These physical processes are accompanied by chemical and biological activity. Chemically, all hydrocarbons are susceptible to oxidation, i.e. attack by oxygen, the rate of which is increased by ultra-violet radiation in sunlight. Many of the resulting products are highly soluble in water, thus assisting the break-up of the slick. Those with a high molecular weight, however, may contribute to forming emulsions and eventually tar-balls. Obviously the extent of these processes will depend on the physical features of the slick; a thin film of oil will degrade through oxidation more quickly than will compact lumps. Biologically, there are micro-organisms in the sea, bacteria and fungi, which feed on the oil, particularly on alkanes, especially in warmer waters and in the first few centimetres of bottom sediments. Again, since this action occurs on the surface of the oil, biodegradation is more effective on thin, extended slicks than on chocolate mousse or tar-balls, where the surface area is small in relation to size.

Finally, the oil comes to rest. If it reaches the shore, a modified form of degradation continues. In oil deposited at high water mark the process is slowed down and the oil becomes a lump of solid tar. If it sinks to the bottom of the sea and is buried in sediment, lack of oxygen prohibits microbial activity.

The effects of oil are thus determined by the state of degradation it has reached and where it is. Spills in the open sea are usually considered the least deadly and are often left to degrade naturally, the 'do-nothing' option. Research, however, does not completely exonerate the poisoners. After the 1975 *Argo Merchant* incident off the north-eastern United States 'fouled zooplankton, moribund fish eggs and a relatively high proportion of oiled birds were observed near the site'.[44] That there were no long-term effects may be due to a lucky coincidence that the oil was not dense enough for much of it to sink to the bottom and that the spill occurred in winter, the slack period for biological activity and fishing.

As for the sea-bed itself, research in the Ekofisk oilfield in the North Sea, where oil 'creeps' into the sediments, reveals ecological changes around some installations but not others; 'but it has not so far been possible to separate the effects of oil pollution from other factors'[45] such as physical disturbance of sediment through discharging drilling muds or burying pipelines. The scientists' dilemma is small comfort to those at the receiving end. Oil may not be the only culprit, but the destruction of one's home is still destruction, whether caused by fire, flood or earthquake. The only certainty is that in nearshore spills such as the *Torrey Canyon* more crustaceans, molluscs and echinoderms died from chemical dispersants than from the oil itself!

With exposed rocky headlands and rock platforms, wave reflection and washing either keeps most of the oil offshore or removes it within a few weeks. Coral reefs are less fortunate. In the Gulf of Eilat 90% of the polyps in shallow water died after unusually low tides in 1970. This enabled scientists to compare recolonization on two reefs, one comparatively free from oil spillings, the second affected by 95 spills between 1971 and 1973 at the rate of one to seven a month. On the first the corals formed a new colony at their normal rate; on the second even species which seize every opportunity for colonization failed. Despite this, the scientists were not satisfied. Discharge of phosphates from a nearby fertilizer plant may have caused eutrophication. The corals, we assume, were not impressed by this inability to reach definite conclusions on the effects of oil.

Shores with rock outcrops, large boulders and stones in inter-tidal areas, whether on headlands or in sheltered fjords, support different communities according to climate and exposure. Their physical features – cracks, fissures, pools – determine whether oil will run back into nearshore waters or be retained. In north-west Europe the most common victims are limpets and barnacles, which oil detaches from the rocks, thereby providing gulls with an unexpected feed and preventing the re-attachment that would otherwise occur. What is good for the gulls is also good for the algae on which limpets graze and which are relatively resistent to oil. A decline in the limpet population leads to an invasion of green algae, followed by brown, which so smother the rocks that barnacles and others have nowhere to settle. 'Recovery', in inverted commas, we are assured, may 'possibly' take place in 5–15 years. As for tropical zones, where oysters abound, together with barnacles, whelks, limpets and coralline and brown algae, 'little is known about oil pollution effects on such shores'.[46]

The extent to which oil affects beaches depends on their type. With fine-grained sand oil does not usually penetrate far into the sediment, so it can be removed mechanically. Where the sand is coarse-grained, oil sinks or is rapidly buried; what remains on the surface is removed naturally within a few months. Mixed sand and gravel beaches, or beaches formed of gravel alone, are more problematic in that oil penetrates quickly, is soon buried, may remain for years and, if heavy, can even form a solid asphalt pavement.[47] Mud and sand flats are more at risk. If waterlogged, flats prevent oil from penetrating, while in those with much sea activity and consequent disturbance, oil may be either buried or washed out; in sheltered flats with no wave action oil penetrates the sediments to remain there for years, gradually leaching out as chronic pollution. The result is the destruction of large numbers of worms, bivalves and crustaceans, particularly where burrowing creatures provide convenient channels through which the oil can seep. As tidal and mud flats are feeding grounds for large numbers of birds and fish, the indirect effects through depleted food supply are even greater.

Because they are usually protected against wave action, polluted salt marshes tend to become oil traps, while the large surface area of marsh vegetation offers an excellent opportunity for oil to interfere with the process by which oxygen reaches the roots. Surprisingly, reactions vary: some plants are killed by one oiling; others take advantage of their disappearance. Most can eventually recover from light coatings of fresh crude oils, or from non-smothering weathered oil, but heavy spills of fresh crude or thick layers of chocolate mousse can be devastating. The effects are not limited to the marshes themselves. Loss of vegetation can cause sediments to become unstable and lead to coastal erosion; wildfowl and wading birds which use the marshes for breeding lose their habitat; and in those parts of the world where salt marshes are used for grazing sheep, cattle or horses, even the human economy is affected.

Most susceptible of all, and most difficult to clean – as the inhabitants of south-eastern Nigeria discovered after the *Funiwa 5* blow-out – are without doubt mangrove swamps. Within three years of the loss of 39,500 barrels of Venezuelan crude oil in the Caribbean from the *Zoe Colocotroni* in 1973, two species of mangroves had lost their leaves and died, though some later recovered. After the spill of 54,000 barrels of crude oil from the *Showa Maru* in Singapore Strait in 1975, there were dead mangroves in bays on two islands, the number of invertebrates was reduced, and hydrocarbon residues were found in sediments. Spills at five different sites in the Gulf of Mexico and the Caribbean produced similar results – defoliation and leaf deformation, deaths of trees and seedlings. The unique feature of mangroves, their ability to grow in salt water, has proved their undoing. The *Funiwa 5* blow-out affected a greater area than any previously poisoned and showed that the effects may not be apparent for some time. Science made a new discovery – that mangroves can die slowly. A survey immediately after the incident reported that large trees had not lost their leaves; fourteen months later mangroves had been killed over an area of 836 acres. Because many of the large trees were also old, recovery will be long indeed.[48]

The Victims

So much for the environments and some of their life forms. What of other living creatures that inhabit them?[49] The deadliness of oil, as we have seen, is not only that it poisons but that it also kills by smothering. Its effects, moreover, may be, in current jargon, both 'acute' and 'chronic'; in plain words, if it does not kill at once, it may have long-term effects on those immediately contaminated or on later generations. And because of the interdependence of one species on another, disturbance at any level upsets the ecological balance. Finally – a point to which we shall repeatedly return, since apologists tend to dismiss the effects of oil itself – poisons do not work alone.

On the smallest organisms, the plankton that form the basis of marine life, an oil spill can have two effects: it may poison directly as light aromatics separate and dissolve in the water beneath a slick; and, if the oil is dense enough, it can 'smother' by reducing the penetration of light so that photosynthesis is impossible. Usually transient in its effects – a slick moves on and plankton reproduce in myriads – a major spill such as the *Amoco Cadiz* caused changes in the proportions of both phyto- and zooplankton that were still discernible two years afterwards. Conversely, there may be little apparent effect; the *Torrey Canyon* was wrecked at a time when the zooplankton contained large numbers of pilchard eggs, yet the pilchard population was barely affected. Additional losses caused by the oil were presumably insufficient to upset the overall loss that normally occurs when pilchards breed.

We have noted GESAMP's concern that plankton such as copepods, which are important in the marine food chain, can be reduced in numbers near offshore platforms, and our ignorance of the possible long-term effects. A single spill may affect only one year class of adults through loss of eggs and larvae, but 'the long-term or ecological significance is not clear'.[50] In short, we may think we can get away with it and so far nothing serious has happened, but we cannot be certain about the future.

Large multicellular algae (macroalgae or macrophytic algae) – seaweeds to the non-biologist – live in inter-tidal and shallow waters. As they need light, they are in danger when such waters are covered by thick oil or mousse, which may also smother them as the tide goes out. While different species vary in vulnerability to the lighter, more toxic, fractions of oil, thin coatings are unlikely to harm them as many seaweeds are covered with a mucus to which oil does not cling. Should it do so, later tides will probably wash off the oil. Even when seaweeds are destroyed, recovery, as we have seen, is comparatively swift; they even benefit from the fact that they recover before the creatures that feed on them, and 'celebrate' by covering a larger area. Humanity is affected in places such as Japan and south-east Asia where *porphyra* cultivation is commercially important.

Oil is more deadly in its effects on invertebrates such as molluscs, crustaceans and worms. In inter-tidal areas, molluscs such as limpets, winkles, cockles, oysters, clams and scallops are either killed by smothering or poisoned by oil that has soaked into the sediment. Lesser effects, e.g. 'tainting' – the presence of an unpleasant smell or flavour – affect their commercial value. Despite this and allowing for variations in the effects of different oils on different organisms, many survivors will have reduced the hydrocarbon level in their tissues to low levels within 30 days; in the laboratory oysters exposed to fuel oil for eight hours lost 90% of the absorbed alkanes in 24 hours when placed in clean sea-water and were almost completely recovered after 28 days. Unfortunately, the sea does not always provide such a convenient method of recuperation.

Crustaceans such as lobsters or crabs living in the sub-tidal zone have the advantage of mobility and escape direct contact with the oil. (Attached crustaceans such as barnacles suffer the fate of molluscs.) Large numbers, however, have been poisoned by oil dissolved in water or have suffered what are euphemistically called 'sub-lethal effects', i.e. loss of appetite and alertness, which upsets feeding and so leads to a lingering death. As with other species, eggs and larvae are the greatest casualties; as little as two parts per million of oil in water can kill off lobster larvae. Between a quarter and half the worms living in inter-tidal sediments may disappear if oil penetrates to this level, while sea-urchins and starfish die in large numbers.

The effects extend up the food chain and last in time. Deprived of mussels, oysters or crabs, human beings can turn to other foods; birds and fish depending on mud flats for worms or crustaceans may find supplies cut off completely.

Fish have three advantages in coping with oil: most species can detect harmful substances in water; like seaweed their outsides are coated with a mucus to which oil does not cling; and they are mobile. Why, then, do so many thousands die from oil spills, particularly in shallow waters, rivers and estuaries? The answer is in part contained in the question. In the open sea 'there is no definitive evidence which suggests that oil pollution has significant effects on fish populations . . . this does not mean that effects do not exist'.[51] The problems of counting the number of fish in the oceans before and after oil spills have so far not been solved and even the omniscient computer cannot include all variables. Shallow waters, where young and adults congregate, are different. Escape is not always easy, thick oils clog the gills and cause asphyxiation, lighter toxic fractions dissolved in water or secreted in sediment are taken internally and accumulate in tissues and body fluids. Once the environment is cleared, however, fish will rid themselves of the greater part of their intake; yet some hydrocarbons and metabolic products remain in the tissues for extremely long periods, causing changes that affect survival. As always, eggs and larvae are most in danger; less than one part per million of oil dissolved in water can affect the numbers of eggs that hatch and consequently the amount of larvae produced. Individual fishes may escape; fish as a species do not.

Sea mammals such as cetaceans – whales, porpoises and dolphins – have smooth, hairless skins to which oil is unlikely to stick permanently and so affect insulation. Thick oil may cover the eyes, but whales, if not immune, are more likely to fall victims to human greed than to poisoning by oil. Mammals with fur, such as seals and otters, are in greater danger, particularly if a slick reaches land at points where they enter the sea. The Santa Barbara blow-out led to a number of oiled seals and California sea-lions; grey seals on Skomer Island off south-west Wales were affected by a spill 'of unknown origin' and some oiled pups died; eleven otters were killed by Bunker–C fuel oil after the *Esso Bernicia* incident at Sullom Voe, Scotland, and another 18 oiled. Even polar bears can suffer long-term effects and death if they attempt to lick heavy deposits of oil from their fur. Nor have domestic mammals escaped; fifty sheep accustomed to grazing on seaweed died after *Esso Bernicia*, and over 2,000 fleeces were oiled. To assert, 'scientifically', that the evidence is inconclusive (the seal pups on Skomer may not have died primarily from oiling) or that these small numbers show clearly that there is no effect on overall populations is to miss the point. Was it really necessary through human stupidity for *any* of these creatures to be lost?

So far reptiles and amphibians have escaped disaster, but there is always the chance. Two small green turtles were found dead, one with tar in its mouth, the other covered with oil. The problem is that, once they leave the beach where they are born, young turtles are so rarely seen that no one really knows what happens to them. Frogs, toads, alligators and crocodiles could also be in danger, especially if oil gets into freshwater habitats, and crocodiles living on estuaries or in nearshore waters are hardly the most mobile of creatures!

Seabirds remain the most spectacular and prominent victims of oil. Not only their deaths but their obvious sufferings have aroused public sympathy and indignation. Oil damages the plumage on which birds depend for insulation and waterproofing, penetrating the open spaces between feathers and skin so that they lose buoyancy, sink and drown. Lacking an insulating layer of air, they lose heat, attempt to compensate for this by increasing the metabolism of food reserves, and, because the oil prevents them from catching food, fail to rectify the balance; they become emaciated, cold and ill. In attempting to preen their feathers, birds inhale poisonous fumes that damage liver and kidneys and lead to difficulty in breathing. 'Stress and shock enhance the effects of exposure and poisoning.'[52] With so many chances of destruction, birds, it would seem, are almost born to be victims of oil.

Most in danger are those birds which spend a great part of their lives on the surface of the sea and dive for food. In western Europe these include divers, grebes, seaduck and auks – guillemots, razorbills and puffins – together with ducks, geese and swans which gather in large numbers in estuaries. Of the estimated loss of 30,000 seabirds after the *Torrey Canyon*, 97% were guillemots and razorbills, many of them still young. In February 1979 two spills between Nova Scotia and Newfoundland, Canada, killed more than 12,000 birds, including 1,500 ducks, together with oldsquaws, red-breasted mergansers, grebes, dovekies, murres, black guillemots, fulmars and common eider ducks, some of whom were killed more than 200 km from the site of the spill after oil had drifted.

Small discharges can be as deadly as large spills. An estimated 40,000 birds, mainly eider ducks and common scoter, died in the Dutch Waddenzee in February 1969 after a spill of no more than 100–200 tonnes. In January 1981, many birds driven by north-westerly gales from their wintering grounds in Scotland took refuge in rocky inlets of the Skagerrak, between Norway and Denmark, only to find themselves trapped. 'Relatively small discharges from, perhaps, two ships resulted in the stranding of an estimated 30,000 oil-damaged birds, some of which were shown by leg rings to be immature birds from Orkney and Shetland.'[53]

Birds, of course, are found the world over. Of the seabirds common to northern waters, even immature gannets make long journeys to the Mediterranean or as far south as Senegal, while razorbills and guillemots probably migrate as much by swimming as by flying, thus exposing themselves to greater dangers. Each autumn Scottish auks appear off the coast of Norway, while colonies from southern Britain move south to Spain.[54]

The greatest danger to these species lies in the nearness of their breeding grounds to recent developments in oil production. Twenty-four species breed in the British Isles alone, while large groups of ducks, geese and swans spend the winter in estuaries and along the coast. According to the RSPB, the razorbill population of 150,000 pairs is about 70% of the total number in the world, and the 2,000–3,000 overwintering great northern divers represent most of Europe's breeding pairs and many of North America's. Oiled birds returning to a nest contaminate the eggs, which then fail to hatch; and since many seabirds produce only one egg per season, the loss is irrecoverable. Even when the parents succeed in hatching the egg, fledglings unable to fly are especially vulnerable to oil. As the Royal Commission on Environmental Protection comments:

> Until the late 1960s these major concentrations of seabirds were relatively remote from the shipping lanes and oil-related industries, but the development of the North Sea oilfields which has led to coastal installations in these regions and the establishment of new tanker routes . . . undoubtedly increases the probability of oil spillages close to important concentrations of birds.[55]

This sober assessment has proved correct. In 1984, when there was no major tanker disaster in British waters, the RSPB reported ten oiling incidents involving more than 50 birds; all but two were off the coast of Scotland or northern England. In 1985 there were a further ten oiling incidents of the same proportions, including that caused by the *Bridgeness*; half of these occurred in the same areas. Of the final 1984 incident in which 943 oiled auks were found on beaches in east Orkney and the Moray Firth, the RSPB commented: 'Many beaches could not be surveyed and it is estimated that at least another 500 birds were affected. An aerial search by the Marine Pollution Control Unit failed to find any oil slicks'.[56] On the incident of October that year in which 893 oiled birds came ashore in Grampian and a further 267 in Orkney and Caithness they conclude: 'No oil slicks were reported by the Marine Pollution Control Unit air patrols and the sources of pollution are unknown'.[57] Here apparently is a new phenomenon – birds can now get themselves oiled even when no one has spilt any oil!

The RSPB sent 49 samples of oil collected in Orkney between March 1984 and May 1985 to the Government Chemist for analysis. Of the 39 samples taken from the plumage of birds, only nine could be traced to two recognized incidents. 'The other 30 were from birds which had probably died as a result of chronic oil pollution (i.e. unspecified small spills). Eighty per cent of the latter samples were identified as being heavy fuel oil.'[58]

Thanks to legal restrictions (see Part 3), the days of major tanker disasters may be over, but underhand discharges from tankers or oil rigs are still with us. They may no longer make the headlines, but birds continue to die. And if this happens in the well documented and policed waters of the North Sea, we may again ask who knows what takes place in the more remote regions of the world, where the fate of birds is still considered of little consequence?

As for that major polluter, humanity, is there no risk that deeds will recoil on the doer, the poisoner become victim of his own action? Unfortunately, too often retribution falls on the innocent rather than the guilty. The most obvious symptom, now rapidly decreasing, or rather, being superseded by more dangerous poisons, is the oiled beach, where tar-balls clutter the rocky shore, dead fish stare from rock pools of thick oil and the holiday-maker bathes in a scum of sheen. This 'loss of amenity' is more than the calculations of clean-up costs or hoteliers' and fishermen's losses, the only quantifiable terms in which it can be assessed. It is an insult to that sector of humanity still affected by the mystique of the sea, an example of oil as excrescence.

As a body of scientists, GESAMP considers two other aspects – the possibility of carcinogenesis and the question of tainting.[59] We saw earlier that polynuclear/polycyclic aromatic hydrocarbons (PNAHs) were carcinogenic and occurred in both crude and refined oils. According to our scientists, 'compared with other sources, oil does not provide a significant proportion of PNAH input to the marine environment on a global scale, but can be a major contributor locally, particularly in sewage discharges and refinery effluents'. How large the proportion has to be before it becomes 'significant' – and to whom and in what way – is not stated, but we can interpret 'locally' as implying that there are places in the world where the results are dangerous. The 'other sources' include the atmosphere from which there is a 'substantial input' as fall-out from burning 'organic material'. 'Relatively high levels of PNAHs' are found, especially in molluscs and algae, and these are 'frequently, but not necessarily, associated with known sources of terrestrial pollution, including oil'. At this point the difference in approach – and language – becomes clear. GESAMP is concerned with the effects of *oil* and so attempts to isolate it; we are concerned with *effects*, irrespective of the poison that causes them.

In simple terms, fish and crustaceans can metabolize PNAHs and later get rid of them by excretion; molluscs cannot, at least not to the same extent. The process is not, however, quite so straightforward. While most PNAHs are discharged, a 'hard core' of one to ten per cent of the intake remains, particularly in shellfish, and 'provides a potential for accumulation by predation', in short, the more shellfish the eater consumes, the greater the intake of PNAHs. Molluscs, in fact, accumulate higher concentrations than any other sea creatures, 'but as these shellfish form only a very small part of the total human diet, their importance to carcinogenic risk might be small' – though considerably greater, one assumes, if one is a pronounced shellfish eater than if one merely has one's average share of the 'total human diet'. Fish do not escape completely; 'there is evidence that the frequency of stomach cancer is significantly (*sic*) increased when the diet is dominated by smoked fish (e.g. in Iceland and Newfoundland) enriched with PNAHs by the smoking process'. Somehow one invariably gets back to the evils of smoking, in this case, of fish, but oil is partially exonerated. PNAHs in 'marine produce do not cause cancer without additional exposure, although they may add to the risk presented by all other sources'.

As for 'tainting', it is equally definitely established that fish, crustaceans and molluscs exposed to oil acquire an oily taste, that the taste is associated with volatile compounds derived from the oil, and that the range and quantity of 'odorous compounds' varies with the type of oil. Beyond these generalities we enter the realm of uncertainty. How much oil is necessary to produce tainting has not been scientifically determined. 'There have been too few studies on the tissue levels of oil components in affected produce for tainting levels to be established firmly.' The layman prefers to trust his senses – he knows 'stinking fish' when he smells or tastes it. The seas may be poisoned, and the fish with them, but on this occasion the potential victim is able to escape.

Oil Around the World[60]

Where, then, is it safe in the seas or on the beaches? Apart from mid-ocean and the great depths, neither of which is prolific in life, the simple answer is that it is not. In its survey of the world's oceans, the only area where, according to GESAMP, 'oil pollution is not a serious problem' (one hesitates to ask what constitutes a 'non-serious' problem) is New Zealand. 'The country is well away from tanker routes and there is only one oil refinery sited in the North Island . . . . Spills so far have been on a small scale only.'[61]

As for the rest of the world, it is unnecessary to do more than state the facts. Wherever there is oil drilling or refining, wherever tankers travel, pollution follows. We noted above how the amounts of floating tar in the Arabian Sea and the southern Bay of Bengal were roughly proportionate to the difference in tanker traffic. Almost 475 million tonnes pass along these routes each year, while 100 million tonnes go through the Suez Canal to the Mediterranean. An estimated 224 tankers are in East African waters at any time, 48 of them VLCCs. Oil deposits and tar-balls on beaches are common sights both in East Africa and further south towards Natal and Cape Agulhas, where they have caused the deaths of many penguins and seabirds. When the East African Oil

Refinery carried out a survey of Kenyan beaches in 1973, they discovered that the worst period was during the south-west monsoon when the tides washed ashore emulsified heavy residues from spillages that had been long enough at sea for the lighter fractions to evaporate. Nor has the region been without its individual spills. Twenty-one in which more than 160 tonnes of oil were lost occurred in 12 years: the Royal Fleet Auxiliary *Ennerdale* lost 40,000 gallons of fuel oil off Mahé, Seychelles; the *Silver Ocean* 18,500 tonnes off the southern tip of Madagascar; the 239,000-ton tanker *Albahoa B* exploded and sank 480 km off Tanzania; and the *Tayeb* released 200 tonnes of heavy oil after breaking up on the reefs of Mauritius. Tankers are not the only problem: in the Mombasa area of Kenya discharges from port operations and refineries have affected the ecosystem to the extent that an invasion of algae has damaged coral reefs; in Tanzania there is pollution near the floating oil mooring in Dar es Salaam, contamination of beaches and damage to coral reefs; and in Madagascar a refinery at Tamatore periodically causes local problems.

On the eastern side of the Indian Ocean tar-balls have affected 100 km of the Goan coast, mangroves have been polluted, and the quantity of oil in water has reached the highest level recorded offshore along the tanker route. In 1973 the *MT Cosmos Pioneer* spilt 18,000 tons of oil when it broke up near Porbander on the Gujarat coast, damaging flora, tainting fish and destroying 70% of the barnacles. Chronic pollution is greatest around Bombay, where port activity and industry, nearness to the tanker route and oil exploration at Bombay High combine to poison the sea. In Pakistan the Manora Channel and adjoining waters have suffered from oil, over 12,000 tonnes of which were discharged into Karachi Port in 1980 and carried by tides and currents to other waters; 'the open coast beaches of Pakistan receive bilge oil, dirty ballast water, and debris from merchant ships awaiting port entry. Oil slicks around ports and fishing harbours are also considered serious problems in Sri Lanka, where proposed offshore crude oil storage facilities threaten to increase the risk of spills. Sri Lanka also collects oil discharges from the 5,000 tankers which pass within five miles of the southern coast each year, carrying 75%–80% of Japan's oil requirements.'[62] Poisoning by oil has caused a number of deaths in the many mangrove areas and coral reefs of the region, among them the Kavaratti reef in the Laccadives and the southern part of Great Nicobar Island in the Andaman Sea.

To the east the Straits of Malacca between Malaysia and Indonesia through which 150 ships pass daily, carrying an estimated 3,000 million tons of goods, including 300 million tons of oil, and in the opinion of the Royal Institute of Navigation in London the area with the highest accident rate in the world, face more dangers, not least to Malaysian fishermen, 70% of whose landings come from its waters. Between January 1975 and April 1979 six tanker incidents alone, three from collisions, one each from grounding, fire or bad weather, resulted in the loss of 20,000 tons of oil. 'Normal discharges' from both tankers and non-tankers, together with effluent from refineries further threaten marine life, and tar-balls are increasingly reported on beaches near the refineries at Port Dickson.[63]

For the Atlantic side of Africa one of the most informative accounts is the survey of marine industrial pollutants in 18 countries, from Senegal in the north to Angola in the south, by specialists of the United Nations Environment Programme (UNEP)'s Regional Seas Programme.[64] The survey gives the estimated quantities of all major pollutants not only by country but, within each country, by the company concerned. Under the heading of 'Oil and grease' they calculate that 71,716,100 kg reach the sea annually. Of this 67,715,242 kg (94.4%) comes from four countries – Nigeria, Gabon, Senegal and Angola. Within this group Nigeria with 54,244,256 kg (or just over 75% of the total) is by far the largest source of pollutants. One company only is responsible – the Nigerian National Oil Corporation (NNOC) from which an estimated 52,500,000 kg of oil/grease enters the sea from crude petroleum production and a further 427,200 kg from refining. The next largest input – a long way behind – is from Gabon. Four companies, all at Port Gentil, are responsible for 5,601,220 kg a year; two only, however, account for most of this – the Terminal Petrolier d'Elf Gabon with four million, arising from washing and storing crude oil, and the Terminal Shell-Gabon with 1,500,000 kg from the same process of salt removal. Senegal with 4,104,095 kg a year, spread over 30 companies, 26 in Dakar and four in Ziguinchor, differs from the others in that the pollutants do not arise from oil production. Two companies are mainly responsible – Lesieur, which produces raw edible oil and discharges 1,100,000 kg and Bata – leather production – with a million kg a year of oil and grease. Finally, Angola with 3,765,671 kg from ten companies, six in Luanda, two in Cabinda and one each at Soyo and Alto Catumbela, again has companies that discharge an estimated million or more kg a year of oil and grease into the sea from washing and storing crude oil – the Gulf Oil Terminal in Cabinda with 2,500,000 kg and the Petrangol/Texaco Oil Terminal at Soyo with one million. The names of Bata, Elf, Gulf, Shell and Texaco are familiar.

Across the Atlantic within the same latitudes, the Gulf of Mexico and the Caribbean, the former a relatively shallow, semi-enclosed basin, have similar problems. Mexico's petroleum reserves, estimated by some to exceed those of Saudi Arabia, are being opened up on the Yucatán Peninsula and offshore in the Bay of Campeche. Refineries will eventually supply about 60% of US requirements, leading GESAMP to conclude that 'a real concern over the extent and potential increase in pollution of the area seems justified'.[65] Off the Atlantic coast of South America that concern has become a reality. Oil refineries and petrochemical factories in the Santos/Volta Redonda/São Paulo region and oil and gas exploration on the continental shelf offshore from Rio de Janeiro and São Paulo in Brazil and the San Jorge Gulf in Argentina are either actual or potential sources of pollution.

Passing from the Atlantic to the Pacific, 'the Magellan Strait, a fragile ecosystem, has suffered heavy oil spills and is a potentially endangered area because of oil pollution',[66] while on the west coast of South America, there have been oil spills, particularly from drilling platforms, in Peru, where there is 'localized' pollution, and in the Guayas Estuary of Ecuador.

The cost to Third World states of supplying industrialized countries with oil while carrying out their own 'development' is indeed high. The fate of the 'industrialized West' is already well known, and we have given adequate examples of tanker disasters, rig blow-outs and pipeline breakages that illustrate the dangers. This summary would be incomplete without mentioning that the North Sea alone receives an estimated 1.4 million tonnes of oil each year, 41% of which comes from run-off from cities and other 'freshwater' sources; that about a million tonnes of oil are discharged annually into that enclosed and slow-moving sea, the Mediterranean, the greatest offenders being the port and refinery areas of Marseilles and Barcelona; that industries near Venice and other north Italian towns discharge oil into the Adriatic, while North African loading terminals and refineries contribute their quota to the southern coasts and there is serious pollution between Cyprus and the Levant coast; that the Baltic, although mainly poisoned by other pollutants, has had several considerable oil spills that have affected beaches and archipelagos; and that the Atlantic coast of North America has suffered similarly from tanker accidents and discharges from refineries. Even the Arctic is not exempt: oil and gas exploration in Canada and the Prudhoe oilfield in Alaska, as well as the Beaufort Sea, still cause concern as to what may happen should there be a major spill in these inhospitable, but ecologically valuable and vulnerable, regions.

The whole world, it would seem, is becoming an endangered planet; and, if that appears an over-alarmist conclusion from our survey of oil, it is because oil is only the first of our poisons. The danger is not from oil alone but from the combined long-term effects of oil in conjunction with human and industrial waste. It is to humanity's individual – and unavoidable – contribution, sewage, that we now turn.

References

1. *OSIR* VIII Nos. 16, 18. 1985
2. GESAMP 15 p. 46
3. Account based on RCEP 8 pp. 5–9
4. RCEP 8 p. 8
5. GESAMP 15 p. 47
6. *OSIR* VIII No. 16. 1985
7. RCEP 8 p. 13
8. Ibid. pp. 13–14
9. ACOPS 1983 pp. 29–30; *TAO* p. 171
10. ACOPS 1983 p. 6
11. ACOPS 1985–6 p. 7
12. *The Times* 20 March 1978
13. McGarr *Memorandum* p. 26. The whole account is based on Judge McGarr's findings
14. Ibid. p. 34
15. Ibid. pp. 72–3

16. Ibid. pp. 89–90
17. Ibid. p. 114
18. Account from *TAO* p. 168
19. ACOPS 1978 and contemporary Press Reports
20. ACOPS 1978, 1980 and contemporary Press Reports
21. Unidentified Press Report 2 March 1975
22. ACOPS 1978, 1979, 1980
23. ACOPS 1979, 1980
24. ACOPS 1980
25. ACOPS 1969
26. ACOPS 1970
27. ACOPS 1977; *Western Mail* 11 October 1977
28. ACOPS 1979, 1980; RCEP 8 p. 105
29. ACOPS 1979, 1980; RCEP 8 pp. 92, 107
30. ACOPS 1980; RCEP 8 p. 92
31. ACOPS 1980; RCEP 8 pp. 108, 110–12
32. *OSIR* VIII. 1985
33. RCEP 8 p. 176
34. GESAMP 15 p. 82
35. RCEP 8 p. 184
36. Ibid. p. 183
37. Ibid. p. 184
38. Ibid.
39. ACOPS 1985–6 p. 6
40. Ibid. p. 7
41. ACOPS *Survey* 1983 pp. 4–5
42. *North Sea Monitor* 86:2. June 1986. pp. 2–3
43. There are numerous accounts of the fate of oil in the sea. I have followed those of Baker 1983 pp. 6–10, 20–25, 39 and RCEP 8 pp. 16–20
44. Baker 1983 p. 20
45. Ibid. p. 21
46. Ibid. p. 22
47. Ibid. p. 39
48. Ibid. pp. 24–5
49. Sources: RCEP 8 pp. 22–38; GESAMP 15 pp. 46–51; Baker 1983 pp. 13–19
50. GESAMP 15 pp. 46–7
51. Baker 1983 p. 15
52. RCEP 8 p. 30
53. Baker 1983 p. 14
54. Anon 1984c p. 317
55. RCEP 8 p. 35
56. ACOPS 1984 p. 38
57. Ibid.
58. ACOPS 1985–6 pp. 64–5
59. GESAMP 15 pp. 47–8 from which all quotations are taken
60. Sources: GESAMP 15 pp. 172–84; *TAO* pp. 172–4; Pathmarajah and Meith 1985 pp. 170, 173, 180–82; *RSRS 13* pp. 96–110
61. GESAMP 15 p. 84
62. Pathmarajah and Meith 1985 pp. 181–2
63. Leong 1982 pp. 66–7

64. *RSRS 2* pp. 75–108
65. GESAMP 15 p. 77
66. Ibid. p. 81

4. In the Shit – Sewage

The spoken word is the clearest indicator of our ambivalent attitude to sewage. When the English north-country gardener asserts that 'there's nowt laik muck', he proclaims the virtues of horse manure. One animal's excrement has become another's fertilizer. His neighbour, on a Mediterranean holiday, who finds himself swimming in a sea of floating or semi-submersible turds and wonders what disease he will bring home as a memento, is not only literally 'in the shit' but also in a metaphorical mess.

Both, of course, are right. It is ironical that, in industrialized countries, the amateur gardener moans about paying for sewage disposal then drives to a garden centre to buy a packet of 'chicken shit'. Nature demands that animal waste matter be returned to the soil so that the soil can regain its fertility. The German chemist Liebig may have exaggerated when he attributed the fall of Rome to the sewers which carried away 'good muck' that should have gone on the fields of the Campagna – but their loss of fertility had its effect, as did similar maltreatment of the land on other early civilizations. So-called 'primitive' peoples and the ancient Chinese knew better; they returned their animal and vegetable wastes to the soil, rather than deposit them in streams or directly into the sea.[1]

Why, then – aesthetics apart – concern ourselves about disease? If manure is good for the garden, why is 'sewage' a poison? The answer is not simply that human beings are not plants; it lies in the nature of sewage itself.

Sewage Good and Bad

The basic fact is that sewage reaching the sea through outfalls or dumping as sewage sludge is a heterogeneous mess. In industrialized countries it contains not only domestic human waste but discharges from industry, storm water and surface run-off. Even in Third World countries, when limited to human waste alone, its contents include both a large amount of organic matter and nutrients such as phosphates and nitrates – the gardener's or farmer's delight – and numerous bacteria and viruses, some of them harmful, together with parasitic worms – the bather's nightmare. The good gardener knows that even the best horse manure has to be 'rotted down', i.e. its undesirable components degraded. When industry adds its contribution of oil, metals and chemicals, they bring their varied forms of toxicity.[2] For that reason, having already considered oil, we shall leave the others until the next chapter.

The problem is complicated by the state in which sewage reaches the sea. In developed countries it may undergo primary treatment – the physical removal of solids, and settlement of the remaining particles to produce a less offensive effluent – and even secondary chemical or biological treatment, which breaks down the organic matter and so reduces its demand for oxygen. The resulting effluent, rich in basic nutrients but still containing what GESAMP calls 'soluble contaminants' is discharged through short or long outfalls into the sea in the hope that natural processes and water movement will complete dispersal and degradation.[3]

Most of the world's sewage, however, especially among coastal communities of Third World countries with growing populations, is simply deposited in the sea as 'raw' or 'untreated' sewage, nutrients and poisons alike. It is here that the greatest danger lies – to both humanity and the seas – as not only the poisons but even the nutrients take their revenge.

Sewage in the Sea

With the nutrients it is a question of over-fertility – feed an organism and you make it grow; overfeed it, and you make it sick. Scientifically, it is a matter of BOD – *biological oxygen demand*.

The seas have a natural method for dealing with organic wastes – decomposition, the breaking down of wastes into inorganic elements. This requires taking oxygen from the water; but as plants are fertilized in the decomposing process, they produce oxygen which replaces that lost. In a balanced ecosystem new production of oxygen compensates for its removal. Introducing large quantities of matter ready for decomposition upsets the cycle by increasing the demand for oxygen – hence eutrophication, the process of over-fertilization that results in mass slaughter of plants and animals, and BOD, the amount of oxygen required for decomposition to take place, as a means of measuring the process.

In the natural cycle fish and other creatures feed on plant life in the water. Removing too much oxygen makes it impossible for animals and fish to survive; in consequence the plants increase in number. As the animals and fish die off, they add more matter for decomposition to existing stocks, further increasing the BOD. The diversity of species on which the whole system depends is now thrown out of gear. The new plant life rarely survives more than a few days; its death brings more material awaiting decomposition, and the ultimate result is an area from which all life is eliminated. In effect, sewage acts as a catalyst, for the BOD of the dead plants can be five or six times as great as that of the untreated sewage. The only survivors are anaerobic (non-oxygen-needing) bacteria responsible for decomposition.

Another unpleasant aspect is the appearance of 'red tides' in coastal areas of the sea caused by a population explosion of red species of phytoplankton. So dense are these tides that they have been known to clog the gills of fish and the filters of shellfish, which, if not killed outright, can accumulate poisons and so endanger human consumers. Even sea-spray from the tides can cause harm and lead to irritations of the skin, mouth and throat. First recorded on the Gulf coast of Florida in 1916, the tides occurred again in 1932 and 1948. This 16-year cycle was broken in the 1950s when they appeared in three successive years from 1952 and then annually from 1957 onwards. Nor have other parts of the world escaped. The tides off Brazil, Sri Lanka and Spain may differ in colour but they have the same causes and effects;[4] off Japan red and other algae, products of industrial and municipal waste, have choked much of the life in the sea around the shores;[5] in 1976 a spectacular explosion occurred off the east coast of the United States in which hundreds of square miles were affected with 'massive mortality' of commercially exploitable fish.[6] And, if this appears unduly alarmist, GESAMP's sober account of 'plankton blooms' offers a warning that cannot be ignored:

> Several genera and species of marine algae can give rise to toxic blooms, and several specific toxins have been identified. Some of these are lethal to marine organisms, whereas others are simply accumulated by them but can cause distress or death to the human consumer of affected fish or shellfish. Such blooms have been recorded from many parts of the world, and indeed in some places they occur regularly, following a seasonal pattern which can be predicted for a given coastal area . . . . Unfortunately, however, prior warning is often impossible so that illness from this cause is not infrequent and death sometimes results.[7]

When GESAMP mentions 'death' twice in one paragraph, even if it only happens 'sometimes', non-scientists know that it is necessary to be on their guard.

These effects come from the 'beneficial' aspects of sewage; there are also the 'soluble contaminants' of the effluent which even treatment does not remove – disease-causing bacteria, viruses and parasites, which survive for hours or days. Viruses tend to remain longer than bacteria, especially if they become attached to organisms at the bottom of the sea. It is at this point that humanity's misdeeds recoil on the doer, for the toxicity of viruses derived from sewage depends entirely on the general health of the human beings from which they come.[8] In the countries of north-western Europe and North America, where health standards are considerably higher than in the Third World, the risk to human beings is proportionately less. In Third World countries it is considerably greater. Ironically, Europeans and Americans are in more danger when bathing in tropical waters, where the local inhabitants may have built up resistance to some of the diseases for which they are themselves responsible but which are unfamiliar to European visitors. Unfortunately, their capacity to build up such resistance is often undermined by lower standards of nourishment.

In the 1950s there were scares in the West that contact with sewage in the sea led to poliomyelitis and typhoid fever. In 1959 the Medical Research Council of the UK published a report[9] which did much to allay these fears by concluding that there was no risk of contracting poliomyelitis from bathing and that only a few cases of typhoid and paratyphoid fevers were due to 'grossly contaminated waters'. These results should not have been surprising. As the RCEP commented in 1984: 'It should be noted, however, that the incidence of typhoid and paratyphoid fevers is now very low in the United Kingdom'.[10] Sewage does not generate the viruses; it merely carries them.

In concentrating on major diseases, the Medical Research Council neglected the minor. We now know that there is a connection between sewage in the sea and milder digestive ailments such as 'traveller's diarrhoea', that children may be more at risk than adults, and that infections of the eyes or of cuts and abrasions can result. Even without direct contact danger remains. Viruses can contaminate shellfish beds or find their way into fish and so reach the human beings who eat them.[11]

Finally, there is the aesthetic aspect. The sight of oil in rock pools is offensive enough – how much more that of human turds on recreational beaches or the stench that comes from an outlet of untreated sewage! Aesthetics may be largely subjective or culturally conditioned; the computer operator's attitude to fertilizer differs from that of the farmer. But human repulsion to a bad smell, especially when behind that smell lurks fear of disease, may well be universal.

From the sea's viewpoint sewage has one advantage over oil. Since humanity is responsible, only those areas nearest to humanity – the immediate coastal regions with large populations lacking proper sanitation – are most in danger. As GESAMP would say, the effects are 'local'. Even when dumped in deeper waters, sewage rarely affects more than the immediate area. Benthic organisms are smothered, sediments disturbed and a patch on the ocean bed made barren. But whales and porpoises are unlikely to suffer the fate of human beings on shore. We must not overestimate the dangers – or underestimate them. Sewage remains a poison; in the sea it is a peripheral poison. Our survey of sewage in the sea is a survey of peripheries – the rivers, estuaries and coastal waters into which humanity drops its excrement. We begin by examining what happens in a developed country – the United Kingdom – and follow it with a Third World area – the Indian Ocean.

Sewage in a Developed Country – the United Kingdom

In July 1981 the *New Scientist* reported the case of Tom Winter and his wife. The Winters went swimming at Lowestoft, a holiday resort on the East Anglian coast. Before entering the sea they noticed turds and contraceptives washed up on the beach. Mrs Winter swam by the pier and later developed cystitis (a urinary disease); her husband contracted an intestinal infection which medical investigation showed was faecally transmitted.[12]

The Winters were unfortunate; others might have swum in the water and got away with it. We cannot, however, escape the fact that, even in a Britain where

96% of householders in England and Wales are connected to sewers[13] and there are regularly emptied septic tanks for those in more remote areas, where sewage works ensure that almost 80% of the sewage produced undergoes secondary (biological) treatment, and where there are Water Authorities (in England and Wales) or River Purification Boards (in Scotland) to regulate and oversee discharges of sewage to rivers, estuaries and the sea, it can – and did – happen. The Winters were *in the shit*.

In the early 1950s Tony Wakefield lost his son from poliomyelitis, caused, he believed at the time, by swimming in the sea near a sewage outfall. In 1958 he founded the Coastal Anti-Pollution League (CAPL) and, when the Medical Research Council published its 1959 Memorandum exonerating sewage as a disease-causer 'except where a beach was aesthetically revolting', challenged them to name beaches in this category. When they refused, he circulated a questionnaire to all coastal authorities, asking for details of their sewage disposal facilities and from the results compiled the first 'Golden List' of beaches. Of 633 beaches surveyed in 1960, 190 were found to be at risk from pollution.[14]

No one disputes the improvements of the last twenty years, or even of the last century. They are necessary prerequisites by which a 'developed country' acquires that status. The relevant questions are: 'Are they enough?' and 'Will they continue to provide adequate safeguards against poisoning the sea with sewage?'

Recent surveys of non-tidal rivers are not reassuring, especially if we consider the stretches in class 3 – waters polluted to an extent that fish are absent or only sporadically present – and class 4 – waters which are grossly polluted and likely to cause a nuisance.[15] In 1980 some 95% of the polluting load of sewage discharged to these rivers was allegedly removed by treatment,[16] yet in 1980/81, 1984/85 and 1985/86, according to figures supplied by the Water Authorities themselves, 10% or more of all rivers were in these undesirable categories. Between 1984/85 and 1985/86 the length of 'poor' or 'bad' rivers actually increased by 130 km. Some areas were worse than others; in North-West a fifth of the river length was in these classes, in Yorkshire 12.6%. In Wessex the proportion of such stretches increased between 1980/81 and 1985/86, almost half the 207 km downgraded being due to poor quality sewage discharges. More disturbing is the proportion of sewage treatment works failing to meet the conditions imposed on them by the Water Authorities when the latter issue 'consents' for discharges. In 1985/86 32% of the West and 13% of the Northumbrian areas did not meet these requirements.[17] The DoE comments that 'the low levels of dissolved oxygen and high levels of ammonia in the rivers Aire and Mersey indicate that these rivers receive large amounts of sewage and industrial effluents'.[18] Both are in class 3. Pollution by nitrates, mostly by run-off from agricultural land, although some nitrates enter waterways from sewage works, is causing concern because it may harm drinking water, especially for children. Over the past 30 years these concentrations have increased and, though the 1975 and 1976 droughts brought a levelling, they are still 'above previous levels'.[19]

And the Government's response to sewage works failing to comply with the conditions set them for discharges? To show its toughness by clamping down on these law-breakers? In October 1986 the Secretary of State for the Environment, Nicholas Ridley, announced in a written answer – a method that generally escapes publicity and avoids the embarrassment of supplementary questions – that, following a review during the previous two years, 1,800 of the 6,000 sewage treatment works were granted *less* stringent conditions for discharges. This relaxation was justified as more cost-effective as it would allow capital investment on projects for improving water quality.[20] But it may not have been entirely unconnected with the fact that, under sections of the 1974 Control of Pollution Act coming into operation, registers of discharges were to be made available to the public – and some public-spirited individuals might even have brought prosecutions against offenders. The Government spared itself embarrassment. When those responsible for carrying out the law are found to be breaking it, the simple answer is to change the law.

What goes into rivers eventually finds its way to the sea, either directly or through estuaries. It may surprise most people in Britain to learn that, in this computerized age, 'there is no regular monitoring of all discharges into coastal and estuarial waters'; however, 'estimates of their sizes can be made'. From such estimates we learn that 'rivers represent the dominant source of discharges' for certain selected pollutants, that discharges into 'the Humber, Mersey and Thames estuaries tended to be relatively high' and that 'the Humber' had the largest discharges for seven of the twelve materials listed'.[21] We learn also that in 1984 6.9 million tonnes of sewage sludge were deposited in 'external waters', mainly in Liverpool Bay, the Thames Estuary, off north-east England and in the Clyde Estuary. (For the sake of completeness, we may add that they were accompanied by 0.7 million tonnes of industrial waste and 18.9 million tonnes of dredging.) The amount of dumped sewage sludge rose from 8.3 million tonnes in 1978 to 8.9 million tonnes in 1980 but has since decreased annually and the proportion of dangerous metals (see next chapter) with it. In contrast, only about five per cent of sewage sludge is discharged into coastal waters through pipelines.

Of the estuaries mentioned by the DoE, the Royal Commission on Environmental Pollution visited the Mersey in June 1982 and described it as 'the worst example' of 'estuarine black spots'. In their Tenth Report they comment:

> The estuary currently receives, untreated, the domestic sewage, trade effluent and surface water from the Liverpool and Wirral conurbations. With a population of almost 1½ million, they comprise by far the largest urban area in the United Kingdom with untreated discharges. There are nearly 50 outfalls in the lower part of the estuary alone and upstream there are further heavy polluting loads from Warrington, Runcorn, Widnes and Ellesmere Port. The Manchester Ship Canal and the River Weaver add smaller, though substantial, loads. The result is that the banks of the estuary are polluted with offensive solids and that the water suffers a serious oxygen deficiency, which can cause smell and, together with persistent and

sometimes toxic industrial effluents, markedly restricts the ability of the estuary to support aquatic life.[22]

By 1986 the Mersey was still in trouble and the Government was forced to act. The major problem was the health hazard caused by the amount of mercury in sewage sludge. We have seen what happened to the Japanese fishermen at Minamata. A Directive from the European Commission laid down that the amount of mercury in fish must not exceed 0.3 ppm. The Government's own scientists and environmental health officers had warned that the quantity of mercury had ranged between 0.25 and 0.28 ppm – too near to the maximum for safety. In February 1986 the North West Water Authority's permit for dumping sewage sludge was renewed – but only on condition that the amount of mercury was reduced by 30%. Inevitably, the Government was in a dilemma. To refuse licences would have saved the sea but caused loss of jobs in sludge processing, notably at Daveyhulme, near Manchester. To grant them without restrictions would have saved jobs at the expense of public health and seen Britain hauled before the EEC as a poisoner of the sea. The result was to compromise and try to keep it quiet; the Government's announcement came in another written answer and so escaped press headlines.[23]

As for the actual dumping, what really happens is anyone's guess. Officially all dumping at sea, whether of sewage sludge, dredging materials or industrial waste, is carried out according to conditions laid down by the Ministry of Agriculture, Fisheries and Food (MAFF), which issues licences specifying the material, quantity and exact position. In practice, as MAFF admitted in evidence to the RCEP, 'in certain areas there is a problem of policing dumping, notably in ensuring that licensed operators do not cut costs by releasing the waste materials nearer to the home port'.[24]

Following its visit to the Tyne–Tees area in March 1982, when the Northumbrian Water Authority drew its attention to the still unsatisfactory quality of tidal waters in both rivers, the RCEP noted that 'the tidal part of the Tees receives discharges of industrial effluent and raw sewage', but the extent of pollution is better gauged from the three targets for improvement set by the Authority 'when resources permit'. The first is to eliminate smells and nuisances, the second to allow the passage of young salmon from fresh water to the sea, and the third to allow the passage of migratory fish at all times. The Tyne, which had also suffered from 'riverside discharges of crude sewage and industrial process water', was likewise improving, thanks to the construction of new sewers and sewage treatment plants. 'Interception of sewage', which had progressed from the mouth of the estuary to the Tyne Bridge, had not only improved water quality but produced 'visual benefit from the removal of sewage solids'. Less euphemistically inclined Tynesiders were also doubtless pleased that you no longer saw shit floating in the water.[25]

The Commission's comments on the Thames Estuary are somewhat complacent. Listing the improvements – from over 80% of tidal waters classed as 'poor' in 1970 to over 83% as 'doubtful' and 16% unpolluted, while the number of different species of fish had risen considerably and two salmon were unwise enough to let themselves be caught in 1983 – they quote the Thames Water Authority's claim that 'the condition of the tidal river has now been substantially restored and is stable'.[26] 'Restored' – undoubtedly; 'substantially' – it may be; but 'stable' – are they really satisfied with 83% in the 'doubtful' category? Surely one should begin to talk in terms of 'stability' when at least 83% is 'unpolluted'.

Others are less impressed. In May 1986, when the Greenpeace research ship, the *Beluga*, carried out a survey of the Thames, it was claimed that pollution had actually been increasing over the past ten years, that the five million tonnes of sewage sludge dumped ten miles off Clacton contained deadly poisons, that the oxygen level in the Thames had dropped so much that the Authority had been forced to pump oxygen into the water to prevent large-scale deaths of fish and that the salmon resulted from restocking the river at an annual expense of £65,000 since 1979.[27]

For swimmers in the sea around the UK there is now a 'Freedom from Faeces' Charter in the 1976 European Community Directive on Bathing Waters (76/160/EEC) which lays down that, in waters where bathing is 'traditionally practised by a large number of bathers', the quality must conform to certain standards. The standards are clear enough: 95% of samples taken must have lower counts of coliform bacteria than 2,000 per 100 ml for faecal coliforms and 10,000 per 100 ml for all coliforms. Coliform bacteria are selected because, although not considered dangerous in themselves, they are comparatively easy to measure and are good indicators that less desirable bacteria are present. The question was: what constituted a 'large number' of people who 'traditionally practised' bathing? At this point the bureaucrats in London demonstrated their superior experience to their colleagues in Brussels. Adopting a 'commonsense assessment', rather than a 'scientific or rigorous definition or analysis', the Department of the Environment decided that, for bathing waters to qualify, first, at some time in the bathing season there should be at least 500 people in the water at the same time (regardless of the length of the stretch of water), and, secondly, that waters where the number of bathers was assessed at more than 1,500 per mile *would* be classified as bathing waters, while those with between 750 and 1,500 *might* be so classified. Actual counting was left to those ambivalent purveyors and regulators of sewage, the water authorities, who had little incentive to identify stretches of water, maintaining the standards of which could mean only more work and expense. The counts, taken in 1979, using on-the-spot counting rather than more accurate methods such as aerial photography, resulted in the 'identification' of 27 bathing waters, 23 of them in southern England, the rest in North Yorkshire and Humberside. Apparently there were no 'traditional' bathing waters in Scotland, Wales or the west coast of England north of the Bristol Channel. Compared with the 600 or so beaches where the Coastal Anti-Pollution League maintain bathing 'regularly' takes place, this paltry figure provoked the derision it deserved. In the May 1986 issue of *Holiday Which?* the Consumers' Association satirically set its readers a quiz on whether they would say that large numbers of people bathed at ten well-known resorts, including Brighton, Eastbourne, Blackpool and Great Yarmouth. Whatever they thought, the Government's answer was 'No' as none of these were 'identified' under the Directive and so need not conform to EEC requirements.

Of the 'identified' waters, in 1985 the DoE commented that, for the five years 1980–84, between 70 and 78% had complied with the faecal coliform limits and between 74 and 93% with the total coliform criteria. Their conclusion magnificently expresses the blandness of their approach: 'Although some bathing waters improved over the period and some deteriorated, there was no significant trend for the 27 waters taken as a whole'. In practice, only 14 of the 27 met the required standard in each of the five years and a further five in four years. Ryde and Shanklin (both on the Isle of Wight) failed every year, Weston-super-Mare (on the Bristol Channel) succeeded in one year only, and four – Bridlington (South Beach), Scarborough (South Beach) (both in Yorkshire), Goodrington Sands (in Devon) and Thorpe Bay (in Essex) – complied in only two years out of five.[28]

It was perhaps not surprising that popular holiday resorts such as Great Yarmouth and Blackpool were excluded from the list. Yarmouth not only attracts tourists but for centuries has been a centre for fishing – the well-known Yarmouth 'bloaters' and shrimps. In the 1930s there were 120 boats seeking shrimps and prawns; by the end of 1985 there were three. The fishermen blame the sewage and industrial waste poured into the Yare, which has killed off all but one of the beds of Ross worm on which the shrimps feed. If the Anglian Water Authority's plans are carried out, the remaining bed, at Caister Hole, half a mile offshore from Caister-on-Sea, just north of Yarmouth, is also doomed, for they propose to shut down the sewage treatment works at Caister, which are affected by subsidence, and pump untreated sewage into the sea through a long outfall. The criterion for satisfactory operation is that there is no discoloration or foaming visible from the shore and no damage to shellfish or conservation areas. (Shellfish are protected under another EEC Directive). Bathers, it is maintained, will not be in danger as the end of the pipeline is nearly a mile from shore and only potential cross-Channel swimmers are likely to reach it. The argument conveniently overlooks the fact that the sea is in perpetual motion – Caister has four tides a day – and that north-easterly gales and strong tides bring sewage back to the beach. To rely on the effects of sunlight and wave movement to degrade the sewage is to ignore the prevalent sea mists and turbidity. Nor is Anglia's record encouraging. With 65% of the population served by unsatisfactory sea outfalls, declining budget allocations for research and development of sewage treatment, and the elimination of all monies for pollution prevention, the only satisfactory item in their accounts would appear to be a £50-million profit in 1984.[29]

We can be more specific about the quality of the water at Blackpool. It is reported that, when the Greenpeace ship, *Beluga*, took samples in July 1986, tests by an independent marine biologist showed that the coliform level was 4.2 times that laid down in the Directive. To maintain, as the resort's director of tourism is alleged to have done, that, by conducting their tests near an outfall pipe, the researchers were obviously going to pick up something, is both to confuse and to concede the issue. The simple question is why there is an outfall directly into the sea a hundred metres from the promenade.[30]

When the matter was raised in Parliament, the Secretary of State for the Environment, William Waldegrave, admitted that there had 'been a problem at Blackpool' but a project had been launched 'with expenditure of over £30 million to put things right'. On further questioning it turned out that the money – now 'about £35 million' – was not solely for Blackpool but also for 'a number of other beaches'. Claims that a certain Mrs Hargreaves had found herself 'swimming in neat sewage off Seaford' (on the south coast) and that 'raw sewage is still discharged into the sea and on to beaches, especially in parts of the south-west that are dependent on tourism' elicited no further response than that 'it is for that very reason that considerable resources are now being committed' and expression of the hope that 'a steady programme of improvement will ensure that by the end of the century virtually all the remaining problems will have been removed'.[31] One wonders why it was necessary to insert the 'now' and what 'problems' will remain under the 'virtually', even at the end of the century.

In the House of Lords the Government spokesman, Lord Elton, demonstrated his ability to have it both ways. When Lord Campbell of Croy asked if the Government was satisfied that beaches used by holiday-makers were free from pollution, Lord Elton referred to the EEC Bathing Waters Directive and Government plans (their response to the ridicule over the 27 'traditional' bathing beaches) to survey more than 350 of these waters. When Lord Cledwyn of Penrhos complained of the 'disgraceful state' of the beaches on the west coast of Wales, Lord Elton courteously pointed out that 'the European directive is concerned with the biological state of the water in which swimmers swim and not with the aesthetic condition of the beaches above the bathing line'. And when Lord Winstanley asked if the Government would take over monitoring coastal pollution between Cardigan Bay and St Bees Head (an area that includes the Sellafield processing plant), Lord Elton politely reminded him that the original question (to which Lord Winstanley's was supplementary and thus restricted to the same topic) was 'about beaches used by holiday makers at resorts in the United Kingdom'.[32] These exchanges not only show clearly the difficulty of getting a straight answer to a straight question but demonstrate the formula for evasion: ask a question about the beach and you get a reply about the sea; ask about the sea and you are told that questions must be about the beach.

Sewage in the Third World – the Indian Ocean

Stretching from the Gulf of Oman and the Bay of Bengal in the north to the East African coast in the west and the shores of Burma, Thailand and Malaysia in the east, the Indian Ocean is bordered by 19 countries inhabited by some 950 million people. As we saw in Chapter 1, it is unique among oceans in that the monsoon winds and surface currents change direction twice a year, thus helping to dilute and disperse the poisons that humanity contributes to its waters.

Compared with Britain, our knowledge of its sewage problem is fragmentary and incomplete. As Meera Pathmarajah concludes in his survey on behalf of UNEP's Regional Seas Programme in 1982, 'At present there is a lack of information on pollution problems in the region . . . . Research on the effects of pollution other than from industrial sources is still scarce'.[33] His efforts and those of his colleagues, together with reports from the Delhi Centre for Science and Environment, enable us to form some estimate of the extent of the problem.

The African states of Somalia, Kenya, Tanzania and Mozambique have a coastline of some 6,800 km and an estimated population in 1980 of over three million in the major urban areas. To these the islands of Comoros, Madagascar, Mauritius and Seychelles add a further 5,150 km of coast and urban populations of 685,000. In most places there is only partial sewerage and the general practice is to discharge raw sewage into streams or rivers leading to estuaries, mangrove swamps and lagoons, or to dispose of it directly into the sea. In Kenya only a fifth of the population of Mombasa is connected to sewers, in Tanzania 15% of the inhabitants of Dar es Salaam and 10% of those of Tanga, in Mozambique a quarter of the people in Beira but only 10% in each of the other coastal towns, and in Somalia, even Mogadishu with a population of 400,000 has no proper sewage system.[34] The majority of people depend on pit latrines, septic tanks or soak pits, which may save the sea in the short term at the expense of the future.

When sewage is discharged into the sea it is usually untreated and in many cases the outfalls are not long enough or sufficiently submerged to prevent their contents from being returned to beaches.[35] In Somalia septic tanks are treated but solid waste is dumped anywhere. Kenya has 150 sewage treatment plants but as the population increases and the tourist industry attracts more visitors these are far from adequate and even the septic tanks and small plants at large coastal hotels have failed to keep up with the expansion. The Mombasa sewage system, now over 25 years old, discharges 1.2 million gallons of sewage daily into the sea, 80% of it with primary treatment, 20% with secondary.[36]

In Tanzania, untreated sewage from Dar es Salaam, Tanga, Zanzibar, Kilwa, Lindi, Pemba and other coastal towns is discharged directly into harbours or into the Indian Ocean. 'It is a common sight to see passers-by and motorists covering their noses due to the stench emanating from sewage-polluted Msimbazi Creek in Dar-es-Salaam and no recreational activity exists in the area.'[37] Faecal coliform counts at five points along the Msimbazi and its tributaries gave readings of from 3,000 to 64,000 per 100 ml. (The EEC standard for qualifying as 'Bathing Water', we recall, is 2,000 per 100 ml.) Mangroves on the estuary of the river are contaminated by both sewage and industrial waste. Swimmers have contracted skin ailments after bathing in Dar es Salaam Bay and there have been incidents of hepatitis, gastroenteritis and even cholera.[38]

In Mozambique nine-tenths of the population use septic tanks or pit latrines.

As the water table is high, these become sources of pollution, as, for example, in Beira. Both Maputo and Beira have ten outfalls discharging partially treated sewage into the sea, which has become so infected as a result that at times, especially during hotter weather, the Government prohibits bathing or fishing. The poisonous waters have caused skin diseases and cholera.[39]

In Mauritius 60% of the population of 150,000 in the industrial area of Port Louis are connected to a sewerage system which discharges through an outfall into a lagoon about 500 metres offshore. Although strong waves disperse the sewage quickly, energy failures and breakdowns have led to the dumping of raw sewage in the sea. Over-fertilization has encouraged excessive growth of seaweed, which, as it decays, not only produces foul stenches but damages corals and benthic organisms.[40]

In Madagascar, with little or no sewage treatment, municipal wastes from Antananarivo (Tananarive) and Nosy Bé are dumped in the sea, increasing the dangers of eutrophication. The local custom of using offshore latrines on stilts above the sea is an unusual example of direct (untreated) human input into the ocean.[41]

In contrast, neither Seychelles nor Comoros have major pollution problems, even if only a small part of the population in the former is linked to sewers and none in the latter. Major tourist hotels in Seychelles have septic tanks, though the waste water eventually seeps into the sea. In Comoros, as with Mozambique, the water table is high and there is danger that seepages from pit latrines may at some point affect the drinking supply.[42]

Despite this, the seas off East Africa are relatively unpolluted compared with those of the Indian sub-continent, especially near the great coastal cities. In Karachi untreated sewage and industrial wastes have been known to affect the city's drinking water to the extent that, in the summer of 1980, there was an outbreak of gastroenteritis and several deaths.[43] Elsewhere the effects are greater on plants than on human beings. At the great port of Bombay it is estimated that 2,000 million cu metres of sewage are discharged annually along the beaches, causing a considerable decrease in the amount of oxygen in the nearer waters with inevitable effects on the sea life deprived of it.[44] Further south in Goa, sewage from the town of Panjim reaching the sea through the Mandovi Estuary has reduced the diversity of plant life and led to dominance by one species.[45] In Kerala sewage affects the Cochin area, particularly the backwaters where salinity is less than one per cent at the height of the south-west monsoon, though tides and currents help increase the amount of oxygen available. Cochin beach is one of the worst places with high counts of faecal coliforms and faecal streptococci. During the south-west monsoon and the months that follow, it is unsuitable for recreation or fishing and becomes particularly obnoxious when the African weed, *Salvinia molesta*, encouraged by over-fertilization, emits rank odours as it decays. Various types of salmonella are found on beaches, if not in the sea.[46] In Sri Lanka raw sewage from Colombo is dumped directly into the Kelani River, thence to the sea, which also receives discharges from other coastal towns.[47] On the east coast, in the Bay of Bengal at Visakhapatnam harbour, sewage discharges have led to an abundance of the benthic worm *Capitella capitata*, which is often used as a pollution indicator and here reaches a density of 50,000 per square metre.[48]

But it is India's rivers and estuaries that the inadequately met needs of its people have turned into drains and sewers in their own right. Every day near Lucknow a 35-km stretch of the River Gomati receives about 180,000 cu metres of sewage, together with wastes from pulp and paper factories. Raw sewage from Hoshangabad in Madhya Pradesh, channelled into the Narmada River, caused an increase in enteric diseases and skin problems among the hundreds of daily bathers. Every day, as the Yamuna passes through the 48 km of the Union Territory of Delhi, it collects nearly 200 million litres of untreated sewage from the capital's 17 outfalls so that, between Delhi and Agra, the water is unfit for either drinking or bathing.[49] As for that largest and most sacred of rivers, the Ganga, the Central Board for Prevention and Control of Water Pollution reported that none of the large cities on its banks has a sewage treatment plant, although most have partial facilities. Over 100 Class I and Class II cities and towns dump largely untreated sewage into the river daily. In Varanasi six major and 61 small drains daily pump nearly 60 million litres of untreated sewage into the Ganga, much of it next to the main bathing area. The pumping station for drinking water is just downstream from the largest drain and the river itself contains numerous cholera, dysentery and typhoid germs. The Kulti Estuary is poisoned by Calcutta's sewage as '48 km of septic tank effluent oscillates in tidal waters without dissipation', reducing the oxygen level to below normal and destroying almost all fish and plant life.[50] At the Hooghly Estuary, where the Indian Ganga reaches the sea, 361 outfalls continuously pour raw sewage into its waters.[51]

How nicely our scientists phrase it! Only when we attempt to picture those 'oscillating' turds, now topping the waves, now descending into the hollows, as the tides ebb and flow, 'without dissipation', can we fully realize that India's sewage is in a mess!

Not all of it, however. The Indians, like the Chinese, are aware of the 'good' aspects of sewage. To the east of Calcutta are about 2,500 ha of fish-ponds in which part of the city's raw sewage is used as a fertilizer. Fish-farmers claim that they get 10–20 tonnes per hectare; one even reported a yield of 28 tonnes. The State Government's fisheries department maintains that these wetlands could support more than 20,000 fish-farm workers, provide more than ten tonnes of fish per hectare, and even treat all the city's sewage by acting as large oxidation ponds.

Human greed, or short-sightedness, however, is unlimited. When fish-farming started in 1930, there were over 10,000 ha of suitable swampland. But as no one likes swamps – nasty places that breed mosquitoes and other noxious insects – when a Yugoslav firm pumped sand from the bed of the Hooghly and filled in 4,000 ha to provide housing plots for Calcutta's growing middle class, the scheme was generally approved – at least until the decline in fish production caused prices to rise. Developers and property-speculators are the same the world over. Not content with what they had, in 1985 it was reported that they now wanted the remaining ponds filled in so that they could build houses for the urban élite. No one disputes the problem of Calcutta's increasing population, though it is the poor who multiply more rapidly than the rich. But, if the fish-ponds disappear, their use for sewage disposal goes with them; not only will fish prices rise still further, the city itself will be even deeper 'in the shit'.[52]

It's the Same the Whole World Over

Beyond India, Malaysia is little better. In 1980 only 14% of the urban population of Peninsular Malaysia had a central sewerage system. In Penang there are no proper treatment plants and the general practice is to discharge raw sewage into the sea to 'dilute and disperse'. How successful this is we can judge from the fact that levels of coliform bacteria are as much as 100 times those recommended for bathing areas in the USA. Pathogenic bacteria are found in shellfish and the greatest public health problem is the high incidence of gastrointestinal ailments. If eating seafood is not responsible for all of these, it is the cause of many.[53] The circle of disease from human inhabitants carried by their excreta into the sea, ingested by shellfish, which are then eaten by human beings, can only widen as the population increases.

In Indonesia, the untreated sewage of over 100 million people poisons the beaches, especially around Jakarta.[54] In Vietnam, epidemics of typhoid and hepatitis along the coast are the result of eating sewage-infected shellfish.[55] We have seen already how Japan's nearshore waters show considerable eutrophication from sewage and other wastes, as 'red tides' choke much of the life in the sea.[56] Even in less densely populated and 'westernized' Australia, Sydney's inadequate system releases sewage so near to its beautiful shores that it is a danger to swimmers.[57]

Across the Pacific, in South America, the problems are the same – too few sewage plants chasing too much sewage! The coast of Peru is badly poisoned, especially near towns, and on the Atlantic coast the increasing population of Brazil, in particular around Rio de Janeiro and São Paulo with more than ten million people, and of Uruguay, where fifteen million live in the Montevideo area, have added the problems of sewage disposal to those of industrial waste.[58]

Of the Caribbean a UNEP report states blandly: 'Less than 10 per cent of total domestic waste receives treatment before disposal. Much of this waste reaches rivers, inland waters, and coastal waters, causing severe damage to fisheries . . . . Several harbours in the Region are experiencing accelerated eutrophication because of the disposal of inadequately treated domestic and industrial wastes.'[59] More specifically, in the 1970s Havana alone was known to pump an estimated 50–100 million gallons of raw sewage into the sea daily.[60] Our survey of tourism in the Caribbean (Chapter 2) highlighted problems of sewage disposal in Barbados.

On West Africa, GESAMP concludes with a reminder of our ignorance. 'Domestic sewage and household waste are frequently dumped into the sea, on beaches and in coastal lagoons. They create amenity problems that interfere with recreation and tourism. The extent to which they pose biological and health problems is not known.'[61] Perhaps not, but from what we have seen elsewhere we may reasonably infer what those problems are, even if, as GESAMP would say, they are not at present 'quantifiable'.

So we return to the seas of Europe and North America, the 'developed' West. Of the latter GESAMP tells us that, 'although at one time it was feared that the large volumes of sewage discharged . . . were destroying the kelp beds of the Southern Californian Bight, they now appear to be recovering in spite of continuing and increasing sewage discharges.' Perhaps the kelp have become accustomed to their new environment – or their function is to distract our attention from the fact that sewage discharges are 'increasing'. The 'cause–effect relationship' between sewage outfalls and fin rot in bottom fish 'has not yet been fully resolved'.[62] A non-scientist's method of 'resolving' this problem would be to remove the sewage – or stop discharging it. That should at least establish whether or not there is a connection. It might even save the fish.

On the eastern seaboard there are considerable discharges of sewage into the sea through direct outfalls or by rivers from the great urban areas of the United States and Canada with the inevitable effects – excessive growth of algae and accumulation of faecal coliforms in sea creatures, notably oysters in Great South Bay of Long Island. Human beings are in less danger because health regulations prevent the oysters from reaching the market.[63] From the oysters' viewpoint, being poisoned by sewage off the coast of industrialized USA is indistinguishable from being poisoned in the non-industrial Third World. No fewer than 45 strains of virus have been found in water off the New Jersey coast; coliform bacteria were detected along the whole length of the Hudson Canyon, which stretches in the sea-bed for 170 km from the mouth of New York's Hudson River to the edge of the continental shelf, thereby shattering the former belief that five kilometres of travel were enough to kill off all bacteria.[64] Sewage sludge is dumped at sea, about nine million tonnes a year off New York and New Jersey, producing oxygen deficiency over 12,000 sq km so that dead fish float in their hundreds near the dumping grounds.[65]

In Europe, governments and scientists continue to argue over whether the North Sea needs protection or whether it can be left to 'clean itself out'. The sewage of some 31 million people goes into its waters at the rate of some 7.3 million cubic metres a day, much of it untreated. In addition, over five million tonnes of sewage sludge are deposited annually, most of it from the UK[66] in the estuarial and coastal waters we have examined. Amid the controversy two things are certain: the most deadly part of the sewage sludge is its concentration of heavy metals; and it is impossible to consider the effects of sewage in isolation from those of its fellow poisons.

As a semi-enclosed area of brackish water, the Baltic is less protected by nature than the North Sea. From the eight moderately populated states on its borders it receives the largely untreated sewage of 18 million people. The effect of organic matter in sewage is made worse by discharges from agricultural fertilizer and leads to a BOD equivalent of 1.4 million tonnes. High phosphorus and nitrogen input produces heavy phytoplankton blooms off Helsinki and

Stockholm, which, when they die, add to the rotting matter at the bottom of the sea. In these cold, slow-moving waters poisons last longer than in warmer climates. Stockholm suffered an epidemic that was traced to a virus in the city sewage. In some areas salmonella have been found in large numbers. Again, the problem cannot be treated in isolation. Sewage is only one poison; heavy metals and organochlorines from industry are even more deadly.[67]

The Mediterranean is notorious as a sea of sewage, especially in tourist areas such as the Bay of Naples in Italy, Barcelona in Spain, and the Gulf of Saronikos in Greece. It is unfair, however, to blame this entirely on the human population of 100 million who live on the coasts and islands, as agricultural and industrial effluent is often discharged with municipal waste. High levels of phosphorus and nitrogen have again caused eutrophication, particularly in the shallow Adriatic where the Po also pours its poisons into the sea. As the currents move anti-clockwise these are carried along the Emilia-Romagna coast to produce frequent algal blooms and kill off all organisms at the bottom of the sea. GESAMP estimates that only an 80% reduction in the level of phosphate in the waste will prevent such blooms. The risk to human health is even greater for the sewage

> contains a full spectrum of enteric micro-organisms excreted by the population . . . . Owing to its climate and socio-economic conditions the Mediterranean has a higher incidence of bacterial, viral and parasitic enteric cases than, for example, northern Europe. For instance, typhoid is about 100 times more frequent in the Mediterranean than in northern Europe. The higher frequency of pathogens in sewage-contaminated waters and the longer immersion of swimmers in the warm water will considerably increase the risk of infection.[68]

We are back to our swimmer in the sea of turds!

If he survives the hazard of direct infection while in the water, he may be in greater danger from eating mussels afterwards. 'The cholera outbreak in Italy was most probably caused by infection from these organisms which are thought to have been contaminated through sewage discharges or releases from ships into illegal mussel beds.'[69]

All, however, is not lost. Encouraged by UNEP's Regional Seas Programme, Mediterranean governments have come to realize that their own interests, including tourism, require them to undertake a massive clean-up, while the construction industry is looking forward to a big boom in building new sewage works. Already Dr Aldo Manos, co-ordinator of the Mediterranean Action Plan, has claimed that the one third of beaches previously considered unhealthy for swimmers has been reduced to a fifth. The first aim of a new programme, agreed in 1986, is to build plants in the 90 coastal cities with more than 100,000 inhabitants; the second, to extend this to the 600 towns with a population of 10,000 or more. Istanbul, Tel Aviv, Alexandria, Naples, Genoa, Marseilles and Nice now have plans for new sewage treatment plants or clean-up schemes.[70] The sewage will still go into the sea, but it will no longer be untreated and the aim is to use long pipelines rather than discharge it near the beaches. One can only hope that the result will not be simply to transfer the problem from coastal waters to where it is no longer seen. But one is still left asking why, when there is much good in sewage, it must go into the sea at all.

Compared with oil, sewage is an unsatisfactory poison to describe. There are no great disasters at sea, no blow-outs or explosions, no monstrous slaughter of birds (dead fish never arouse the same sympathy); their common concern is to desecrate beaches and waters near the shore. There is another major difference: some day the oil will run out and we shall be free from that menace; but, as long as humanity exists, the excremental element in sewage will remain. It is the unavoidable pollutant.

In this chapter we have concentrated on this aspect, on the nutrients that over-fertilize the oceans and so bring decay and death, and on the viruses that endanger human health. But, as we said at the outset and have been continually reminded in our survey, sewage is a heterogeneous mess. Many outfalls contain not only human waste but those from agriculture and industry – wastes that include poisons far deadlier than humanity's viruses: the heavy metals, organochlorines and other chemicals that are the subject of our next chapter.

References

1. Moorcraft 1972 p. 62
2. GESAMP 15 p. 59; *TAO* p. 173
3. Ibid.
4. Moorcraft 1972 pp. 63–6
5. *TAO* p. 173
6. GESAMP 15 p. 62
7. Ibid.
8. Ibid.
9. Medical Research Council 1959
10. RCEP 10 p. 87
11. Ibid. pp. 86–7
12. *New Scientist* 16 July 1981
13. DoE *Digest* 1985 p. 18
14. CAPL Report in ACOPS 1985–6 pp. 53–4; Gowen 1985
15. Explanations from: The Welsh Office 1985 p. 31
16. DoE *Digest* 1985 p. 18
17. *ENDS* No. 138. July 1986. p. 4
18. DoE *Digest* 1985 p. 21
19. Ibid.
20. *Hansard*. House of Commons. 31 October 1986
21. DoE *Digest* 1985 p. 21
22. RCEP 10 p. 70
23. *Guardian* 3 March 1986
24. RCEP 10 p. 26
25. Ibid. p. 71

26. Ibid.
27. *Guardian* 24 May 1986
28. RCEP 10 pp. 88–90; DoE *Digest* 1985 pp. 23–4; *Holiday Which?* March 1986
29. Gowen 1985
30. *Guardian* 5 July 1986
31. *Hansard.* House of Commons. 23 July 1986
32. *Hansard.* House of Lords. 8 April 1986
33. *RSRS 13* p. 139
34. *RSRS 8* pp. 23–4 Table 7
35. Ibid. p. 22
36. *RSRS 13* pp. 110–11
37. *RSRS 8* p. 38
38. Ibid. p. 36
39. Ibid. pp. 25, 36–8; Pathmarajah and Meith 1985 p. 176
40. *RSRS 8* pp. 24–5, *RSRS 13* p. 111
41. *RSRS 13* p. 111
42. *RSRS 8* p. 25; *RSRS 13* p. 111
43. *RSRS 13* p. 123; Pathmarajah and Meith 1985 p. 186
44. *RSRS 13* p. 116
45. Ibid.
46. Ibid.; Pathmarajah and Meith 1985 p. 186
47. *RSRS 13* p. 111; Pathmarajah and Meith 1985 p. 186
48. Pathmarajah and Meith 1985 p. 183
49. Agarwal et al. 1982 pp. 20–22
50. Pathmarajah and Meith 1985 p. 181
51. Agarwal et al. 1982 pp. 23, 25; 1985 p. 48
52. Agarwal et al. 1985 p. 45
53. Leong 1982 pp. 68–9
54. *TAO* p. 173
55. Ibid.
56. Ibid.
57. Ibid.
58. GESAMP 15 pp. 80–81; *TAO* p. 172
59. *RSRS 14* p. 13
60. Moorcraft 1972 p. 173
61. GESAMP 15 p. 76
62. Ibid. p. 79
63. Ibid. p. 78
64. Moorcraft 1972 pp. 66–7
65. *TAO* p. 172
66. *TAO* p. 174; GESAMP 15 p. 73
67. *TAO* p. 175; GESAMP 15 p. 71; Moorcraft 1972 p. 132
68. GESAMP 15 p. 75; *TAO* p. 177
69. *TAO* p. 177
70. *The Times* 26 August 1986; *Lloyd's List* 23 September 1986

5. Toxic Technology: Hazardous Chemicals and Heavy Metals

The *Dana Optima*, *Ariadne* and others

On 13 January 1984 the Danish cargo ship *Dana Optima* on a regular voyage from Newcastle upon Tyne, England, to Esbjerg, Denmark, ran into hazardous force twelve storms then sweeping over northern Europe. A fault developed in a supercharger, causing it to lose power and the ship to drift dangerously close to oil rigs in the Norm field. Helicopters were alerted to evacuate the rig crews, but the *Dana Optima* recovered power and went on her way. Not without loss, however: 38 containers and trailers carried on deck were swept overboard, among them 80 drums containing 16 tonnes of a highly toxic weedkiller, Dinoseb.[1]

Ten days later the Danish Government sent a rescue ship, the *Gunnar Seidenfaden,* to try to recover the drums. With no definite location and the possibility that some containers were already buried in the sea-bed, the search was unsuccessful and on 3 February the *Gunnar Seidenfaden* decided it was useless to continue. Fishermen's organizations, aware of the risk to their members, thought otherwise. Under their pressure the Danish Government ordered a further search and on 14 February the *Gunnar Seidenfaden* was joined by Dutch naval vessels, who found some of the cargo, but not the drums. A month after this second attempt began, the Danes again abandoned their efforts, leaving it to the Dutch Navy to carry on. Pressure, however, continued, and on 19 March, more than two months after the loss, the Danish Minister for the Environment announced yet another attempt to find the drums.

Ironically, it was neither the rescue ship nor the Dutch Navy that discovered the first drum but a Dutch fishing boat from Urk which, on 27 March, found one in its nets. Next day a second fishing vessel 'caught' another, and on 30 March a third Dutch ship found 11, which the rescue ship recovered, only to return to port because of bad weather. A Dutch naval vessel, the *Haarlem*, eventually located the remainder. Not all were recovered immediately; the 68th found its way into a fisherman's net on 14 May, four months and a day after the accident. A fortnight later fishermen recovered a further three; nine remain in the sea, waiting until the containers corrode and their poisons spill into the waters. On 15 May the Dutch and Danish Governments officially announced an end to the search.[2]

Unlike the tanker incidents described earlier, the loss of Dinoseb from the *Dana Optima* was not due to 'human error' and only indirectly to mechanical failure. Hazardous cargo watchers, however, quickly pointed out that the accident would have been avoided had the drums not been stored on deck where they were most likely to be washed overboard in rough seas. To which the reply was that human lives came first. The deadliest cargoes are commonly stored on deck so that, if the ship is in danger, they can be easily jettisoned. The dilemma is obvious: faced with a choice of losing his ship and crew or poisoning the sea, the ship's master opts for the safety of his vessel and men. The deeper issue of whether we can afford to risk destroying the environment in the process is thrust into the background.

The Dutch and Danish Governments were doubtless aware that Dinoseb, in use since 1948, was highly toxic, but not even they could have known the full extent of the danger. To farmers it was an excellent herbicide, particularly effective in killing broadleaf weeds when sprayed on soya beans, potatoes, cotton, peanuts, alfalfa, beans, peas, grapes or almonds. To commercial gardeners it was equally useful with irises, gladioli, tulips and roses and for cleaning drainage ditches. Yet in October 1986 the US Environmental Protection Agency (EPA) abruptly banned its sale in the USA under an emergency order, the third pesticide ever to receive this treatment. The UK followed in December, suspending all approvals for sales pending a full review by the Advisory Committee on Pesticides. Studies completed the previous May showed that Dinoseb, the chemical dinitrophenol, fed to pregnant rabbits at a rate of 10 milligrams per kilogram (mg/kg) of body weight, produced defects in the brain, spinal cord and skeletal system of their offspring, and caused infertility in males by interfering with the basic actions of cells. Farmers and agricultural workers using Dinoseb had been exposed to similar or higher levels than those used in the study; hence the need for emergency action.

In the USA Dinoseb was sold under a variety of appropriately startling trade names – Dinitrix, Klean Krop, Dynamite and Hel-Fire; in the UK it appears as Chafer, Farmon, Fletchers Duby Amine, Herbon and Marks DNBP. In Britain Dinoseb ingredients are manufactured by S. H. Marks of Bradford and Universal Crop Protection; in France by SNPE and in the FRG by Hoehst, who, in September 1986, ordered their US subsidiary to stop production.[3] No one is accusing these chemical manufacturers of poisoning the seas – their product is intended for the land – but, in transporting it across the North Sea on the deck of a cargo ship in a force 12 gale, they narrowly escaped that invidious distinction. More pertinently one might ask why such poisons are not given the rigorous tests to which the EPA submitted them *before* being placed on the market.

The *Dana Optima* incident ended with no known casualties. In August 1985 the inhabitants of Mogadishu, Somalia, were less fortunate. On the 24th of the month the 24,198-ton dwt Greek-owned, Panamanian-registered *Ariadne*, carrying 9,925 tonnes of containers and general cargo, 645 tonnes of fuel and 162.5 tonnes of diesel oil, grounded in Mogadishu harbour. The ship drifted nearer to land and, on Saturday 28 September, broke in two, the stern remaining afloat, while the bow section, known to contain certain dangerous chemicals, sank and split again. Much of the cargo fell into the harbour and the inhabitants were warned against eating fish from the area or bathing in the sea. A United Nations Environment Programme team arrived to identify and assess the danger from the chemicals, which an Information Ministry spokesman described as toxic and explosive. They were found to include both chlorinated and non-chlorinated solvents, pesticides, and the highly poisonous tetra-ethyl lead, none of which were bound for Mogadishu. Analysis of the water showed increasing chemical poisoning, as did the number of dead fish washed up on the beach. Since there was both danger of an explosion and the possibility of a cloud of poison gas forming, the Government made plans to evacuate between 200,000 and 300,000 people. Two hundred were moved from private houses on the waterfront, the central prison and the hospital; shops and seafront hotels closed and the British Embassy shut its doors. To the Somalis the European response to appeals for technical assistance seemed slow, if not dilatory. Murri International Salvage Operation Company, which began the attempted recovery of the cargo, had joined forces with Smit International; their *Giant 3* salvage barge, fitted with a floating crane for retrieving the chemicals, was not due to sail until early October and eventually arrived on the 20th, eight weeks after the grounding. When he visited London at the beginning of the month, the Vice-Minister of Marine Transport, Abdulahi Mohomed Mire, was unsparing in his criticism. 'If this had happened in Europe, there would have been a swift and decisive response. But because of who and where we are there has been no sense of urgency at our plight'.[4] Privately, officials at the International Maritime Organization agreed. Having spent the greater part of the previous summer listening to the wranglings of governments as they attempted to put together a Hazardous and Noxious Substances Convention covering liability and compensation for loss of just such chemicals, only to find the issue deferred, an *Ariadne* incident in European waters might have provided the same impetus for action on 'HazChem' as did the *Torrey Canyon* for oil. Apparently humanity not only needs a disaster to bring it to its senses; for speedy action that disaster must take place in the West, not in the Third World.

Nine years earlier a similar disaster in the Adriatic, with the same chemical, did lead to decisive action. In October 1976, off the coast of Otranto at the entrance to the Adriatic Sea lay the sunken Yugoslav ship *Cavtat*; inside it 900 drums of tetra-ethyl lead were known to be corroding. Divers reported that small quantities had already leaked out to add to the 64% of Italian industrial effluent poured into the waters, including, at the northern end of the Adriatic, the poisonous heavy metals lead, mercury, cadmium and zinc. On the Emilia-Romagna coast huge quantities of fertilizers, washed down by the autumn rains, combined with effluent from food factories and distilleries to produce a massive growth of seaweed, among which stinking masses of dead fish, molluscs and shellfish offered an unexpected feast for gulls. In Venice the health authorities impounded large quantities of tuna fish containing dangerous amounts of mercury, while off Manfredonia police and naval launches patrolled the sea to stop fishermen from entering an area poisoned by an arsenic compound from a chemical factory.[5] At the heart of the Mediterranean the lake of Santa Gida near Cagliari, capital of Sardinia, was found to be poisoned with mercury. The lake is one of three large salt lakes visited by 10,000 water birds to feed and breed, including avocets, stilts, wild duck, gull-billed terns and the rare purple gallinule. It is also the repository for effluent from petro-chemical factories on shore. The appearance of dead fish early in the summer prompted scientists to seek out the causes. They found that the lake had five times more mercury in it than the law allowed; eels contained 4.67 mg/kg as opposed to the permitted 0.7 mg/kg. Driven to extreme action, the Regional Government decided to prevent poisoning of the sea in the Bay of Cagliari by blocking off the exit from the lake, removing all fish and dredging the bottom until all traces of mercury were eliminated.[6]

The outcome was a determined attempt, both from self-interest – tourism is important economically – and for ecological reasons, to 'clean up the Med.', which led to the Barcelona Convention and the practical measures of the Mediterranean Action Plan.

The dangers, however, remain. The poisoning of the Adriatic occurred in 1977, the *Dana Optima* and *Ariadne* incidents in 1984 and 1985. Together these events illustrate the subject of this chapter: the heavy metals – mercury, cadmium, lead and zinc – and the hazardous chemicals and chlorinated hydrocarbons with polysyllabic names. Not only are all deadly in their effects, they have a further common factor – they are products of modern agro-industrial technology and apparently inseparable from the aims of increased efficiency and higher profits. Before continuing our search for the poisoners, it is useful to know more about these poisons and their effects.

Parade of Poisons

Of the poisonous chemicals entering the sea the most notorious are the chlorinated hydrocarbons or organochlorines known by their initials DDT and PCB.

DDT – dichloro-diphenyl-trichloro-ethane in full,[7] which is sufficient to explain general use of the acronym – is a synthetic product, first made in 1874 but not generally recognized as a pesticide until 1939, after which its ability to control pests was so widely recognized that manufacturers, farmers, forestry workers and health authorities proceeded to let it loose on a worldwide scale. In the USA alone production rose from 4,400 tonnes in 1944 to 81,300 tonnes in 1963 with an estimated manufacture of 1.22 million tonnes between 1944 and 1968.[8] GESAMP gives a more conservative figure of 60,000 tonnes for worldwide production in 1974,[9] by which time, following arguments at the UN Food and Agriculture Organization, even its major users were beginning to reconsider its desirability.

That pests are a nuisance to farmers and malarial mosquitoes a danger to human beings is undeniable; and the efficiency of DDT in eliminating them is not, at least at the outset, in doubt. The case against DDT is that the major methods of use – spraying crops or houses – is both wasteful and dangerous, that the poison itself is highly persistent, and that, because of this, we still do not know the final consequences of its use.

Spraying, either from the ground or the air, is the method commonly used for killing insects harmful to crops and for 'protecting' trees and human beings from disease-carriers. But, as all who have watched can see for themselves, only a minute proportion of the spray actually reaches its target. Some is carried away by air currents, droplets landing on leaves evaporate into the air, and most of the remainder falls on the ground, where it either evaporates or is taken in by the soil, to be leached away into water courses, thence to rivers and the sea. The details of what ultimately happens are uncertain. DDT is highly persistent and non-biodegradable; in plain terms, it lasts for up to fifty years and cannot be broken down by living creatures into harmless elements. The changes it undergoes result in production of its 'metabolites', DDD and DDE; the latter is even longer lived and equally noxious.

Even scientists were shocked to discover how far air transport carried DDT or DDE. They have been found in rain water, in Antarctic snow and in soils and lakes many thousands of miles from possible spraying. Amid the unknown or partly-known aspects of their movements, one fact is certain. Because the oceans make up 70% of the earth's surface and operate as a unit with the atmosphere, they receive the greater part of the poison, not only as with sewage, in immediate coastal areas, but in the open expanses of the great oceans, which, in GESAMP'S words, become 'the ultimate sink of non-degraded residues'. Not even our distinguished scientists are prepared to tell us what finally happens. 'There are still gaps in knowledge of the circulation and fate of DDT and its analogues in the environment as a whole.' Tropical climates may cause the 'formation of several still unknown metabolites. Very little is known of the toxicological properties of these conversion products'. In short, those Third World countries where DDT is still used are exposed to unknown dangers which the 'advanced' West has avoided by restricting its use, while chemical manufacturers continue to rake in their profits by exporting these known killers to places where, through ignorance, necessity, or the complicity of their governments, they remain 'acceptable'. Ironically, one can detect the workings of natural justice in GESAMP's disclaimer which follows admission of ignorance: 'However, it should be noted that even less information exists on the environmental fate of many other pesticides, *including those that are now being substituted for DDT*, such as toxaphene, which is used, for example, in cotton-growing areas. Residues of this pesticide, which is a mixture of chlorinated compounds, are being reported in marine fish far away from where it is applied'[10] (my stress). When environmentalists succeed in getting one poison banned, the chemical industry has a ready answer – produce another – and deadlier; it can be marketed before its effects are realized. And the Third World will still be available even when the 'faddists' have got a new ban accepted elsewhere.

At least the major effects of DDT on life in the sea are undisputed. We know that it enters plankton through their porous cell walls and is stored in their fat, which dissolves the poison more readily than water, and that, as one progresses up the food chain, concentrations increase. Predatory birds that eat fish-eating birds have higher concentrations than the birds or fish eaten at intermediate stages in the process. Yet the effect on even lesser creatures can be disastrous. The eggs of copepods fail to develop into adults so that the population declines. Shrimps continuously exposed to low levels die off, and the growth of molluscs such as oysters is retarded. Fish continue to die off, even when transferred to clean water; eggs and fry are particularly in danger because of the fat-loving properties of DDT. Seabirds are affected when the shells of eggs become so thin that they break while being hatched.

As for human beings, the case remains unproven. The scare caused by the discovery that milk in the breasts of American mothers contained higher quantities of DDT residues than those allowed in bottled milk has died with the imposition of restrictions. And GESAMP is sanguine that 'it is unlikely that tolerance levels for man will generally be exceeded by consuming marine food'.[11] 'Unlikely', we note, but not 'impossible'; and 'generally' implies that there may be exceptions; GESAMP admits 'there is the risk that in some coastal zones residue levels are being reached in some marine organisms which might make them unacceptable as human food'.[12] Provided, of course, the human beings are given warning of their 'unacceptability' and it is not considered necessary for men, women and children to die before 'proof' can be established.

Finally, two facts about DDT to ponder over. Unlike plankton, fish, birds or human beings, the only creatures to date to have 'benefited' are those it was designed to exterminate; malarial mosquitoes have developed a DDT-resistant strain, thereby not only making the whole process futile but also impeding research into more natural methods of control. Secondly, because of their persistence and accumulation, even if the production and sale of DDT and DDE ceased worldwide tomorrow, there will still be huge quantities in the air and seas for the next fifty years – or even longer. The battle against use – if not production – of DDT may have been won in the West, but DDT is far from defeated.

Polychlorinated biphenyls (PCBs)[13] are less familiar to the non-scientist who at least knows an insecticide when s/he sees one, but fails to find GESAMP's explanation that 'PCBs consist of a large number of homologues and isomers of chlorinated biphenyls'[14] particularly helpful, though, from its glossary, we may conclude that these are chlorine-based compounds with different structures. Chlorine, we know, is unpleasant.

Why have PCBs suddenly acquired such prominence that in 1983 the Paris Commission, responsible for controlling land-discharges into the North Sea and the north-east Atlantic, recommended an end to their use, while the Helsinki Commission proposed limitations leading to a complete ban in the Baltic? What in fact, were their uses and why the rush?

The answers offer little encouragement for confidence in scientists, who identified PCBs in the environment only as late as 1966. For the previous twenty years – PCBs first appeared in 1944 – scientists had included them among the different forms of DDT, and their discovery came as a shock, especially when PCBs were found not only in coastal areas near industry but in mid-Atlantic throughout the whole of its range. The problem was that, unlike DDT, PCBs are not pesticides and so could not have been 'lost' in aerial spraying. Their main uses are in manufacturing paints, plastics, adhesives, coating compounds, hydraulic fluids and electrical equipment, with widespread use in transformers. The only way they could have reached the sea was through the air – from inadequate protection in the incineration of 'used' paints, varnishes or discarded electrical products.

PCBs are even more persistent than DDT so that, whatever governments have now done to stop their use, those already in the sea will be around for a long time. Scientists have shown that micro-organisms can actually break them down but the process is so slow that, for practical purposes, we can disregard it. Once they enter the sea PCBs collect on the sediments at the bottom and are gradually released into the water above. This poses a double danger to marine life, which is poisoned both by taking in water and by eating lesser creatures already infected. Like DDT, PCBs are attracted to fatty tissue, where they remain, so that concentrations increase as one passes up the food chain. Their effects vary according to the type of PCB and the extent of their concentration. While they have spread worldwide, research now shows that they are most common in coastal areas near industrialized countries, where they can kill fish, particularly young ones and fish fry. Invertebrates are even more liable to be affected, while mammals such as sea-lions risk losing their young, as happened in California in the early 1970s, or of having them born deformed, as occurred more recently in the Baltic and Dutch Waddenzee. Inevitably, fish-eating seabirds acquire the poison; 12,000 washed up on the west coast of Britain in 1969 contained unusually high levels of PCBs. Where they are not killed outright, the same effects as with DDT appear in eggshell thinning and subsequent loss of young. Similarly, PCBs can affect that ultimate mammal, humanity; in developed countries supplies of seafood are now checked for their presence and, where 'safe' limits are exceeded, consumption is banned. In 1971 the US Food and Drug Administration were forced to destroy 50,000 turkeys and 80,000 chickens fed on PCB-poisoned fishmeal, together with 60,000 eggs. What happens elsewhere is unknown – or fails to appear in the Western press. GESAMP reports complacently that 'there appear to be no confirmed records of illness from this source'.[15] 'Unconfirmed' reports are, of course, 'unscientific'; but do we really need a Bhopal before we wake up to the chemical poisons that industry daily discharges into the environment?

The problem, as so often, is our ignorance. We go on using things, convinced that they are harmless, until someone establishes a connection between them and damage to fish, birds or mammals. Many yachtsmen were surprised to learn that the highly effective anti-fouling paint they applied to the hulls of their boats to keep them free from barnacles and worms was also effective in less desirable ways. So were lifeboatmen and fishermen on inshore vessels who also used the paint. The main danger, however, came from pleasure craft moored for long periods in estuaries so that the organotin content, especially tribultyn tin (TBT) leached into the water, extensively damaging marine life, in particular shellfish. In Europe France took the lead by banning use of the paint in 1982. The UK followed by restricting the amount of organotin in anti-fouling paints and by setting a water quality target of 20 nanogrammes per litre (ng/l) for TBT. The disturbing feature is that, while this was considered a level at which shellfish would not be affected, in mid-1986 scientists discovered that, for some species of shellfish, even this standard was still inadequate. Moreover, despite the curbs on anti-fouling paints, the level of poison in some estuaries used by large numbers of pleasure craft had not fallen sufficiently. In the summer of 1986 the level of TBT in the Crouch Estuary in Essex varied from 50 to 130 ng/l, more than six times the target; five out of eight estuaries investigated by MAFF exceeded the limit, as did parts of the Norfolk Broads, even where there was no heavy boat traffic. The only solution was a complete ban on the use of TBT in anti-fouling ·paint, a suggestion that had already provoked an inter-departmental argument between the DoE and the DTI, who attempted to delay imposition of the ban because of its effects on the paint industry.

This is not the only occasion on which TBT has proved dangerous. At a conference in Washington in September 1986 one of the papers showed how use of TBT biocides in fish pens had resulted, again through leaching, in the deaths or retarded growth of salmon at Alaskan fish-farms. Further studies showed that salmon reared in such pens and available on the open market contained between 0.081 and 0.20 micrograms per gram (μg/g) of organotin, mostly TBT, only 24% of which was removed by different methods of cooking. What effect this would have on human beings who ate the fish is not known, though we do know that very small concentrations of TBT can break down the membranes of red blood cells.[16] Again we ask why such research is not carried out *before* such dangerous products are sold to the public.

Organotins in paint provide a convenient bridge to our second group of poisons, 'heavy metals',[17] a term used loosely, with the alternative of 'trace elements', to cover such substances as mercury, cadmium, lead, selenium, tin, arsenic, copper, cobalt and manganese. To the non-scientist their most striking feature is their contradictory character; in small quantities many heavy metals are either essential or helpful to metabolic activity in living creatures; in heavy concentrations they are deadly poisonous. At times the gap between the amounts required is comparatively narrow.

As with oil, heavy metals reach the sea from natural sources following weathering in rocks, gaseous explosions or volcanic activity, and from bottom sediments dissolving in water. For a few, notably mercury and lead, the atmosphere is an important mode of transport. Large quantities, however, are the result of human activities and reach the sea through poisoned rivers, direct discharges or deliberate dumping. In the water they may concentrate near the surface or, attaching themselves to particles of matter, sink to the bottom, to remain in sediments long after the original source has ceased; later they are released into the water, often in a different, more dangerous, form.

For scientists wishing to determine the effect of a particular heavy metal the problem is complicated by the fact that they rarely enter the sea alone. As we saw in the last chapter, industrial waste containing heavy metals is often discharged with sewage or detergents. Life then becomes troublesome for the scientist seeking an answer to the effect of mercury or cadmium on the environment, but not half as troublesome as to the creatures of that environment owing to the phenomenon of *synergism*. Put simply, this means that, when two heavy metals are in conjunction, the resulting poisonous effect is considerably greater than the 'sum' of the two poisons concerned. A further complication – from the viewpoint of the possible consumer – is the form of the metal at any time. Trace metals attached to particles, for example, are most readily taken in by filter feeders, such as oysters, while those dissolved in water find their way, like DDT and PCBs, into the fatty tissue of living creatures.

What actually happens is best seen by describing some metals in more detail. To the non-scientist mercury is the silvery substance used in thermometers, which, if broken, discharge it as globules that entertainingly amalgamate or divide. Actually, this is only one form of mercury – metallic mercury or quicksilver. Mercury also occurs naturally in rocks as cinnabar and in a number of minerals as a substitute for other elements such as copper. The non-scientist learns further that the 'natural' home for mercury would appear to be the atmosphere into which an estimated 25,000–150,000 tonnes are released annually from degassing of the earth's crust and from the oceans. Human activities – the burning of fossil fuels, waste disposal, mining operations, the use of biocides, and industrial uses, particularly in chloro-alkali plants – are responsible for releasing an estimated 10,000 tonnes into the environment. Concentrations in the atmosphere are generally higher over urban areas than over semi-enclosed seas, such as the Baltic, the North Sea and the Mediterranean, which in turn have higher concentrations than over the open ocean. In fact, only about a fifth of the mercury reaching the surface of the earth actually remains there, the rest is returned to the atmosphere.

Entering the sea as part of effluent discharged through outfalls or from waste dumped directly into the water, mercury tends to attach itself to particles which sink and collect in the sediments. Some may escape to the open sea, but the most likely course, in estuaries or shallow coastal waters, is for the mercury to concentrate at the bottom of the water. Here under bacterial action, it is converted into the poisonous methylmercury, which, as we saw in the Prologue, brought infamy and death to Minamata.

Mercury is not irremovable; phytoplankton can take up to 20% of it annually in estuaries and one per cent in the upper 100 m of the open ocean; of the remainder less than five per cent in the water reaches the sediments during 100–1,000 years, a period long enough, one would assume, for some of it to be taken in by lesser sea creatures and so passed up the food chain in greater concentrations. The results are either death or reduced ability to survive with, as usual, younger generations in greater danger than adults.

Concern in the West over mercury began with the discovery in 1964 of high levels in the corpses of freshwater fish and birds. Sea fish, including mackerel, herring and cod, were also contaminated and in 1970 governments started to analyse food in shops. In the USA the discovery of dangerous amounts of methylmercury in tins of tuna fish caused a million tins to be withdrawn from sale. Continued surveys and prompt action have so far prevented disaster and enabled GESAMP to conclude that, while there is 'no general threat to average consumers from metals in the sea, . . . only for mercury and only for certain groups of consumers who eat larger than normal amounts of fish is there a significant risk'.[18] After Minamata it would be difficult to maintain otherwise. Even GESAMP is not happy about how much we really know. If its scientists assure us that 'there is clearly at present no general health risk', they add that, so far as epidemiological studies of the effects of mercury on fishermen and their families are concerned, 'further research is required to assess these data'.[19]

The trouble is that, as with TBT in paint, far from increasing our confidence in scientific assessment, 'further research' often discovers that things are worse than expected. Take, for example, lead. Everyone in the West knows that lead in paint and lead in petrol are undesirable, but what of lead in the sea? We know that 150,000 tonnes enter the water annually from natural sources, but how much reaches it through the atmosphere as a result of human activities remains debatable, except that, until the recent curbs on emissions, concentrations in mid-ocean were increasing. Our point here, however, is less with discharges than effects. While the industrial standard for workers in an advanced country, the UK, takes a level of 80 micrograms of lead per decilitre of blood as the threshold for lead poisoning, a survey by the US Harvard School of Public Health, published only in mid-1985, shows that, at above half this level, there are serious effects on the mood of workers, including depression, irrational bouts of anger, fatigue, instability of mood and periods of confusion. At higher levels but still within currently accepted safety standards, certain functions of the brain – verbal ability and number memory – are affected; neither do victims recover rapidly when levels of lead in the blood are reduced.[20] This means that, since the 1930s, we have been prepared to allow possible exposure to damage from lead at levels which, fifty years later, are discovered to be unsafe. Who knows what further discoveries will upset present conclusions in fifty years' time?

Unlike most heavy metals cadmium has no known useful purpose for living creatures. When it enters the human body, it builds up in liver and kidneys as well as replacing calcium in bones and making them brittle. It can cause high blood pressure, and deaths from cardiovascular diseases have been associated with high concentrations of cadmium in the kidneys, as have areas with a high death rate from such diseases with high concentrations of cadmium in the atmosphere. The worst case of cadmium poisoning through water was again in Japan, where 500 people died; a zinc-smelting works discharged the cadmium waste produced into rivers, whence the cadmium found its way into rice paddies and so into food. In the UK there was considerable concern at one time over the amount of cadmium in fish caught in the Bristol Channel, again as the result of zinc smelting.

Humanity is responsible for about half the cadmium reaching the sea, with equal proportions entering through the atmosphere and from rivers. Ninety per cent of the latter remains in areas of the coastal shelf, only a tenth reaches the open sea, where it may be carried by detritus or faeces to the bottom, then returned to the water, to be joined by other cadmium entering via the atmosphere. As the amount entering the water from both sources exceeds that permanently deposited on sediments, the quantity of cadmium in the ocean is gradually increasing.[21] This long-term process may not affect us now, when the greater danger is from cadmium already in estuaries and coastal waters, but the future may bring yet another of those unpleasant surprises for which we cannot plead we were unwarned.

Already environmentally conscious governments are taking action. In 1982 Sweden introduced curbs on the uses of cadmium to stop its increasing accumulation. In 1984 Denmark announced a similar programme; this prohibited products containing cadmium pigments and plastics with cadmium stabilizers from 1 January 1987, but allowed their outdoor use for a further year, with cadmium-plated objects banned from the beginning of 1989. Switzerland planned to restrict the use of cadmium in plastics, to impose general bans on cadmium-plating from 1 September 1988 and on products with cadmium-plated components from 1 September 1990, and to introduce a labelling, collection and disposal scheme for nickel–cadmium batteries from September 1987.[22] Such actions may halt or reduce the entry of poisons from land into the environment; only a complete reversal of industrial practices will prevent the occurrence of incidents that, too often, are presented as beyond human control.

Accidents at Sea – and on Land

If the majority of dangerous chemicals or heavy metals reach the sea through industrial effluent and river run-off, the *Dana Optima* and the *Ariadne* remind us that this is not the only source. Because of their worldwide use in modern industry and agriculture, poisons need to be taken from where they are manufactured to where they are used and, after use, to where the residues will be disposed of. Inevitably there are accidents.

In December 1979 the motor vessel *Sinbad* lost 51 cylinders of chlorine gas during heavy seas 15 miles off the Dutch coast near IJmuiden. A search at the time failed to find them. In August 1984 three of the missing cylinders turned up in the nets of offshore fishermen. This led to a renewed attempt which, by the end of September, had located 13 cylinders, now so corroded that explosives were used to destroy them.

At the end of 1984 25 cylinders were still either unlocated, or, if located, not recovered or destroyed. Using side-scan sonar equipment, the searchers identified 50 possible places where missing cylinders might be found. By mid-February 1985 ten had been discovered and destroyed. The remaining 15 lie buried in the sand among an unknown quantity of other objects. Heavy gales may wash them out of the sand; calmer seas allow them to be buried again. The danger remains.[23]

The *Sinbad*'s story, like that of the *Dana Optima* which it resembles, is no isolated incident. During gales on the night of 24–25 October 1984, the *Forum Hope* lost 2,500 drums in the Bay of Biscay, some of them known to contain dangerous chemicals; three weeks later, on 16 November, the *Brigitta Montanaru*, with a cargo of hazardous chemicals on board, sank in gales in the Adriatic. What follows these incidents is more disconcerting because unexpected. On 18 November a 45-gallon drum of methyl ethyl ketone (MEK), washed ashore with eleven others, exploded on the beach at the holiday resort of Lyme Regis, Dorset, England. MEK is a volatile oxidizing agent, widely used in the chemical industry. Next day, two drums, washed ashore at nearby Portland, also exploded. Coastguards and fire-brigades warned people not to go near any drums they found and to report them at once. Emergency services mounted a sea watch and fire-brigades carried out several controlled burnings. In all, 22 drums of MEK reached British shores; 19 were recovered.[24]

The greatest danger is from a double ignorance – ignorance of the contents of such drums, so that authorities do not know what steps to take, and ignorance of how widespread is the phenomenon as a whole. It seems reasonable to assume that, if explosive chemicals are washed ashore in the UK or lost off the Dutch coast, similar incidents must occur elsewhere where the local authorities are less prepared. Yet even in 'advanced' Western countries there are no systematic data available on the quantities of dangerous substances reaching their shores. In one of the few surveys carried out, the Keep Britain Tidy Group (KBTG) of the UK showed that, in the 12 months after 1 September 1982, local authorities recovered 254 packages from beaches, of which 131 contained substances listed in the International Maritime Dangerous Goods (IMDG) Code, another 21 were suspected of containing such goods, and a further 42, mostly metal drums, contained various fuel and lubricating oils. The most dangerous, four drums containing 842 litres of ether, which is both narcotic and inflammable, were washed up on the Welsh coast, while a plastic container of acetaldehyde, which is also inflammable and dangerous if swallowed or the vapour inhaled, was found on a beach near Brighton. Fifty-nine packages contained substances classed as of 'medium danger', i.e. compressed gases, inflammable liquids, oxidizing agents, corrosives and other poisons. Twenty-one contained suspected hazardous chemicals, including some dysentery tablets found at Kimmeridge Bay, Dorset. While 64% of the packages carried proper warnings, on only 13% were there markings to identify the contents.

This absence of information was most noticeable on metal drums, as the loss from the *Forum Hope* showed. Of 31 drums of inflammable liquids washed ashore in the UK, only one had a visible marking or label. Ninety per cent of the 140 packages reaching the coast had no indication of whether or not they were dangerous or what they contained. Later they were identified as receptacles containing hydrogen peroxide, concentrated hydrochloric acid and inflammable liquids. One drum exploded on the beach near enough to a woman out walking to singe the fur of her dog. Three children, four council workers and a fireman received minor chemical burns from handling packages of hydrogen peroxide. Ironically, on 21 November Dorset County Council were informed that some of the packages had come from the *Forum Hope* – almost a month after the loss occurred.[25]

Twelve months later, on 7 December 1985 and in the days that followed, 26 five-gallon drums of concentrated hydrochloric acid were washed ashore on the Scilly Isles and the Lizard Peninsula of Cornwall. Fourteen of the drums, which appeared to have been made in the Federal Republic of Germany and were bound for Beirut, were full.[26] In February 1986 a 'dangerous chemical' alert was sounded on the east coast of Britain between Skegness and north Essex after four 25-gallon canisters of the industrial cleaner Vecom B–20 were washed ashore in two places. The chemical explodes on contact with the air.[27]

These were not the only 'explosive devices' to reach British beaches or coastal waters. Quoting figures provided by the Ministry of Defence, the KBTG report reveals that, during the period of their survey, 2,396 items were collected and later disposed of by Royal Navy Explosives Ordnance Disposal (EOD) teams. These included 12 bombs, 75 mines, 62 shells, 15 torpedoes and 2,204 'assorted pyrotechnics', including military smoke-generating devices and non-military ship distress signals which, becoming outdated, had been jettisoned as a convenient method of disposal. In a single incident affecting south Devon and Cornwall in July 1983, 26 military devices made in the Netherlands drifted ashore without warning, causing the local authorities to take emergency action at the height of the tourist season.[28] And in November 1986 people in the Isle of Wight were warned not to touch any aluminium canisters after five of them – flares used by submarines and containing a poisonous and explosive chemical – were washed up on beaches.[29] Seldom has the concept of the 'sea as dustbin' been better illustrated. The only difference is that the land-dweller does not normally put live fireworks into the rubbish and then tip it into the neighbour's garden.

Not all 'military devices' reach the shore. On 4 August 1986 the suction dredger/sand carrier *Arco Tees*, at work ten miles off Great Yarmouth on the east coast of the UK, drew in through its suction pipe an object which it was later concluded was a wartime bomb. The bomb exploded, blowing out the bulkhead doors, depriving the ship of electricity and radio, and causing a leak in the engine room. One of the crew, with burns on the legs, was taken to hospital by helicopter; others were evacuated when it appeared that the ship would sink. Fortunately, the combined efforts of a second dredger, the *Arco Swale*, and the Gorleston and Caister lifeboats saved the vessel, which later berthed at Lowestoft.[30]

That the *Arco Tees* should suck in an unexploded bomb, dropped from an unknown source more than forty years before, may be dismissed as a chance in a million. The fact remains that, whatever odds our personal prejudices favour, we have no knowledge by which to prove or disprove them. How many dangerous objects are buried at the bottom of the world's seas, awaiting the arrival of some luckless dredger, or, having broken loose, are now drifting towards land, is a question to which all answers are guesswork. The only reliable, if limited, information on military dangers is that for deliberate dumping. According to the *Times Atlas of the Oceans*, '. . . the dumping of waste material from military installations and shore industries has increased alarmingly since 1945. Military waste, including nerve gas, has been dumped for several years. In 1958, for example, the *William Ralston* was scuttled in the Atlantic carrying 8,000 tonnes of mustard gas'.[31] The authors could have added that the German military began dumping mustard gas in the Baltic shortly after the First World War and that, after World War II, the Allies sank 179,000 tons of Nazi poison gas off Norwegian fjords, including canisters aboard the cruiser *Leipzig*, which was scuttled. In March 1987 Norwegians were reported as attributing part of the blame for increased cancerous tumours in fish to leaks from the canisters.[32]

Accidents at sea in which hazardous chemicals offer immediate danger are at least fewer than those on land – if only because there are fewer opportunities for them. But even with land installations we are constantly reminded of how much we do not know. Not until Bhopal prompted them into action did the US Environmental Protection Agency (EPA) set up an inquiry to discover how accident-prone was the chemical industry in the USA. The results, incomplete as they are since they cover only New Jersey, Texas, California, the Midwest and Ohio, are more than disturbing. In the five years to 1985 there were no fewer than 6,928 accidents involving toxic chemicals, three-quarters of them at plants, the rest during transportation; more than 135 people were killed and nearly 1,500 injured – an average of five accidents a day throughout the period. The leading consultants, Industrial Economics Inc., of Cambridge, Massachusetts, maintained further that, had the whole country been covered, the figure would have been two and a half to three times as great. As it was, spills and emissions resulted in the loss of 420 million lb (190 million kg) of chemicals, bringing death or injury to 468 people and causing the evacuation of 217,457.[33] In the world's most advanced capitalist country where emphasis is on technological progress, the investigators found that storage tanks, valves, pipes and other equipment failed on average five times daily. Presumably it was someone's job to ensure that they didn't! Before the West condemns the Indians or Russians for their inefficiency it would do well to scrutinize its own operations more closely.

Why, for example, when, in August 1984, Gibson Chemical Ltd. of Wokingham, Berkshire, England, discharged a mixture of detergent, bleach and caustic soda from damaged drums into a surface drain leading to Emm Brook and thence to the River Loddon, killing up to 17,000 fish and completely destroying all life in the water, did they do so under the impression that the poisons would be carried to a 'foul sewer' and thus cause no damage?[34]

Some potential dangers at least are prevented – or diverted. On 1 July 1986 at Immingham Dock, Humberside, England, a tank of highly poisonous ethylenediamine being unloaded from the Swedish ro-ro *MV Baldwin* sprang a leak, contaminating some 200 metres of the quayside and causing a large area to be evacuated. The chemical had apparently expanded with the heat. For four hours firemen swilled down the quay with high-pressure hoses before the tank was sealed and removed.[35] And the chemical? Naturally, it was washed into the water.

Cold weather can be as disastrous as hot. In February 1986 15 tank cars on the 'acid train' that travels regularly from the Falconbridge Factory in Sudbury, Canada, along the shore of Lake Huron to Ohio, USA, jumped the tracks near Parry Sound about 100 miles north of Toronto. Each car, containing up to 11,000 gallons of sulphuric acid, plunged through the ice into the waters on either side of the tracks. An Ontario Environment Ministry official announced that one of the cars leaked at least 4,000 gallons. The response was to bring up 15 cars of limestone and empty those into the lake to neutralize the acid.

The incident in itself may or may not have been dangerous. The real hazard arises from the cumulative effect of such incidents and their impact on regular and continuous discharges of poison. The previous autumn Dow Chemical of Canada spilled about 3,000 gallons of perchloroethylene, used in dry-cleaning, into the St Clair River, which flows from Lake Huron to Detroit. Add the effects of acid rain from coal-burning plants in Ohio[36] across the border and one has the ingredients for a disaster, the nature and extent of which will remain unknown until it happens.

As for the ability of individual plants to act in an emergency, habitual secrecy under the guise of 'confidentiality' has led to public disquiet and distrust of the chemical industry. It was with incredulity that the British viewing public learned from a television programme in April 1986 that the Imperial Chemical Industries plant at Runcorn, Cheshire, which stores chlorine gas in giant tanks of up to 300 tonnes, had no emergency plans for handling an accident to such tanks as this was 'not a credible event'. The worst spill that they planned to counter was some 20 tonnes from a fractured pipe. According to ICI the 300-tonne tanks were 'built like battleships', could not explode from high pressure and were surrounded by barriers. The only way to rupture one would be for an aircraft to fall 20,000 or 30,000 feet and make a direct hit.[37] The comparison was perhaps unfortunate; battleships have been known to explode – if not in urban areas with a large population; the 'incredible' has happened – too frequently in recent times. One sometimes wonders whether Bhopal ever occurred.

In the UK even the law has been misinterpreted so that people did not know what was happening. Until June 1986 factory inspectors were not allowed to reveal details of accidents, or even where dangerous chemicals were manufactured and stored, without permission from the company concerned. The Health and Safety Executive based its policy on the 1974 Health and Safety at Work Act which referred to the need to have 'the relevant consent' of the company before disclosure. Reinterpretation of the Act revealed that officials had the duty to inform the public about pollution and potential risks to safety.[38] Perhaps we should be grateful that victims may now be informed beforehand rather than told that the accident never happened.

Toxic Technology in the Developed World

Accidents are by definition unpredictable. The daily doses of poison which industry and agriculture discharge into the atmosphere and into the seas of the world are the direct result of modern technological processes. If the Western world is at least aware of the danger, the increasing spread of industry and the discharges of chemical waste and heavy metals accompanying it, together with the ever growing use of pesticides in agriculture, more than counter attempts at control.

How far have things changed in the West? Has alleged environmental consciousness been translated into action? Are the regulations of governments, anxious to placate public opinion but determined not to offend industry or farmers, really effective? The US report on accidents in the chemical field is hardly reassuring. In the UK a survey of poisons found in marine life produced by MAFF's Lowestoft research unit in 1984 – the latest information available on trends – is more optimistic. It concludes that in the 1970s contamination of coastal waters by heavy metals and pesticides declined following withdrawal from use of PCBs, a voluntary ban on Dieldrin and other killers, and increased control over the dumping of heavy metals. This claim is backed by a series of graphs which, for most substances, show declining trends from the early 1970s, when industrialists, aware that the UN Stockholm Conference on the Environment would make life harder, dumped as much as they could in the sea while the going was good.

Unfortunately, for those who want to know what is happening in the 1980s, the report ends at 1976. In that year the procedures for monitoring the data were changed to include greater detail. More recent figures are promised in due course, which will be related to the old, but it seems remarkable that the Fisheries Directorate, which rushed out an account of the effects of Chernobyl on UK waters within weeks of that incident, were unable to produce information on some of the intervening years. The report concludes that, after an early peak, levels of mercury in fish and shellfish declined between 1970 and 1976, that PCBs probably followed a similar pattern, but that for Dieldrin, DDT, lead and cadmium there was little change. The aim, of course, is to discover 'trends', a task in which the game of plying statistics is used with professional expertise. Not only are the graphs based on three-year average trends, thereby ironing out any untoward effects, but levels of contamination considered so high that they would 'distort the overall sample' are omitted from the calculations, some of which place a strain on the meaning of the word 'decrease'. The mean concentration of Dieldrin in cod, for example, in 1970, 1975 and 1976 is given respectively as 0.15, 0.40 and 0.53 mg/kg; in whiting it was 0.28 in 1970 and 0.36 in 1976; and in plaice 0.24 (1970) and 0.37 (1976). This 'decrease' is obtained by excluding highly contaminated samples which contained 2.4 mg/kg of Dieldrin in 1970 and 3.4 mg/kg in 1976.[39]

The non-scientist can only remain sceptical of such 'improvement'. Dependent on scientists for figures, yet uncertain whether 0.15 mg/kg of Dieldrin in cod is a danger to the fish or to anyone eating it (scepticism extends to the 'safe limits' set by establishment scientists), s/he knows that Dieldrin is not good to eat, that 1976 was later than 1970, and that 0.36 is an increase on 0.28. Admittedly, two figures do not make a 'trend', but when the relationship between figures for three types of fish is in the same direction – upward – it needs more than a scientific mystery to explain why the overall trend is said to be in the opposite direction!

Scepticism increases when one reads that, in August 1984, more than 4,000 fish, including both young salmon and adults up to 15 lb in weight, were killed in a six-mile stretch of the River Mawddach, near Dolgellau in mid-Wales, just above where the ten-mile estuary flows through mountains to the sea. Welsh Water Authority scientists discovered high levels of zinc, cadmium and copper consistent with effluent discharges from mining for non-ferrous metals that have been worked here for over a century. Three years ago a gold mine reopened at Gwynfynydd. The mine manager disclaimed responsibility for the deaths of the fish.[40]

When Greenpeace investigated the Manchester Ship Canal in July 1986, it found that the amount of oxygen in the water – less than two per cent – was insufficient for fish to survive. Of the industries using the canal as a dustbin – quite legally, since the Water Authority grants permission – Associated Octel, which produces lead for petrol, discharges about 80 kg of lead daily as a liquid, while ICI Castner Kellner of north Runcorn has 21 discharge pipes, 16 of them licensed to discharge mercury. In 1979 2,400 birds died on a sandbank from eating lead-contaminated worms. Associated Octel were awarded the Queen's Award to Industry for services to exports.[41]

Documents released by the House of Commons Select Committee on Agriculture in November 1986 showed that the Anglian Water Authority had found concentrations of the highly poisonous insecticide, Lindane, in drinking water 350 times higher than what is permitted under EEC regulations. Both the Water Authority and the Department of the Environment denied that there was a danger to human health. The Water Research Centre, however, warned that bottle-fed babies were at risk from pesticides in drinking water.[42]

These examples are not the result of unforeseeable accidents but of everyday operations in the chemical industry, mining and agriculture. From lakes and rivers poisons pass to the sea, from spraying on land they leach into drinking water. The amount of poison in nearshore waters may or may not have declined between 1970 and 1976, but one of these events occurred in 1984, the other two in 1986.

The UK is only one contributor to the poisons entering the North Sea. Dumping of industrial waste, factory effluent carried by rivers, and discharges released into the atmosphere from industrial complexes on its shores combine to produce an amalgam of poison, the extent and effects of which are still uncertain. Dumping includes waste from the titanium dioxide industry (now being curtailed by EEC regulation), mineral tailings, acids and alkalis. A Norwegian study estimated that in the 1970s about 3,600 tons of chemicals were discharged into the sea annually. Pipelines and river systems contribute their share of DDT and PCBs, while 45,000 tonnes of zinc, 14,000 tonnes of lead, 10,000 tonnes of copper, 5,000 tonnes of chromium, 4,000 tonnes of nickel and 1,000 tonnes of mercury enter the waters every year. Most of these metals are contained in other wastes – the seven million metric tons of industrial waste dumped by ships, the 73 million tonnes of rubble, the 150 million tonnes of dredged spoil and the five million tonnes of sewage sludge encountered earlier. The heaviest dumping occurs at the mouth of the Rhine and off the north Brittany coast.

The most remarkable features of this massive input of poisons to a comparatively shallow portion of the world ocean are, firstly, despite anti-pollution legislation, it is all legal, and secondly, that the opinions of scientists on its effects vary according to who and where they are. GESAMP concludes that 'despite these various inputs, . . . the extent of pollution in the North Sea is not large' and 'confined mainly to coastal areas, with "hot spots" such as dumping grounds and polluted estuaries'. In such areas 'there is evidence of elevated levels of metals in fish or shellfish'. Having conceded this, they add ambiguously that 'generally the levels found are not much higher than in most specimens from the coastal zone'. They do, however, admit that 'seals and porpoises living in some parts of the Waddenzee have high concentrations of PCBs and mercury in their tissues, and populations of these mammals have been declining continuously in recent years'.[44]

Similarly, the *Times Atlas of the Oceans*, after calling the North Sea 'one of the worst polluted sea areas in the world', maintains that, 'apart from specific incidents, such as the decline in inshore plaice stocks near estuaries, there is no conclusive proof that the living resources of the North Sea have, as yet, been seriously affected by pollution'.[45] One wonders how 'conclusive proof' differs from other forms of proof (except that it *sounds* more convincing) and at what stage 'living resources' are 'seriously affected' as opposed to 'affected'. One also notes the inclusion of an ominous 'as yet'.

The Council of Experts for Environmental Problems in the FRG, in their 1980 report for the Minister of the Interior on 'Environmental Problems of the North Sea', had fewer doubts. They found pollution in some areas alarming, especially in coastal regions: 'emissions of chemical wastes and sludges have extended so much that the situation can no longer be tolerated'.[46] And a Scientific Conference for the Protection of the North Sea, held in June 1984, produced evidence which suggested that not only coastal areas but the open sea is directly endangered. 'The stocks of some fish species decrease, while those of other less sensitive species increase. Ill or parasitized fishes, birds and other sea animals are becoming increasingly common'.[47]

The argument continues between governments. The FRG demands preventive action before it is too late, the UK resists action without 'conclusive proof'. The environmentalist concludes that, by the time the British Government gets its 'proof', it will probably be 'too late'. Statements from the Netherlands Institute for the Investigation of Fishery published in October 1986 that 40% of a sample of 20,000 flounders, dab and plaice had cancerous tumours or bacterial skin diseases from chemical contamination and were unfit for eating were apparently insufficient, even if they corroborated a German figure of 42% diseased fish in a survey earlier in the year. The British stonewalled, arguing that MAFF's regular surveys did not show this extent of the disease and that the Netherlands research referred only to the east side of the North Sea. In consequence, there was no need to issue health warnings to the British public. The Dutch disagreed.[48]

When environmental ministers from North Sea states met in London in November 1987, the result was a *quid pro quo*. The Germans agreed to halve the volume of heavy metals and agricultural chemicals deposited by the Rhine within seven years, the British to stop discharging dangerous liquid chemical wastes into North Sea waters by 1989 and to ensure that levels of poisoning did not rise above those of 1987. Incineration of toxic wastes at sea was to be phased out by 1994 and the overall volume of toxic substances and agricultural chemicals discharged into the sea halved by 1995. An attempt to declare the North Sea a specially protected area under the 1973/78 MARPOL Convention (see Part 3) failed. In plain terms, the poisoning will go on; it will be reduced, but will the reduction be enough?

Until the regulations of the Helsinki Commission begin to bite, that other northern sea, the Baltic, will remain even more poisoned. In the seven countries around its shores are industries engaged in copper smelting and the manufacture of aluminium, arsenic, lead, steel, textiles, petroleum, chemicals, zinc and chlorine, together with paper- and pulp-making plants, and food-producing factories. Between them they discharge some 68,000 tonnes of zinc, 27,000 tonnes of copper, 14,000 tonnes of lead and 60 tonnes of mercury into the water, alongside waste containing PCBs and DDT. Mercury also enters the sea through the air. The results are predictable. Scientists have found concentrations of metals, DDT and PCBs in fish, and birds have suffered eggshell thinning. Both the white-tailed eagle and the osprey are in danger, and the grey seal population has been decimated not only by hunting (which, in 1982, the Commission recommended should be banned) but because of damage to their reproductive capacity from eating PCB-infected Baltic herring.[49]

The Mediterranean Action Plan mentioned in the opening section began with the compilation of an inventory of poisons actually there. The results, published by UNEP in 1984,[50] show clearly not only the extent of pollution but also the difficulties of determining the source. When industries discharge their waste through municipal sewerage systems, when coastal cities release their sewage into rivers so that it is included as part of the river run-off, and when the whole process is complicated by input from natural sources, as with some mercury, controlling the poisoners becomes highly complex. The main industries identified included iron and steel in the Marseilles, Genoa and Athens areas, chemical complexes in a number of regions of concentrated industry, leather tanning and finishing along the Spanish and Italian coasts and near Athens and Alexandria, and textile manufacturing, food processing and canning, and pulp and paper factories throughout the region. Of the major poisons, chloro-alkali plants at Livorno in Italy and Haifa in Israel discharge mercury, lead enters from the Barcelona region, and zinc and copper in the

Gulf of Saronikos, Greece.[51]

The UNEP experts conclude that every year 25,000 tons of zinc, 4,800 tons of lead, 2,800 tons of chromium and 130 tons of mercury enter the Mediterranean from the land, together with 90 tons of organochlorine pesticides. These figures include estimates of natural discharges as those who receive the poisons do not distinguish the source. Of the organochlorines about a third are DDT and its associates. Even now, the information is incomplete; there are no estimates for cadmium 'owing to an almost complete lack of data for all source categories'.[52] If this means that those who put this highly toxic poison in the sea did so without knowing how much is there and with no regard for the consequences, it is the height of irresponsibility.

Of these consequences GESAMP mentions high concentrations of mercury of up to four parts per million (ppm) in blue fin tuna and six ppm in striped mullet and in Norway lobster. All are commercially important and all exceed official limits. If these limits were imposed, it would mean confiscating a large part of the catch. Not surprisingly, fishermen, fish-sellers and their families have high levels of mercury in their blood and hair, 'the potential risk [of which] has still to be assessed'. Humanity, however, is partly exonerated. The poisons occur in fish 'caught far away from anthropogenic [man-made] mercury sources' and the high concentrations 'are considered to be derived from natural sources'.[53] GESAMP's precision, exemplified in specific figures for 'parts per million' of poisons in fish, becomes a vague 'far away' when applied to industry. The Mediterranean, hardly the largest of seas, is not an area where one can easily get 'far away' as in the Pacific. One needs more reassurance before attributing the potential poisoning of fishermen and their families to unavoidable Acts of God.

Across the Atlantic heavy metals and chemicals from industry on the north-eastern seaboard of the USA and Canada have affected coastal waters. GESAMP blandly reports:

> Metal-containing wastes from such operations as electroplating and metal-processing plants are discharged from most urban centres along the Atlantic coast of North America. In the Canadian maritime provinces, metals are released from mines and smelters. Leaching of lead and zinc from mine tailing piles in the Miramichi River drainage basin [leading to the St Lawrence Gulf] has affected the Atlantic salmon run in this stream.
>
> Chloro-alkali plants using mercury cells and pulp mills using mercurial slimicides contributed mercury in some of the streams and coastal waters of the Canadian maritime provinces and Quebec before 1970. Action was taken to stem these sources in 1971 and the discharges of mercury are now very low. However, sediments continue to exhibit high mercury concentrations in some areas.[54]

In broad terms GESAMP is correct and Canada has succeeded in presenting to the world an image of concern for the environment. 'Locally', as GESAMP would say, there are exceptions. One of them is the Wabigoon River, where the industrialized world meets the indigenous inhabitants.

In 1961 Reed Paper Ltd. of Toronto, the Canadian subsidiary of the British

Reed International (which has interests in 44 countries ranging from building materials to newspapers), acquired a controlling interest in a paper mill at Dryden. Shortly afterwards, they installed a chloro-alkali plant using mercury to break down brine into caustic soda (for use in producing pulp) and chlorine (for bleaching the paper). Theoretically, all mercury was recycled in the plant; in practice, in the next eight years 20,000 lb of mercury escaped, either into the atmosphere or through underwater outlets into the Wabigoon River. The river passes through Clay Lake, 55 miles from the plant, to join the English River system, where there are two Indian reserves – Grassy Narrows and Whitedog. Reed was operating legally; until 1972 there were no Government regulations prohibiting discharges of mercury, and no standards for levels of mercury in commercially available fish.

In 1969 a Norwegian zoologist discovered levels of mercury in the livers of ducks in Clay Lake up to 100 ppm; further investigations by the Ontario authorities throughout the area showed levels of 12–14 ppm of mercury in wall-eyed pike, a favourite food of the local Indians and of the many rich tourists who came to fish. The 'safe limit' for wall-eyed pike in both the USA and Canada is now 0.5 ppm. Smaller fish were found to have 9.2 ppm, and mercury from other chloro-alkali plants – 16 operated in Canada at the time – was also found in waters in the south-west of the province.

In the spring of 1970 – the action to which GESAMP presumably refers – the Federal Department of Fisheries and Forestry began a survey of mercury in fish throughout the country. The results enabled the minister responsible to claim confidently in April that they had caught the mercury problem in time before there was any real danger to human beings. Nor need tourists stay away from their favourite resorts – all they were required to do, for their own safety, was not to eat the fish. In August the Ontario Government expressed the hope that by the following summer the problem would be over; they had eliminated the sources and were satisfied that there was no longer a loss of mercury.

The Government was optimistic. Mercury will remain in the river system for 70–100 years. Their own studies, completed in February 1972, showed that levels of mercury in fish were up to 30 times the limit and concluded that all fish-eaters in north-west Ontario were in danger. The report was not released until November 1974 after parts had been made public on a CBC programme. In 1972 also, the Federal Government, following the Minamata example, fed 16 cats with contaminated fish. All showed signs of poisoning – but it was three years before these results were made known. In March 1975 the medical services branch of the Ontario Government sent a letter to all Indians who were known to have high levels of mercury in their blood advising them not to eat more fish than usual and preferably to eat smaller ones, as these contained less mercury. A month later, the same Indians received another letter, strongly advising them not to eat *any* fish; the previous advice was now 'out of date'.

The Ojibway Indians have been more than unfortunate in their encounters with industry. First, they were moved from their previous home to make way for a dam; now, having adapted to new occupations as fishermen, or as guides, cooks and attendants in the tourist complex, they found fishing banned or restricted and the tourists no longer keen to visit the mercury-poisoned waters. In the year that the Government declared the danger over, out of a population of about 1,000, 50 fishermen ceased work and 250 Indians in the tourist industry lost their jobs. Between 1970 and 1972 welfare payments almost doubled. Bored and idle, the men took to drink; in the same period, two at Grassy Meadows died of alcoholic poisoning. In March 1972 five Indians died and one was blinded after boosting their cheap liquor with antifreeze. Alcoholism complicated medical investigations and enabled the health authorities to claim that no one had actually died from mercury poisoning. Not even if the circumstances it produced drove one to drink! Finally, in 1977, the largest tour operator in the area not only shut down his camp after 25 years in business but opened a lawsuit against Reed International Ltd. and Reed Paper Ltd. of Toronto, demanding compensation for loss of the Indians' jobs as a result of the mercury discharges which had led to a ban on fishing and caused the rich tourists to shun the area.[55]

The Ojibways are not the only indigenous people to have suffered – or complained. Two years later, in May 1979, the Council of the Haudenosaunee or Six Nation Iroquois Confederacy, issued a 'Statement to the World' in which they lambasted Western industrialization for destroying the land. On the poisoning of inland waters and lakes they declared:

> Brothers and Sisters: Our ancient homeland is spotted today with an array of chemical dumps. Along the Niagara River dioxin, a particularly deadly substance, threatens the remaining life there and in the waters which flow from there . . .
> The fish of the Great Lakes are laced with mercury from industrial plants, and fluoride from aluminium plants poisons the land and the people. Sewage from population centers is mixed with PCBs and PBs in the watersheds of the Great Lakes and Finger Lakes, and the waters are virtually nowhere safe for any living creature.[56]

The Ojibways and the Haudenosaunee may not be coastal peoples, but the waters from which they suffered flow into the Great Lakes and thence to the sea. As always, the first victims of toxic technology are those already unfortunate.

Third World Waters

The Atlantic
Is the Atlantic in any better state where it washes the shores of Third World countries?

Of West Africa – the Atlantic coast from Senegal to Angola – GESAMP states only that 'industrial wastes are discharged into the sea, without treatment, from assorted manufacturing operations for such products as sugar, soap, beverages, textiles and wood pulp, and from extractive industries such as those for aluminium and iron'.[57] The 1982 UNEP survey of industrial pollutants gives estimated discharges of phenols, chromium, fluoride and cyanide. Of the 18 countries visited only the smaller and less industrialized – The Gambia, Guinea-Bissau, Equatorial Guinea and São Tomé & Principe – are exempt from the charge of poisoning the waters off their coasts. The greatest offenders are Senegal, Ivory Coast, Ghana, Togo, Nigeria, Cameroon and Gabon, making the Gulf of Guinea potentially the most polluted part of the region. Into these waters the Ivory Coast, Ghana, Togo and Cameroon discharge an estimated 3,915,668 kg per annum (kg/a) of fluoride, and, with the addition of Nigeria, 191,255 kg/a of phenols and 146,064 kg/a of chromium, for which Nigeria is responsible for 90% and 85% respectively. Nor is this all. Cameroon discharges 95,097 kg/a of lead and cadmium. These five countries have almost half – 31 out of 66 – of the industrial activities listed throughout the region as responsible for these forms of poisoning. Thirteen are concerned with the manufacture of textiles, seven with steel or aluminium, five with petroleum refining, and the remainder with fertilizer, asphalt, phosphates and plywood. Heading the list in terms of quantity of potential poisons is the Office Togolaise des Phosphates at Kpémé, Togo, which washes seven million tons of phosphate mineral annually and in the process discharges into the sea an estimated 2.3 million kg/a of fluoride and seven million kg/a of phosphorus. This is followed by Volta Aluminium at Tema, Ghana, which produces 187,440 tons of aluminium annually and discharges 1,250,225 kg/a of fluoride. Between them these two enterprises, in adjoining countries, are responsible for 90% of the fluoride entering the water throughout the entire region, a process which the local inhabitants can hardly view with equanimity when they learn that the adjoining waters at Lomé receive 9,000 kg/a of cyanide from steel production and steel rolling by the Société Nationale de Sidérurgie (SNS). For phenols and chromium in the Gulf of Guinea, Nigeria's National Oil Corporation's textile activities lead the way with 110,643 kg/a of phenols and the same quantity of chromium, though the latter figure is exceeded on an individual basis by the Bata company at Dakar, Senegal, which discharges 134,000 kg/a of chromium into the Atlantic waters from leather production.

Even if the UNEP estimates are challenged, the data show clearly that these polluting industries are almost all concentrated in a small area of the country, thus intensifying local dangers. All 15 enterprises in Senegal are in Dakar, all 11 in the Ivory Coast in Abidjan, those in Ghana in the Accra–Tema area except for one at Takaradi, and Nigerian production is confined to the east Atlantic coast. Obviously industry is sited where it can operate most conveniently; it is also sited where its discharges make the greatest local impact on the sea.[58]

No such details are available for the South American shores of the Atlantic. We know, however, that there is river pollution in north-east Brazil and Central America caused by discharging waste from sugar-cane alcohol production,[59] that there are chemical and petro-chemical factories, and iron and steel mills, in the industrial complex of Santos, Volta Redonda and São Paulo,[60] and that Argentina's steel and paper mills, chemical and food-processing factories, although sited inland, discharge highly toxic waste through the Río de la Plata, threatening the water supply of Buenos Aires, killing thousands of fish in the estuary and making bathing impossible. If industrialization, as GESAMP claims, 'is at a relatively early stage',[61] one hesitates to think what will happen as 'development' gets under way.

The Indian Ocean

Technological development on the shores of the Indian Ocean, with almost all countries at different stages of industrialization, foreshadow a bleak future for a large part of the Third World. Of the East African coast UNEP's experts bluntly report:

> Most of the factories often discharge their waste without treatment directly into estuaries, lagoons, bays or the sea. Some discharge their wastes into rivers which flow into coastal waters. The industrial policy is geared towards providing employment and satisfying domestic needs. Little attention seems to be given to the question of pollution.[62]

It is the old story – jobs before safety, profits before protection of the environment, a short-sighted policy that, in the name of 'development', of ostensibly benefiting the peoples of these countries, is prepared to sacrifice their future for immediate material gains.

Of East African countries and islands, only in Somalia, the Seychelles and the Comoros is there little industry. There are, however, other dangers. In Somalia effluent from slaughterhouses on the coast at Marka and Mogadishu is either discharged directly into the sea or leaches there from a large open pond. As a result sharks have appeared offshore where they were not found previously. At Mogadishu also solid waste is dumped on a large tip near the abattoir; the tip is uncontrolled, infested with vermin, and provides a potential source of poison through leaching, especially in the rainy season.

In the Seychelles two furniture factories in the Mont Retraite area have dumped sawdust in the bay, coating the sea-bed with a four-metre thick carpet of dust over an area 100 metres by 20 metres. Although biodegradable, the sawdust has a high demand for oxygen and life in the waters cannot be unaffected. The Seywood Factory also discharges about 20,000 litres of spent wood preservative liquor with high levels of copper and arsenic in it four times a year. These additions to the waters are supplemented by discharges of caustic soda from cleaning vats at the local brewery. Yet more disturbing was the discovery in 1981 of levels of mercury in twelve commercially important types of fish up to double the recommended limits; some local people had mercury in their blood close to the danger level. 'The source of these elevated concentrations has not been established', and, while the inhabitants are the largest fish-eaters in the region, 'no epidemiological studies have been undertaken to assess the public hazard'.[63]

The Comoros have similar problems with their saw mills and distillery. At Moroni it is apparently the practice to dump abandoned motor vehicles in the sea. This different type of 'heavy metal' may not be particularly toxic – the practice may even be justified, like similarly disposing of abandoned oil rigs, as providing artificial reefs for fish – but it is less appreciated by bathers and boatmen.

In Kenya, according to a 1977 Ministry of Local Government Report, industries are medium-scale and mainly agrarian so that discharging low volumes of untreated waste into the sea has not led to any 'significant pollution problems'.[64] Inevitably, the word 'significant' arouses suspicions. What actually happens? From Nairobi and the industrial sector of Kiambu, wastes from slaughterhouses, cement factories, tanneries and coffee factories drain into the Athi River and eventually reach the Indian Ocean to join other wastes from Mombasa and Kisumu; these come from dairy processing plants, fertilizer factories and tanneries which discharge large quantities of chrome salts and solids, thus increasing the BOD. Mining and smelting operations produce cyanide; coffee and sisal plants, and pulp and paper mills, produce lots of organic waste, while the use of zinc to coat iron sheets for roofing leads to heavy metal poisoning. In agriculture 25,000 tonnes of mercury compounds are used each year as seed dressing; the use of pesticides increased tenfold between 1966 and 1982 with the Athi River again collecting run-off from Kiambu; DDT is used extensively in aerial spraying of cotton fields around Margarini in Malindi and for disinfecting harbours. 'Organo-mercuric fungicides which have been banned in the developed countries due to mercury toxicity are currently [1982] in use, though in limited quantities.'[65] Finally, there is no control on leaching from either of the two solid waste tips in Mombasa – an uncontrolled landfill at Makupa Creek used for dumping hazardous wastes, expired medicines from hospitals, old toxic chemicals and animal corpses, and a second, also at Makupa, for solid wastes from foreign ships, including unclaimed cargo containing toxic chemicals. Perhaps these data will allow us to form our own definition of 'significant pollution' in interpreting the Kenya Government's assessment.

Tanzania is rightly regarded as mainly an agricultural country. Seventy to eighty per cent of its small industries are in and around Dar es Salaam, where the waste waters from some 30 factories – textiles, abattoirs, breweries and chemical plants – are discharged untreated into rivers, creeks and bays of the sea. Tanzanian distilleries discharge about 36,000 litres a day of spent molasses into Dar es Salaam harbour, thereby increasing the oxygen demand. The Msimbazi River, whose unsavoury qualities were noted in discussing sewage, receives waste from chemical works manufacturing pesticides such as DDT and from a bicycle factory using cyanide and chromium. A local rubbish tip on the banks of the Luhanga River, which flows into the Msimbazi, receives all types of waste, including hazardous substances; seepage and leaching, especially in the wet season, ensure that Luhanga–Msimbazi acquire a variety of poisons adequate enough to guarantee some form of synergism. Products containing DDT and dieldrin are used in aerial spraying to control tsetse fly.

In Mozambique effluent from cotton and textile factories drains directly into Lourenço Marques Bay at Maputo; high levels of iron, copper, lead and nickel from loading methods used in the harbour, though generally short-lived in their effects, are a potential danger to bivalves and shrimps; the Matola River, which flows into the Bay, receives untreated effluent from food-processing factories; and emissions from a cement factory near Matola harbour may be responsible both for air pollution and subsequent arrival of poison-bearing particles in the sea. Like other countries of the region, Mozambique continues to use products containing DDT and dieldrin for aerial spraying of tsetse fly, alongside other 'ecologically unsafe' herbicides, including one containing dioxin.

Madagascar resembles Kenya in that effluent from sisal and sugar-cane industries, tanneries, plastics and textile factories, and paper mills are all potential sources of pollution, which could affect shrimp fisheries on the west and south coasts. The sugar-cane industry uses about 20,000 tonnes annually of some 50 types of pesticide, including DDT, HCH and phosphoric and sulphuric compounds, while DDT and endrin are used for spraying houses.

Mauritius is exposed to danger from its 21 sugar-cane processing factories, which discharge untreated mixtures of cane fibres, ash, soot and molasses into rivers and the sea, causing considerable oxygen deficiency and killing fish. The Monloisir sugar estate has grossly polluted the estuary of the River Rempart. Every day the Solitude Distillery discharged 200 cubic metres of waste water, high in organic matter, into the River Citron, which in turn feeds a prawn and fish pond. Life in the river has disappeared and the pond itself is affected. Large quantities of pesticides – 1,160 tonnes in 1977 – are used in the sugar industry and for 'protecting' food crops, including chlorinated and other pesticides prohibited elsewhere. Unique to Mauritius is its thermal power station, waste oil from which passes to the St Louis River, where there is danger that it may be accompanied by PCBs used for electric capacitors and transformers.

Compared with major Western centres of heavy industry, the sugar and sisal factories of East Africa, its slaughterhouses, distilleries, saw mills and food-processing plants are both smaller and more limited in their effect – but so are the restrictions on them. The most disturbing factors in the limited data available are the lack of concern for the consequences of allowing untreated effluent to pass into rivers and estuaries or leach from uncontrolled tips of dangerous solid waste, and the continued use of pesticides that are known to be harmful and, in consequence, banned elsewhere. For this the ultimate blame lies with the manufacturers and suppliers, who are prepared to foist upon Third World countries those poisons for which the home market is now closed.

Across the Indian Ocean lie the growing industrial conurbations of Karachi and Bombay.[66] More than half the industry of Pakistan is situated around Karachi, where 800 different industries – food, metal, non-metal, paper and pulp, rubber, tobacco, petroleum and chemical products – are responsible for over 80% of the effluent discharged. Factories release untreated mercury, lead compounds, chlorine, and hydrochloric acid into the rivers to join the sewage already there. From Bombay's 100 industries about 75 million cubic metres of industrial effluent is discharged every day, through creeks into the Kalu River and so to the sea. Monitoring of seaweed along the coast of Goa reveals concentrations of nickel, lead, cobalt, copper, tin, manganese and zinc; the last four occur also in waters of the Cochin backwater. In the sea at this point relatively high levels of mercury, attributable to natural causes, occur in the muscles of sharks, while zinc, copper and iron are found in oysters. The Chaliyar Estuary in Kerala to the south is poisoned by effluent from the Gwalior Rayons factory at Mavoor; the 54.8 million litres of effluents discharged into the river contain both organic and inorganic matter, together with zinc, so that fish have died from lack of oxygen.

On the eastern side, discharges from a caustic soda plant into the Pinnakayal Channel, Tamil Nadu, have destroyed fish and left large quantities of chlorine in the water. The Bay of Bengal is even more polluted with mercury than are western waters (apart from Bombay and Cochin). The Hooghly Estuary in particular suffers from discharges of effluent, 80% of it untreated, from paper and pulp mills using jute and salar grass as raw materials. Prominent in this waste is lignin, which is fatal to fish, so that there are stretches of the estuary where few fish are found. Part-way between the Hooghly and Madras to the south, Vishakhapatnam harbour receives industrial effluent from fertilizer factories, which in the mid-1970s were allegedly responsible for more than one mass slaughter of fish by discharges containing ammonia, fluorides, phenols and heavy metals. In Sri Lanka high levels of copper have been found in industrial effluent in Colombo – this directly affects drinking water – while discharges from paper and flour mills, and ilmenite mines, flow directly into coastal waters. The use of modern technology in agriculture, though restricted mainly to fertilizers and pesticides, which are also applied to 'protect' human health, reflects the East African experience. 'Remarkably high concentrations of DDT and hydrocarbons were found in air and water samples off the western coast of India, indicating their heavy use in tropical countries of the region both in antimalarial programmes and in order to sustain food supplies.'[67]

The Citizens' Reports for 1982 and 1984–5 from the New Delhi Centre for Science and Environment corroborate this disturbing outline. On the use of pesticides, which increased 20 times between 1960 and 1980 and by 1989–90 is expected to average 120,000 tonnes a year, they comment:

> In terms of tonnage, at least 70 per cent of all pesticides consumed on Indian farms are banned or severely restricted in Western countries and identified by the WHO as excessively toxic or hazardous . . . Current annual consumption of DDT is 3,500 tonnes in agriculture used over an area exceeding 2.5 million hectares and 4,000 tonnes in public health . . .[68]
>
> Another dangerous substance is BHC, two and a half times as toxic as DDT, banned in European Economic Community (EEC) countries, suspended and cancelled in the US, and also a suspected carcinogen, but which covers eight per cent of the country's net sown area; estimated consumption in 1982: 33,000 tonnes. Methyl parathion, 20 times more toxic than DDT, is also banned in the West, but 3,000 tonnes is consumed every year in India, over 12 million hectares, the highest coverage for any pesticide. Heptachlor, three times more toxic than DDT, banned in the US and withdrawn from the UK, is still consumed in India . . . Herbicide

2,4–D is a basic ingredient of 'Agent Orange', the defoliant used with brutal effect in Vietnam. India has an installed manufacturing capacity of 1,135 tonnes for this herbicide, and an annual coverage of 3.33 lakh [100,000] hectares.[69]

The 14,000 tonnes of DDT produced in India annually generate 28,000 tonnes of sludge which, even after treatment, still contains nearly 14 tonnes of DDT. 'This sludge is usually dumped on low lying areas and the leachate pollutes both ground and surface water.'[70] In 1980 11 major phosphatic fertilizer plants produced some 3.5 million tonnes of the by-product phospho-gypsum (BPG), four fifths of which,

> containing thousands of tonnes of heavy metals and toxic substances such as cadmium, chromium, copper, lead, manganese and fluorides, was used for land filling or dumped into lagoons in the form of slurry. The available land for disposal is nearly exhausted, . . .the lagoons are overflowing into surface waters like streams and ponds and toxic substances are leaching from dump sites into groundwater.[71]

The reports contain numerous examples of poisonous substances deposited by industry in inland and coastal rivers and in estuaries. The authors quote from a university study of the 256-km stretch of the Ganga between Barauni and Farakka, which identifies the point of 'maximum pollution' as near Makamah Bridge. Here 'effluents from the Bata Shoe Factory, the McDowell Distillery, the Oil Refinery, the Thermal Power Station and the Fertilizer Factory are discharged into the river'. The Bata Shoe Factory and the distillery discharge 250,000 litres of unprocessed waste daily, waste so toxic that fish placed in the mixing zone of effluents from the Bata factory died within 48 hours, those in effluents from the distillery within five hours.[72]

In Orissa, on the east coast, the small coastal river, the Rushikulya, is deprived of fish as the result of discharges of chemical wastes from Jayshree Chemicals Limited (JCL), which manufactures caustic soda. The amount of fish caught by fishermen – 200 kg a day in 1967 – is now reduced to five kilograms a day. In Kerala to the south, the Periyar receives 170 million litres of effluent containing suspended solids, metals, urea, ammonia, fluorides, chlorides and other chemicals from factories on its lower banks which produce fertilizers, chemicals, metallurgical objects and rayon.[73]

If the report on accident rates at chemical plants in the USA is disturbing, information on conditions in India is far worse. Fears of a second Bhopal spurred some state governments to action. The West Bengal Pollution Control Board surveyed 55 hazardous industries in Calcutta and 26 elsewhere. These included leading companies such as Chloride India, Bata India, Kesoram Rayon, Bengal Chemicals, Titagarth Paper Mills, Reckitt and Colman, Calcutta Chemicals, Shalimar Paints, Guest Keen William, Hindustan Motors, Standard Pharmaceuticals, Wimco, Bengal Distilleries and East India Paper. The Board reported that 'All these companies were found releasing hazardous effluent into rivers and sewers. At Chloride India's Shyamnagar plant, for instance, the lead in effluents was 0.4 ppm as compared to the Board's stipulation of 0.1 ppm. Bata India's effluents contained chrome and Kesoram Rayon's zinc.'[74]

In Bombay the Environmental Safety Committee set up by the state Pollution Control Board found that 'almost every factory it inspected was deficient in safety measures', yet, with one exception, all were consistently making profits and not short of funds. At the Calico Chemicals plant at Chembur, which handles inflammable materials and highly carcinogenic substances such as vinyl chloride, the Committee found that the valves, pipelines and storage vessels of the chlorine and caustic soda plant were so corroded that they considered the plant unsafe to operate. The Bombay Soap Factory had no effluent treatment plant, although it was in a densely populated area; the BOD, COD and chlorine levels in the effluent were very high compared to the set standard; there was no separate fire-fighting group; and the highly dangerous chemical, hexane, was stored in large quantities even when the plant was not operating. The Committee recommended an immediate move to a more suitable site. India Explosives Ltd., manufacturing dyes and chemicals, was criticized for not monitoring emissions and for not having a proper effluent treatment plant. There was no round-the-clock fire-fighting group and butanol was stored in a highly dangerous way near the cyanide handling unit. The Committee concluded that it was not safe to continue operating the plant. Among other criticisms of the Excel Industries Ltd. plant at Iogeshwari, manufacturing industrial and agricultural chemicals, was that the quantity of mercury released in the effluent exceeded the required standard, while Burroughs Wellcome, manufacturing medicines, was found storing highly dangerous and inflammable substances, including hydrogen, phosgene and sulphur dioxide, many of them in the open and close to each other. The Hindustan Ciba Geigy plant, making dyes and chemicals, did not monitor emissions and there was no system for measuring the temperature of chloroform in the storage tank, which needed to be relocated away from a railway line.

If this is the situation among reputable industries in 'advanced' Bombay, we can imagine what happens where the authorities are less vigilant. So far investigators have concentrated – rightly– on the more immediate dangers to human beings working in the factories or living nearby. But the waters off Bombay are already highly poisoned, and, without action now, it will not be long before some accident increases that poisoning to a point at which it will be impossible not to label it 'significant'. Even if the chances of a major accident are reduced, insidious poisoning by effluents containing hazardous chemicals and heavy metals still goes on.

'Modernization' has brought inevitable developments further east in Malaysia. In his 1982 paper to an Environmental Protection Society of Malaysia seminar, Dr Leong Yueh Kwong points out that, while the effects of persistent organochlorine pesticides have not been documented, we can reasonably assume that increasing use of pesticides means that part of these chemicals will eventually reach the sea. Fresh waters are already affected and fish have been killed in paddy-fields, while poisoning of estuarial waters by heavy metals from the Peral Industrial Estate, although 'local' in its effects, has reduced the income from fishing by two thirds in the village of Kuala Juru. Levels of cadmium and chromium were above recommended limits, those of nickel, lead and mercury considered high. The paper concludes that 'industrial pollution will be an increasing problem with the increased tempo of industrial development and that the fishes caught in some industrial areas, such as Kuala Juru, Tikam Batu (in Kedah) or Kamunting (in Perak) may one day be unfit for human consumption, if industrial pollution is not checked'.[75]

The Pacific

Lack of data prevents a full assessment of the Pacific. Of the South American coast GESAMP reports only that 'many towns and industries discharge directly into the ocean or to rivers', that Ite Bay in Peru is polluted by mining waste and Chimbote Bay by organic pollution from fishing plants; Chile also discharges mining wastes.[76] Unfortunately, there is no information on their effects. Australia has 'localized pollution' near major industrialized cities, such as in the Derwent Estuary, Tasmania, or Corio Bay and Hobsons Bay, Victoria. With inside knowledge rather than available data GESAMP adds that 'Botany Bay and the Parramatta River estuary at Sydney, NSW, are not listed, more due to lack of reported measurements than to their cleanliness. This must be true of a number of other locations around the coast of Australia'.[77] New Zealand, while lacking 'major industrial discharges containing metals' and having no metal ore mines in operation, is responsible for arsenic in the water from geothermal developments, while aluminium smelters, one in operation in the North Island, one planned for the South, produce fluorides that are discharged both into the air and as liquid effluent.[78]

Ironically, thanks to the work of local scientists and of UNEP, we know more of those one-time last outposts of innocence, the islands of the South Pacific, which have not escaped the effects of toxic technology. The impetus came from within – to use their hidden mineral wealth to finance 'development', including the laudable aims of protecting crops and people from diseases and pests; the means came from without – the deadly pesticides and herbicides of the West and the mechanical means of acquiring minerals. Today countries in the Pacific are threatened by these innovations whose long-term capacity for destruction they must weigh against immediate economic benefit.

Like Africa and India, the Pacific Islands have been caught up in the great pesticide boom. In the past ten years the number of pesticides available has risen from 162 to 589 – and this excludes household 'bug-killers'. In Papua New Guinea alone, the number, in terms of active ingredients, rose from 65 to 226. How much is actually used is difficult to assess as there are few reliable data. We know, however, that Papua New Guinea and Fiji use the most. In 1981 Fiji imported 500 tonnes of pesticides, in 1982 Papua New Guinea about 300 tonnes of active ingredients, the equivalent of 930 tonnes of pesticide. In 1982–3 even little Tonga received 20 tonnes, a third of it in relief aid after a hurricane.[79]

As in Africa and India also, the most disturbing feature is that many of these pesticides are prohibited in their countries of manufacture: 'Of 589 compounds available in the South Pacific, 34 are classified as "extremely hazardous" by WHO; another 52 are "highly hazardous"; 16 are "banned, withdrawn, not approved" in the USA; 24 are "severely restricted" in the USA; 57 are for "restricted use" in the USA; and 55 are banned, withdrawn or not approved elsewhere in the world.'[80] Yet the makers are prepared to let these loose on peoples lacking both experience in their use and specialists to guide them.

In 1982 Papua New Guinea used pesticides that included, in terms of active ingredients, more than 50,000 kg of paraquat, over 40,000 kg of DDT and more than 5,000 kg of 2,4–D, MSMA and malathion; in 1982–3 Tonga used more than 2,000 kg of manoozeb, 1,000 kg of malathion and over 800 kg of paraquat. Not surprisingly, there have been poisonings and even deaths – in Western Samoa, Fiji and Papua New Guinea, mainly from paraquat. Some were accidental – from storing paraquat in unlabelled drinking containers; others reportedly deliberate – if mercury in their rivers drove Ojibway Indians to drink, pesticides in the local store provide South Pacific islanders with a new way to suicide. More insidiously, low levels of aldrin, dieldrin, DDT and HCH (among others) have been found in the breast milk of women in Papua New Guinea. As for the waters around these islands, 'since very little is known about the fate of pesticides in small island ecosystems, there are doubtless other effects on the fauna and flora of the region about which we are completely unaware'.[81] Once again poisons are released into the environment which we know must affect the sea, but of both immediate and ultimate consequences of that release we are ignorant.

The second great danger, which effects the island paradise of Papua New Guinea, is from mining.[82] In 1971 Bougainville Copper Limited (BCL) began extracting copper at Panguna in the eastern province of the North Solomons. In 12 years the mine produced 600,000 tonnes of waste, a third of which was stored on land, and two-thirds dumped in the Jaba River under the impression that it would be carried out to sea. No one assessed the environmental implications of the project. The wastes have collected on sediments that extend six kilometres into Empress Augusta Bay. They contain not only unextracted copper, now in solution, but also quantities of zinc, chromium, lead, cadmium, arsenic and smaller amounts of mercury. 'The fate of these is unknown and has been ignored.'[83] The river and its mouth no longer contain any life.

Estimates for a proposed gold mine at Wau in Morobe Province reveal that during nine years of operation, it will discharge as waste 281,000 tonnes of copper, 2,700 tonnes of lead, 14,000 tonnes of zinc, 162,000 tonnes of iron, 2,000 tonnes of arsenic, 38,000 kg of cadmium and 4,700 kg of mercury. Independent experts maintain that, downriver from the mine, there exists 'such a variety of environmental conditions that the metallic compounds may be deposited as banded sediments and consequently re-dissolved'.[84] Non-experts are not heartened to learn further that mining companies use cyanide extensively in extracting and purifying gold and that there have already been accidents – 2,700 sixty-litre drums of sodium cyanide lost at the mouth of the

Fly River in western Papua New Guinea when a carrying barge capsized, and only 138 recovered. On another occasion about 1,080 cu metres, containing 300 mg/l of free cyanide, were released into the OK Tedi River, producing estimated levels of 200–500 µg/l and destroying hundreds of fish and prawns.[85]

These incidents arose from operations of Papua New Guinea's most controversial plant, OK Tedi Mining Limited in Western Province, close to the Irian Jaya border. Since May 1984 the company has extracted gold on the OK Tedi River, which flows into the large Fly River running eventually into a delta on the Gulf of Papua where there are major breeding grounds for baramundi, other commercial fish, and crustacea. To protect the environment, the PNG Government required OK Tedi to submit a detailed study of the impact of mining, as the result of which the company was instructed to build a tailings dam. The theory was that any cyanides remaining after passing through a cyanide destruction tower would be retained by the dam and break down. Particles containing heavy metals were also expected to settle in the dam.

Unfortunately, in January 1984, one of PNG's numerous earthquakes caused a landslide that destroyed the site of the dam. As an interim measure the Government allowed OK Tedi to treat tailings with hydrogen peroxide – to lower the concentrations of cyanide – and dump them into a nearby valley, while finer tailings were discharged into the Fly River system under strict monitoring. The plan might have worked but for the unexpected discovery of a large amount of copper in the mine, which led to an increased use of cyanide and hydrogen peroxide and consequent increase in the quantities of heavy metals and cyanides released in the finer tailings. Monitoring showed high levels of heavy metals, and levels of cyanide up to 50 µg/l as far as 80 km downstream. 'What effect these levels have on aquatic life is not easy to predict. Nor is it known how far the effects reach down the river. Recently, however, Australian scientists have expressed a concern that the Great Barrier Reef could be polluted.'[86]

On 1 February 1985, unhappy with the company's record and uncertain of its intentions, the PNG Government ordered OK Tedi to stop operations. Seven weeks later, after the company had reaffirmed its intention to build a permanent tailings dam and the Government conceded that the dam need not be built until January 1990, the mine was allowed to reopen. Increased gold production led to an even greater discharge of 'finer tailings' into the river system. Even if the dam is eventually constructed, it is impossible to predict what will happen. Torrential rains in the area are almost certain to cause considerable leaching and one prefers not to think of the consequences of another earth tremor when the dam is working to full capacity.

Meanwhile, in September 1986, it was reported that Bougainville Copper Limited had recently introduced a more efficient method of blasting which required large quantities of nitric acid. The Bermuda-based firm, Sea Containers, has organized a fleet of 18 nitric acid tanks that will be rotated monthly on a BCL ship between Sydney, Australia, and Panguna. Some of the tanks will be used for storage on the island. Sea Containers have a high reputation and the tanks are specially designed for carrying high-strength nitric acid.[87] The Pacific at this point is one of the world's most beautiful oceans, dotted with small coral atolls that delight the traveller who sights them through the translucent waters while flying from Port Moresby to Brisbane. All one can do is . . . keep one's fingers crossed – and hope!

Pesticides and mining are not the only dangers that threaten the Pacific. There is yet a third and possibly greater – radioactivity. But that affects other places also, and requires a chapter to itself.

References

1. ACOPS 1983 pp. 6–7
2. ACOPS 1984 pp. 1–2
3. *New Scientist* 16 October p. 19; *Guardian* 5 December 1986
4. *Lloyd's List* 30 September 1985, 2, 5, 8 and 17 October 1985
5. *The Times* 14 October 1976
6. Ibid. 6 November 1976
7. Account based on Moorcraft 1972 pp. 71–81; GESAMP 15 pp. 42–4
8. *Chemical Economics Handbook* cited Moorcraft 1972 p. 72
9. GESAMP 15 p. 43
10. Ibid.
11. Ibid. p. 44
12. Ibid.
13. Sources for PCBs: Moorcraft 1972 pp. 82–5; GESAMP 15 pp. 41–2
14. GESAMP 15 p. 41
15. Ibid. p. 42
16. *Observer* 16 September 1984; *ENDS* No. 142 November 1986 p. 6
17. Sources: GESAMP 15 pp. 26–35, 49–51; Moorcraft 1972 pp. 89–94
18. GESAMP 15 p. 51
19. Ibid.
20. *Guardian* 13 August 1985
21. GESAMP 15 pp. 31, 35; Moorcraft 1972 pp. 92–3
22. *ENDS* No. 142 November 1986 pp. 23–4
23. *North Sea Monitor* 84.4 pp. 10–11; 85.1 p. 7; 85.2 pp. 4–5
24. ACOPS 1984 pp. 5, 7; *Guardian* 31 October 1984, 19, 20 November 1984
25. KBTG 1985
26. ACOPS 1985–6 p. 9
27. *Observer* 16 February 1986
28. ACOPS 1984 p. 66; 1985–6 p. 97
29. *Guardian* 14 November 1986
30. *Lloyd's List* 6, 7, 8, 9 August 1986
31. *TAO* p. 172
32. Moorcraft 1972 p. 95; *Observer* 8 March 1987
33. *New York Times* 4 October 1985
34. *Guardian* 21 August 1984
35. *Lloyd's List* 3 July 1986

36. *Guardian* 14 February 1986
37. Ibid. 17 April 1986
38. Ibid. 18 June 1986
39. Tucker. A. 1984a
40. *Guardian* 27 August 1984
41. Ibid. 8 July 1986
42. Ibid. 21 November 1986
43. *TAO* p. 174; Action Conference 1984 pp. 4, 8
44. GESAMP 15 p. 74
45. *TAO* p. 174
46. Action Conference 1984 p. 4
47. Ibid. p. 5
48. *Guardian* 6 October 1986
49. *TAO* p. 175
50. *RSRS 32* p. 21
51. *TAO* p. 176
52. *RSRS 32* p. 21
53. GESAMP 15 p. 75
54. Ibid. pp. 78–9
55. Pringle 1977
56. *Akwesasne Notes.* Spring 1979
57. GESAMP 15 p. 76
58. *RSRS 2* Annex III Tables 1–18
59. *TAO* p. 172
60. GESAMP 15 p. 80
61. Ibid.; *TAO* p. 172
62. *RSRS 8* p. 15; Data for East Africa from Pathmarajah and Meith 1985 pp. 174–6, 178, 207–8; *RSRS 8* pp. 14–20, 25–8, 36–8; *RSRS 13* pp. 69–71, 123–8
63. *RSRS 8* p. 38
64. Cited *RSRS 8* p. 19
65. *RSRS 8* p. 28
66. General data on India and Pakistan from Pathmarajah and Meith 1985 pp. 181–5, 187; GESAMP 15 pp. 82–3; *RSRS 13* pp. 72–87, 128–32
67. Pathmarajah and Meith 1985 p. 187
68. Agarwal et al. 1985 p. 201
69. Ibid.
70. Ibid. p. 199
71. Ibid.
72. Agarwal et al. 1982 p. 24
73. Ibid. p. 22
74. Agarwal et al. 1985 p. 229
75. Leong 1982 p. 69
76. GESAMP 15 p. 81
77. Ibid. p. 84
78. Ibid. p. 85
79. Data on pesticides from Mowbray 1985 pp. 13–19
80. Ibid. p. 16
81. Ibid. p. 14
82. Data on mining from Hewitt, Flores and Pohei 1985, and Mowbray 1986
83. Hewitt et al. 1985 p. 41

84. Ibid.
85. Mowbray 1986 p. 13
86. Ibid.
87. *Lloyd's List* 2 September 1986

6. The Future in Danger – Radioactivity

Radiation and Other Mysteries

When, in July 1984, Sir Douglas Black, commissioned to investigate the relationship between discharges from the Sellafield (formerly Windscale) nuclear plant and the incidence of leukaemia in the area, reached a verdict of 'Not proven', the nuclear industry welcomed his findings and the British Government accepted them with a speed unique in the history of official reports. Nineteen months later the Health Minister, Barney Hayhoe, revealed that the figure of 400 grammes of uranium discharged into the atmosphere in the early 1950s, provided by British Nuclear Fuels Ltd. (BNFL) and given to Sir Douglas by the National Radiological Protection Board (NRPB), was incorrect; it should have been 20 kilogrammes.

The new data did not affect the report's conclusions. Those who had accepted them continued to do so; those who were sceptical had their scepticism confirmed. Attitudes to the mysteries of radiation are not changed overnight, even when the figure turns out to be fifty times greater than that actually used. Preferring common sense to science, environmentalists were not impressed by Sir Douglas's remark to the British Association on the relationship between Sellafield and childhood cancers that 'Common sense dictates that there should be a connection, but common sense is not science.'[1]

This was not the first, or last, example of incorrect or misleading information. In June 1985 Members of the Advisory Committee on the Safety of Nuclear Installations were reportedly disturbed by ministerial assurances given to the British Parliament that safety checks on nine 20-year-old Magnox reactors working beyond their expected life span were being carried out. While the checks were doubtless taking place, their own information was that, owing to staff shortages in the Nuclear Installations Inspectorate (NII), they would not be completed for a further five years.[2]

The following month the Ministry of Defence admitted to Alec Falconer, a former worker on Polaris submarine refits at Rosyth, Scotland, now a Euro-MP, that the radiation transfer record sent to him on leaving employment did not include details of the overdose he received in 1971. His inquiry had revealed 'a number of similar omissions' which were being 'rectified'.[3] And at the end of 1986, in promoting its new image of a cleaned-up, high technology industry,

BNFL were caught out, if not lying, at least being economical with the truth. The British Advertising Standards Authority upheld a complaint against BNFL for describing Calder Hall, Sellafield, as 'the world's first commercial nuclear power station', while failing to mention that it also produced plutonium for nuclear weapons. In fact, as stated in the official history of the Atomic Energy Authority (AEA), it was set up primarily for that purpose.[4]

It is the cumulative impact of minor incidents such as these, as much as major accidents – the 1957 Windscale fire, Three Mile Island, the 1983 Sellafield discharges – that produces an atmosphere in which, on one side, secrecy, contradiction and obfuscation combine with arrogance, contempt and ineptitude to arouse on the other suspicion, scepticism or cynical distrust of everything nuclear. When Chernobyl polluted the world's atmosphere, Western governments accused the Russians of failing to 'come clean'. The truth is that nowhere does the nuclear industry 'come clean' unless it is forced to do so. In discussing radioactive poisoning of the sea, we must be prepared for new revelations that will outdate anything written here; judging from the past such revelations will not be for the better.

We can at least begin with the facts about radioactivity which (at present) are not in dispute. Everyone now knows that the atom consists of a nucleus surrounded by negative particles, electrons, and that within the nucleus there are positively charged protons, and neutrons with no charge.[5] The number of protons – the atomic number – is fixed for a particular element, but the same element may have different numbers of neutrons. As the atomic number increases, i.e. the more protons there are, the number of neutrons exceeds that of protons to such an extent that the nuclei become unstable and disintegrate in an attempt to achieve stability. The process, known as 'radioactive decay', leads to emission of 'ionizing radiation'.

This appears in three forms: alpha particles, given off, for example, by plutonium, are emitted at high speed, do not travel far, cannot penetrate the skin and can be stopped by a piece of paper. If, however, they are emitted *inside* a human body, e.g. from plutonium in the bone, they are extremely harmful and rated 20 times more hazardous than X-rays.

Beta particles are high energy, electrically charged negative particles, much smaller and lighter than alpha; they travel faster, can pass through human skin and penetrate the body, but can be stopped by a fairly thin sheet of lead or aluminium. Incorporated into tissues, they deposit their energy over a small volume and are rated as dangerous as X-rays. They are emitted by radionuclides such as iodine–131, the presence of which in milk aroused concern in many European countries after Chernobyl, and by krypton–85, which forms part of the emission from nuclear power plants.

Gamma rays are similar to radio waves or visible light, but have a much shorter wavelength. They are of very high energy, travel very fast and are extremely powerful and penetrating so that they can pass right through the body and be stopped only by thick sheets of lead, many feet of concrete, or water. Caesium–137 and 134 emit gamma rays.

All forms of radiation are 'potentially dangerous to living matter',[6] even that emitted by the tube of a television set or when a patient has an X-ray in hospital. How readily we accept radiation risks without probably even being aware of them is shown by a report of the United Nations Scientific Committee on the Effects of Atomic Radiation, which revealed that, in 1982, 800,000 old luminous wristwatches containing radioactive radium were still in use in the United Kingdom.[7]

The obvious common sense questions are – why, if all radiation is dangerous, produce it? At what point does it become *undesirably* harmful? And, once it is released into the environment, how long will it last?

The short answer to the first question is that there are two sources of radioactivity, humanity and nature, and that, while we can control what humanity does, we have no similar power over nature. 'Radioactive uranium and thorium are found in the earth; some radiation comes from cosmic rays in space; and some radioactive gases are produced in the atmosphere by the sun. Even the sea is naturally radioactive and contains alpha, beta and gamma emitters.'[8] Recently scientists have begun to investigate a colourless, odourless and tasteless gas, radon, seven and a half times heavier than air, which originates from the decay of uranium in the earth's crust and finds it way into houses, most frequently into those built on fissured granite through which the gas escapes. They now estimate that up to five million houses in the USA may be dangerous; a sitting room in Cornwall, England, contained concentrations of radioactivity 4,000 times the level in the air outside, and the health centre of Chagford village, Devon, on the edge of Dartmoor National Park, contains what it claimed to be Britain's most radioactive loo![9]

The Holliday report maintains that 'about 87% of the radiation to which the population of the UK is exposed comes from natural sources . . . the remaining 13% is man-made resulting from the treatment of cancer and medical diagnosis (11.4%); fallout from atmospheric weapon testing in the 1950s and 1960s (0.5%) and routine power plant operations and uses in scientific research, defence and industry (1.1%)'.[10] The figures are reassuring to the inhabitants of the British Isles and to the nuclear industry. If 87% of the radiation received is unavoidable, because natural, what difference will be made by an additional one per cent from industry? The answer is: probably very little – if this were all we have to consider and if we were concerned only with 'global issues'. Frequent comparisons to 'background radiation' tend to obscure the fact that natural radiation has already been supplemented by fallout from atmospheric testing of nuclear weapons and from nuclear-powered satellites (see below). The figure of 0.5% for weapon testing may not be statistically impressive, but common sense suggests that the addition was sufficiently alarming to governments to jolt them into agreeing to ban such tests.

Nor is the figure of 11.4% for those admirable activities, cancer treatment and medical diagnosis, quite so admirable when translated into practical terms. Comparative research led to the surprising discovery that levels of radioactive iodine–125 were as high in the thyroids of both animals and human beings in the 'safe' area of Weybridge, Surrey, England, as in the neighbourhood of 'contaminated' Sellafield. Further discovery that the isotope occurred in local drinking water, supplied from the River Thames, and its presence in swans living on the river, led to the conclusion that it could have come only from research establishments and hospitals which flushed contaminated material into sewers. As the choice of Weybridge for investigation was purely fortuitous,[11] research elsewhere might have found a safe area – or worse. The point is that, until such research is carried out, an unlikely prospect on a wide scale, we are entering an area where, however reassuring the percentages, the Douglas Black syndrome is always with us. The only certainty is that we do not know.

In considering how long radiation decay will take before the nucleus reaches stability, we are on more certain, if disconcerting, ground. Scientists tell us that the rate of decay is proportional to the number of atoms, and express the time required as the 'half-life' of the element, a concept which again reveals that science is not common sense. While in normal linguistic usage a 'half-life' would be that period which, if doubled, would give us the 'whole-life' (causing one to ask further why we could not be given this figure in the first place), scientists use the term for the period over which *half the material* will have decayed. The process, moreover, is continuous; we cannot expect the remaining half to have decayed over a similar, succeeding period, only *half* of it. A gramme of radium–126, for example, with a half-life of 1,600 years, will have decayed to half a gramme at the end of that time, to a quarter of a gramme after 3,200 years and to an eighth of a gramme after 4,800 years. Additional information that 'the radium will be decaying to its "daughter products" . . . many of which are also radioactive',[12] means in effect that though radiation from the original source may be reduced, we shall never be rid of it completely. Nor need the results of deterioration be desirable. Thorium–234 has a half-life of 24.1 days, i.e. after 24.1 days 12 grammes will have become six, and so on; but thorium–234 decays, through a short, intermediate stage, to uranium–234, which has a half-life of 250,000 years! As the stock of thorium decreases, that of uranium will actually be increasing.[13] Not surprisingly, the non-scientist is baffled, if not awed, by mysterious phenomena in which the more you take away, the more remains.

To discover at what level radioactivity becomes undesirably harmful, we must know how scientists measure radiation. At this point the non-specialist tends to give up, especially as, under the recently adopted Système Internationale (SI), the terminology has been changed.

We need to know three types of measurement: first, the activity of the disintegrating element. This is measured by the *becquerel* (Bq) (familiarly known as 'buggerall') which is one disintegration per second. Secondly, there is the quantity of radiation *absorbed*; this is measured in terms of the *gray*, which is equivalent to one joule per kilogramme of tissue (the joule being the standard unit for measuring energy). Thirdly, there is the *effective* radiation dose; this differs from the quantity absorbed by taking into account the way in which radionuclides behave in the body, in which organs they tend to concentrate, how long they remain if undisturbed, and how much the body can get rid of. As the 'effectiveness' varies with the form of radiation (see p. 173), the unit of the *sievert* (Sv) is obtained by multiplying the dose in grays by a quality factor of one for beta particles and gamma rays, ten for neutrons and 20 for alpha particles. Radioactivity in milk, water and other foods is often given as so many becquerels per litre, and the same unit is used for measuring discharges of radioactive effluent to the sea. The effective dose to human beings is usually given in *milliSieverts* (mSv), i.e. thousandths of a sievert, as a 'radiation limit' for workers in the nuclear industry or the general public.

Under the previous system the activity of the disintegrating element was measured by the *curie* (Cu/Ci) which equalled 37 thousand million disintegrations per second, the absorbed quantity of radiation by the *rad* (one hundredth of the present gray) and the effective dose by the *rem* (one hundredth of the present sievert).

The existence of two systems enables those in authority to bamboozle the public – in the interests of science and mathematical accuracy – by playing the Fun-with-Figures game and by making non-common-sense semantic distinctions. The figures of discharge limits for nuclear plants in the UK, for example,[14] show that the Sellafield sea pipeline is allowed an annual discharge of 200,000 Ci of beta activity, 600 Ci of alpha, 40,000 Ci of ruthenium–106 and 20,000 Ci of strontium–90. The limits for Berkeley power station are, however, expressed as: Total activity 200 Ci, Tritium 1,500 Ci, leaving the non-mathematician wondering how the amount of tritium can be more than seven times as great as the 'total'. A small, raised figure [1] against 'Total activity' then directs one to the explanatory footnote: '1 excluding tritium'. So the *real* total is not 200 Ci but 1,700 Ci. Tritium, it appears, is now shown separately because it is considered 'much less radiotoxic than other beta-active wastes', its effect being 'a thousand times less than that for caesium–137'.[15] At first sight Hartlepool and Heysham power stations are much less dangerous than others since each has a total activity of '4'. This, of course, excludes not only tritium, with a figure of 1,850, but also sulphur 35, with a figure of 7.5. The unit has, moreover, been changed from Ci to TBq – teraBecquerels, i.e. units 1,000,000,000,000 (or 10^{12}) times as large as the becquerel, or equivalent to 27 Ci. Translated into the same units as used in most of the table, the seemingly small figures turn out to be, respectively, 108, 202.5 and 49,950 Ci, giving a total discharge limit of 50,260.5 Ci, which is higher than Winfrith's 30,000 Ci or Dounreay's 24,000 Ci. Amersham International's laboratory at Cardiff, which discharges into a sewer discharging into the Severn Estuary, has limits expressed even more confusingly as beta/gamma activity 96 GBq (giga-Becquerels = 1,000,000,000 Bq); carbon–14, 2 TBq; tritium, 1,400 TBq; or what would be, for comparative purposes, 37,856.6 Ci, were it not that the beta/gamma activity figure excludes not only tritium and carbon–14 but also 'radioisotopes of calcium and strontium'. Which type of strontium is not specified, nor are any figures given. It is not surprising that measurement of radiation has acquired an aura of mystery.

Given that all radiation is potentially harmful and that there is no 'safe' level, the ultimate issues are who determines these limits and on what basis. All countries producing nuclear power either have their own statutory bodies or accept the findings of the International Commission on Radiological Protection (ICRP). The composition of this body is thus all important. The UK's DoE describes it as 'an independent scientific body of experts drawn from a number of countries',[16] the Holliday Committee more cautiously as 'formed from recognized experts on the effects of radiation on man'.[17] Holliday also draws attention both to the fact that the ICRP has become the ultimate authority and to the way in which statements on risk from radiation are phrased in consequence. 'It is common for risk estimates to be expressed solely in terms of ICRP limits, rather than in the more readily understandable terms of numbers of health effects or probabilities of cancer.'[18] Perhaps 'ready understanding' – by the public – is not a priority aim of governments committed to nuclear power. No Minister for Energy is likely to assert that a proposed reprocessing plant may cause x number of cancers over y years, when he can claim that discharges conform to ICRP limits – even if the two statements mean the same.

Holliday describes the ICRP system as based on principles which include, firstly, that 'no practice shall be adopted unless its introduction produces a net positive benefit', and, secondly, that 'all exposures shall be kept as low as reasonably achievable (the ALARA principle), economic and social factors being taken into account'.[19] We note that the principles do not state for whom the practice will produce a 'net positive benefit', and that the exposures need not be as low as *technically* possible, only 'reasonably', however that is interpreted, bearing in mind the 'economic and social factors', which, as the cynics would say, include what profits the enterprise will produce and how much they can get away with so far as safety standards are concerned.

Holliday comments on these principles:

> In calculating recommended limits, it will be evident that the ICRP cannot use scientific judgements alone, and value judgements are necessary. ICRP has aimed to set a 'permissible' or 'acceptable' upper limit such that the risks to individuals from the radiation hazard are similar or lower than the risks commonly accepted in everyday life. *This approach assumes, however, that the practice which gives rise to the risk is commonly 'accepted', and that the health effects are also comparable.*[20] (My stress.)

In plain terms, experts in one field – science – are required to make decisions in a different field – values – that affect the lives, and deaths, of millions of people throughout the world, as the ICRP defines, not the 'safe', but the 'acceptable', limits. One wonders in which countries people have had the chance of 'accepting' or 'not accepting' the risks which the nuclear industry thrusts on them. One wonders how many are aware that their 'acceptance' is assumed, and that, when they are told that a particularly unpleasant action is 'within ICRP limits', they have really only themselves to blame for the unpleasantness.

As to actual membership of the ICRP, Rosalie Bertell maintains further that:

Membership of the ICRP is highly selective and controlled. Prospective members must be recommended either by current ICRP members, or by members of the International Congress of Radiology and then approved by the ICRP International Executive Committee. *Through this structure participation in standard setting has been dominated by colleagues from the military, the civilian nuclear establishment and the medical radiological societies, who nominate one another. . . . People in all these categories have a vested interest in the use of radiation and depreciation of the risks in its use.* There is the added problem of military secrecy in many countries, including the USA, about radiation health effects, since these are the results of a nuclear bomb. This again limits the pool of 'experts' available to ICRP. There is no independent body, even the World Health Organisation, which can place a person on the ICRP. *It is, in every sense of the term, a closed club and not a body of independent scientific experts.*[21] (Stress in original.)

Inevitably, the values of such a 'club', in deciding 'acceptability', are those of the establishment, not of the world's peoples. Can one really expect otherwise? The only 'experts' in such matters, like their colleagues in government ministries, are those who have become prominent for their work in the nuclear industry or defence establishments. Logically, one might suggest that they should be joined by an equal number of 'experts' in 'values', but the prospect of distinguished clergymen, sociologists, specialists in ethics, trade union officials, health workers or even university vice-chancellors ever becoming members of the IRCP may be dismissed as beyond 'acceptable' limits, i.e. limits 'acceptable' to the IRCP.

Even at the purely scientific level the problem is lack of information. The only 'experiments' on human beings that have been monitored over a number of years (but see below) were those at Hiroshima and Nagasaki. Unfortunately, scientists have now decided that the data obtained need reassessment. Some houses apparently offered more protection than had previously been thought; in consequence, some illnesses were caused by lower doses of radiation than assumed; more mysteriously, certain individuals survived unharmed, while others, in the same room, succumbed.[22] Meanwhile, until the reassessment is completed, we must 'accept' the present limits, though even on these non-scientists are faced with confusion.

Why, for example, in March 1986, did the UK National Radiological Protection Board issue new guidelines on dose limits for members of the public? These are now set at one mSv a year with an overall lifetime dose of 70 mSv. Previously, it was 'acceptable' to go beyond this limit and receive doses of up to five mSv in some years, provided that the lifetime limit was not exceeded. Why, further, is the limit for the public set at one mSv in the UK, but at 0.25 mSv in the USA and 0.3 mSv in the Federal Republic of Germany? Are the British more radiation-resistant than Americans or Germans? The official answer is that the methods of calculation are different. Apparently the figure of five mSv for the public was derived by dividing the 'safety limit' for nuclear workers by ten.[23] To this example of 'scientific method' the non-scientist can only retort, 'Think of a number. . . .' Further, what does one conclude from a

1985 report by the UK Medical Research Council, following investigation into 3,000 deaths among 40,000 workers at the UK Atomic Energy Authority's research centres throughout the country, which warns that 'risk estimates used to set radiation standards may be 15 times too low'?[24] The only certainty is that the members of the London School of Hygiene who conducted this inquiry will not be selected for inclusion in the ICRP.

Most of the natural radioactivity in the sea comes from potassium–40, with a half-life of 1.3×10^9 or 1,300 million years. Collisions between cosmic rays and atoms in the atmosphere produce short-lived radionuclides such as tritium, with a half-life of 12.4 years, while some deep sea sediments are themselves radioactive. The problem is complicated by the addition of man-made elements and by differences in behaviour between radionuclides. Iodine, caesium and tritium, for example, are highly soluble in water and, in consequence, become diluted and distributed widely by currents. Conversely, plutonium and americium tend to attach themselves to particles and sink to the sea-bed where they remain.[25]

To assess potential risks to human beings, scientists have developed the concept of the *critical pathway*. One such pathway, the biological, is the food chain by which greater creatures feed on smaller, and so on, up to the greatest predator of all, humanity. In the Holliday example a worm, feeding on contaminated mud, is eaten by a crustacean, which in turn is eaten by a small squid. As squid are often cannibalistic, the small squid is eaten by a larger squid, which becomes food for surface feeding fish such as tuna, which eventually find their way into a tin in someone's larder.[26] The problem of calculating the risk is obviously extremely complex. If one were concerned only with the amount of radioactivity in the original worm passing up the food chain, by the time it reached humanity, its relative proportion would be minuscule. Unfortunately, life does not consist of one worm, one crustacean, one small squid, etc. One needs to know, for each link in the chain, whether it feeds entirely or only partly on the previous contaminated species, what happens biologically within the organism itself, how much is retained, how much excreted, and how the weight of the food eaten relates to the weight of the animal. Since much of what we know about these processes is derived from research in comparatively shallow waters, there is the added uncertainty that extrapolation may not apply to deep waters. The chain, moreover, may not have the completeness of the model. Human beings do not only eat fish that have themselves fed upon lesser creatures but crustaceans which are nearer the original poison. Worse still, as we saw in Chapter 1, some sea creatures have the ability to concentrate poisons rather than pass them on in diluted form.

The biological is not the only pathway; there is the chance of contamination by direct physical contact, for example, through fishing gear or, where radioactive effluent is discharged into the sea, from sand and silt in inter-tidal areas. Finally, there is the sea's own discharge into the atmosphere through bubbles which burst as they reach the surface and through sea-spray, both of which, as noted earlier, have the ability to concentrate poisons before returning them to humanity. Obviously the people most at risk, the *critical group*, are those fishermen and their families, or dwellers in houseboats on tidal flats, who also eat a lot of fish.

The critical pathway approach has one further effect. By directing our attention to the end of the chain, it is diverted from the links. Humanity can avoid eating poisoned fish, the fish cannot escape contamination – or its effects. Individuals have a limited lifespan, but the radionuclides may last for thousands of years. By discharging radioactivity into the sea we have started a gigantic experiment that cannot be stopped. What will happen to the next generations of fish is uncertain – they may adapt themselves, or die off, or produce deformed monstrosities. Whatever humanity decides to do *now*, their future is already in danger.

Subs, Satellites and Fallout

The human contribution of radioactivity to the sea arises from five sources: atmospheric testing of nuclear weapons; dumping of nuclear waste; regular discharges of effluent from industrial installations; operation of nuclear-powered military vessels; and accidents to nuclear-powered satellites. The Holliday Committee quotes figures of 0.6% addition and 0.005% addition to overall background activity as the respective results of weapons testing and dumping or coastal discharges.[27] Such statistics, however reassuring in overall terms – what is an extra 0.005% in 1,205,600,000 cu km of water? – become increasingly meaningless when we consider those parts of the ocean immediately affected.

Turning first to those sources about which we know least, submarines and satellites, we saw in Chapter 2 that there are now an estimated 585 nuclear-powered submarines in the world. How many are at sea at any time, where they are and how much radioactivity they discharge in normal operations are questions it is impossible to answer. Nuclear submarines prefer secrecy to newspaper headlines; that is their milieu. At times, however, secrecy is impossible, as when, in the early hours of 10 June 1985, the British submarine, *HMS Resolution*, carrying Polaris missiles for testing, and cruising on the surface off Cape Canaveral, collided with an American yacht, *Proud Mary*, a 40-ton converted fishing boat. The impact merely knocked a bit of plastic fairing off the submarine's steel hull, but caused it to 'light up like a Christmas tree'; the yacht had to be towed into harbour by the US Coastguard, three members of its crew injured.

On 2 May 1986 the Pentagon admitted that two US nuclear-powered submarines had run aground within the previous two months; on 13 March the *USS Nathaniel Greene*, armed with 16 Poseidon missiles, touched bottom in the Irish Sea, damaging the rudder and an external ballast tank. On 29 April the nuclear-powered attack submarine *USS Atlanta* damaged its ballast tanks and suffered other external damage when it ran aground in the Strait of Gibraltar. Both vessels limped to safety, one to the Holy Loch, Scotland, the other to

Gibraltar. The authorities denied that there had been any damage to either of the nuclear power plants or to the nuclear missiles.

Less fortunate was the Soviet submarine which, on 3 October 1986, caught fire 960 km off Bermuda. It surfaced, was taken in tow, but, becoming filled with water, was scuppered 1,088 km from Bermuda and some 2,000 km from New York. Experts described it as having two nuclear reactors and capable of carrying 16 nuclear missiles. Inevitably there were reassurances for the public. Since the reactors were housed in 'massive heavy steel', they would take 'forever to corrode', while in the vastness of the ocean ten to 100 pounds of nuclear material 'would not make much of a difference'. With the Reykjavik summit only a few days distant, American commentators suddenly discovered a vast improvement in Soviet technology since their Chernobyl misgivings less than six months before. The Pentagon now admitted that it had lost two of its own submarines and regularly monitored where they had gone down. A few dissidents suggested that, if the reactor cooling system became blocked, this could lead to an explosion, but their arguments made as little impact as those of most dissidents.[28] One thing is certain – not even the ICRP knows how much radioactivity now enters the sea, or may one day enter it, from submarines.

In the choice of two evils, the environmentalist prefers satellites; at least they can be seen, even if one has no idea what they are up to. By 1983 no fewer than 55 satellites carrying nuclear power generators had been launched.[29] For obvious reasons they are intended to fly in a low orbit; at the end of their mission the various parts are made to separate and the nuclear reactor, using the thrust from its own rocket engine, moves for safety to a higher orbit, where it can go on circling the earth for some 500 years, time enough, say the scientists, for its radioactive contents to decay.

Unfortunately, practice does not always follow theory. The satellite *Cosmos 954* failed to achieve a higher orbit and on 24 January 1978 entered the earth's atmosphere and partially burned up, poisoning the atmosphere with radioactivity. Debris landed in and contaminated northern Canada. Earlier a US Navy satellite, launched on 21 April 1964 and carrying a nuclear power generator using plutonium 238, failed to orbit and re-entered the earth's atmosphere in the southern hemisphere. The power generator burned up and the resulting radioactive particles were distributed about 50 km above the earth. Some 95% of the radioactivity, estimated at 17,000 Ci (630 TBq), eventually reached the earth where the fallout in the southern hemisphere was 2.5 times that in the northern. How much landed in the Pacific, Atlantic and Indian Oceans is uncertain, but the plutonium 238 fallout from this satellite was nearly twice that which resulted from atmospheric testing of nuclear weapons to the end of 1970.[30] Somehow the incident, like those affecting other satellites, has escaped inclusion in those overall surveys which tell us how much radioactivity enters the sea and from which source.

On 28 December 1982 *Cosmos 1402*, launched on 30 August, split up some time between its 1,920th and 1,926th orbit. The following month the Soviet news agency Tass announced that, after receiving commands from the earth, it had divided to isolate the active part of the reactor, thus ensuring its 'subsequent complete combustion in the dense atmospheric strata'. This would not, however, prevent some radioactivity from reaching the earth.

After the *Cosmos 954* accident, President Carter pledged that the US would pursue a ban on nuclear power in space, only to withdraw the proposal later. The US Subcommittee on the Peaceful Uses of Outer Space, together with Russian scientists, carried out a technical study of the use of nuclear power in satellites. Their main recommendation was that 'appropriate measures for adequate radiation protection during all phases of the flight of a spacecraft carrying a nuclear power source should be primarily based on the existing and internationally recognized standards of the ICRP'.[31] The Subcommittee took particular note of the ICRP principle that 'no practice shall be adopted unless its introduction produces a postive net benefit'. B. R. Jasani of the Stockholm International Peace Research Institute comments: 'It is difficult to imagine how the current practice of using nuclear power sources on board military satellites – which mainly enhances the efficiency of weapons, particularly nuclear weapons – can have any positive benefit'.[32] The world has moved forward since his account. Reagan has replaced Carter. With Star Wars the possibility of 'accidents' in space is not mentioned.

One part of the world ocean has received more than its share of radioactivity from the skies – the Pacific.[33] In 1947 the USA took over the Marshall Islands, 3,200 km south-west of Hawaii, as United Nations trust territory. They celebrated their trust by exploding 66 atomic and hydrogen bombs. The French began with atmospheric testing and, from 1975 onwards, carried out underground tests, first at Fangataufa atoll, then, since April 1976, at Moruroa in French Polynesia.

Against this background one reads with surprise that, according to scientists of the South Pacific Regional Environment Programme's (SPREP's) Technical Group on Radioactivity in the South Pacific Region, exposure to radiation from atmospheric weapons testing 'is on the average lower, perhaps two to three times lower, in the South Pacific region than it is for the world as a whole',[34] while, for radiation from natural sources, the average figure is approximately 1,000 mSv a year – half the world average. They attribute this to three causes: background radiation is considerably lower in coral-based soil than elsewhere; concentrations of radon over the ocean are considerably lower than over continental land masses; most people live in well-ventilated houses and spend much time out of doors, thus avoiding exposure to concentrations of radon indoors.[35]

Unfortunately, the South Pacific is not peopled by 'average' human beings, nor is there an 'average' nuclear explosion. The Americans began by blowing up and contaminating the atolls of Bikini and Enewetak. US Navy records show that a 1946 nuclear blast left 500,000 tons of radioactive debris in Bikini lagoon. The Bikinians had been evacuated, first to Rongerik, where some of the fish were poisonous and the vegetation was inadequate, thence to the US support base at Kwajalein, and finally to the island of Kili, about a sixth the size of Bikini. In 1971, after a radiological survey by the US military had declared their island 'safe', about 150 returned. A second survey in 1978 revealed that, after eating food grown in Bikini soil, the islanders had experienced a 75% increase in caesium–137 contamination in their bodies. The US Government declared Bikini uninhabitable for another 50 years and in September 1978 the islanders were moved elsewhere.

Enewetak, with 43 nuclear detonations offshore, was even more contaminated. In September 1979 the US Department of Energy advised the former inhabitants that what was left of their northern islands would be uninhabitable for at least 30 years. After a considerable clean-up the islanders were allowed back in 1982, but not to Runit Island, where a large crater had been blasted to contain radioactive sand and debris, and sealed with concrete. Runit Island, it is estimated, will be outside human visitation for the next 25,000 years.

The third group affected were the people of Rongelap, not because the US decided to use their island for testing, but because they had the misfortune to get in the way. On 1 March 1954 the US exploded the Bravo hydrogen bomb at Bikini with a strength about 1,000 times that of the Hiroshima and Nagasaki bombs. The radioactive cloud drifted over Rongelap, about 160 km away. Official reports attributed this to a change in wind, but US weathermen on Rongerik later disputed this version. The story of how the children on Rongelap, ignorant of any danger, enjoyed themselves in the unexpected 'snow' has passed into nuclear history. Both water and food were contaminated and the inhabitants evacuated three days later. By that time many had contracted radiation burns.

In 1957 the islanders were returned to Rongelap. A report by the US Brookhaven team of scientists declared that 'the habitation of these people on the island will afford most valuable ecological radiation data on human beings'.[36] The following year, while admitting that radiation levels were higher than those found in other inhabited places, they announced that Rongelap was 'considered perfectly safe for human habitation'.[37] Suggestions that the Rongelap islanders were deliberately and callously exposed to radioactive fallout and later returned to the islands as part of a concerted plan to use them as guinea pigs in investigating the effects of radiation on human beings have been dismissed as 'conspiracy theory', anti-US propaganda or, more simply, on the grounds that no civilized people would copy the medical 'experiments' perpetrated in Nazi concentration camps. What, then, are we to make of the report of a US House of Representatives Subcommittee, details of which appeared in the UK press only in February 1987, that, for three decades after the 1940s, experiments were carried out at reputable US institutions on hospital patients with low prospects of survival, elderly inmates of an Age Centre or prison inmates, in which they were injected with plutonium, uranium salts, radium or thorium, or given X-ray doses of up to 600 rads (6 grays) on the testicles to discover the effect on fertility?[38] We may still not know much about the effects of radiation. But for the greater freedom of information in the US compared with the UK or the USSR we should still not know of these inhuman practices carried out in the name of medical science. Now that the world has been told, the anger of the US Administration when Greenpeace evacuated the Rongelap islanders in May 1985 acquires a less self-righteous and more sinister explanation.

Secrecy surrounds both atmospheric and underground French tests in Polynesia. We know at least that, during the atmospheric testing, in September 1966 the New Zealand National Radiation Laboratory reported radioactivity of 135,000 picocuries (4,995 Bq) per litre in rainwater in Western Samoa, 3,200 km downwind from the test site. We know further that, in August 1968, scientists attributed high levels of radioactivity in fish along the Baja Peninsula of Mexico to the French tests. On the effects of underground tests at Moruroa, which are still going on, we are less certain. It has been suggested that an increased incidence of cyclones in the area following a heating of the water may not be unconnected and that another alarming phenomenon, increased fish poisoning, was otherwise inexplicable. Even SPREP's scientists, while giving the French a clean bill of health, have their reservations. They concluded that 'one should be concerned about the possible long-term effects, such as leakage of radionuclides into the ocean, especially if the testing programme and the accumulations of radionuclides underground are to continue into the future'.[39]

This statement is the more remarkable in view of the scientists' attitude, as revealed in the reaction of their chairman, Dr Michael P. Bacon, to the Prime Minister of Papua New Guinea's call for a nuclear-free Pacific:

> The Prime Minister may very well have sound political reasons for his statement, but his is an intellectually rigid stand that a scientist would not take. [The art of 'politics', like 'common sense', is not 'science'.] I believe that most scientists who have thought about the question would at least consider it a hypothesis worth testing that the oceans are a resource that can serve mankind, in part by serving as a receptacle for some of the wastes produced by human technology. The amounts that can be assimilated by the ocean may be close to zero for some kinds of waste or very large for others, *but we will never know if we reject the opportunity out of hand.*[40] (My stress.)

In plain terms – go on dumping poisons in the ocean, even if the amounts it can assimilate may be 'close to zero', because, unless we do, we shall never find out whether the sea can take it or not. And supposing the answer is 'not'? Are we then to be left with parts of the sea that, like Runit Island, are 'out of bounds' to humanity for the next 25,000 years? Except that, unlike Runit Island, the sea cannot be isolated; ocean currents will ensure that poisoned areas mingle with non-poisoned and so contaminate the whole.

Of the tests at Moruroa, Dr Bacon finds it understandable that debate 'tends to be irrational and full of emotion' because *we really are in ignorance*, and that condition always arouses suspicion and activates the imagination'.[41] (My stress.) One can only marvel at the ways of modern science which enable statements to be made minimizing the dangers of radiation in the Pacific, while admitting to ignorance about one of the major causes of that radiation and arguing that we shall never know how much the sea can absorb if we 'reject the opportunity' to find out.

Scientists reading this section will doubtless point out – rationally – that inflicting doses of radiation on South Pacific islanders is not poisoning the seas. Admittedly, the people concerned suffered contamination direct rather than from eating poisoned fish. But the radioactive 'snow' that fell on Rongelap fell on the intervening waters; seepages from sea-bed dumps and underground explosions go directly into the ocean. The Pacific has only itself to blame. It should not be so large. Besides, it is a long way from France.

Poisonous Power

The method of producing power through *nuclear fission* is basically no more incomprehensible than understanding radiation.[42] When a neutron strikes an atom of uranium 235, it sets off a chain reaction in which that atom splits, releasing other neutrons to strike more atoms, which split in turn, releasing more neutrons, and so on. The process releases a huge amount of energy in the form of heat. The aim is to make use of this energy.

There are two obvious problems – how to convert the heat into electric power, and how to control the fission process. The first is carried out by using the heat to convert water into steam, which then turns a power generator; the second by inserting control rods to absorb the neutrons and so prevent them striking more atoms.

This process affects the sea through the waste it produces. In the first place, it creates far too much heat energy – only about a third of it is needed to generate electricity – and the excess is disposed of as 'thermal pollution', i.e. released into water where it causes a considerable rise in temperature. Secondly, the water or liquid coolant used acquires radioactive particles and also requires disposal. Usually it is kept back until short-lived isotopes have decayed and, after further treatment, discharged as effluent. Thirdly, there are the spent fuel rods; the outer covers are removed and the rods dissolved in nitric acid, a process that produces considerable high-level solid and liquid waste. Both normal operations and reprocessing lead to the fourth form of waste – gaseous emissions into the atmosphere, when, after filtering and holding them back to allow time for radioactive elements to decay, the gases are released. If we emphasize waste rather than the advantages of electricity, we do so because, at different times and places, the sea has been the recipient of these wastes – thermal discharges and effluent at the site of operation, solid waste through dumping, and gaseous emissions through atmospheric precipitation. The last contain nitrous oxide – now notorious as a source of acid rain – radioactive iodine and other fission products such as krypton, tritium and carbon–14. The radioactive solution left after the gases are released contains a mixture in which strontium–90, caesium–137 and exceptionally long-lived actinides predominate. Effluent from normal operations, e.g. the Sellafield pipeline, contains strontium–90 and ruthenium–106, while that from 21 other plants in the UK includes tritium.[43]

According to figures published in February 1986, there were 361 nuclear power reactors in operation worldwide at the end of 1985 and a further 144 planned for the next ten years, an increase of 28.5%.[44] How many of these will be completed or how many old reactors decommissioned (35 are scheduled for retirement by 1995) is impossible to say. In the post-Chernobyl era, with nuclear policy in flux, disillusion has already caused changes in national programmes. Of plants currently operating 35.0% are in Western Europe, 32.9% in the USA and Canada and 17.9% in the USSR and Eastern Europe. If we add Japan and South Africa, this means that almost 95% of nuclear capacity is concentrated in the developed world. Third World countries, with 18 plants now working, plan – or planned – to add a further 26 by 1995, thus increasing their share of the total from 5.3% to 8.5%.

Not all reactors are situated by the sea, but an analysis of plant sites in Europe shows that no fewer than 53 are within 50 km of national borders.[45] Belgium, for example, has four nuclear power stations at Doel on the estuary of the River Scheldt, less than four kilometres from the Dutch frontier, while the French are building two reactors at Chooz at the tip of a 24-km long and five-km wide stretch of territory jutting into Belgium. Great Britain, having no land borders with other European states, has placed the majority of its reactors around the coast, including the Dounreay complex in the remote north of Scotland. Not surprisingly cynics have suggested that nuclear power planners have so little faith in their installations that they prefer to have them as far as possible from their major centres of population. The radioactive cloud from Chernobyl showed that even this safeguard was illusory.

As with tankers and oil, discharges from nuclear plants occur during 'normal operations' and by accident. As with tankers also, there are those mysterious discharges that occur when no one is looking. Inevitably, one begins with the British Nuclear Fuels plc (BNFL) plant at Sellafield, formerly Windscale, Cumbria, UK. The Sellafield complex officially includes the Windscale nuclear reprocessing plant, which handles all spent magnox fuel from UK power stations and some from abroad, the Calder Hall magnox-type nuclear power station, and fuel element storage and decanning plants. Discharges reach the Irish Sea by pipelines which extend 2.1 km beyond low water mark.[46]

In its report of March 1986 the House of Commons Environment Committee had few doubts about these discharges:

> The UK discharges more radioactivity to the sea than any other nation. As the Ministry of Agriculture confirmed to us, Sellafield is the largest recorded source of radioactive discharge in the world and as a result the Irish Sea is the most radioactive sea in the world.[47]

In the Fifth Annual Report of the Radioactive Waste Management Committee, published in July 1984, Sellafield had already been described as having the highest radioactive discharge in Europe. The Committee considered it unduly high with a dose level in 1981 up to 69% of the internationally recommended level.[48]

Following improvements, in July 1986 a House of Lords Select Committee was able to quote figures showing that peak discharges in the 1970s of approximately 4,900 curies per annum (Ci/a) (181 TBq) for 'total alpha' activity and 250,000 Ci/a (9,260 TBq) for 'total beta' had come down to current rates of 200 Ci (7.4 TBq) and 20,000 Ci (740 TBq) respectively, and by the early 1990s would be 20 Ci (0.75 TBq) and 8,000 Ci (296 TBq).[49] This development compared favourably with the similar French plant at Cap de la Hague, across the Channel, 'where discharges are currently, and are expected to remain, at a level of 30,000 curies [1,111 TBq] a year "total beta" and 20 curies [0.75 TBq] a year "total alpha"'. With patriotic imbalance they conclude that 'whereas Sellafield is currently ten times worse than Cap La Hague [*sic*] in respect of total alpha, and slightly better in terms of total beta activity, by the early 1990s Sellafield will be at the same level as the French in respect of total alpha and at about a quarter of their level in respect of total beta'.[50] The fact that these discharges will continue and add their poisons to those already there is dismissed by Their Lordships as ancient history. 'The accumulation of radioactivity as a result of the operations at Sellafield is, to a far greater extent than is generally appreciated, a legacy of the past'.[51] Unfortunately, with a quarter of a ton of plutonium lying at the bottom of the Irish Sea that legacy will affect future generations for almost a quarter of a million years. Once again observers see what they wish to see. The Lords Committee looked at nuclear energy with the eyes of those who thought it a 'good thing'; the Commons Environment Committee looked at radioactive waste – and decided they didn't like it.

The Commons Committee was also mystified by how actual rates of discharge are determined. Officially these are authorized on the basis that there is no hazard to health. The Committee, however, was forced to admit that

> We do not know how the discharge limits currently in force for UK nuclear plants relate to the present principal dose limit of 1 mSv recommended by the ICRP/NRPB, nor indeed to the 5 mSv per annum [see earlier]. We therefore do not know how relevant the current discharge limits are to the most recent objectives for radiological protection. Almost all discharge limits were fixed by MAFF/DOE before ICRP issued their most recent (1985) advice[52] [on the 1 mSv standard].

They add that, since they were set 'some time ago', discharge limits 'may well have been fixed with regard to what the operator could manage at that time and with somewhat less regard for objectives of radiological protection'.[53] At Sellafield 'authorised alpha discharge limits were increased in the mid-1950s and again in 1971 to accommodate the increased level of discharges from the plant'.[54] As the accompanying diagram shows that actual discharges after 1971 exceeded the pre-mid-50s limits, one is left wondering whether the sea's capacity to 'dilute and disperse' has increased, despite the poison meanwhile injected into its system. Perhaps a Mithradatic syndrome operates in the Sellafield area so that, by gradually accustoming itself to poison, the sea is able to absorb more of it. One thing is certain – that Sellafield discharges will always be 'within authorized limits' – even if those limits have to be fixed so high that, without being breached, they can include the 1983 injection that poisoned 25 miles of coastline.

As for more reprehensible discharges, not until 1986 was it revealed that, between May 1952 and March 1953, without warning to the public, large quantities of plutonium were discharged into the Irish Sea as an 'experiment' to see what would happen. The effluent was pumped out at the 'recommended maximum permissible discharge', the results analysed and pronounced satisfactory.[55] Given what we now know about what was taking place at the same time in the Pacific and in hospitals and prisons in the USA, the experiment appears more sinister than 'satisfactory'.

Over thirty years later a team of scientists from the University of East Anglia and the UK Atomic Energy Authority reported that radioactive bubbles carrying plutonium were popping up in the Irish Sea between two and ten km from the Sellafield discharge pipe. Radioactive particles concentrate in air bubbles in the water which burst when they reach the surface, releasing the plutonium, which, in the samples of air examined, was of concentrations up to 600 times higher than in water. The scientists found particles of plutonium–239 and 240 (half-lives of 24,000 and 6,600 years), plutonium–238 (half-life of 86 years) and americium, a breakdown product of plutonium (half-life 460 years).[56]

It is the secrecy surrounding operations at nuclear plants, a product of the original research into nuclear weapons, together with the arrogance of those in authority, as seen in the Sellafield 'experiment', plus the mystique of nuclear physics and the releasing of monstrous invisible powers of destruction, that causes public concern. Accidents, at least if sufficiently large, cannot be hidden and the Sellafield complex, where some of the earliest buildings were constructed with more regard for speed than safety in the attempt to ensure British participation in the nuclear age, has been distinguished by an ignominious record. The House of Commons Environment Committee, while 'somewhat reassured' by proposed changes, admitted that, 'whatever the uncertainties about routine discharges, the possible effects of accidents are worrying'.[57]

With some 300 recorded incidents in the course of its existence, Sellafield qualifies as more than a source of worry. The most notorious was the 1957 fire in the No. 1 plutonium production reactor, caused when a physicist threw a switch too soon. For 42 hours it passed unnoticed and was then sprayed with carbon dioxide which only fed the flames. The fire raged for a further 24 hours before being put out, releasing emissions to the atmosphere which caused the Government to order the destruction of two million litres of milk. The report of the inquiry into the accident has never been published. In the 1970s there was a leak of radioactive caesium and strontium from silo B–38, found only by chance during building work; it had been going on for probably four years. Investigation revealed a second and larger leak in an adjoining building, which had probably been there for seven years. In 1979, fire in building 204 during the cutting of obsolete pipework led to the fiasco of discovering that the fire alarm had been removed, that the only line to the fire station was engaged and that, when the brigade eventually arrived, its training and equipment were defective. In 1981, radioactive iodine was released from building 205 during reprocessing of six fuel rods which had not been kept long enough in storage. This was the fault of the Central Electricity Generating Board (CEGB), who also failed to provide adequate documentation. But BNFL failed to inform either the Nuclear Installations Inspectorate (NII) or the Ministers responsible before restarting the plant. In 1983 came the deliberate discharge of crud and solvent, and subsequent beach closure, with Ministers not being informed until a week after it occurred. In February 1986, for only the second time in its history, Sellafield was placed under amber alert following the escape of plutonium nitrate during the repair of a pump in building 205, the formation of a plutonium mist and contamination of up to 15 workers.[58]

Despite these incidents and repeated promises to reform, when, at the end of 1986, the Health and Safety Executive (HSE) published the report of a 12-man team of inspectors, they found that safety standards were not up to those of the chemical industry or of other sectors of the nuclear industry. 'The condition of the plant seems to have been subordinated to the requirements of current production, is unsatisfactory and demands planned new investment to enable it to perform for a further 10 years and beyond without unnecessary hazard to workers, and in the extreme to the public.' If significant advances were not made within a year, the HSE would order the closure of the reprocessing plant until safety was improved.[59]

Close down Sellafield! A large new Thermal Oxide Reprocessing Plant (THORP) is being built at a cost of £1,300 million as a major source of revenue through reprocessing spent fuel not only from the UK but from Europe. Reprocessing is also *the* major source of radioactive waste, as the Commons Environment Committee pointed out in recommending that, if analysis of the financial and unemployment consequences did not warrant its continuation, THORP should be abandoned.[60] The Tory Government rejected this proposal even before it had answered the Committee's other recommendations. In November 1985 the Prime Minister, Margaret Thatcher, made flying visits to four nuclear sites, including Sellafield, in what was described as a bid to help the industry with its image problem.[61] In March 1986 she wrote to the Irish Prime Minister, Dr Garret Fitzgerald, who had expressed concern over incidents at Sellafield and the dangers of radiation in and around Ireland. In her letter, she blamed the media for exaggerating the recent incidents out of all proportion to the real risks to health and safety 'in an apparent effort to discredit the nuclear industry', which was very conscious of the need to maintain high standards of safety and whose record was 'excellent'.[62] Somewhere between the Health and Safety Executive's report and the Prime Minister's letter words have either lost, or changed, their meaning.

Sellafield is not the only nuclear plant in the world to have accidents, or near accidents. As long ago as December 1950 there was a hydrogen explosion at the NRX reactor at Chalk River, about 240 km north-west of Ottawa, Canada, in which the reactor was largely destroyed and a million gallons of radioactive water flooded the building.[63] In a second incident at the same reactor in 1958, overheated uranium fuel rods ruptured inside the core and, in removing them, a piece of burning uranium was dropped in a shallow maintenance pit, showering fission products inside the building and causing contamination downwind.[64] What happened at Kyshtym/Chelyabinsk in the Ural Mountains of the USSR in the winter of 1957–8 is still not fully established but it is generally accepted that a major disaster followed the explosion of stored nuclear waste.[65] Protests failed to stop construction of the Fermi 1 Breeder Reactor, near Detroit, Michigan, USA, which uses plutonium instead of uranium and which even the Atomic Energy Commission had refused to declare safe. In 1966 there was a major accident and the reactor came close to showering plutonium over the city of Detroit.[66] Had this occurred, the disaster would have been far greater than the better-known incident at No. 2 reactor, Three Mile Island, near Harrisburg, Pennsylvania, on 28 March 1979. This was a Pressurized Water Reactor (PWR), using a double loop system in which water under pressure in one loop boils at a higher temperature and is used to convert water in the second loop into steam. An accidental shutting-off of the water cooling system caused temperatures to rise to 2,816°C (5,100°F), producing a partial meltdown of the nuclear core. Escaping radioactivity led to the evacuation of an estimated 150,000 citizens, mainly pregnant women and children.[67]

The nuclear industry, however, seems either unable or unwilling to learn. In May 1986 a member of the US Nuclear Regulatory Commission (NRC), James Asselstine, reportedly declared that in the previous 12 months the nuclear industry had its worst safety record since the 1979 incident with about 10% of plants experiencing significant mishaps or management problems. Among incidents cited in the NRC's annual report to Congress was that of 9 June 1984 at the Davis–Besse plant near Toledo, Ohio, which lost its feedwater system so that, as at Three Mile Island, the reactor core started to overheat and was saved only when the auxiliary pump was started in time.[68] According to another report, when inspectors from the NRC visited the plant unexpectedly the previous April, they found, among other things, an unlicensed operator asleep in the main pump room. When the incident occurred the only back-up pump also stopped as, contrary to regulations, its power came from the same source. Fourteen other pieces of equipment also failed and, in the chaos that followed, engineers pushed the wrong set of buttons at least once before rushing out to start the auxiliary pump. This was the eighth major emergency of the year at Davis–Besse. Twelve minutes passed before they restarted pumping; at Three Mile Island the reactor went out of control in eighteen.[69] And on 3 October 1985, after years of public protest and litigation, the undamaged No. 1 reactor at Three Mile Island resumed operations.[70]

Seven months later came Chernobyl. Among the verbal fallout in the West – assurances that 'it couldn't happen here', that Western technology and safety measures were superior – came rumblings of potential problems at the N–reactor of the US Hanford Government Reservation Facility, Washington. The reactor was one of several plants in the US that, like Chernobyl, had no containment structure to prevent the release of radioactivity. Like Chernobyl also, it used graphite as a moderator in the cooling system. To this ominous combination was added a warning on 26 April 1985 in a United Nuclear Industries report of 'serious deterioration' of the valve discs in the primary cooling system. The valves could break off and partially obstruct the pipes, 'a risk which must be avoided to assure nuclear safety and reactor production continuity'. On this occasion Chernobyl concentrated the minds of those concerned more speedily than official reports. Plans to replace the faulty valves in the 1988 financial year were suddenly aborted. In December 1986 an expert panel from the Energy Department recommended a six-month shut-down to make improvements in safety. They also recommended a permanent shut-down within five years.[71]

How much poison did Chernobyl itself add to the sea? According to the World Health Organization, after the rain of 28–29 April 1986, Gävle, on the east coast of Sweden, received a number of radioactive substances that included caesium–137, iodine–131, plutonium–239, ruthenium–103, barium–140, tellurium–132, zirconium–95 and strontium–90. The WHO placed Gävle at the top of its 'hit list' outside the USSR with a deposit for caesium of 137,000 Bq per square metre – 27 times the amount of radioactive material received from all nuclear weapons testing since World War II. From corresponding figures of 9,000 Bq/sq m for Finland, 13,000 Bq/sq m for Trondheim on the west coast of Norway, 2,500 Bq/sq m for Scotland and 15 Bq/sq m for England we can make our own estimates of possible precipitation in the two nearest seas, the Baltic and the North Sea.[72] British scientists at least rose to the challenge, if not to the satisfaction of those preferring a common sense approach. Introducing its 'Monitoring of Fallout from the Chernobyl Reactor Accident', MAFF's Directorate of Fisheries Research informs us that, 'as the aim of this assessment has been to evaluate the dose from Chernobyl fallout it has been necessary to subtract the contribution to radioactivity from UK radioactive waste discharges'.[73] How correct they are! If one wants to find out how much actually came from Chernobyl, one must disregard what was already there. Unfortunately, this exercise in scientific accuracy does not have the same practical benefit for the fish, shellfish, molluscs, etc. at the receiving end who find it impossible to separate their normal Sellafield intake from the abnormal foreign matter. Nor is this all. 'These data can only be regarded as being approximate since no direct data on deposition into the marine environment are available at the time of writing. Estimates have been made by extrapolation from observations over land.'[74] After that admission it would be invidious to quote figures.

Nuclear plants at least provide their own form of humour. For example, on 5 September 1985, while bringing in lobster pots off the north coast of Scotland, fishermen in the 30-ft *Northern Lights* hauled up a 60 cm section of the Dounreay reactor's waste discharge pipe. Readings inside the pipe were 15,000 times 'background' radiation. The lobsters were sent for analysis, but their fate went unreported.[75] There have also been problems with jellyfish. In April 1985 they clogged the tunnel for drawing in sea water used to cool the two CANDU reactors at the Madras Atomic Power Plant, India, forcing the plant to close. This had happened before, when in 1983, four weeks after the plant opened, a similar invasion forced it to shut down for a week. On 7 September 1984 (US Labour Day) a 36 square km slick of jellyfish crept into the intakes at the Florida Power and Light St Lucie nuclear power station, Fort Pierce, Florida. Plastering themselves against the 15-cm-thick steel filter screens, they caused such an obstruction that the screens were sucked inward. The plant was closed for eleven days. At the Dungeness nuclear power station on the south coast of England sprats put the filter system out of action seven times between 1969 and 1980. The 'exhaust' end of the process fares better than the 'intake'. Discharges of warm water attract fish, and at St Laurent, France, provide the right conditions for breeding goldfish and exotic koi carp. It has even been suggested that the Tricastin nuclear plant should breed crocodiles to support local tanneries and shoe manufacturers.[76] Where humanity is concerned, the destructive element is inevitable. If effluent discharges fail to kill fish, we can always breed creatures for destruction at the intake pipe.

Poisonous Power Outside Europe and North America

The Mediterranean, polluted by sewage and hazardous chemicals, receives its share of radioactive effluent from nuclear power plants in southern France, Spain and Italy. According to UNEP estimates, 2,480 Ci (92 TBq) of tritium and 138 Ci (5 TBq) of other radionuclides are discharged annually into western and central waters from both coastal sources and major rivers. They admit, however, that this is an underestimate. The river data do not include discharges into the Rhône from plants operating before 1977; information on 'nuclear research work going on in a number of countries, together with a widespread use of radioisotopes in medicine' is also omitted. Israel's nuclear capabilities are not mentioned.[77]

In the Far East, China and Japan have chosen different paths. Even before Chernobyl, China had decided not to build any large new plants until the early 1990s beyond the two already agreed, one of which is at Daya Bay near Hong Kong. The decision surprised Kraftwerk Union of West Germany, who had anticipated supplying two new reactors, and shattered US hopes of getting into the market.[78] Chinese nuclear practices would appear to resemble those of the rest of the world. In April 1986 the BBC in London monitored a broadcast by Peking Radio which admitted that 'over the past few years, as a result of poor management systems, the municipality has experienced the loss of radioactive elements and an accident, in which the radiation operators were irradiated unusually, occurred.'[79] One reported accident concerned the spillage of a highly radioactive solution on to the floor of a non-ferrous metal research institute near Peking. The floor was subsequently covered with another layer of concrete, only to have the building collapse on it during the 1976 Tangshen earthquake. On the deputy director's instructions the party secretary of Dongtian village in Hebei province disposed of 25 tons of the concrete with radioactive levels 100 times above normal by throwing them down a dry well where it could have contaminated the nearby Xidaying reservoir. China, however, is not Sellafield. The deputy director was dismissed and the secretary expelled from the Party.[80]

Even after Chernobyl, Japan, which already operates 32 power plants, has ten reactors under construction and plans a further six, the majority discharging radioactive effluent either directly or through rivers into the sea, demonstrated its determination to qualify as a member of the 'West' by announcing that it would go ahead in making nuclear power its 'number one energy source'. Already Japan has problems in disposing of its high-level radioactive waste. In August 1986 the water supply system at the No. 5 reactor of a plant in Fukushima prefecture, 114 km north-west of Tokyo, failed to work properly and the reactor was shut down. Inevitably, no damage or injuries were reported.[81] Taiwan, with four reactors working and two more under construction, is one developing country relying heavily on nuclear power, which produces 59% of its energy requirements.[82]

In South and Central America, Argentina, Brazil and Mexico are taking the nuclear path. Mexico plans to build two reactors, Brazil has one in operation and two being built, but high costs will probably prevent construction of the nine which the former military regime planned for 1990. Argentina has two reactors and plans to complete a third. With a plentiful supply of uranium and knowledge of nuclear technology, it has provided Chile, Colombia and Uruguay with small research reactors. Add to these Cuba's Soviet reactor[83] and a future picture emerges of the South Atlantic and Pacific receiving unwanted discharges of radioactive effluent to swell the poisonous sewage and industrial waste already there.

With six reactors already working and another five under construction, the Indo–Pakistan sub-continent is the most 'advanced', and, to the seas, potentially dangerous area of the Third World. In Pakistan the Karachi Nuclear Power Plant on the west coast of the harbour near Paradise Point, Hawks Bay, discharges radioactive substances into the Arabian Sea. Reporting in 1982, UNEP noted that so far these had remained 'within permissible limits' and that no contamination to fauna and flora had been noted.[84] This may be due as much to political difficulty as to technical efficiency. Having announced that it is able to enrich uranium, and so ultimately produce an atomic bomb (if it has not already done so), Pakistan has problems in keeping its reactor working. Following its refusal to sign the nuclear non-proliferation treaty, its main backer, Canada, has become reluctant to supply parts and technical support.[85]

Even without their other problems, India's plants at Trombay, near Bombay, and Tarapur, 100 km further north, are already poisoning the Arabian Sea. The Trombay research station, with four reactors, thorium and uranium plants, a reprocessing plant, isotope production facilities and laboratories, has a daily discharge of 140,000 litres of radioactive effluent and 2,950 litres of thermal effluent. Bottom sediments and coastal organisms are already contaminated with caesium–137, curium–144 and rubidium–106. The thermal discharges cause an oxygen deficiency near the outfall, leading to plankton blooms and changes in the composition of species.[86]

India's problems are both political and technological.[87] Except for Tarapur, all reactors are of the CANDU type and use heavy water. Although more capital intensive, the Atomic Energy Commission (AEC) preferred them to light water reactors because they use natural, as opposed to enriched, uranium, of which India has its own resources and can thus be independent. The political problem is basically the same as Pakistan's. In 1974 India used spent fuel rods from a CANDU reactor to manufacture and explode an atomic bomb at Pokhran. Canada, which had sponsored the nuclear power programme, refused to supply heavy water for a second reactor and India set about producing its own without US or Canadian help. Later experience in Canada showed that CANDU reactors, having begun with great promise, had developed an unwanted propensity for accidents. After only 12 years' operation, the Pickering 1 reactor burst a pressure pipe in 1983, spilling 240 gallons of heavy water into Lake Ontario. A month later the Douglas Point reactor leaked 594 gallons of heavy water into Lake Huron and was permanently closed after 17 years' service.[88] In India faults in design of the Vadodara heavy water plant caused an explosion during its 1977 trials that put it out of action until 1981. In 1983 the *Times of India* carried a front page report claiming that workers at the Tarapur Atomic Power Station (TAPS) had been subject to higher than permissible radiation levels. Others considered it the most polluted atomic power plant in the world. Built by the US, the reactor is one of the most poorly engineered ever to be traded overseas.

As with pesticides and dangerous chemicals, but with far greater lethal potential, the Third World is used as a dumping ground for obsolete or hazardous European products.

> For the nuclear industry of western Europe, now desperate for orders, Tarapur may turn out to be a boon. According to well-documented reports West German companies are eager to hawk sub-systems of the scrapped Gundreommingen reactor, also of Tarapur's lineage, to the DAE [Department of Atomic Energy] as spares; the French are equally keen on exploring nuclear export possibilities. Evidently what is patently unsafe and dangerous in Europe – KRB Gundreommingen was scrapped in 1980 for safety reasons – is perfectly safe for India.[89]

At Tarapur there were 38 failures, emergencies or accidents in the first five years of power generation; by 1980 there were 344, of which three-quarters were due to 'equipment or design deficiency', including 128 in the reactors themselves. The Rajasthan Atomic Power Station unit 1 (RAPS–1) reactor, which inherited all the faults of Douglas Point, had to be shut down 251 times during ten years of operation; in March 1982 cracks were discovered in the end shield and the plant had not restarted three years later. Narora Atomic Power Station, on the banks of the Ganga in a densely populated area, has the added distinction of being in a Grade IV seismic zone, only 50 km from the epicentre of a 1956 earthquake. The water table is only four or five metres below ground level and there is no rock for a stable foundation. With records like these for its nuclear stations, the outlook for India's seas as recipients of their waste products is gloomy indeed.

Mining uranium is essentially hazardous owing to the ever-present danger of inhaling radon gas. Even more environmentally dangerous are mine tailings which, at Jaduguda processing mill in Bihar, are dumped into a 25-ha pond, decanted and, together with mine water containing uranium, radium and maganese, channelled into a nearby nullah (ravine). When the effluent reaches the River Subarnarekha, which flows into the Bay of Bengal south of the Hooghly estuary, the uranium and radium concentrations have increased. Health physicists claim that the levels are 'below permissible limits', but occasional discharges of tailing slurry from the pond directly into the water system leave little ground for optimism.

Great as they are, India's potentialities for disaster appear minimal when compared with those of the Philippines. Among the more ignominious acts of former President Marcos was his sanctioning of the construction of a Westinghouse-designed pressurized water reactor at Morong on the shore of the Bataan Peninsula, 80 km in a direct line from the capital, Manila.[90] Not only is Morong in a major earthquake zone, it is at the foot of Mount Natib, a dormant volcano. As the International Atomic Energy Authority pointed out: 'The Morong site is unique in the nuclear industry with respect to the risks presented by nearby volcanoes; the eruption of Mt. Natib is a credible event.'[91] The fact that the proposed reactor was of the Three Mile Island type did little to make it more acceptable to local inhabitants. Had it ever gone into operation, the presence of the sea on its doorstep would have offered a challenge to Sellafield in the contest for the 'Most Radioactive Sea in the World'.

On 1 May 1986 the British press reported two 'nuclear' incidents. At the Indian heavy water plant at Talcher in eastern Orissa a devastating fire had broken out, only five months after production started. Problems of 'equipment malfunction' and 'design' had delayed the plant's opening. The fire reportedly destroyed the control room and a pumping station and caused hundreds of families to flee the area. It also set back India's attempts to produce heavy water for its nuclear reactors. The same day, President Corazon Aquino announced that the Philippines Government had decided to scrap the Morong reactor. She gave as reasons that it was unsafe and the cost at US$2.1 billion outrageously high. Westinghouse had already acknowledged that they paid a former Marcos associate a large sum, varying from US$17 million to US$35 million in order to help them secure the contract.[92]

The Sea as Dustbin – Dumping

On 18 July 1977 the Nuclear Energy Agency (NEA) of the Organization for Economic Co-operation and Development (OECD) announced in Paris that the UK had completed a radioactive waste dumping operation in the north-east

Atlantic. Some 3,000 tarred concrete containers, with metal drums inside them, enclosing 2,250 tonnes of radioactive waste were dropped into the sea at an approved site 700 km from the European coast where the water is more than 4,000 m deep. The previous month the Netherlands and Switzerland had dumped 4,180 containers. Britain's contribution meant that, between 1967 and 1977, eight European countries had dropped a total of 46,000 tonnes of radioactive waste into the sea.[93]

Britain began dumping at sea as early as 1950. Radioactive sludge from the Aldermaston Atomic Weapons Research Establishment and other sources was placed in containers designed to release their contents for dispersal and dropped into the Hurd Deep in the western English Channel, a site previously used for disposing of unstable ammunition. Annual dumping at this site stopped in 1963 because the water was less than 2,000 m deep, the minimum recommended by the IAEA. By that time about 15,300 tonnes of waste had been dropped containing 14.4 TBq of alpha activity and 41.2 TBq of beta and gamma.[94]

Across the Atlantic, wartime secrecy in nuclear matters continued into the post-war era. Not until 1981 did George Earle IV, a former US Navy lieutenant-commander, reveal how, in October 1947, he flew three secret missions to drop half a dozen large metal canisters, each weighing 2–3 tons, into the sea 160 km from Atlantic City, New Jersey. For 25 years the US used planes and barges to dump radioactive waste at sites within a few hours' boat ride from New York, Newark, Boston, Los Angeles and San Francisco. When the canisters failed to sink, sailors reportedly punctured them with bullets; when the seas were rough, they dropped them in San Francisco Bay. A 1961 study of the California dumping site revealed that 36% of the drums were damaged and four of the nine concrete blocks demolished. The US Atomic Energy Commission (AEC) claimed that 94% of 162 canisters tested were intact. After nearly 50,000 canisters of radioactive waste had been dumped near the Farallon Islands, 37 km from San Francisco's Golden Gate, the US Environmental Protection Agency (EPA) revealed in 1980 that radioactivity in bottom sediments was 2,000 times greater than 'background radiation'. At least this compared favourably with the site off New Jersey where levels were 260,000 times greater. The US followed up its scuttling of the *William Ralston* – contents, mustard gas (see Chapter 5) – by sinking the nuclear submarine *Sea Wolf* about 190 km off the Delaware–Maryland coast – contents, one complete nuclear reactor with about 33,000 Ci (1,222 TBq) of radioactive material.[95]

Meanwhile, until 1983 authorized dumping continued at the north-east Atlantic site under the co-ordination of the NEA. Belgium, France, the FRG, Italy, the Netherlands, Sweden, Switzerland and the UK took part in joint operations, although only the UK and the Netherlands used the sea as dustbin every year. The greatest dumping occurred in 1980 and 1981 when radioactive waste containing 150 TBq of alpha activity and over 12,000 TBq of beta and gamma, including tritium, was deposited in the 24-month period. In both years the UK was responsible for almost all the alpha activity and for more than half the beta/gamma. Three-quarters of the alpha-emitters dumped between 1949 and 1982 are various forms of plutonium (238, 239, 240 and 242), more than half the beta/gamma-emitters tritium, three-quarters of the remainder plutonium–241. The latter arises mainly from reprocessing, whereas alpha-active waste comes from both nuclear fuel processes and the production of radionuclides for special purposes.[96]

By 1983 France and Germany had turned to deep land burial for disposal of their waste; the Netherlands had stopped sea dumping when it became publicly unacceptable; Sweden was considering a central depository in rock 50 m below the sea-bed ready for operation in 1988, and, despite the wishes of the US Navy to dump 100 obsolete nuclear submarines at sea, the United States had not dumped wastes at sea since the 1970s. Japanese plans to dump 10,000 tonnes of waste in the Pacific were frustrated by opposition from the countries most likely to be affected and their plan to make the Pacific a nuclear-free zone. Of the European countries only the Governments of Belgium and the UK remained committed to dumping at sea.[97]

So far we have written of 'radioactive waste'; it should be made clear, however, that, while all wastes are obnoxious, some are more obnoxious than others. The most deadly is high-level waste (HLW), the spent fuel rods and contaminated liquids that must be isolated for 100,000 years or more and which, in consequence, are usually stored on site in special ponds or, where technology permits, 'vitrified', i.e. 'bonded' into glass, to await deep burial. At the opposite end is low-level waste (LLW), lightly contaminated gloves, clothing, equipment, etc., which, in the UK, has been given shallow burial. Between these two is the catch-all intermediate-level waste (ILW) with half-lives between those of LLW and HLW, which has been the main object of sea dumping. According to the UK Department of the Environment, by the end of the century, in Britain alone, there will be 4,300 cu m of HLW (to be left in its tanks to cool), 85,000 cu m of ILW (some of which may eventually be treated as LLW) and a monstrous 500,000 cu m of LLW. In the USA almost all the 12,000 tonnes of spent fuel already produced is still stored in water-filled ponds and it is estimated that this amount will quadruple within 15 years. The NEA in Paris estimates that OECD countries will have accumulated 160,000 tonnes of spent fuel by the year 2000.[98]

This is basically the fault of the nuclear industry itself. In the UK the RCEP recommended in its Sixth Report that 'there should be no commitment to a large programme of nuclear fission power *until it has been demonstrated beyond reasonable doubt* that a method exists to ensure safe containment of long-lived, highly radioactive waste for the indefinite future'.[99] (My stress.) The industry not only ignored this recommendation but promoted expansion at the expense of research. In his evidence to the Lords Select Committee, Lord Marshall, Chairman of the CEGB, belatedly 'regretted that progress with development and demonstration of waste disposal methods had not taken place much earlier. He regarded the decision, taken many years ago, to leave the problem on one side for the time being, as a bad policy mistake'.[100] The British Government not only acquiesced in this unwarrantable prognostication but actively impeded its solution. In December 1981, while the USA, Canada and Sweden were examining the possibilities of deep land burial, it abruptly cancelled an extensive programme of test drilling to assess the suitability of geological formations throughout the country as repositories for HLW, thereby antagonizing not merely environmentalists but geologists at the Institute of Geological Sciences.[101]

The Government, moreover, ensured that more waste was created than necessary by encouraging reprocessing. When four cubic metres of spent fuel elements are reprocessed, they become 600 cu m of LLW and 40 cu m of ILW, while still leaving 2.5 cu m of HLW.[102] The original purpose of reprocessing was to extract plutonium for making atomic bombs; the contemporary 'justification' is to recover uranium for use as fuel and contaminated plutonium for possible use in fast breeder reactors. Even more important, reprocessing is profitable commercially. European countries prefer to get rid of their HLW by shipping it to the UK for reprocessing and the nuclear industry makes money as a result. In monetarist terms it is logical that the British Government should reject abandoning the THORP project, even if, as the Commons Environment Committee stated, reprocessing at Sellafield creates 'in volume terms, 76 per cent of the UK's LLW, 62 per cent of ILW, 77 per cent of HLW' and that 'the real reason why BNFL is anxious to go ahead with an expanded reprocessing programme is because it has done so in the past and to ensure its own commercial success in that field'.[103]

In the same terms, it is equally logical that 'the Government appear quite eager to resume the sea dump', which had been stopped by a resolution at the 1983 meeting of the parties to the London Dumping Convention (LDC), 'and do not regard the LDC resolution as legally binding. MAFF officials admitted to us [the Commons Environment Committee] that the Government would have ignored the moratorium, had it not been for the NUS [National Union of Seamen] and other unions blacking the practice'.[104] In plain terms, while others have attempted to find technical solutions to the problem, the British Government and nuclear industry have not only disregarded it but adopted a deliberate policy of creating more waste, because it is profitable, and, in the disposal of that waste, would have been prepared to flout majority world opinion by using the sea as a dustbin and were only prevented because they knew British seamen would not carry out their instructions. The union's objection was on more than environmental grounds: 'the NUS queries the morality of any nation . . . using international waters as a disposal site for its nuclear waste, when the environmental repercussions of such a policy would not respect national boundaries'.[105] The NUS argument against dumping at sea is no longer fashionable among politicians; in simple words, they regard it as *wrong*. At this level discussion is impossible, for supporters and opponents of dumping not only view the world with different eyes but do not speak the same language. The Government's return to 'Victorian values' conveniently omits the Victorians' insistence on public, no less than private, morality.

'Dumping' is, in any case, a misnomer. Common sense usage implies that by 'dumping' something we get rid of it. When radioactive waste is dumped at sea, it may be conveniently out of sight, and even out of mind, but it is not out of action. At the north-east Atlantic site the drums used for disposal contained waste packed in concrete or bitumen and surrounded by a metal container, i.e. they were given sufficient protection to ensure safe handling on their journey to the site and to the ocean floor. Holliday describes what happens afterwards:

> There is no firm information to predict when the packages will disintegrate once dumped into the sea. It is judged that the outer mild steel drum will have a life of 30–40 years and the reinforced concrete lining will last for about 300 years or even longer.
> The packages may thus remain intact on the seabed for a long period of time. They are widely scattered over a large area, and it would be practically impossible and extremely expensive to recover even a significant proportion of them. . . . Once their contents have been released, recovery of the radioactivity would not be possible by any means of which we are aware.[106]

In short, dumping is really prolonged storage leading to ultimate discharge, a discharge of whose effects we of the present generation will be conveniently spared but which we have the arrogance to offer, without choice, to our great-great-great-great-grandchildren. It is impossible to be more precise. We do not *know* when these packages will disintegrate and spread their poisons in the waters. Scientists have made 'predictions' and 'judgements'. The only certainty is that, once the radioactivity is released, we cannot call it back. Fortunately for them, the perpetrators of this stupidity will not be around to face the 'judgements' of future generations.

Dumping thus becomes a delayed instance of 'dilute and disperse', the disposal option about which, in considering its merits against those of 'containment', the Commons Environment Committee expressed itself 'in general, anxious about any methods based on [this] philosophy'.[107] Meanwhile, the scientists work on their task of raising public morale by calculating what will happen when dispersal occurs and radiation is eventually released. Common sense accepts their conclusions that the greatest concentration will be round the canister itself. It seems reasonable also to assume that ocean currents will move a diluted radioactive plume away from the site and that some particles on to which radionuclides are adsorbed will sink to the sea-bed. One can accept also that water with radionuclides in it will eventually reach the foot of the continental slope and continue, at the same level, on a 20-year circulation round the deep waters of the ocean basin.[108]

At that point, as scientists cannot actually go down into the sea and measure what is happening, they have evolved a series of computerized models, which, to the non-scientist, are impressive as much for what they omit as for what they include. GESAMP has established a number of principles which it considers should apply to model-making.[109] When it states that models should include 'only those [processes occurring naturally in the sea] which are essential in determining the concentrations of radionuclides over volumes of the ocean for periods of time in which they may be important', this strikes one as a euphemistically erudite version of the common sense axiom that you omit the irrelevant. On reading the negative formulation – 'it is unnecessary for any model to incorporate specifically all the processes or all the motions which occur in the ocean' – one is not happy; and when one reads further that 'it follows that the models should contain a considerable degree of simplification', one begins to wonder at what point the 'considerable degree' becomes 'oversimplification'. Finally, when one is told that, for future concentrations of radionuclides, 'the fluctuations tend to be less important than the mean value when averaged over periods of time and volume over which the fluctuations persist', one hears a 'mean' little voice whispering, 'I may be only an *average* individual, but, as "fluctuation" implies variation between greater and lesser than average, suppose I happen to be the unfortunate one who gets caught in a greater "fluctuation"? Will that help *me* any?' Sellafield 1983 was only a 'fluctuation' within approved limits.

We are back to the old question of 'local' and 'general'. Concerned with producing models for general application, scientists tend to overlook the local excesses that mar their calculations and will not fit neatly into little boxes. It must be great fun dividing the world ocean into a three-dimensional box model based on temperature, salinity and water flow and moving the pollutants from one box to another, as in a complicated game of ludo. The results are doubtless as accurate as human ingenuity and computerization can contrive. But one still has no desire to be a member of some shoal of fish encountering an unwarrantably high fluctuation about which the model gives no warning because it is excluded from the original data.

The Reverberations of 'Hex'

When the French cargo ship *Mont Louis*, carrying 200 tons of uranium hexafluoride in 30 heavy steel containers, collided with the cross-channel ferry *Olau Britannia* on 25 August 1984 and sank in 14 m of water 18 km off Ostend, Belgium, immediate concern was with potential radioactive contamination or a possible explosion. In retrospect, since all containers were recovered intact, the incident is more important for the revelations it brought on the transport of nuclear cargoes, both at sea and on land.[110]

The salvage operation by the Dutch firm, Smit Tak International, and the Belgian Union de Remorquage et de Sauvetage was a highly competent technological exercise. Delayed by bad weather, the splitting of the *Mont Louis* in two in early September and the discovery of a plate blocking access to some containers, and confronted by a scare from local yachting enthusiasts that the ship lay just above the wreck of a World War II ammunition ship, the *Washaba*, which sank in 1944, the salvage crews succeeded in manoeuvring two huge pontoons, Titans 8 and 9, and a great floating crane, Taklift One, into position, used explosives to blast a hole in the side of the ship, fitted new guards over their potentially dangerous valves, and by stages retrieved the canisters. On 4 October the thirtieth, and last, container was salvaged and taken to Dunkirk.

With the secrecy and obfuscation that surrounds all nuclear matters it is probable that, but for the sinking of the *Mont Louis*, the true nature of its cargo, described, according to one report, as 'medical supplies', might have remained unknown. Warned that the ship was carrying radioactive cargo, the crew had demanded extra payment; the owners, Compagnie Générale Maritime, refused, but issued each member with a gauge to show how much radioactivity he was receiving. The Paris Greenpeace office was the first to issue a statement claiming that the ship contained radioactive cargo; later it produced a copy of the ship's manifest. Meanwhile the owners had telexed Belgian coastguards at Ostend, who in turn warned all shipping of the wreck, adding, mistakenly as it happened, that the *Mont Louis* contained radioactive waste packed in yellow drums marked IMCO 7 – the international mark to denote radioactive cargo and the colour used for the two most dangerous of three categories of radioactive strength. The French Government, which had kept silent, defended its action not to reveal the nature of the ship's cargo by claiming that it did not wish to alarm the public.

According to the ship's manifest there were in all 52 cylinders, 22 of them empty (some of these escaped to sea and were washed up on shore). The 30 full cylinders all contained uranium hexafluoride, more familiarly known as 'hex', though not in the same state throughout. Nine cylinders contained normal hex, used for making material for nuclear fuel or weapons production; in 18 the hex was in a depleted form; but the remaining three contained partially enriched uranium in which were minute traces of plutonium, tritium and strontium. From the radioactive standpoint, these three were potentially the most dangerous, although their radioactivity was given at the low figure of 180 Ci (6.6 TBq). Despite publication of the manifest, the Belgian Government offically admitted their existence only on 29 August, four days after the collision. To increase confusion and speculation, the state-owned French company responsible for the shipment, Cogema, had made no distinction in labelling between these cylinders and the rest, causing the more suspicious-minded to view this as an attempt at deceit, the less charitable to conclude that they could not be bothered to indicate the difference, and the more tolerant to decide that, given the small amount of radioactivity, this was a non-issue.

At this point, and continuing sporadically throughout the period, a diversionary argument arose over whether this was a 'radioactive' incident, as claimed in the original Greenpeace statement and taken up by the press, or should more properly be classed as a 'chemical hazard' and thus removed from the emotive atmosphere of matters nuclear. In reality it was both; the greatest immediate danger came not from the small quantities of plutonium, but from the chemical properties of hex, even if, in this context, hex was associated with the nuclear process (and for that reason is included in this chapter).

The consensus of scientific opinion is that hex, in its solid form at normal room temperature, is a highly corrosive and dangerous substance, which at 56.5°C becomes a gas. It must be transported in extremely strong containers since, on contact with water, it produces a violent chemical explosion. The danger from hex leaking into the sea during salvage operations thus warranted references to a potential 'chemical bomb'. Sceptics felt this diagnosis confirmed when they read the French Atomic Energy Commission's statement that any contents released from a container would be quickly diluted and that scientists at BNFL predicted at worst a 'vigorous fizzing'. To complete the diversion, Con Allday, Chairman of BNFL, maintained that the 400 tonnes of oil on board were a greater pollution hazard. As it happened, he was right; conservationists reported that up to 500 seabirds were killed by mid-September during spraying of an oil slick from the *Mont Louis*, while Brussels and Flemish provincial authorities were worried about holiday beaches.

To call hex 'nuclear waste', as did some reports, is to put it at completely the wrong end of the process. It was the unravelling of the role of hex in production that revealed some of the lesser known, and more bizarre, aspects of nuclear transport.

The key to the process is the uranium isotope 235. In natural uranium this forms less than one per cent of the total, but for use as fuel the percentage must be increased and for nuclear weapons it must reach over 90%. Hence the need for 'enrichment', which is where hex comes in. In the early days of nuclear history only the US, the UK, the USSR and France had enrichment plants as part of their weapons programme. Britain closed her Capenhurst plant in the late 1950s as her civil nuclear reactors used natural uranium and did not need the enriched type. France, in need of enriched uranium for its PWR programme and having serious problems with its first plant, entered into agreements with the USSR for hex to be processed for use in French reactors. Hence, further, the *Mont Louis* with a cargo of uranium hexafluoride en route from Le Havre to the Soviet port of Riga.

Anticipating major nuclear expansion throughout the world, the UK reversed its policy and, together with the FRG and the Netherlands, set up an international enrichment company, Urenco, while France, with Belgium, Italy and Spain as partners, became the dominant figure in Europe, with an enrichment plant at Tricastin, France. Unfortunately for the nuclear industry, disillusion rather than expansion followed, leading to aggressive commercial rivalry between the consortia, whose only point of agreement was that neither the other, nor the rest of the world, including as far as possible, the IAEA, should know what they were up to. With the development of nuclear reactors, if not at the rate anticipated, and the establishment of enrichment plants in the FRG, the Netherlands, China, Japan, South Africa, Australia, and possibly Israel, India, Pakistan, Argentina and Brazil in addition to the four original countries, trade in hex and other by-products of nuclear activity has become internationalized and the sea a major route for the transport of the world's most dangerous substances. How much is involved in total no one knows, though one report alleges that 'perhaps nine million separate movements of nuclear cargoes are notified to the International Atomic Energy Authority annually'.[111] Commercial secrecy and fear of terrorism combine to ensure that the public knows as little as possible.

In the revelations following the *Mont Louis*, people in Britain were surprised to learn that the CEGB, under an agreement signed in the 1970s and valid until 1994, sends about 10% of its hex to the Soviet Union for reprocessing. BNFL sends convoys of lorries, each with one 15-tonne conainer of hex, to Ellesmere Port, Cheshire, for two or three shipments each year. The South of Scotland Electricity Board sends rather more than the CEGB, to give a total of about 350 tonnes a year. Larger quantities, amounting to 100 tonnes a week, go to Hull, Immingham and other east coast ports for shipment to the Urenco plant at Almedo in the Netherlands. Even more unusual was the admission by BNFL that quantities of uranium, unenriched on the outward journey, enriched on the return, up to 1,200 tonnes or more, were carried by Sealink passenger ferries to both France and Holland. At first BNFL had denied the report, but, presented with a document naming them as consigners of two containers of uranium on the *MV Senlac* on 28 February 1984, described the activity as 'on quite a regular basis', adding that, 'It's not dangerous in its containers'.[112] A rival claim, in a letter to the *Guardian* newspaper of 1 September, on behalf of the 'infinitely more dangerous radioactive plutonium nitrate, eight shipments of which from Dounreay on the north of Scotland to Sellafield' had allegedly taken place since June 1981,[113] passed almost unnoticed. No holiday-makers accompanied these consignments.

The Sealink revelation was not the only setback for BNFL. On 28 August 1984, three days after the *Mont Louis* sank, it was reported that in Panama the port authorities had refused port services to the *Pacific Fisher*, a British ship carrying spent nuclear fuel from Japan to Sellafield for reprocessing. According to BNFL, shipments had been passing through the canal for years and facilities had never been refused before. The point, of course, is not the current stoppage but the information that this traffic had gone on 'for years'.

The ultimate in the bizarre was Greenpeace's claim that the Soviet Union played a vital role in manufacturing plutonium for American missile warheads, using the seas of the world for transport. The process for one consignment worked as follows: uranium from Canadian mines was shipped to France, where it was processed into hex and sent to Riga for enrichment. The enriched uranium then found its way, via Cap de la Hague, France, to Seattle, USA, where it was turned into uranium oxide and sent to New Jersey for conversion into fuel rods. In turn the fuel rods were shipped back to Europe for use in West German reactors and the spent fuel sent to Cap de la Hague for reprocessing. From this activity depleted uranium went back to the Soviet Union for enrichment (on the *Mont Louis*?) but the plutonium extracted was sent to the USA, where the Government had reserved the right to use it for warheads and Senate records show that plutonium obtained in this way is used for the American weapons stockpile.[114]

Seldom have the contorted ways of the nuclear industry – and their governments – been so ruthlessly exposed as in this scenario. Whatever the validity of the Greenpeace argument – and one is tempted to cry 'A plague on *all* your houses' – the *Mont Louis* served a useful purpose if it set them tracing the path of nuclear cargoes to and fro across the Atlantic, back and forth through the heavy shipping lanes of the English Channel to the North Sea and the Baltic. One can only hope that, when the next collision occurs and a cargo of hex finds its way to the sea-bed, we shall be as fortunate. The world cannot afford a *Mont Louis* on the scale of the *Torrey Canyon* or the *Amoco Cadiz*.

References

1. *Guardian* 24 July 1984, 2 September 1984, 17 February 1986
2. Ibid. 26 June 1985
3. Ibid. 9 July 1985
4. Ibid. 7 January 1987
5. Numerous accounts of radiation are available. That given here draws largely on Holliday 1984 pp. 5–9 and Tucker 1986. For more detail, especially health aspects, see Bertell 1985 pp. 15–63
6. Holliday 1984 p. 7
7. Lean 1985
8. Holliday 1984 p. 6
9. Lean 1986a; McKie 1987
10. Holliday 1984 p. 6
11. Lean 1987
12. Holliday 1984 p. 6
13. Bertell 1985 p. 34
14. Hunt 1986
15. Holliday 1984 p. 14
16. DoE *Digest 1985* p. 25
17. Holliday 1984 p. 7
18. Ibid. p. 49
19. Ibid.
20. Ibid. p. 50
21. Bertell 1985 p. 173
22. BBC *Panorama* Programme 12 May 1986
23. *Guardian* 13 March 1986, 24 May 1986
24. Ibid. 17 August 1985
25. Holliday 1984 pp. 6–7
26. Ibid. p. 39 and Fig. 6.5
27. Ibid. p. 7
28. *Guardian* 12 June 1985, 3 March 1986, 6, 7 October 1986; *Lloyd's List* 3 March 1986; *Observer* 5 October 1986
29. Jasani 1985 pp. 240–53
30. Ibid. p. 246
31. Ibid. p. 252
32. Ibid.
33. Data for the Pacific from: Bacon 1984 pp. 31–38; Bertell 1985 pp. 70–76, 99–103; Brown 1985; Gristwood 1986
34. Bacon 1984 p. 33
35. Ibid.
36. Quoted Gristwood 1986
37. Quoted Bertell 1985 p. 76
38. Tucker 1987
39. Bacon 1984 p. 37
40. Ibid.
41. Ibid.
42. Data on processes and reactors from: Bertell 1985 pp. 105–7; House of Lords 1986 pp. 15–20
43. Hunt 1986 pp. 6–7 Table 1

44. *Nuclear News* February 1986. Quoted Pollock 1986 p. 8 Table 1
45. Steele 1986a
46. Hunt 1986 p.6
47. House of Commons 1986 para. 116
48. *Guardian* 5 July 1984
49. House of Lords 1986 para. 82
50. Ibid. para. 83
51. Ibid.
52. House of Commons 1986 para. 147
53. Ibid. para. 155
54. Ibid.
55. Lean 1986b
56. *Guardian* 11 September 1986
57. House of Commons 1986 para. 129
58. Lean 1986b
59. *Guardian* 12 December 1986
60. House of Commons 1986 para. 216
61. *Guardian* 2 November 1985
62. Ibid. 8 March 1986
63. Bertell 1985 p. 170
64. Ibid. p. 171
65. Ibid. pp. 175–180
66. Ibid. p. 197
67. *Guardian* 31 May 1985
68. Ibid. 5 May 1986
69. Jackson 1985
70. *Guardian* 4 October 1985
71. Ibid. 13 December 1986
72. Mosey 1986
73. Camplin et al. p. 15
74. Ibid. p. 17
75. ACOPS 1985–6 p. 12
76. Highfield 1985
77. *RSRS 32* pp. 18–20, Table 8
78. *Guardian* 15 March 1986
79. Ibid. 23 May 1986
80. Ibid.
81. *Lloyd's List* 27 August 1986, 17 October 1986
82. Steele 1986b
83. Ibid.
84. *RSRS 13* p. 132
85. Steele 1986b
86. Pathmarajah and Meith 1985 p. 188
87. Except where stated Indian data from Agarwal et al. 1985 pp. 282–97
88. Bertell 1985 p. 107
89. Agarwal et al. 1985 p. 288
90. Watts and Taylor 1985 pp. 32–6
91. Quoted Watts and Taylor 1985 p. 32
92. *Guardian* 1 May 1986, 16 May 1986
93. *The Times* 20 July 1977; Holliday 1984 p. 12

94. Holliday 1984 p. 11
95. Bertell 1985 pp. 302–4
96. Holliday 1984 pp. 11–15
97. Ibid. pp. 19–20; Bertell 1985 pp. 304–6
98. Pollock 1986 pp. 14, 19
99. RCEP 6
100. House of Lords 1986 para. 85
101. Smith 1985
102. Fairhall 1986
103. House of Commons 1986 paras. 176, 210
104. Ibid. para. 37
105. Quoted ibid. para. 78
106. Holliday 1984 p. 19
107. House of Commons 1986 para. 79
108. Holliday 1984 pp. 25–9
109. GESAMP 19, quoted Holliday 1984 pp. 35–6
110. Account based on press reports: *Guardian* 27, 28, 30 August 1984, 3, 11, 12, 14, 15 September 1984; *The Times* 13 September 1984; *Observer* 16 September 1984; with particular reference to Fairhall 1984a, 1984b; Tucker 1984b
111. Samstag 1984
112. *Guardian* Diary 20 September 1984
113. Letter from Andrew Bluefield. *Guardian* 1 September 1984
114. *Guardian* 29 August 1984

Part 3:
The Deeper Malady

The deeper malady is better hid; the world is
wounded at the heart.

Wordsworth

7.   Portents and Possibilities

Long-range Forecast

At a conference in Villach, Austria, in October 1985, scientists from 29 countries warned governments that it was time to intensify research programmes and develop social and economic strategies ready for changes in the world's climate in the first half of the next century 'greater than any in man's history'. According to their predictions a rise in surface temperature of 1.5°C–4.5°C at the equator – greater at higher latitudes – will take place within the next 45 years. As the result of thermal expansion and melting ice, the level of the sea will rise by 25–145 cm. During the following century the melting of glaciers will cause a further rise of 20 cm, and, while a global rise of 4.5°C is unlikely to cause the western Antarctic ice sheet to melt, if this does occur, the sea will rise by a further *five metres* over several hundred years.[1]

Not everyone accepts this prognostic in its entirety. Dr Rhodes Fairbridge of Colombia University and Dr Walter Newman of New York University argue that, while the average sea level has risen by more than a millimetre a year over the last 50 years, increased water storage on land has absorbed almost this amount for the last 30 years and there is substantial scope for diverting huge volumes of the sea into drainage basins such as the Dead Sea, the Qattara Depression, Egypt, and Imperial Valley, California.[2]

The process, however, is not a simple one of rising temperatures causing the polar ice caps to melt and cause a Second Deluge. In fact, the opposite occurs. Not only is the Antarctic ice sheet increasing in size but the Hubbard glacier in southern Alaska, advancing at the astounding rate of 34 metres a day, has closed off the sea end of a fjord 55 km long to form an inland lake. The explanation of this apparent contradiction is sufficiently simple for even the non-scientist to grasp. The first effect of a rise in temperature is to increase evaporation of sea-water; this leads to increased precipitation over the cooler parts of the earth, heavier snowfalls in the polar regions and consequent expansion of the ice cap. The fact that the sea level is actually rising is thus attributed to thermal expansion and the melting of small glaciers at lower altitudes. As for the sea itself, while scientists readily admit that the long-term effects of warmer oceans on marine ecosystems, fisheries and food chains are virtually unknown, they have already made one discovery: 'On a recent research cruise in the North Pacific, oceanographers discovered that the plankton were blooming to such an extent that two to three times more organic matter is being produced by photosynthesis than has been measured before'.[3]

We thus face the prospect that, not only are the seas being poisoned by oil, chemicals, sewage, heavy metals and radioactive waste, but their existence as we know it is now threatened with unprecedented change. This potentially catastrophic future – the inundation of low-lying coastal cities and farmland, mangrove swamps, river deltas and estuaries, with conjoint effects on vegetation and such areas of forest as remain – results from the well known 'greenhouse effect' caused by the release of carbon dioxide and other gases into the atmosphere. In pre-industrial times the concentration of carbon dioxide was 280 ppm of air by volume; by 1980 it had reached 340 ppm, and between the middle and the end of the next century it is expected to have doubled to 560 ppm.[4] The gases act as a coat that keeps us warm – a little too warm for comfort. Recent research suggests that the 'other greenhouse gases' rather than carbon dioxide are a cause of concern. .Before their warming effect was appreciated, scientists thought that carbon dioxide alone would not generate such a rise in sea level until the last half of the next century. They have now decided that the effect of the other gases, which are rapidly increasing, will be to advance considerably the date of significant warning.[5] In short, humanity has been caught out. We thought that this was something we need not bother about because it would happen only when we were no longer around. Now we discover that, unless something is done quickly, it will affect, if not ourselves, at least our children and grandchildren.

Discussion of these gases, mainly chlorofluorocarbons or CFCs, leads, on the one hand, to such domestic products as aerosol sprays, hamburger cartons, refrigerators and air-conditioning, and, on the other, to that fascinating topic for contemporary scientific speculation, the 'hole' in the ozone layer above Antarctica.[6] The ozone occupies a band between 40 and 50 km above the earth's surface and, from our anthropocentric viewpoint, is usually described as screening harmful ultra-violet rays from the sun, thus protecting humanity from skin cancers and other diseases. Any depletion in ozone sufficient to allow increased penetration will thus affect human beings. Ecologically, however, as the stratosphere, in which ozone occurs, acts as a 'lid' on the weather systems of the troposphere below it, any changes in the stratosphere can produce changes in our weather as yet unknown.

Scientists of the British Antarctic Survey, analysing data collected by balloon since 1957, first discovered the 'hole' in 1985. Their findings were confirmed by the American satellite *Nimbus 7*, which had actually been measuring the decline in ozone since 1979, only to have its reports rejected by NASA's computers as 'incredible'! Discovery of the hole aroused considerable controversy over its causes. Was it due to CFCs or nitrogen oxide, both of which 'soak up' ozone, or did it arise naturally in conjunction with sun-spot fluctuations? And what were the implications of later discoveries that the 'hole' consists of a series of 'layers' of different concentrations? A number of facts were, however, indisputable: first, that CFCs are squirted from aerosol tins and used to puff up plastic foam fast-food boxes, for cooling refrigerators and cleaning computers, and in air-conditioning systems and fire extinguishers; secondly, that, molecule for molecule, CFCs are 10,000 times more effective than carbon dioxide in increasing the 'greenhouse effect'; thirdly, that, once released into the atmosphere, they remain in existence for more than 100 years; and finally, that, if we are to bring about a return to 'normal', a cut-back of 85% is required.

Despite the lack of a proven connection between CFCs and the 'ozone hole', in an attempt, largely at the instigation of UNEP, to conclude a protocol to the 1985 Vienna Convention on the Ozone Layer, the US Environmental Protection Agency (EPA) proposed a freeze at current levels of production, leading to an eventual ban. The EPA argued that a continued 2.8% per annum growth in output would lead to 40 million extra skin cancers, 12 million extra eye cataracts and 800,000 deaths in the US alone from exposure to higher levels of ultra-violet radiation over the next 90 years. The USSR, the Scandinavian countries and the FRG, despite the importance of Hoechst as a manufacturer, favoured a phasing out. Until March 1987 official EEC policy was for a freeze, the main opposition to further action coming from Spain and the UK, whose attitude was described as barely distinguishable from that of Britain's biggest producer, Imperial Chemical Industries. In March, however, when new data suggested that the ozone shield over Western Europe and much of the northern hemisphere was disappearing four times faster than predicted by computer estimates based on the quantity of chemicals released, the British Government made an environmental half-turn. Overcoming opposition from the Department of Trade and Industry, the environment minister, William Waldegrave, met his colleagues in Brussels with a mandate to accept cuts that resulted in a compromise agreement of a single 20% cut in CFC production by 1990, followed by a scientific review. The 1990 reduction met UNEP requirements, but British opposition to UNEP plans for further cuts of 20% every four years with a complete ban by the year 2000 threatened to undermine the consensus necessary for agreement under UN rules. On this occasion the US could afford to be on the side of the angels; its major producer, DuPont, had allegedly patented safer alternatives, leaving the UK to follow its customary obstructionist line against the majority.

When legal experts met at The Hague in July, the Director of UNEP, Dr Mostafa Tolba, was still confident of an agreement. The British based their opposition on the view that the cause of the hole was not yet known and in August published the first report of an official Stratospheric Ozone Review Group as scientific backing for their stand. Among the signatories to the report was Dr Joe Farman, Director of the British Antarctic Survey, who first discovered the hole. Angered by the way in which the DoE had used the Report's executive summary to claim that 'the use of CFCs at present rates is unlikely to lead to a reduction of the stratospheric ozone layer', while ignoring its conclusion that, though little immediate change could be expected, after 20 or 30 years 'ozone decreases could be substantial', Dr Farman pointed out that the report had been written some months previously and that subsequent

American research now placed responsibility firmly on CFCs. Unable to reject the latest scientific evidence and bombarded by an informed press campaign and expressions of public concern, within a fortnight the British Government agreed to withdraw its opposition to signing a new protocol calling for a 50% reduction.

By the end of August it almost appeared that humanity was about to act sensibly. The final negotiations in Montreal, however, ran into a number of snags which, unexpectedly, came from some of the treaty's main supporters. The US, on President Reagan's initiative, demanded that it should not come into effect until ratified by countries that produced 90% of the chemicals. This would have given the EEC, Japan, the US or the Soviet Union the chance to block the treaty by failing to ratify it. In turn, the USSR insisted on changes to bring the timing into line with its current five-year plan, and certain Third World countries, led by Argentina and Brazil, demanded exemptions that would allow production to rise for a period to enable them to increase their consumption.

On 16 September 1987 the parties reached the inevitable compromise – a treaty that satisfied everybody and nobody. Some hailed it as 'the first world-wide pact ever signed to reduce pollution'; others derided it for being as full of 'holes' as the ozone layer itself. Under the agreement consumption in the developed world is to be cut by 50% in two stages by the year 2000; production, however, will be cut by only 35% over the same period owing to the insistence of US and British producers on the need to increase exports to the Third World. The treaty even allows leading producers to *increase* their output by ten per cent until 1990, while the USSR will be allowed to complete two CFC plants in line with its five-year plan. Finally, the agreement only comes into force after ratification by 67% of the participating countries.

Critics were not slow to point out that the treaty's provisions could be circumvented by companies building plants in non-signatory countries and exporting the products back to the developed world. The non-specialist gives a feeble cheer for the 50% cut-back in consumption in the developed world but remains puzzled as to how the ozone layer will distinguish between CFCs from this quarter and those from the Third World. The figure of an immediate cut of 85% considered essential to prevent further damage seems to have disappeared with the missing ozone. So far as the seas and humanity are concerned, our great-grandchildren living on low-lying coasts may well thank our present far-sighted statesmen that the rising waters will not come up to their necks, only to their knees.

That other source of atmospheric poisoning, carbon dioxide, caused mainly by the burning of fossil fuels, oil, coal and gas, is, moreover, still with us. Attacking the use of these as sources of energy, the Energy Panel of the UN World Commission on Environment and Development (WCED) maintains that 'carbon dioxide output globally could be halved by energy efficiency measures over the next 50 years or so without any reduction of the tempo of economic growth',[7] but for a body whose aim is to produce a 'global strategy for sustainable development', their conclusion that 'nuclear energy could also have an important role to play in attacking fossil-fuel related issues'[8] seems rather like casting out a known and familiar devil only to bring in an unknown and even more dangerous one. The seas will not be saved by slowing down their thermal expansion only to poison them with nuclear waste, even if human beings are required to cut down on aerosols, hamburger cartons and fridges.

Enter the Law – Softly, Softly

Leaving the scientists to argue over the ozone hole, we turn to the activities of their colleagues in the protection of the sea – the lawyers. Between 1926, when an International Maritime Conference in Washington produced the first international convention on oil pollution, which no one ratified, and 1984, when an International Maritime Organization (IMO) Conference in London failed to agree on a convention for 'Hazardous and Noxious Substances' (HNS), i.e. chemicals, so that there was nothing to ratify, governments have put their signatures to no fewer than 50 major legal conventions or agreements affecting, directly or indirectly, the entry of poisons into the sea (see Figs. 7.1, 7.2). Of the 26 international conventions, applicable throughout the world, if we extend the category to include 'defects' in ships and those who sail them, all but two dealt with what lawyers referred to as 'vessel-source pollution', only one (not yet in operation) with 'land-based sources'. Of the 22 regional agreements or conventions, laying down regulations for specified parts of the world ocean, 16 also dealt with ships, but 11 covered discharges from land. Of the poisons considered in the previous chapters, 16 international and 15 regional documents concerned oil, 17 regional but only six international heavy metals, chemicals, DDT, PCBs, etc. and 15 regional but only three international (two of them not yet operative) sewage, 'garbage' and plastics. Radioactivity and the disposal of radioactive waste appear in five international and three regional documents.

Obviously not all agreements are equally important. The well known MARPOL 73/78 Convention (see p. 219), which aims at a comprehensive reduction in pollution by oil, bulk chemicals, sewage and garbage, is more far-reaching than the 1966 Load Lines Convention, which ensures that ships do not carry more than is good for them. Nevertheless, this broad statistical analysis suggests that discussions at international level have concerned ships and oil, those at regional level both land and sea with more attention to other poisons. In one sense this is not surprising. Sewage and industrial waste affect coastal waters or enclosed seas such as the Baltic or Mediterranean more readily than the open ocean; but the absence of international agreement on carrying packages of hazardous chemicals on deck, while regulations for their carriage in bulk are only now (1987) taking effect is no matter for congratulation, especially when contrasted with ten international agreements on liability and compensation for damage caused by oil.

There is a further difference. Of the 20 international conventions now operative, three took ten years to come into effect and the overall delay between

Figure 7.1
INTERNATIONAL CONVENTIONS

				Source				Pollutant				Other		
	Date / Short Title	Operative	No. of Contracting States[1]	Ship	Land	Offshore/ sea-bed	Dumping	Oil	Chemicals/ HNS	Sewage/ Garbage/ Plastics	Radioactivity	Ship Construction	Seamanship	Liability & compensation
1	1954 OILPOL	1958	72	×				×						
2	1957 Limitation of Liability	1960		×				×						×
	Geneva Conventions:													
3	1958 High Seas	1962		×				×						
4	1958 Continental Shelf	1964				×		×				×		
5	1962 Liability of Operations of Nuclear Ships	NY		×							×			×
6	1966 Load Lines	1968	108	×								×		
7	1969 CLC	1975	57	×				×						×
8	1969 Intervention	1975	50	×				×						
9	1971 Fund/FC	1978	34	×				×						×
10	1971 Carriage of Nuclear Materials	1975	11	×					×		×			
11	1972 Collision Regulations	1977	95	×									×	
12	1972 LDC	1975	61	×			×		×	×				
13	1972 Safe Containers	1977	43	×										
14	1973 MARPOL	1983[2]	39	×				×	×	×				
15	1973 Intervention Protocol	1983	20	×				×	×					
16	1973 Transport of Radioactive Materials	?		×							×			
17	1974 SOLAS	1980	94	×								×		
18	1976 CLC Protocol	1981	22	×				×						×
19	1976 Fund Protocol	NY	14	×				×						×
20	1976 Limitation of Maritime Claims	1986	13	×										×
21	1978 MARPOL Protocol	1983	39	×				×	×	×				
22	1978 SOLAS Protocol	1981	58	×								×		
23	1978 STCW	1984	51	×									×	
24	1979 SAR	1985	25	×									×	
25	1981 SOLAS Amendments	1984		×								×		
26	1982 LOSC	NY		×	×	×	×	×	×	×	×			
27	1984 CLC Protocol	NY		×				×						×
28	1984 FC Protocol	NY	1	×				×						×

[1] IMO Conventions only, as at mid-1986
[2] Oil only

Figure 7.1. KEY – Full titles of International Conventions and Agreements

1. International Convention for the Prevention of Pollution of the Sea by Oil 1954
2. (Brussels) Convention on the Limitation of Liability of Owners of Sea-Going Ships 1957
3. Geneva Convention on the High Seas 1958
4. Geneva Convention on the Continental Shelf 1958
5. (Brussels) Convention on the Liability of Operators of Nuclear Ships 1962
6. International Convention on Load Lines 1966
7. International Convention on Civil Liability for Oil Pollution Damage 1969
8. International Convention Relating to Intervention on the High Seas in Cases of Oil Pollution Casualties 1969
9. International Convention on the Establishment of an International Fund for Oil Pollution Damage 1971
10. International Convention Relating to Civil Liability in the Field of Maritime Carriage of Nuclear Materials 1971
11. International Regulations for Preventing Collisions 1972
12. International Convention for the Prevention of Marine Pollution by Dumping of Wastes and Other Matter 1972
13. International Convention on Safe Containers 1972
14. International Convention for the Prevention of Pollution from Ships 1973
15. Protocol Relating to Intervention on the High Seas in Cases of Marine Pollution by Substances Other than Oil 1973
16. International Atomic Energy Agency Regulations for the Safe Transport of Radioactive Materials 1973
17. International Convention for Safety of Life at Sea 1974
18. 1976 Protocol to the 1969 International Convention on Civil Liability for Oil Pollution Damage
19. 1976 Protocol to the 1971 International Convention on the Establishment of an International Fund for Oil Pollution Damage
20. (London) Convention on Limitation of Liability for Maritime Claims
21. 1978 Protocol to the 1973 International Convention for the Prevention of Pollution from Ships
22. 1978 Protocol to the 1974 International Convention for Safety of Life at Sea
23. International Convention on Standards of Training, Certification and Watchkeeping for Seafarers 1978
24. International Convention on Maritime Search and Rescue 1979
25. 1981 Amendments to the 1974 International Convention for Safety of Life at Sea
26. (United Nations) Law of the Sea Convention 1982
27. 1984 Protocol to the 1969 International Convention on Civil Liability for Oil Pollution Damage
28. 1984 Protocol to the 1971 International Convention on the Establishment of an International Fund for Oil Pollution Damage

Figure 7.2
REGIONAL AGREEMENTS

#	Date	Short Title	Oper-ative	Area	Source: Ship	Land	Offshore/sea-bed	Dumping	Pollutant: Oil	Chemicals/HNS	Sewage/Garbage/Plastics	Radio-activity	Other: Ship Construction	Sea-manship	Liability & compensation
1	1957	EURATOM	1959	EEC								X			
2	1969	Bonn Agreement	1969	North Sea	X				X						
3	1972	Oslo Convention	1974	W. Europe & N-E Atlantic				X				X		X	
4	1974	Helsinki Convention	1980	Baltic	X	X	X		X	X	X	X			
5	1974	Paris Convention	1978	North Sea & N-E Atlantic	X	X			X	X	X	X			
6	1976	Barcelona Convention	1978	Mediter-					X	X	X				
7	1976	& Protocol	1978	ranean			X		X	X					
8	1976	Liability for Oil Pollution Damage	NY	North Sea			X		X				X		
9	1978	Hague Memorandum	1979	N-W Europe	X		X								
10	1978	Kuwait Convention	1979	Gulf	X				X	X	X				
11	1978	& Protocol	1979		X		X		X	X	X				
12	1979	Bonn Extension		North Sea	X	X				X					
13	1980	Athens Protocol	1983	Mediter-ranean		X	X			X	X				
14	1981	Abidjan Convention	1984	West & Central Africa	X	X	X		X	X	X[Land]				
15	1981	Lomé Protocol			X				X	X	(X)				
16	1981	Lima Convention	1986	S-E Pacific	X		X	X	X	X	(X)				
17	1982	Jeddah Convention	NY	Red Sea & Gulf of Aden	X		X	X	X	X	X		X		
18	1982	& Protocol	1982												
19	1982	Paris MOU on PSC		EEC + Finland Norway Sweden									X		
20	1983	Quito Protocol	1986	S-E Pacific	X	X			X	X	(X)				
21	1983	Cartagena Convention	NY	Caribbean	X	X	X		X	X	(X)				
22	1983	& Protocol			X				X		X				

Figure 7.2 KEY – Full Titles of Regional Conventions and Agreements

1. European Atomic Energy Community Treaty 1957
2. Bonn Agreement for Co-operation in Dealing with Pollution of the North Sea by Oil 1969
3. Convention for the Prevention of Marine Pollution by Dumping from Ships and Aircraft 1972
4. Convention for the Protection of the Marine Environment of the Baltic Sea Area 1974
5. Convention for the Prevention of Marine Pollution from Land-Based Sources 1974
6. Convention for the Protection of the Mediterranean against Pollution 1976, and
7. Protocol concerning Co-operation in Combating Pollution of the Mediterranean Sea by Oil and Other Harmful Substances in Cases of Emergency 1976
8. (London) Convention on Civil Liability for Oil Pollution Damage from Offshore Installations 1976
9. Hague Memorandum of Understanding between Certain Maritime Authorities on the Maintenance of Standards on Merchant Ships 1978
10. Kuwait Regional Convention for Co-operation on the Protection of the Marine Environment from Pollution 1978, and
11. Protocol concerning Regional Co-operation in Combating Pollution by Oil and Other Harmful Substances in Cases of Emergency 1978
12. (Extension to) Bonn Agreement for Co-operation in Dealing with Pollution of the North Sea by Oil (1979)
13. Protocol concerning the Protection of the Mediterranean Sea against Pollution from Land-Based Sources 1980
14. Convention for Co-operation in the Protection and Development of the Marine and Coastal Environment of the West and Central African Region 1981, and
15. Protocol concerning Co-operation in Combating Pollution in Cases of Emergency 1981
16. Convention on the Protection of the Marine Environment of the South-East Pacific 1981
17. Regional Convention for the Conservation of the Red Sea and the Gulf of Aden Environment 1982, and
18. Protocol concerning Regional Co-operation in Combating Pollution by Oil and Other Harmful Substances in Cases of Emergency 1982
19. Paris Memorandum of Understanding on Port State Control 1982
20. Supplementary Protocol to the Agreement on Regional Co-operation in Combating Pollution of the South-East Pacific by Hydrocarbons or other Harmful Substances
21. Convention for the Protection of the Marine Environment of the Wider Caribbean 1983, and
22. Protocol concerning Co-operation in Combating Oil Spills in the Wider Caribbean Region 1983

signing and operation was, on average, 5.5 years. Against this, while one regional agreement took six years to become effective and two others five, even if these are included, the average for 14 is 2.7 years, half the time for international conventions. The law, at whatever level, moves slowly, slowly, even if it moves faster regionally than internationally.

Two events, neither concerned solely with the seas, provided an impetus and an opportunity for all concerned with the well-being of the world ocean. The Stockholm UN Conference on the Human Environment (UNCHE) in June 1972 produced a *Declaration* that includes, as one of its 26 principles:

> States shall take all possible steps to prevent pollution of the seas by substances that are liable to create hazards to human health, to harm living resources and marine life, damage amenities or to interfere with other legitimate uses of the sea.[9]

More importantly, 'Stockholm', itself the culmination of several years of preparation, embodied an upsurge in public concern about the environment which governments could no longer ignore. On the practical side, an *Action Plan* provided the basis for establishing the UN Environment Programme so that, from 1974 onwards, UNEP's Regional Seas Programme was able to bring about regional agreements covering the Mediterranean, the Atlantic off West and Central Africa, the South-East Pacific, the Red Sea and Gulf of Aden, and the wider Caribbean. In Europe, the Baltic countries signed the Helsinki Convention (1974) to protect that much-poisoned sea, the EEC and Nordic countries followed earlier agreements on co-operation to deal with oil spills (Bonn, 1969), dumping (Oslo, 1972) and pollution from land (Paris, 1974) with arrangements for inspecting ships for seaworthiness (Paris, 1982) that include powers of detention until faults are put right.

The Third UN Conference on the Law of the Sea, that series of meetings, arguments, compromises and attempts at consensus from 1973 to 1982, which began with the idealistic concept of the sea as the 'common heritage of mankind', progressed to practical methods of exploiting the sea-bed while preserving the waters, and ended in rancour as the Reagan Administration overturned previous agreements, produced in the 1982 Law of the Sea Convention (LOSC) a document embodying the Stockholm principles. The Convention gives coastal states the right to protect the seas within both an extended territorial sea of 12 miles and a 200-mile Exclusive Economic Zone (EEZ) as well as laying down new provisions for the rights and responsibilities of coastal, flag and port states concerning ships in port, in inland waters, in the new legal zones and on the high seas. By April 1986, 159 states had signed the Convention and 27 had ratified it.[10] Conspicuous near the end of the alphabetical list as two who had not were the United Kingdom and the USA.

But it was disasters at sea, particularly in European waters, as much as positive concern by the environmentally conscious, that led to speedy action. The Intergovernmental Maritime Consultative Organization (IMCO), established as a specialized UN agency in 1958, had called conferences in Copenhagen in 1959 and in London in 1962. Only when the *Torrey Canyon* foundered in 1967 did its members adopt the 1969 Convention on Intervention on the High Seas in Cases of Oil Pollution Casualties, the Civil Liability Convention (CLC) of the same year and the 1972 International Regulations for Preventing Collisions at Sea. In Europe the disaster brought about the 1969 Bonn Agreement for Co-operation in Dealing with Pollution of the North Sea by Oil, while the *Stella Maris* incident speeded up conclusion of the Oslo Dumping Convention in 1972, to be followed swiftly by its global application that same year, the London Dumping Convention (LDC), and its counterpart to deal with dangers from land, the Paris Convention of 1974.

The year after Stockholm saw the most comprehensive attempt at global level to curb pollution from ships. The 1973 International Convention for the Prevention of Pollution from Ships, invariably referred to as MARPOL, not only laid down regulations for discharging oil at sea, provided for detailed records of operations to be kept in an Oil Record Book, gave states at which ships arrived the right to inspect them, and insisted that reception facilities for waste oils were provided at ports and loading terminals, but also designated the Baltic, Mediterranean, Black and Red Seas and the Gulf as 'special areas' in which discharging oil was prohibited; separate annexes applied appropriate provisions to liquid chemicals in bulk, 'hazardous and noxious substances' in packages, sewage, and garbage from ships.

In practice MARPOL was too comprehensive. Not only was there opposition from the shipping industry, which objected to the additional expense, but many Third World countries found the cost of installing reception facilities for oil residues beyond their means. So the years passed, the tankers grew larger and the number of accidents increased. Concerned at this trend, in February 1978, the IMCO called a conference on Tanker Safety and Pollution Prevention. The following month the *Amoco Cadiz* grounded on the rocks off Brittany. Before the year was out there was not only a new convention, aimed at improving standards of seamanship, the International Convention on Standards of Training, Certification and Watchkeeping for Seafarers (STCW), but also a Protocol to MARPOL, which allowed a stage-by-stage process of implementation. The regulations on oil were put into operation first, though not until ten years after the original agreement.

A glance at the terms and mode of operation of one regional and one international agreement shows both the strength and weaknesses of the legal approach. On 24 March 1974 the seven states bordering the Baltic Sea signed the Convention on the Protection of the Marine Environment of the Baltic Sea Area (Helsinki Convention). This comprehensive set of regulations covers pollution both from ships, including pleasure craft (Article 7) and from the land (Articles 5 and 6), lays down conditions for discharging oil and chemicals carried in bulk, and makes reception facilities obligatory. Annex IV to Article 7 covers discharges of sewage and garbage from ships and the provision of reception facilities for their disposal. Article 6 and Annex III deal with direct discharges from land through sewers, the carrying of solid substances in rivers and agricultural run-off, and list 16 groups of substances, including heavy metals, persistent pesticides and radioactive materials, significant (*sic*) quantities of which cannot be discharged without special permits from the appropriate national authority. Article 10 calls on Contracting Parties to take measures to prevent pollution from exploration and exploitation of the sea-bed, while Article 9 prohibits dumping, except to save human life or of dredged spoils not containing significant quantities of the harmful substances listed in Annexes I and II. Special permission for such dumping is given by the appropriate national authority according to provisions specified in Annex V. The Convention operates through an intergovernmental agency, the Helsinki Commission (HELCOM), which meets annually to agree recommendations which are then passed to national governments.

The Law, as laid down in the Convention, is satisfactory to the point of superfluity. The clause to prevent pollution from exploration and exploitation of the sea-bed, as HELCOM admits, has applied mainly to removing sand and gravel, since there has been little exploration for oil. But when one looks closely at the 'get out' clauses and how things work in practice, doubts emerge as to the effectiveness of the whole operation. There is One Law for the entire Baltic region, but no One Body with the power to enforce it. HELCOM makes 'Recommendations' to the seven national governments, the recommendations call on the Contracting Parties to report on action taken and set a date for them to do so. But HELCOM has no powers to demand that action is taken, to penalize recalcitrant governments, or to call to account those whose actions are unsatisfactory. Even within the terms of the Convention the discretionary powers given to national governments are such that, without their goodwill and positive co-operation, the whole aim of the Convention is frustrated. Discharges of heavy metals, persistent pesticides and radioactive materials are controlled – an excellent and necessary precaution that is immediately contradicted when we read that governments can issue permits authorizing the discharge of 'significant' quantities. The same proviso applies to dumping, which is banned, except that national governments may again issue permits for dumping dredged spoils not containing 'significant' quantities of certain harmful substances. Everything depends on how 'significant' is interpreted, who determines the level of 'significance' and how widely the results are accepted. The official procedure is for 'national authorities' to 'collaborate in finding common criteria for permits and in collating information on the effects on the marine environment of inputs from different sources'.[11] In practice government scientists get together to discuss the results of research and to draw up a list of substances and quantities. Government scientists have dual loyalties – to science and to their government. Fortunately for them, the two rarely conflict; their entire training and education leads them to adopt an establishment world view which can accommodate national interests and scientific 'objectivity', even if it arouses dissension among independent scientists with loyalties to a broader view of the interests of humanity as a whole.

Meanwhile the shadow-boxing continues as international bureaucrats compliment themselves on the effectiveness of their actions. A 1986 issue of

IMO News gives the 'encouraging information' on the implementation of MARPOL that, in 1984, of 119 ships boarded in Norway, 95% had a 'valid International Oil Pollution Prevention Certificate, 99 per cent complied with Oil Book Requirements and all ships carried the necessary pollution control equipment'. Corresponding figures for 7,709 ships inspected in the USA in 1985 were 99.17% for the IOPP Certificate, 98.98% for the record book and 98.77% for pollution control equipment.[12] From a less self-congratulatory viewpoint this means that, if no ships were inspected in both places, there were at least 70 ships sailing the world's seas whose 'equipment, systems, fittings, arrangements and material' were not in 'efficient order' for carrying oil, 80 not keeping records of cleaning or discharging dirty ballast, and 95 without pollution control equipment.

Under that regional agreement for ensuring safer ships, the 1982 Paris Memorandum of Understanding on Port State Control, between 1 July 1984 and 30 June 1985 there were 10,044 inspections in Western Europe on 7,665 ships from 112 different countries; 428 ships were delayed or detained for some defect or deficiency. Over 40% of the 'deficiencies' concerned 'life-saving appliances', over 30% 'fire-fighting appliances' and over 22% 'navigational equipment'. Contrary to the US experience there were increased 'deficiencies' for the IOPP Certificate from 315 for 1983–4 to 900, and for the Oil Record Book from 6 to 234. The increases may reflect more efficient inspecting but the numbers leave no room for complacency. Not that much can be done about it once the 'deficiency' has been rectified and the ship allowed on its way. The statistics remain statistics, the identity of the culprits unknown. The Secretariat of the MOU takes refuge in confidentiality; 'as it was never intended that the Memorandum should divulge confidential information, the statistics omit any reference to specific ships'.[13] The Laws of the Sea are strange indeed. While the common housebreaker's name is blazoned in the local paper even before he is called to trial, the ship's captain whose negligence could affect not only his crew but endanger others at sea and on land is allowed to carry on anonymously to the next port of call.

No international convention has aroused more heated passions or exposed governments in a truer light than the 1972 London Dumping Convention (LDC), especially on the question of radioactive waste. The aim of the Convention is as clear as the compromises of international agreement and legal phraseology permit. Under Article 1 contracting parties 'pledge themselves to take all practicable steps to prevent pollution of the sea by the dumping of waste and other matter that is liable to create hazards to human health, harm living resources and marine life, to damage amenities or to interfere with other legitimate uses of the sea'. In short, the Convention is designed to uphold the Stockholm principle. The limitations and opportunities for argument are, however, obvious. As no supra-national authority exists to enforce the Convention, governments merely 'pledge' their support, i.e. acceptance of decisions is voluntary; as long as these suit the government concerned, or do not interfere too strongly with its interests, it will go along with the majority.

When it disagrees, there are a number of fall-back positions; it can argue, on 'scientific' grounds, that the proposed measures are not 'liable to create hazards', etc; it can maintain that they are not 'practicable'; and, finally, it can simply disregard the decision.

Article 2 defines 'dumping' as the deliberate disposal at sea of wastes from ships and other man-made structures, while Article 3 excludes wastes from 'normal operations'. Even this seemingly straightforward definition of 'dumping' has aroused contention, as we shall see. Annex I lists substances that may not be dumped. These include organohalogen compounds, mercury and cadmium and their respective compounds, persistent plastics and other persistent synthetic materials, crude oil and its wastes, refined petroleum products and mixtures, high-level radioactive waste and other high-level radioactive matter (as defined by the IAEA) and materials produced for biological or chemical warfare. Again there is a 'let out' clause; the ban does not apply to 'substances rapidly rendered harmless by physical, chemical or biological processes of the sea', e.g. sewage sludges and dredged spoils containing only trace quantities of these substances. The obvious problem is – how much is a 'trace'? Annex II lists poisons considered to be less deadly – arsenic, lead, zinc, copper, cyanides, fluorides and pesticides not covered by Annex I, together with substances which, though not toxic, may 'harm amenities' if dumped in sufficiently large quantities. These substances may, however, be dumped under 'prior special permits' issued by national authorities according to criteria set out in Annex III. Finally, dumping on the high seas is controlled solely by the flag states of ships carrying out the dumping. The Convention includes provisions for agreements on mutual enforcement, but no such agreement has been reached and in ratifying the Convention, a number of states, including France, the FRG and the UK, stated that it did not allow coastal states 'to assume by unilateral action control over zones of the High Seas beyond the limits provided by international law'.[14] In short, if a Third World country, anxious to protect its coast and inshore fishing, declares a 200-mile EEZ under the LOSC, which is not yet operative as international law, the matter can be disputed or, if necessary, disregarded.

Two issues have dominated recent meetings of the parties to the LDC – the dumping of low-level radioactive waste at sea, and the possible disposal of HLW under the sea-bed. Concern over the effects of European dumping at the north-east Atlantic site and the prospect of the USA and Japan taking similar action came to a head in 1983 when, by 19 votes to six, the parties agreed to a two-year moratorium on dumping LLW, while a scientific review body undertook to assess the risks to the sea and to human health. The four European countries immediately announced that they would ignore the moratorium. The Netherlands later changed its position, while trade union blacklisting and boycotts effectively blocked all attempts to resume dumping elsewhere. When the moratorium expired, the panel of scientific experts, nominated by the International Council of Scientific Unions (ICSU) and the IAEA, and later expanded to include representatives of governments and international organizations, had failed to agree either on matters of substance or on what action to recommend. As the parties gathered for the 1985 meeting and it became known that 22 of the 60 members supported a total ban on dumping, the UK threatened to resume dumping, if the moratorium was not lifted, and to pull out of the LDC if dumping was outlawed. Not surprisingly the meeting failed to reach consensus and a resolution, proposed by Spain with support from Australia and New Zealand, was carried by 25 votes to six. This called for an indefinite suspension of dumping until all studies were completed. The studies, moreover, now included wider political, legal, economic and social aspects, while at the scientific level the onus of proof was transferred from those who opposed dumping of radioactive waste showing that it was dangerous to those who favoured it proving that it was safe. Canada, France, South Africa, Switzerland, the UK and the USA voted against the resolution. The UK was particularly appalled by three features – the indefinite suspension, the intrusion of 'politics' into what was considered a matter of 'science', and the terms for proving dumping acceptable, which were virtually impossible to carry out. The British Government's desperation was evident in the head of their delegation's statement that the LDC decision was not legally binding.[15] In 1986 the LDC meeting formally set up a panel to consider the wider aspects, the costs and risks of land-based options and whether it could be proved that dumping would not harm human life or cause significant damage to the marine environment.[16] Somehow, we are back to what is 'significant'!

There was a similar line-up on the question of disposing of HLW in the sea-bed and an additional legal wrangle over whether or not the sea-bed was covered by the Convention. As the technical means – 'shooting' canisters into the land under the ocean, as opposed to dropping them on to it – did not exist when the Convention was written, it was obviously not mentioned. The lawyers were thus able to enjoy themselves arguing whether 'deliberate disposal at sea', the definition of 'dumping' given in Article 2, referred only to leaving waste *in* the sea to sink to the sea-bed, or whether it covered using the sea as a transit route with sea-bed emplacement as the ultimate objective. Against this others argued that the proposal was not only against the spirit of the Convention, if not the letter, but that disturbance of the sea-bed would affect the sea itself. The only matters on which they agreed were that the LDC Consultative Meeting was the proper place to discuss the issue, and that no disposal should take place unless and until it was proved to be 'technically feasible and environmentally acceptable'. The Catch-22 aspect was how to prove it 'technically feasible' if one was not allowed an experimental 'emplacement'.

The 1984 meeting ended with two draft resolutions: the first, from France, Japan, the Netherlands, the UK and the USA, accepted a moratorium until 'research' demonstrated the feasibility of sea-bed emplacement; the second, the 'Nordic Resolution', wanted the definition of 'dumping' extended to include such emplacement and demanded that HLW 'should not be emplaced into the sea-bed as part of experimental operations'. The dilemma has not been resolved. The 1985 meeting adjourned the matter for a further year and in 1986 the parties agreed that, 'in the light of current activity on this subject, no additional action was needed at this stage'.[17] Perhaps 'current inactivity' would be more accurate. In Britain the Thatcher Government was spared the prospect of standing up to majority world opinion. After two attempts in October 1984, plans to use the research ship *Discovery* to 'shoot' two-metre long, torpedo-shaped 'penetrators' through six-and-a-half kilometres of sea before burying themselves 30 metres deep in the sediments of the sea-bed, 480 km off Madeira, were abandoned when the NUS crew refused to sail the ship and dockers from the Transport and General Workers Union (TGWU) to load it. Within four months the UK Government had come up with another scheme – to bury ILW in potentially retrievable canisters in boreholes in the sea-bed, using oil-drilling technology.[18] That, at least, would by-pass the NUS.

Finally, the 1986 meeting also discussed the question of producing an inventory of radioactive waste entering the sea *from all sources*. This common sense idea of actually finding out what was going into the sea, even possibly of what was actually there, and so providing 'an information base against which the impact of radioactivity on the marine environment could be more adequately assessed' had been discussed – and tried – on previous occasions, only to founder on the 'poor response from States to comply with requests for information'.[19] Inevitably, the legists pointed out that the LDC concerned dumping, not discharges from all sources. The Netherlands delegation stated that, as its dumping activities were already covered by the LDC and its other discharges by the Paris Convention, it was quite willing to provide the information. Others were less enthusiastic and accepted the diversion of an IAEA announcement that, jointly with WHO, it was asking members to submit data on radionuclides released from Chernobyl for preparation of a computerized data base as a first step towards an inventory. So perhaps at some future date we may have some idea of how much radioactivity goes into the sea, even if, by that time, it is too late to do anything about it. The plain facts are that at present we do not know and the so-called responsible governments of the world are not prepared to help us find out.

The Law remains only the Law, which, until translated into national laws and given effective enforcement, is so many words on paper, the results less of idealistic expression than of compromises and bargaining. In interpreting the inevitable ambiguities, national governments act according to their own interests, which may, or may not, coincide with the welfare of the sea. At its best, the Law can only prevent; it can never cure. Crime statistics rise, even in societies with rigorous laws and an efficient police force. No law can prevent accidents, even if stricter application can reduce those 'human errors' that are too often their cause. If we are to grapple with the problem of poisoning the seas, more is needed than even the most efficient 'legal regime'. We must get to the cause of the pollution, not merely tamper with its effects.

Triple Ignorance and Multiple Ignominy

Looking back at our survey of the seas, we find a number of continually recurring themes. Prominent among them is the admission by experts of their ignorance, or inadequate knowledge, of the sea and its poisons.

Firstly, despite the research of the last fifty years, what we know of the sea itself is far from complete. As the specialists of the *Times Atlas* admit, we still do not fully understand the 'complex behaviour of the tides' or the 'chemical balance of the oceans'; our 'quantitative knowledge of wave conditions' is incomplete as are data on the nature and extent of life in deep ocean trenches.[20]

Secondly, we are ignorant about how much poison goes into the world's seas and what happens to it. We have just noted the lack of an inventory of radioactive substances in the sea. GESAMP's scientists maintain that our knowledge of fundamental processes by which poisons are carried is not 'extensive enough for the identification or quantification of the oceanic pathways of many substances' and call for further work on the spreading of poisons from coastal areas to the deep ocean and on 'hot spots' of the world, particularly salt marshes, mangrove swamps and coral reefs. They add that there is 'very little information' on the levels of poisons in the minute but important organisms in the thin surface layer of the sea. As for the poisons themselves, 'there are still gaps in knowledge of the circulation and fate of DDT and its analogues in the environment as a whole', while 'even less information exists on the environmental fate of many other pesticides, including those that are now being substituted for DDT, such as toxaphene'.[21]

At the regional level UNEP's specialists comment on the 'lack of information on pollution problems' in the Indian Ocean[22] and on discharges of both cadmium and radionuclides into the Mediterranean;[23] the British Royal Commission was baffled in its attempts to estimate how much oil reaches the sea in operational discharges from ships,[24] and the Netherlands Government by those from oil rigs.[25] Other unsolved questions range from the fate of pesticides in small island ecosystems of the Pacific[26] to the source of mercury in commercially important fish in the Seychelles[27] and to the number of fish killed by oil in the open ocean.[28] There are even doubts on the methodology used – on the validity of extrapolating data on food chains obtained from shallow waters to those of the deep ocean,[29] the relationship between discharge limits for nuclear plants and radiation limits for human beings[30] and the 'acceptability' of such limits in terms of 'values'.[31]

Thirdly, we do not know, or have inadequate knowledge of, the effects of actual and potential poisons, both on a global scale and locally. Unsolved general problems include the long-term effects of oil on plankton, the amount of oil required to produce 'tainting' in fish, the full effects of mercury on fishermen and their families,[32] the effects of thermal energy plants on sea creatures at intake and outlet pipes and by the discharge of biocides,[33] the timing and effects of the dispersal of radioactivity from ocean dumping[34] and land discharges,[35] and the timing and effects of an overall rise in the level of the sea.[36] 'Locally', experts admit to ignorance on the effects of oil on shores in the tropics,[37] the extent to which the dumping of West African sewage in the sea poses 'biological and health problems',[38] the effect on the public of mercury in fish sold in the Seychelles,[39] and the effect in the Pacific of French nuclear testing at Moruroa.[40]

The significance of this varied and uneven catalogue of 'ignorance' is that it comes entirely from reports of official bodies or scientific specialists and *reflects the results of research carried out*. It reveals not what we do not know, but what scientists have failed to discover when they actually looked. Even more important are questions to which we do not know the answers because no one has yet looked for them – how many bombs, explosives and other military objects have been dumped at sea, where are they and what is their condition? How many packages or drums of hazardous chemicals have been 'lost' at sea, how dangerous are they, and what will happen to their contents? We cannot escape the double conclusion that not only have we so far failed to find answers to questions that scientists have posed but that we are ignorant of even the extent of our ignorance. We do not know how much we do not know.

Despite this we are prepared to go on allowing poisons to be discharged into the sea, dismissing these lacunae in our knowledge as of minor importance and hopeful that, though with decreasing assurance, in the vastness of the world ocean the poisons will 'dilute and disperse'.

The common sense response when faced with something we do not know is to find out. The problem is – how? Here our three categories of ignorance differ. To extend our knowledge of the ocean or of the nature and amount of poisons entering it is to investigate existing facts; to assess the impact of those poisons on the seas, the creatures living in them and ultimately on humanity is more problematic. In our arrogance we test medicines that may be dangerous to ourselves on 'lesser' mammals before pronouncing them 'safe'. Unfortunately, there are no 'lesser' seas and we have just seen doubts cast on the method of using coastal waters to discover what happens in the deep ocean. The only way, it would appear, is to follow the procedure, advocated earlier by Dr Bacon, of testing the hypothesis that 'the oceans are a resource that can serve mankind, in part by serving as a receptacle for some of the wastes produced by human technology' and that 'we will never know if we reject the opportunity out of hand'.[41] We have already asked what will happen if, on Dr Bacon's own admission, the quantities of some substances which the ocean can absorb are 'close to zero'. Our concern here is with the 'deeper malady', the flaw in the Baconian world view, which regards the oceans as a 'resource' whose function is to 'serve mankind'.

Basically, the issue is a moral one. Who are *we* to claim that, because we have the power, the seas are there for our *use*? In making his covenant with Noah after the flood, the God of the Old Testament gave him dominion over 'every beast of the earth . . . every fowl of the air . . . all that moveth upon the earth' and even 'all the fishes in the sea', but not over the seas themselves, for which the only promise was that there would not 'any more be a flood to destroy the earth',[42] a promise that humanity is now contriving to unmake. One wonders which modern divinity has elevated those who adopt Dr Bacon's world view above the status of the Old Testament patriarch.

Not all scientists share this attitude. In its response to the World Conservation Strategy launched in 1980 by the International Union for the Conservation of Nature and Natural Resources (IUCN), the World Wildlife

Fund (WWF) and UNEP, the British Review Group appointed to consider 'marine and coastal waters' observed, on the same subject of nuclear waste, that 'at present the UK discharges more transuranic radioactive materials than any other country into the marine environment, and does it into a relatively enclosed shallow sea area where dispersion is poor'. Anticipating 'pressure to license an increase in the quantities discharged', they concluded that, 'if there is uncertainty on a matter of this sort, it would be wise for the UK to play safe and reduce its discharges'. Against critics who claimed that discharges conformed to ICRP recommendations they argued that 'in an uncertain situation where there is a large time lag between an action and its consequences, it is better to be cautious'.[43]

The Review Group was not concerned with research but with present and future actualities. Nevertheless, its attitude is clear – the risks are too great. Unlike the Sellafield scientists who discharged the maximum amount of plutonium into the Irish Sea to find out what would happen, they prefer to 'play safe'.

The argument resembles that between the pro-dumping lobby at the LDC who maintain that dumping should continue unless it is shown that it harms the environment and the anti-dumpers who want it stopped until others can prove that it is safe. At a further remove it is the argument between those who maintain that the issue should be judged solely on 'scientific grounds' and those who insist that it is also a question of 'values'. The expressions of the Review Group that 'it would be wise', that it is better to be 'cautious', reflect an attitude that embodies identifiable, if unexpressed, values. At bottom the distinction between our categories of ignorance is simple: acquisition of knowledge, about the sea and its poisons, allows a degree of objectivity in discovering the facts. What one scientist does can be checked, verified or corrected by another. In considering actions, whether to allow discharges or dumping to continue so that we can find out, we cannot separate the action from consequences that can be assessed only in terms of value, whether the action is, or is not, desirable, whether we have the right to risk endangering future life on earth.

We can go further. Our apparently grudging statement that the acquisition of knowledge allows a 'degree of objectivity' calls for explanation. Why not 'complete objectivity'? The answer is suggested by a challenging paper to the 1982 Rättvik Conference, in which Dr Viktor Sebek of the London-based Advisory Committee on Pollution of the Sea lists among priorities for action the need for 'independent advice to policy-makers'. Dr Sebek argues that

> it may be difficult to ensure that national governments receive independent advice since they not only rely on their scientists within the civil service for briefings, but also use them for the inevitable bargaining process at diplomatic conferences . . . There nevertheless exists a need for a steady input of data and evaluations from the independent scientific community to relevant national and international bodies.[44]

Why this need for 'independent scientists'? Is Dr Sebek suggesting that the MAFF experts who decide the quantities of radioactive waste to be dumped or those at the Department of Transport who advise on oil are incompetent, or not to be trusted? The answer can only be that with which we began. As members of the human race, scientists cannot escape holding, however unconsciously, certain values that determine their world view. For those within the civil service or industry this is an establishment view; for 'independent' scientists it need not be. Whatever view they hold inevitably affects what they perceive and the conclusions they reach. The strength of the government scientist is that he not only believes in the myth of his 'objectivity' but that this myth is accepted by the public. The strength of independent scientists is that they recognize the impossibility of value-free conclusions; their weakness is that they rarely occupy the positions of power from which to promulgate an alternative strategy.

This diagnosis – and Dr Bacon's honesty – enable us to see the fallacy in his argument. In asserting that the seas should 'serve mankind', he is making a value-judgement, not a scientific statement, but using his prestige as a scientist to ensure its acceptability. Government scientists who take part in diplomatic conferences are too intelligent, or too cunning, to be caught out in this way. In making statements based on the same value system, they are unlikely to reveal it so readily. As non-scientists we welcome and accept the factual conclusions of specialists proficient in techniques of investigation of which we are incapable and who can thus add to our knowledge of the world in which we live. But it is illogical to extend such acceptance to statements made, or to the assumptions underlying them, about matters that are not primarily scientific, but on which they pronounce with the same authority. As human beings we question the capability of scientists to make value-judgements that have greater validity than those of other human beings. Where, from our own standard of values, we disagree, not with the verifiable facts they produce, but with the presentation of those facts and the recommendations for one value-determined course of action rather than another, the basic premise is that we are as capable as the 'experts' in the formulation of values. Only from this standpoint can we challenge the assumption that the seas are there 'to serve mankind'.

In the context of his statement, by 'serving' humanity Dr Bacon implies that we are entitled to use the sea as a dustbin. The advantage of dustbins is that the contents are taken away and we have got rid of our waste; the disadvantage is that there are quantitative limits to what we can dispose of in this way. Plastic dustbins carry a warning, that householders ignore at their peril, against putting 'hot ashes' in the bin. While we may not *know* with certainty what will happen if we ignore the warning, most people consider it 'wise' to 'play safe' and 'be cautious'. Only the Baconians would satisfy their scientific thirst for knowledge by insisting that we do not 'reject . . . out of hand' this method of dumping hot cinders. Fortunately, new dustbins are available; the problem is that new seas are not.

The conflict between the cautious and the risk-takers, the Don't-do-it-until-you-know brigade and the How-shall-we-know-if-we-don't-do-it group goes deeper than this particular expression of their antagonism. At bottom it is the struggle between the life-preservers and the death-bringers, between those who are concerned about the future of the planet of which they consider themselves part and those whose arrogance allows them to regard, not only the seas, but the earth's entire resources, including the majority of the human race, as existing for their benefit. To justify this assertion we must look further at questions that our survey makes inevitable. Who are the poisoners of the seas? What are the ultimate causes of poisoning? To what extent are the seas already poisoned? And what are the conditions for recovery or survival? Our answers will take us beyond the seas themselves to the nature of modern technology, the relationship between the industrialized and the Third World, the poisoning of the atmosphere, misuse of land and resources, deforestation, the problems of energy and sustainable growth. The seas are only a. beginning. Their future cannot be considered in isolation, for in the global world of the 1980s and 1990s everything is interlinked. We turn from ignorance to ignominy, from the seas to their poisoners.

Our ignorance of the seas is paralleled by inadequate knowledge of those who poison them. Nevertheless, despite its inadequacies and the impossibility of the task, our survey reveals the identity of some of those who have been, or still are, responsible. A number have already felt the force of the law – Standard Oil Company (Indiana) for negligence causing the loss of the *Amoco Cadiz* and the oil spill that followed; British Nuclear Fuels plc for managerial deficiencies leading to the discharge of radioactive crud and solvent to the Irish Sea, and the Showa Denko factory, Kanose, Japan, for allowing mercury-containing waste to poison fish so that those who ate them became ill or died. The charges brought against these offenders were not, however, that they had poisoned the sea, but that they had broken statutory regulations under which they operated (BNFL) or were liable for claims for damages (Standard, Showa Denko). Others have been 'criticized' or 'disciplined' by the appropriate authorities – the master of the *Argo Merchant* for 'navigational incompetence' resulting in the grounding of the tanker and loss of oil, the captain of the *Christos Bitos* for 'gross negligence' leading to the loss of his ship and spillage of oil, Total for inadequate maintenance of the *Betelgeuse* and Gulf Oil Terminals (Ireland) Ltd. for poor safety standards at Bantry Bay terminal and attempted deception after the *Betelgeuse* disaster.

The most remarkable feature of our survey, however, is that many poisoners of the sea are doing nothing wrong. When Associated Octel, England, discharges lead and Imperial Chemical Industries, Runcorn, mercury into the Manchester Ship Canal, they are operating within the law, as are the Nigerian National Oil Corporation; Terminal Petrolier d'Elf, Gabon; Terminal Shell–Gabon; Gulf Oil Terminal, Cabinda; Petrangol/Texaco Oil Terminal, Soyo, Angola; and the Lesieur and Bata companies, Dakar, Senegal, with their chronic discharges of oil and grease into the Atlantic off the West African coast; or Bougainville Copper, Ltd. and the OK Tedi Mining Ltd. in Papua New Guinea, the first in dumping waste so that heavy metals collect in the sediments of Empress Augusta Bay, the second in releasing mine tailings containing heavy metals and cyanides into the Fly River and so to the Torres Strait. And who will arraign the

US and French Governments for exploding nuclear weapons in the Pacific, the US Government for dumping radioactive waste off both its coasts or for scuttling the nuclear submarine *Sea Wolf* off Delaware–Maryland, the Governments of Belgium, France, the FRG, the Netherlands, Italy, Sweden, Switzerland and the UK for dumping nuclear waste in the north-east Atlantic, or even the UK Secretary of State for the Environment, Nicholas Ridley, for allowing less stringent conditions for discharging sewage into the sea? Who can dispute that all these actions have increased the poisons entering the sea and that, if we are to speak plainly, they should be labelled 'poisoners of the seas'?

In defending their actions our poisoners will doubtless argue that they are merely doing what everybody does, that the waste has to go somewhere and that, provided the operation is properly controlled, no great harm will be done to the seas, their resources or to human health. Past calamities were the result of accidents for which present safeguards and efficient training of seamen, workers and management in industry or agriculture will reduce the risk of 'human error'. As for that 'unavoidable pollutant', sewage, improved treatment plant and better medical facilities will eliminate the bacteria and viruses that are the real danger. Admittedly some coastal areas and even seas, the Mediterranean and the Baltic, for example, have not been treated with sufficient care, but regional monitoring and safeguards will ensure adequate protection in the future.

Let us be fair to our poisoners and examine their case, beginning with a question of intent. Summoning the manufacturers of DDT, dieldrin, aldrin, Dinoseb and other pesticides now banned or restricted in the developed world, we ask – are you prepared to stop supplying these highly toxic and dangerous pesticides to Third World countries? We have mentioned those of East Africa, and given figures for India and islands of the Pacific; we shall be surprised if the practice does not extend elsewhere. We ask further – are you prepared to carry out the necessary tests to ensure that replacements, such as toxaphene, are completely safe before retailing them on the world market? And to the makers of nuclear technology we ask – will you discontinue exporting to Third World countries reactors and components that have been scrapped in the West because they are considered unsafe? We refuse to accept the excuses that you are not acting illegally, that, in today's highly competitive society, you cannot afford to let pass any opportunity for trade, that retraction on your part means a better chance for your rivals, that increased exports are necessary in the national interest, that such action would lead to unemployment at home, that the practice is not limited to pesticides, fertilizers or nuclear technology but applies to cars and their spares, refrigerators, electrical equipment, machinery, in short, that the Third World is a dumping ground for what cannot be marketed at home because it is dangerous or defective.

When our poisoners produce evidence of their good intentions, they will have done something to establish their credibility. Until that time we shall continue to regard their actions, however legal in terms of national or even international laws, as crimes against humanity and the seas.

To argue that the waste must go somewhere is to provoke a series of further questions. Must it be discharged or dumped at sea? Are there not other places for disposal? What about incineration? Which is the Best Practicable Environmental Option? Cannot the amount of waste, instead of increasing, be reduced or at least brought under control through more efficient technology? All these are, however, *second level* questions. They arise only from the fundamental question – why the waste in the first place? Why do manufacturing industries, distilleries, tanneries, pulp and paper mills, jute mills, chemical works, nuclear power stations and reprocessing plants *need* to discharge poisonous effluents into drains, sewers, coastal rivers and estuaries so that their noxious contents infect the seas around us or the atmosphere above us with results about which we become daily less certain? Why, throughout large expanses of land used for growing crops, are pesticides sprayed so wastefully that they fall on to the soil, leach into aquifers and so drain to the sea or evaporate into the air to join other poisons which eventually descend on land or water?

The simple answer is – this is the way things are; this is how modern technology works; the waste – and its poisons – are inevitable products of the way we live now. If they were not, the whole process would have stopped as soon as human beings realized the danger.

The answer, of course, is simplistic, but it contains a general truth. In socio-economic terms both the technological means of production and the social organization of the relations of production, whether in capitalist, socialist or mixed economies, disregard the environmental consequences. Globally, we are still ignorant of the amount of waste that modern technology produces, of how much enters the seas and of what will happen to it. Two things are certain – that the poisons humanity releases into the world ocean and into the atmosphere are increasing, and that, unless we end the process – perhaps even before we have ended it – there are some nasty surprises in store for humanity. Not until 1985 did scientists discover the hole in the ozone layer above Antarctica. Only in mid-1987 did they explain the phenomenon and its causes. But ten years previously the ordinary users of aerosols, refrigerators and hamburger cartons would have dismissed as nonsense the suggestion that they were 'poisoners of the air' and in part responsible for a future rise in the level of the sea.

The issue of waste is inseparable from the problem of energy, for it is in the use of particular forms of energy to produce the material goods that humanity now demands that the waste arises. According to the WCED's Energy Panel's investigation of future energy strategies, adopting a 'high energy scenario' will require a 'tripling of global energy consumption over 1980 levels by 2020'. To reach this, production of oil and natural gas will need to be doubled, that of coal increased by 80% and 150 large nuclear reactors of 1,000 MWe per annum capacity installed. With a 'low scenario' of only ten per cent increased global energy consumption by the year 2020, 'oil and coal would be used at rates approximately 20 per cent less than in 1980, and only nuclear, hydro and natural gas would increase above 1980 levels by factors of 2.4, 1.4 and 0.8

respectively'. Environmentally the high scenario consumption of coal will more than double the production of carbon dioxide in the atmosphere and hasten major climatic changes, while increased use of fossil fuels at power stations and in cars will aggravate the acid rain problem. Conversely, the low scenario will see a small decrease in the rate of carbon dioxide production. The panel discusses at length the threats of high-level fossil fuel consumption – air pollution, acidification of the environment and climatic change, including the rise in the sea level – and attempts to make the doubling of nuclear power palatable by calling for international co-operation in solving the problem of waste, and the use of recently developed 'relatively small reactors'.[45] Their report leads inevitably to yet another dimension of our problem – the increased use of fuelwood, particularly in Third World countries, which has added to the inroads on existing woodland made by agriculture, industry and an expanding population. The resulting deforestation has removed protective cover from large parts of the earth, denuded the soil, caused erosion, and led to the silting up of rivers and estuaries, thus changing the coastal ecosystem.

Important as they are, this is not the place to discuss these problems. Our concern is to demonstrate the interrelationship of technological, social, political and environmental factors. The action of a South American peasant, forced by expanding urbanization and the establishment of factories into more and more marginal land, in hacking down trees to create a new farmstead, adds a contribution, however minute, to the forces that will determine the future of the seas, as does the Indian entrepreneur whose pharmaceuticals factory discharges effluent into a coastal river, the European city council that constructs a new pipeline to take its sewage out to sea, or the educated Nigerian whose aerosol spray ejects its proportion of CFC into the ozone layer.

The sea is being poisoned not only by the immediate injection of oil, heavy metals, hydrochlorines or radioactive waste, but the cumulative impact of countless actions of people, many of whom have never seen the sea. And while specialists have studied the effects of individual poisons, the unknown factor of this *cumulative impact* causes the greatest concern.

Are the seas poisoned? We do not know because not all the poisons have done their work. The experts assure us that, even if enclosed seas and coastal areas are dying because of human activities, the open expanses of the ocean are still 'sound'. How long they will remain healthy depends on the actions of humanity. If we adopt a 'high energy scenario', double the production of oil and natural gas, increase coal production and set up the required 150 nuclear power plants, we can expect a future in which climatic change will cause the seas to rise with the inevitable catastrophic consequences for low-lying mangrove swamps, salt marshes and agricultural land. We can expect increased discharges of poisons from expanding industries, renewed demands for the dumping of nuclear waste in the sea and a successsion of accidents at nuclear power stations that will affect both land and water. Humanity has got itself into a cul-de-sac, enticed by the label of 'Development' in brilliant neon lights at the entrance and lured by the prospect of bigger and better cars, videos, stereos, and bank accounts, to pay for which the poor must become poorer, the earth be depleted of its resources and the seas poisoned. Poverty, depletion and poisoning are part of the same syndrome.

Ultimately it is a question of the relationship between humanity and the natural world. The assertion that the seas are there to 'serve mankind' has as its corollary that the minerals of the earth and the creatures of the air exist for our benefit. It is no coincidence that the industrialist relaxes by shooting pheasants. Traditional fishermen catch fish – to eat; but they know they must throw back the immature to let them breed. Only the modern factory ship scoops up the lot.

The young Karl Marx foresaw and analysed the problem as long ago as 1844. In discussing 'alienated labour' he distinguished four aspects of modern humanity's predicament:

> (a) man is alienated from *nature*, i.e. as producer, he is alienated from the product of his work and thus, from the sensuous external world;
> (b) he is alienated from himself in that his activity offers no satisfaction either in or by itself, but only through its sale to another;
> (c) he is thus alienated from himself as a member of the human species:
> (d) he is alienated from other human beings.[46]

Later, Marx offered his view of a future in which 'need or enjoyment have lost their *egotistical* nature, and nature has lost its mere utility by use becoming *human* use'.[47] (Italics in original.)

The Hegelian phraseology reads strangely to modern ears, but the conclusions are clear:

> 1) Economic, social and political issues cannot be divorced from the environmental, or the environmental from economics, sociology and politics;
> 2) Humanity's treatment of the natural world as 'mere utility', as existing to 'serve mankind', is itself the result of our alienation from nature.

The problem of the seas is essentially a human problem, the outcome of a misplaced relationship between human beings and the planet on which we live, of an arrogance, short-sightedness and stupidity by which the human animal negates the evolutionary links between humanity and other creatures, only to find itself negated. It is as much a part of twentieth century ills as are the more familiar aspects of social, political and economic exploitation. Poisoning of the seas and poisoning of the air cannot be ended through legal palliatives or even the current panacea of renewable resources because they are inherent in our present system of social organization. Exploitation of the seas is only one facet of that global exploitation of the soil, forests, minerals and other human beings, which arises from their treatment as objects of 'mere use', a treatment made possible only by the dehumanization of those in power who are thus able to regard these objects as 'mere things'.

Exploitation of the seas will end only with the end of all exploitation, with the establishment of a social and economic order embodying a new relationship between humanity and the natural world and between human beings themselves, an order which, if we follow our argument to its logical conclusion, can be attained only through a reversal of modern technological trends and acceptance of the fact that present methods of producing material goods, which the world's peoples are induced to think they want, or even the food they actually need, will inevitably, through the toxic waste they discharge into the seas and the poisonous fumes they release into the air, lead to human suicide.

In a world where human greed has destroyed or depleted the earth's natural resources and human short-sightedness poisoned the seas, anti-capitalist, anti-imperialist and anti-neo-colonialist movements must no longer aim at taking over the means of production only to perpetuate and even expand the existing technology of destruction, but develop new technologies appropriate to today. With the clamour in the 'developed' world for more material goods, a clamour echoed by the élites of Third World countries, where the wretched lack even the food to survive, as the gap widens between North and South and dominant groups increase their stranglehold, the omens are not propitious.

Beginning the End

'The authentic question,' wrote Theodor Adorno, 'will somehow almost always include its answer.'[48] Throughout this book we have sought to alert, to provide essential information, and to pose those authentic questions in which the answers may be found. The overall *strategic* aim of a total transformation of society, of achieving a renewed harmony between the human race and Planet Earth, will not be achieved overnight. In this final section we turn to *tactical* issues, the more immediate steps which, because of differences in geography, climate and economic development, vary in priority from one region to another. Their implementation is only a beginning to the end of poisoning the seas but it offers identifiable targets.

Any programme for progress involves three interrelated aspects: arousing awareness, acquiring knowledge and taking action. In the past, awareness was often a temporary reaction to disaster rather than anticipation of future catastrophe. Only when an *Amoco Cadiz* struck the rocks, a *Funiwa 5* spewed its oil into Nigerian mangrove swamps or a *Mont Louis* lost its cargo of hex did the world pause in its preoccupation with other horrors to take a few days' notice and then only to thank its gods, stars or leaders that what happened was not in its backyard.

In Western industrialized nations awareness of environmental issues is now greater than it has ever been. Repeated opinion polls show clearly that many ordinary citizens are worried about their future. In the FRG 89% of those polled agreed with the statement that 'Mankind is severely abusing the environment'; in England the figure was 80%, in the USA 77%.[49] Of the Third World it is more difficult to generalize. Those who suffer most have least to say or are in no position to say it. We have quoted from intellectuals in India and Malaysia who are aware of the problem, from the Prime Minister of Papua New Guinea in his attempt to face up to it, and from the Government of Kenya which dismisses it. Many academics, particularly in Africa, re-fighting the battles of their fathers, are inclined to dismiss environmental issues as peripheral and, with a smattering of Marx to support them, give primacy to economics without considering the *context* within which society operates. Yet it was Engels who attacked the bourgeois concept of 'the *absolute immutability of nature*', graphically described the death of the solar system and depicted deforestation in words that read like a handout from Friends of the Earth.

> The people who, in Mesopotamia, Greece, Asia Minor and elsewhere, destroyed the forests to obtain cultivable land, never dreamed that by removing along with the forests the collecting centres and reservoirs of moisture they were laying the basis for the present forlorn state of those countries.[50]

Perhaps awareness will come only the hard way as the encroaching desert moves southward and the trees, planted in response to exhortations from traditional rulers, are hacked down for firewood to replace the already denuded bush.

Awareness cannot become effective without knowledge. The facts presented and the questions posed in our survey include as answers a sevenfold programme. We present it, not as a 'solution' or system of priorities, but as a summary of those answers contained in questions already asked.

Preventing Pollution

In the beginning the poisoner got away with it for there was nothing to prevent him. Out of legal conferences has come the *Polluter Pays Principle* (PPP), now given at least lip service throughout the Western world, which means what it says – the person responsible for poisoning the seas pays for the damage caused. The PPP has three weaknesses: 1) it operates only *after* the event and does nothing to prevent it; 2) it is framed in the only terms the West appears to understand – monetary values. The poisoner does his poisoning and, if found out and convicted, pays up; 3) it does nothing for the environment. Fishermen may claim for loss of catch, but the fishes killed, birds poisoned or the ecosystem destroyed have no lawyers at their disposal to assess 'environmental damage'.

PPP is useful, but inadequate. It needs to be extended and reframed as PPPP – the *Prevention of Potential Polluters Principle*. This takes as its starting point the historic decision of the 1985 LDC meeting in which a majority laid down three conditions for the dumping at sea of nuclear waste. Extended to all forms of poison – hydrocarbons, sewage, chemicals, heavy metals and radioactive materials – whether through discharges from land, by dumping or through the atmosphere – this would imply: 1) indefinite suspension of such activity until studies on the effects of the poison had been completed; 2) the studies should include not only scientific but political, legal and social aspects, particularly that of 'acceptability' to the communities affected; and 3) scientifically the onus of proof should be transferred from showing that potential poisons are dangerous to demonstrating that they are safe.

PPPP will be dismissed as unrealistic, a long-term aim rather than an immediate practical step. The powerful forces represented by those governments that opposed the LDC resolution, particularly the USA, the UK and France, will denounce it as demanding the impossible. Industry – and agriculture – will claim that they could not operate under these conditions.

To this the answer is – that depends on the development of technology. If power stations and motor vehicles can be adapted so that they no longer emit poisonous fumes into the atmosphere, why should we not find the technological means to prevent the discharge of poisons into rivers, estuaries and coastal waters? The real objection is that the necessary research and installation would cost money and so cut into profits. Yet even self-interest demands that a start be made now. Enlightened industrialists know that one cannot go on poisoning the seas indefinitely and in numerous ways have already demonstrated that 'conservation' can, in their own pet phrase, be as 'cost-effective' as continued poisoning. What is lacking is the will and effective political leadership.

At bottom PPPP is plain common sense. If, as individuals, we suspect that too much sugar is affecting our internal organs or the occasional whisky upsetting our liver, we cut down on sugar and cut out the whisky, not wait until they have 'proved' themselves harmful. Decent human beings do so not only out of concern for themselves but to avoid becoming a nuisance to others – the 'social aspect' of self-poisoning that is dismissed as non-scientific. The alleged dichotomy between the 'social' and the 'scientific', between values and science, is at best a farce, at worst a tragedy. Readers can decide for themselves in which category they would place the following incident.

In 1986 the British Government announced its intention to bury low-level nuclear waste at four rural sites in England – Fulbeck, Lincolnshire; Bradwell, Essex; South Killingholme, Humberside; and Elstow, Bedfordshire. Overriding all-party opposition from local people, which in places even went as far as passive resistance, the Nuclear Industry Radioactive Waste Executive (NIREX) went ahead with its investigations until May 1987 when, with enquiries still incomplete, the Environment Secretary, Nicholas Ridley, reversed his decision – on grounds of rising costs. The NIREX Chairman, John Baker, explained that the change in costings arose from a Government decision to build a 'Rolls Royce' standard depository when faced with 'the need to respond to public perception' rather than from 'any technical considerations'. The Government, which had opposed the introduction of 'non-scientific' factors at the LDC, now admitted their validity in making its decision. 'Public perception' of this policy reversal went further. If early questions on the issue provoked the customary response that it would be premature to answer until investigations were complete, the fact that the announcement was made suddenly, before NIREX had finished its work, caused more perceptive members of the public to sense that a General Election was imminent and that, far from being made solely on financial or technological grounds, the reversal was not unconnected with a decline in Government support in the constituencies affected, one of which was that of the Government Chief Whip. Whatever the outcome, public reactions are now as much a part of 'science' as are becquerels and the outdated curies.

Eliminating Accidents

In a world of contingency, accidents to oil tankers, liquid gas vessels and carriers of hazardous chemicals or nuclear cargo are inevitable. The large majority, however, as our survey shows, need not, and should not, have happened. The two most immediate causes are sub-standard or inadequately maintained ships and 'human error', as reinforced by the Flags of Convenience (FOC) system. Already international regulations exist – SOLAS 1974 lays down rules for ship construction, STCW 1978 stipulates training requirements and standards of competence for ship's officers and men (see Figures 7.1 and 7.2). Regional arrangements for ship inspection such as the 1983 Paris MOU of PSC, aim to ensure that defects in ships and their operation are made good before the vessel is allowed to go on its way. Any form of control that reduces the number of rogue captains or rogue ships is welcome, but the urge to cut costs and corners in today's highly competitive world, to ensure maximum use irrespective of maintenance or men, inevitably leads to taking risks, whether on chemical tankers or cross-Channel ferries. The immediate practical needs are to increase the number and severity of inspections, to insist that all ships are brought up to international standards or taken out of service, and that the secrecy by which defaulters are concealed as statistics is brought to an end. Not only must the names of ships be revealed but those of their nominal and real owners where these are hidden behind the facade of a subsidiary. Only in this way will the real poisoners of the seas be forced to take action. The unwanted, if unavoidable, publicity given to Townsend–Thoresen over the *Herald of Free Enterprise* disaster at least ensured tougher safety measures. Similar action for ships carrying goods rather than people can prevent loss of bird and marine life and of human livelihood.

We have already noted the increase in the FOC system. When Gibraltar and even the Isle of Man become adherents to this lucrative option, it is time to demand an end. The cynical admission of the reasons for its operation – using cheap labour without the cost of paid holidays or insurance contributions and with no union opposition to secure the competence or safety of crews – reveals the lengths to which operators go in placing profits before people, 'enterprise' before the environment. The system exists only because of that wider system in which the victims of world unemployment are offered a chance to work rather than remain idle. Ending it would not only make the seas safer but aim a blow at those enemies of society to whom the world exists primarily for the pickings.

Strengthening the Law

Of the many aspects of the present legal regime we select three for attention. First, it is intolerable that the Law of the Sea Convention (LOSC) signed at Montego Bay in December 1982 after eight years of argument, bargaining and compromise in an attempt to produce an acceptable 'package' deal, should now fail to become effective, largely owing to the opposition of the US and British Governments to its deep sea-bed mining provisions, which become daily less relevant. The argument against incorporating environmental provisions into customary law and ignoring others is that they form part of the 'package'. Articles in the Convention were watered down or expressed in general terms in order to achieve consensus; acceptance in this weakened form while yielding nothing on other issues would be for the majority to take the easiest course in the face of opposition from the powerful minority and to make a mockery of the effort, idealism and common sense that went into the protracted discussions of the Conference. The LOSC exists: it is a minimum charter for all aspects of the world ocean, including its protection; it must be given a chance.

Secondly, there is a need to plug gaps in existing legislation. The most obvious and urgent of these is the carrying of chemicals in packages, especially on the docks of ships. While MARPOL 1973 includes 'Control of Pollution by Noxious Liquid Substances in Bulk', i.e. chemical tankers, only the regional Barcelona Convention for the Mediterranean covers the release or loss overboard of harmful substances in packages, freight containers or portable tanks. Rectifying this omission is a priority activity on which international lawyers can work for an acceptable solution.

Thirdly, our scepticism over the effectiveness of the law and our conviction that laws alone are not enough do not exclude that, as an immediate measure, existing laws should be effective. The greatest need in the legal field is not for a new batch of laws, but, once the gaps are filled, for more effective enforcement of existing laws. With more than half a century of agreement on what needs to be done, it is time for the lawyer to hand over to the policeman and ensure that it *is* done.

An End to Hazardous Exports

Western governments should take immediate steps to ensure that the sale to Third World countries of toxic pesticides or hazardous fertilizers either banned or placed under severe restrictions in the countries of their manufacture is subject to the same conditions abroad as at home. Similar restrictions should apply to the export of technology, particularly in the nuclear field, when it has been discarded on grounds of safety. Present practices, justified in the name of 'free' trade, are not only immoral but a danger to life, both on land and in the seas.

At the same time there should be a rigorous, long-term testing programme of research into substitute pesticides *before* they are marketed; only when they are shown to be safe should their use be allowed. It is futile to cast out the devil of DDT, only to replace it with another devil that is seven times worse.

Safeguarding the 'Hot Spots' of the World

It is fascinating, if futile, to speculate as to which areas of the sea need most urgent protection. The framers of MARPOL made their priorities for oil the banning of discharges in such threatened seas as the Mediterranean and the Baltic. Others would favour the coastal zones of industrial states where all forms of poison reach the sea in as many combinations as there are outlets. Industrial development, however, often leads to regulations that safeguard the health of local inhabitants, especially where they become vocal in their protests and make their voices heard.

We suggest that the parts of the sea needing immediate protection are the 'defenceless' hot spots where regulations are non-existent and human inhabitants absent or disinclined to protest – the salt marshes, mangrove swamps and coral reefs of the Third World. The first two are perpetually at risk from discharges of oil, the third have the added danger that their beauty attracts thoughtless tourists who trample all over them or purloin their treasures. We need a special programme to ensure that these areas receive the protective treatment they need and deserve.

Continuing Research

Every chapter of this book highlighted those areas of ignorance or incomplete knowledge which we have stressed in this chapter. An ongoing programme to continue and expand existing efforts should concentrate on three areas – extending our knowledge of the sea itself, establishing an inventory of all poisons entering it, and determining their effects, both individually and cumulatively.

Research, we have suggested, cannot and must not remain in the hands of those whose interests lie in perpetuating the status quo, whether government scientists or establishment-minded members of industry, any more than the setting of safety standards can be left to bodies such as the ICRP. It must not only claim to be independent but be seen to be independent; the bodies undertaking research must thus include non-specialist members of the public on the lines of the UK RCEP but even more broadly based. Only in this way can we bridge the gap between science and the citizen.

Industry and Energy

Our programme for discharges requires a new approach from industry. Even before it becomes effective there should be steps to increase the use of 'clean' technology. The ambiguous and ineffective ALARA – as low as reasonably achievable – principle, applied in the UK for discharges of radioactive waste, must be replaced by ALATA – as low as technically achievable, and extended to all discharges into the sea and air in an effort to reduce such discharges to zero.

At the same time the search for positive, non-harmful sources of energy must continue, both on environmental grounds of eliminating the hazards now facing humanity and from self-interested preparation for the ultimate end of those natural resources on which industry depends. Humanity will need not only those alternative sources of energy from the sea, whose advantages and disadvantages we outlined in Chapter 2, but others such as solar or wind power.

An immediate target, not only for the safety of the seas but because it is a risk that humanity cannot afford, is to ensure that all existing nuclear plants are closed at the end of their lifetime and that no new ones are built. The fear that ran through the world after Chernobyl has passed and we resume our normal complacency, too engrossed in the personal struggle to exist, lulled by continued propaganda that it can't happen here, or acquiescent that it can but there is nothing we can do about it.

The unavoidable fact is that Chernobyl is not yet over. Its effects, whether in additional deaths from cancer or in damage to the environment, are still with us. A year after the disaster, in the UK alone, 2,000 miles from the accident, 465 farms and 250,000 sheep in Cumbria and North Wales remained affected. In North Wales levels of caesium in sheep, instead of decreasing, rose from 1,400 Bq per kilo in July 1986 to 2,000 in October and 2,900 at the beginning of 1987, with tests suggesting a steady *increase* throughout the summer. Nearly thirty years ago research on atomic bomb fallout showed that upland grass retained its deadly contents far longer than that in the lowlands, yet the Ministry of Agriculture used computer predictions based on the behaviour of caesium in lowland soils as the basis for action and allowed six weeks to pass before imposing restrictions. In August 1987 the Government reintroduced controls on the movement and slaughter of sheep in several areas where they had previously been lifted; in September, 17 months after Chernobyl, it imposed controls on three districts of Northern Ireland *for the first time*. What happens when the 'Chernobyl lambs' themselves start lambing in 1988 is, at the time of writing, too frightful for farmers to contemplate.[51] Extend this example around the world and, even allowing for the self-satisfied incompetence of the British Ministry of Agriculture and the fact that Cumbrian soil was already polluted by fallout from atomic bombs and Sellafield, it is obvious that this nuclear stupidity should be stopped. We cannot risk another disaster.

Our Programme for Action deals only with aims, not means. How we can accomplish it, where we make a start and what priorities we choose depends on who we are and where we are. In many Third World countries sewage or oil is as urgent as nuclear waste in the West. One thing is certain – we can expect little but opposition from the governments of industrialized countries or from the élites now ruling much of the Third World.

Nor should we underestimate their power.

In a 1985 Gallup poll in the UK, commissioned by ENSEC, Ltd., a group of companies favouring disposal of nuclear waste in boreholes in the sea-bed, 76% of 2,000 people interviewed opposed the dumping of low-level waste at sea and 54% were against more nuclear power stations until a safer system of disposal was found than burying waste in shallow trenches.[52]

In the 1987 General Election 57% of those who polled voted against the Thatcher Government which, thanks to the British electoral system, returned to office with a majority sufficient to ensure it the power to ignore those who stand for cleaner seas and cleaner air with the same obstinate obstructiveness it has shown in the past.

With nearly eight out of ten people against dumping and almost three out of five against Thatcher, is Britain destined to live by Ovid's dictum: *Video meliora proboque; Deteriora sequor* – I see the better things and approve of them; I follow the worse? Must the cry of the 1990s be a baleful parody of Shaw's Saint Joan? Not 'When will the earth be ready to receive Thy saints? How long, O Lord, how long?' but 'When will the earth be ready to save its seas? How many more do we need? How many more?'

References

1. *Siren* 31 July 1986 p. 4; WCED pp. 24–5
2. *Guardian* 1 April 1986
3. Data and quotation from Gribbin 1986
4. WCED p. 24
5. Ibid. pp. 24–5
6. Data on the ozone hole from *Guardian* 2 January 1987, 13 March 1987, 19 March 1987, 29 April 1987, 7 August 1987, 19 August 1987, 17 September 1987; *Observer* 15 March 1987, 22 March 1987, 5 July 1987, 6 September 1987, 13 September 1987; *ENDS* No. 142, November 1986, p. 24
7. WCED p. 26
8. Ibid. p. 27
9. UNCHE 1972 *Principle 7*
10. *UN Law of the Sea Bulletin* No. 7. April 1986
11. HELCOM 1985
12. *IMO News* No. 3. 1986. p. 6
13. *MOU 3.* 1986
14. Cmnd. 8486. pp. 18–20
15. *Guardian* 27 September 1985
16. *LOS Report 1986* p. 16, para. 60
17. *LDC 10/15*, p. 23, para. 5.7
18. *Guardian* 1, 2, 3, 10 October 1984, 4 February 1985
19. *LDC 10/15*, p. 14, paras. 5.9, 5.10
20. *TAO* pp. 58, 60, 66, 72
21. GESAMP 15 pp. 3, 5, 16, 43
22. *RSRS 13* p. 139
23. *RSRS 32* pp. 19, 21
24. RCEP 8 p. 184
25. *North Sea Monitor* 1986 pp. 2–3
26. Mowbray 1985 p. 4
27. *RSRS 8* p. 38
28. Baker 1983 p. 15
29. Holliday 1984 p. 39
30. House of Commons 1986 para. 147
31. Holliday 1984 p. 50
32. GESAMP 15 pp. 46, 48, 51
33. GESAMP 20 pp. 12–19
34. Holliday 1984 p. 19
35. *LDC 10/15*, p. 14, paras. 5.9, 5.10
36. WCED pp. 24–5
37. Baker 1983 p. 22
38. GESAMP 15 p. 76
39. *RSRS 8* p. 38
40. Bacon 1984 p. 37
41. Ibid.
42. Genesis, Chapter 5, Verses 3, 11
43. WCS 1983 pp. 275, 288
44. Sebek 1983 p. 120
45. WCED pp. 10–11, 13–25, 43
46. Meszaros 1970 p. 14

47. Marx 1973 p. 139
48. Adorno 1973 p. 63
49. Kessel 1984 Table 9
50. Engels 1968 pp. 341, 350, 363
51. *Observer* 3 May 1987; *Guardian* 13 August 1987, 16 September 1987
52. *Guardian* 1 October 1985

Epilogue:
Chernobasel on the Rhine[1]

On 1 November 1986, at about 1 a.m., a fire broke out in building 956 of the Sandoz A.G. manufacturing complex at Schweizerhalle, nine kilometres south-east of Basel, Switzerland, on the banks of the Rhine. The building, a warehouse, was used for storing agricultural chemicals and raw materials. Ten metres away, a second store contained sodium, acid chloride and other substances that explode on contact with water. The warehouse had no containment dam, no automatic sprinklers and no automatic smoke or heat warning system.

In dowsing the fire, the firemen inevitably hosed into the river 30 or more tons of chemicals, including dinitro ortho creosol, ethylparathion and 200 kg of mercury-based herbicides. While some of the mercury sank to the bottom, the river carried the mass of poisonous chemicals out of Switzerland and through Germany and the Netherlands to the North Sea. Behind it remained 200–250 km of biologically dead water, tens of thousands of dead fish and 150,000 dead eels.

Official reaction to the Rhine poisoning was slow and uncooperative. According to the West German account, two hours after the fire started environmental officials in Basel telephoned news of the outbreak to the water protection office in Mannheim, adding that there was no reason to set off the International Rhine Warning System. At 11 a.m., ten hours after the fire began, the Swiss Embassy informed the Bonn Government that contaminated water had escaped into the Rhine, but again added that there was no cause for alarm. The Germans claim that chemicals were not mentioned. On their instigation the Mannheim office, as the centre for the alarm system, tried to contact Basel but failed to reach anyone responsible. Attempts to send a telex were no more successful – the number had been changed two days previously and no one informed. At that point the West Germans activated the alarm.

At 9.30 in the evening Basel told the Mannheim office that the pollution was worse than expected and that it was a good thing they had set off the alarm. Not until 7.25 the following evening, 2 November, did the Swiss send their first telex to authorities down the Rhine – the reason for the delay was, of course, that they did not wish to cause panic – and when the International Rhine Commission met in Colmar on 3 November, the Swiss delegate was unable to say immediately what had gone into the Rhine or how it happened.

For days afterwards, as the 40-km stretch of poisoned water made its way to the sea, waterworks were shut down, cattle removed from grazing near the river, and the 12,000 inhabitants of Unkel collected their drinking supplies in buckets from the local fire brigade. Since 1970 they had contributed to the £14,000 million spent to clean up the Rhine waters, which had so improved that pike, perch, roach, carp, trout and minute shrimps were thriving in the water. Riverside inhabitants could even go for a swim and tourists were again buying eels. They now estimated the loss of eel stocks at £3.5 million.

Forewarned, the Dutch were able to shut the sluice gates to the IJsselmeer Lake (the former Zuider Zee), where there are many varieties of fish and a number of bird sanctuaries, and send 90% of the water along the quickest channels to the North Sea. Early in the evening of Saturday 8 November, a monitoring station in the east of the Netherlands detected the first traces of poisoned water. By 11 a.m. on Monday the 10th it had reached the sea east of the port of Rotterdam. The poisons were now heavily diluted and no fish died; the only likely casualties were water fleas and other micro-organisms.

The incident had other repercussions. Eyewitnesses at the fire revealed that drums of chemicals, thrown into the air by explosions in the burning warehouse, punctured the roof of the adjoining building where the sodium was stored. In trying to stop the fire from spreading, firemen naturally soaked the store, unaware that, had the water come into contact with the sodium, according to fire brigade experts, the resulting explosion would have removed the entire Sandoz plant, including tanks of the deadly nerve gas, phosgene, 250 metres away. The result, in the words of the West German Social Democrat MP, Michael Müller, the party's expert on the chemical industry, 'would have put Bhopal in the shade'. Not surprisingly, the inhabitants of Basel named the incident 'Chernobasel'.

As the first wave of poison from Basel reached the sea, a second wave, the result of a further leak of up to 50,000 litres of chemically poisoned effluent from Sandoz on 7 November reached Mannheim. Analysts identified mercury and 35 other chemicals, herbicides or pesticides. Four days later the largest Swiss chemical firm, Ciba–Geigy, admitted that, 24 hours before the Sandoz fire, 400 kg of the herbicide Atrazine had escaped from a production unit at their Schweizerhalle factory, and, while confined to the filter plant, had been leaking into the river in small quantities. Apparently it took five days to discover the leak and as only one milligram per litre reached the river, while the toxic limit was five mg/l, Ciba had not registered the incident with the authorities as soon as it was discovered. They admitted the leak only after West German scientists had found high concentrations of Atrazine in the Rhine and the University of Karlsruhe published data showing that the same high concentrations were found near Schweizerhalle between August and October 1985, suggesting that the 'leaks' had gone on for some time. On 14 November the Basel authorities confiscated Ciba's records on the production of Atrazine. They eventually concluded that the leak had in fact begun four hours before the Sandoz fire but their report gave no explanation of why the toxic concentrations in the Rhine were higher than those expected from 400 kg of weedkiller.

Recalling how, in the 1970s, tankers had seized the opportunity of genuine accidents to discharge waste oil, the European Commissioner for the Environment, Stanley Clinton Davis warned on 13 November that unscrupulous chemical firms could use the Sandoz incident to dump their own waste in the river.

A week later Ciba were involved in a second incident at Schweizerhalle, when, following the addition of too much catalyser while producing 500 kg of resin, a cloud of phenol gas escaped and floated over Basel. The authorities warned residents to keep doors and windows shut as the extent of the danger was not immediately clear.

Next day, the West German firm BASF announced that 1,100 kg of the herbicide dichloro–phenoxyacetic acid had leaked into the Rhine from its Ludwigshaven factory. Pressure from the environmental authorities forced BASF to admit that this estimate was 900 kg below the true level, a discovery that led the North Rhine–Westphalia Environment Minister, Klaus Matthiesen, to call their information policy 'scandalous'.

A day later, after a private environmental group had discovered high concentrations of the solvent chlorobenzol in a Rhine tributary, the Main, the West German firm Hoechst admitted that their Kelsterbach plant had spilled 850 grammes of the solvent into a drain from a leaky tank. The amount did not necessitate their notifying the authorities.

On 27 November the West German chemical company, Bayer, also admitted that it discharged up to 200 kg of a chloride disinfectant into the Rhine through defective filters on the 25th and 800 kg of methanol alcohol into the river on the 26th. Neither substance, it claimed, endangered drinking water supplies. The admission was again made only after environmental groups had drawn attention to the poisons.

Finally (?), on 2 December the chemical firm Lonza announced that more than 1,000 gallons of polyvinyl–chloride latex had been accidentally discharged into the Rhine near Waldshut. The company claimed that the chemical was 'not at all dangerous'. Tests by the Baden–Württemberg State authorities showed that the solution contained a carcinogenic substance.

Meanwhile, there were further revelations about the Sandoz incident – on 26 November the company admitted that, during the fire, a 'very low concentration' of highly poisonous dioxin was released into the air. They had also discovered the cause of the fire – 'an animal' gnawing on wiring in the building. Sandoz had done well in 1985 with net profits up by 28% to a record 530 million Swiss Francs (£223 million); Ciba–Geigy were not so successful: their profits rose by only 20%.

On Sunday 14 December, six weeks after the fire, over 30,000 people demonstrated against the poisoning of the Rhine. Along parts of the 30-km southern stretch of the river in West Germany, where many of the chemical firms are situated, more than 10,000 formed a human chain. On a ship in Rotterdam harbour environmentalists handed the Dutch Transport and Waterways Minister, Nellie Smit-Kroes, a petition urging the banning of 120 dangerous chemicals. Their demands had been anticipated by the West

German Environment Minister, Walter Wallmann, who had taken up a twelve-month-old opposition proposal, which, at the time, the Government had dismissed as 'not necessary', to carry out a radical overhaul of regulations on accidents in the chemicals industry. He would not even exclude a production ban on 'certain especially dangerous' substances. Earlier in the week the Swiss President and Interior Minister, Alphons Egli, went further and envisaged a debate on 'what risks our modern society is prepared to take'.

While people demonstrate and politicians pontificate, the poisoning goes on . . .

Had the unnamed rodent causing the Sandoz fire delayed its action for another four months, it would have been twenty years since the *Torrey Canyon* grounded on the Seven Stones reef. *Plus ça change* . . .

References

1. Sources: press reports in *The Times, Guardian, Lloyd's List* and *Observer* for the period 8 November–15 December 1986; and the *New Scientist* of 27 November 1986.

Bibliography

In alphabetical order of Author or Acronym used in References

ACOPS   Advisory Committee on Pollution of the Sea *Annual Reports/ Yearbooks.* Various years as specified
————— *Survey. Survey of Oil Pollution around the Coasts of the United Kingdom 1983*
Action Conference North Sea. International Conference of Environmental Organizations in Bremen. *The North Sea Memorandum.* 1984
Adorno, Theodor W. (1973) *Negative Dialectics.* Translated E. B. Ashton. London. Routledge and Kegan Paul.
Agarwal, A., Chopra R. and Sharma, K. (Eds.) (1982) *The State of India's Environment 1982. A Citizens' Report.* Centre for Science and Environment, New Delhi.
Agarwal, A. and Narain, S. (Eds.) (1985) *The State of India's Environment 1984-5. The Second Citizens' Report.* Centre for Science and Environment, New Delhi.
Albrecht, V. G. (Comp.) (1983) *Weyer's Flotten Taschenbuch 1983/4, Warships of the World.* Munich. Bernard and Gaefe Verlag.
Anon. (1984a) 'Report on the Symposium on the Denuclearization of the Ocean and *Pacem in Maribus*'. *Ocean Yearbook 5.*
————— (1984b) Editorial. *Industry and Environment* 7,1 p. 1.
————— (1984c) *Book of British Birds.* London. Readers Digest.
————— (1986a) 'Prediction of the Risk to Platforms from Errant Vessels'. *Focus* 53
————— (1986b) Editorial. *Industry and Environment* 9,1 p. 1.
Bacon, Michael P. (1984) 'Pacific Radioactivity: a Scientist's View'. The *Siren* 26 pp. 31-38.
Baker, J. M. (1983) *Impact of Oil Pollution on Living Resources.* Commission on Ecology Papers No. 4. International Union for the Conservation of Nature and Natural Resources.
Bates, J. H. (1985) *United Kingdom Marine Pollution Law.* London. Lloyds of London Press.
Bell, John (1986) 'Death of an Oil Platform'. *New Scientist* 27 February 1986
Bertell, Rosalie (1985) *No Immediate Danger.* London. The Women's Press.
Borgese, Elizabeth Mann and Ginsburg, Norton (Eds.) (1985) *Ocean Yearbook 5.* Chicago and London. University of Chicago Press.
Brown, E. D. (1982) 'Decommissioning of Offshore Structures: Legal Obligations under International and Municipal Law'. OPP 1,1.

Brown, Lester R. (1985) 'Maintaining World Fisheries' in (Ed.) Starke, Linda. *State of the World 1985.* A Worldwatch Institute Report on Progress Toward a Sustainable Society. New York, London. W. W. Norton.

Brown, Paul (1985) 'The Legacy of a Snowstorm in Paradise'. *Guardian* 15 May 1985

Bruce, Maxwell (1985) 'Ocean Energy: Some Perspectives on Economic Viability'. *Ocean Yearbook 5.*

Camplin, W. C., Mitchell, N. T., Leonard, D. R. P. and Jefferies, D. F. (1986) *Radioactivity in Surface and Coastal Waters of the British Isles. Monitoring of Fallout from the Chernobyl Reactor Accident.* Aquatic Environment Monitoring Report No. 15. MAFF Directorate of Fisheries Research. Lowestoft.

DoE (Department of the Environment) (1985) *Digest of Environmental Protection and Water Statistics No. 8.* London. HMSO.

DoE Radiochemicals Inspectorate (1984) *An Incident leading to Contamination of the Beaches near to the British Nuclear Fuels Ltd. Windscale and Calder Hall Works, Sellafield, November 1983.* London. HMSO.

Engels, Frederick (1968) 'Introduction to *Dialectics of Nature*' and 'The Part Played by Labour in the Transition from Ape to Man' in *Karl Marx and Frederick Engels Selected Works* pp. 338–64. London. Lawrence and Wishart.

Fairhall David (1984a) 'All Hands to Keep the Powder Dry'. *Guardian* 30 August 1984

────── (1984b) 'UK Cuts Costs with Soviet Nuclear Deal'. *Guardian* 31 August 1984

────── (1986) 'Half a Million Cubic Metres of Trouble'. *Guardian* 20 February 1986

FAO UN Food and Agriculture Organization. Rome. (1983) *INOFISH Marketing Digest No. 5*

────── (1983) *Review of the State of World Fishery Resources*

────── *Yearbook of Fishery Statistics.* Catches and Landings/Fishery Commodities. Various years as stated.

Gerlach, S. A. (1976) 'The Sea in Danger' in (Ed.) Grzimek, B. *Grzimek's Encyclopedia of Ecology.* New York. Van Nostrand Reinhold.

GESAMP UN Joint Group of Experts on the Scientific Aspects of Marine Pollution: — 15, Reports and Studies No. 15. *The Review of the Health of the Oceans.* UNESCO. 1982

────── 19, Reports and Studies No. 19. *An Oceanographic Model for the Dispersion of Wastes Disposed of in the Deep Sea.* Quoted Holliday 1984 pp. 35–6.

────── 20, Reports and Studies No. 20. *Marine Pollution Implications of Ocean Energy Development.* New York. United Nations. 1984

────── 22, Reports and Studies No. 22. *Review of Potentially Harmful Substances: Cadmium, Lead and Tin.* WHO. 1983.

Gowen, Patrick (1985) 'Beside the Sewage, Beside the Sea'. *Guardian* 30 November 1985

Gribbin, John (1986) 'The Longer Range Forecast'. *Guardian* 15 August 1986

Gristwood, Sarah (1986) 'America's Nuclear Shock for a Pacific People'. *Guardian* 2 May 1986

Gulland, J. (1984) 'How much of the World's Fisheries Lie Within EEZs?' *Marine Policy* 8,4.

Hansard. Parliamentary Reports House of Commons – 22 January 1986, 23 July 1986; House of Lords –8 April 1986.

Health and Safety Executive (1984) *Contamination of the Beach Incident of British Nuclear Fuels Ltd. November 1983.* London. HMSO.

HELCOM. The Helsinki Commission. (1985) *Ten Years of the Helsinki Convention.* Helsinki. HELCOM.

Hewitt, B. R., Flores, Aleni, and Pokei, Yaru (1985) 'Ore mining? Or What?' The *Siren* 29 pp. 39–44

Highfield, Roger (1985) 'Hooked on Power'. *Guardian* 11 July 1985

Holliday, F. G. T. (Chairman) (1984) *Report of the Independent Review of Disposal of Radioactive Waste in the North-east Atlantic.* London. HMSO.

House of Commons Environment Committee (1986) *First Report. Radioactive Waste.* London. HMSO.

House of Lords Select Committee of the European Communities (1986) *Eighteenth Report. Nuclear Power in Europe.* London. HMSO.

Hunt, G. J. (1986) *Radioactivity in Surface and Coastal Waters of the British Isles 1985.* Aquatic Monitoring Report No. 14. MAFF Directorate of Fisheries Research. Lowestoft.

Jackson, Harold (1985) 'Cores and Effect'. *Guardian* 4 October 1985

Jackson, Ivor (1986) 'Carrying Capacity for Tourism in Small Tropical Islands'. *Industry and Environment* 9,1 pp 7–10

Jasani, B. M. (1985) 'A Note on Ocean Surveillance from Space'. *Ocean Yearbook 5*

Kasoulides, George (1986) 'Decommissioning of Offshore Structures'. Unpublished paper for ACOPS.

Kessel, Hans (1984) *Environmental Awareness in the Federal Republic of Germany, England and the United States.* Berlin. International Institute for Environment and Society/Internationales Institut für Umwelt und Gesellschaft. Discussion paper 84–4.

Kimball, L. (1985) 'Conference Reports: Short-term Dilemmas and Long-term Prospects at PrepCom'. *Marine Policy* 9,1

KBTG Keep Britain Tidy Group (1985) *Survey of Packaged Dangerous Goods, Munitions and Pyrotechnics Recovered on the Beaches and in the Nearshore Waters of the British Isles (1 September 1982–31 August 1983)*

LDC 10/15 (1986) *Tenth Meeting of the Contracting Parties to the London Dumping Convention 13–17 October 1986.* London. International Maritime Organization

Lean, Geoffrey (1985) 'Your Daily Dose of Radiation'. *Observer* 13 July 1985

——— (1986a) 'Radon: Second Largest Cause of Lung Cancer'. *Observer* 13 July 1986

——— (1986b) 'Edge of Darkness'. *Observer* 23 February 1986

——— (1987) 'Stockbroker Belt Worse than N-Plant'. *Observer* 8 February 1987

Leong Yueh Kwong (1982) 'Marine Ecosystems in Malaya – 10 Years after Stockholm' in (Eds.) Gurmit Singh and Tun Peck Woon. *Proceedings of epsm Seminar: The Malaysian Environment 10 Years after Stockholm.* Epsm.

Lloyds of London (1986) *Lloyd's Register of Shipping*

LOS Report (1986) UN General Assembly. *Law of the Sea Report of the Secretary-General.*

McGarr Memorandum (1984) *Memorandum Opinion and Final Judgment Order on the Issue of Liability by United States District Judge Frank J. McGarr in the United States District Court for the Northern District of Illinois Eastern Division*, MDL Docket No. 376, 18 April 1984

McKie, Robin (1987) 'Scientists Flush Out a Bizarre Nuclear Inconvenience'. *Observer* 8 February 1987

Marx, Karl (1973) *Economic and Philosophical Manuscripts of 1844.* Translated by M. Milligan. London. Lawrence and Wishart.

Medical Research Council (1959) *Sewage Contamination of Bathing Beaches in England and Wales.* Memorandum No. 37. London. HMSO.

Meszaros, I. (1970) *Marx's Theory of Alienation.* London. Merlin Press.

Moorcraft, Colin (1972) *Must the Seas Die?* London. Temple Smith.

Moore, J. E. (Ed.) (1983) *Jane's Fighting Ships 1983/84*

———— (1984) *Jane's Fighting Ships 1984/85* London. Macdonald and Jane's.

Mosey, Chris (1986) 'Gävle Wakes Up to a Dreaded Legacy'. *Observer* 1 June 1986

MOU 3 (1986) *Third Annual Report on the Implementation of the Memorandum of Understanding on Port State Control (1 July 1984 - 30 June 1985).* The Secretariat. The Hague.

Mowbray, David (1985) 'The Poisoning of the Pacific'. The *Siren* 29 pp. 13–19

———— (1986) 'OK Tedi'. The *Siren* 31 pp. 11–14

OSIR - Oil Spill Intelligence Reports. Volume, number and year as indicated.

Pathmarajah, Meera and Meith, Nikki (1985) 'A Regional Approach to Marine Environmental Problems in East Africa and the Indian Ocean'. *Ocean Yearbook* 5

Pearce, D. G. and Kirk, R. M. (1986) 'Carrying Capacities for Coastal Tourism'. *Industry and Environment* 9,1 pp. 3–6

Pollock, Cynthia (1986) *Decommissioning: Nuclear Power's Missing Link.* Worldwatch Paper 69.

Pringle, Peter (1977) 'The Scandal of Wabigoon River'. *Sunday Times* 1 May 1977

RCEP Royal Commission on Environmental Pollution - 6, *6th Report: Nuclear Power and the Environment.* 1976

———— 8, *8th Report: Oil Pollution in the United Kingdom* 1981

———— 10, *10th Report: Tackling Pollution - Experience and Prospects* 1984

Romeril, Michael (1984) 'Coastal Tourism - the Experience of Great Britain'. *Industry and Environment* 7,1 pp. 4–6

RSRS United Nations Environment Programme Regional Seas Reports and Studies - 2, *Survey of Marine Pollutants from Industrial Sources in the West and Central African Region.* 1982

———— 8, *Marine Pollution in the East African Region.* 1982

———— 13, Pathmarajah, Meera. *Pollution and the Marine Environment in the Indian Ocean.* 1982

———— 14, *Development and Environment in the Wider Caribbean Region: A Synthesis* (in co-operation with the Economic Commission for Latin America). 1982

———— 32, *Pollutants from Land-Based Sources in the Mediterranean.* 1984

Salm, Rodney (1986) 'Coral Reefs and Tourist Carrying Capacity: the Indian Ocean Experience'. *Industry and Environment* 9,1. pp. 11–14

Samstag, Tony (1984) 'But Who Carries the Nuclear Can?' *The Times* 13 September 1984

Sanger, Clyde (1986) *Ordering the Oceans.* London. Zed Books.

Sebek, Viktor (1983) 'Bridging the Gap between Environmental Science and Policy-making'. *Ambio* 12,2 pp. 118–120.

Sindiyo, Daniel M. and Pertet, Fred N. (1984) 'Tourism and its Impact on Wildlife Conservation in Kenya'. *Industry and Environment* 7,1 pp 14–19

Smith, Peter J. (1985) 'How the Waste was Dumped'. *Guardian* 30 May 1985

Steele, Jonathan (1986a) 'The Nuclear Shock'. *Guardian* 19 May 1986

1986b 'Fallout Leads to Shutdown'. *Guardian* 16 May 1986

TAO Couper, A. (Ed.) (1983) *The Times Atlas of the Oceans.* London. Times Books.

Tucker, Anthony (1984a) 'Fishing for Trouble'. *Guardian* 15 November 1984, based on MAFF *Aquatic Monitoring Report No. 10.* Lowestoft.

———— (1984b) 'How "HEX" Underpins Nuclear Power'. *Guardian* 28 August 1984

———— (1986) 'A Guide to the Language of Invisible Death'. *Guardian* 7 May 1986

———— (1987) 'America's Guilty Secret'. *Guardian* 13 February 1987, based on *American Nuclear Guinea Pigs. Three Decades of Radiation Experiments on US Citizens.* Subcommittee Report for the Committee of Energy and Commerce. US House of Representatives.

UNCHE United Nations Conference of the Human Environment (1972) *Declaration on the Human Environment.* Stockholm.

Van der Burgt, Cees (1984) Introduction to *The First Decade.* Oslo and Paris Commissions.

Watts, Simon and Taylor, Conrad (1985) 'Morong Nuclear Reactor, Philippines: Playing with Fire'. *Inside Asia* 3/4 pp. 32–36.

WCED World Commission on Environment and Development (1987) *Energy 2000.* Report to the World Commission on Environment and Development. London. Zed Books.

WCS World Conservation Strategy (1983) *The Conservation and Development Programme for the UK: a Response to the World Conservation Strategy.* London. Kegan Paul.

Welsh Office (1985) *Environmental Digest for Wales* No. 2. London. HMSO.

Index

Note: to avoid duplication, topics and sub-topics are grouped together without showing location, e.g. birds: on beaches; and DDT; and oil; and mercury, etc., while entries for countries, seas, etc. give details of relevant topics, e.g. Seychelles: coral reefs and tourism; industrial discharges; sewage.